D1564155

PERSPECTIVES ON WESTERN ART

Perspectives on Western Art

Source Documents and Readings from the Ancient Near East through the Middle Ages

Edited by
Linnea H. Wren and David J. Wren
with Janine M. Carter

ICON EDITIONS

1817
HARPER & ROW, PUBLISHERS, New York
Cambridge, Philadelphia, San Francisco, Washington
London, Mexico City, São Paulo, Singapore, Sydney

 For information address Harper & Row, Publishers, Inc., 10 East 53rd Street, New York, N.Y. 10022. Published simultaneously in Canada by Fitzhenry & Whiteside Limited, Toronto.

FIRST EDITION

Designer: C. Linda Dingler
Copy editor: Ann Finlayson
Indexer: Sylvia Farrington

Library of Congress Cataloging-in-Publication Data

Wren, Linnea Holmer.
Perspectives on Western art.

(Icon editions)
Bibliography: p.
Includes index.
1. Art—History. I. Wren, David. II. Carter, Janine M. III. Title.
N5303.W74 1987 709 85-45244
ISBN 0-06-438942-1 87 88 89 90 91 HC 10 9 8 7 6 5 4 3 2 1
ISBN 0-06-430154-0 (pbk.) 87 88 89 90 91 HC 10 9 8 7 6 5 4 3 2 1

Contents

Acknowledgments

We wish to express our appreciation to the many people who have assisted us throughout the preparation of this volume. The idea for the book resulted from the participation of the senior co-editor with two colleagues, Claus Buechmann and Clair Johnson, in an interdisciplinary program for teaching the humanities at Gustavus Adolphus College. Our discussions about the relationships among Western literature, religion, and art did much to suggest the need for a volume of this kind and point to its eventual shape. We are indebted to many colleagues for their assistance and insight. William Freiert, Marleen Flory, and George Rochefort offered valuable advice on the documents related to Classical art. Kathleen Mitchell, Conrad Rudolph, and Charles Buzicky guided us in the selection and interpretation of readings related to medieval art. All have reviewed portions of the manuscript and offered useful criticisms.

We would also like to acknowledge the contributions of our students in art history and philosophy, who responded willingly and cheerfully to their role as the initial audience for our endeavors. Two students, Karen Dykstra and Kristen Ersland, undertook additional research, related to areas of special interest to them. Special thanks are due to a former student, Janine Carter, who provided enthusiasm, hard work, and good judgment at every stage of this project.

We also wish to express our gratitude to the staff of the Folke Bernadotte Library at Gustavus Adolphus College: to Michael Haeuser for his willingness to put the resources of the library at our disposal; to Howard Cohrt, Jeris Cassel, and Norma Hervey for their help in locating research materials; and, most especially, to Kathie Martin and Susan Gravelin for their unceasing efforts to locate documents and archival sources.

Assistance in the physical preparation of the manuscript was received from Clarice Ziebarth and Janine Genelin of the typing service at Gustavus Adolphus College and Maurine Hatting of the typing service at the College of St. Catherine. The staff of the computer center at the College of St. Catherine, and in particular Jim Jones, has been of significant assistance.

Financial support for this project was provided by the National Endowment for the Humanities and by the Committee for Research, Scholarship and Creativity of Gustavus Adolphus College. Additional support was provided by the Office of Faculty Development of the College of St. Catherine from a grant received from the Bush Foundation. A sabbatical leave from Gustavus Adolphus College further assisted the completion of the manuscript.

We are deeply in the debt of Cass Canfield, Jr., at Harper & Row. His encouragement and enthusiasm, his patient and careful nurturing of the idea for the anthology, and his thoughtful advice during its preparation have been crucial contributions to the work. We also wish to express our appreciation of the skillful editing of Ann Finlayson. In matters both of style and substance, her comments and suggestions have resulted in many improvements in the text.

Linnea H. Wren
David J. Wren
May 1987

Preface

The purpose of this anthology is to unite the study of Western art history with the understanding of Western social and cultural history. Painting, sculpture, architecture, and other forms of the visual arts are, like literary documents, primary sources that reveal the thoughts and abilities of individuals and that record the fundamental concerns of their age and culture. Works of art and written documents are related in this volume in order to demonstrate to the undergraduate student how the visual and literary records of Western intellectual history illuminate each other. Studied together, they enlarge our knowledge of our past and enrich our understanding of the creative and intellectual life of the West.

Most textbooks in art history have emphasized the stylistic development of the visual arts. Examples of art have been analyzed primarily in terms of formal qualities such as line, color, light, space, and composition. The twentieth-century stress on the aesthetic qualities of art works and the enjoyment derived from them has frequently resulted in a lessened emphasis on the social purposes art has served in the past. Until the nineteenth century, few works of art were created exclusively to be appreciated for their beauty. Most either depicted a subject or narrated a story to serve broader purposes: to convey the spiritual convictions of an age, to commemorate a historical event, to further the ambitions of an individual, or sometimes—though more rarely—to give shape to the personal vision of the artist. The artistic tradition of the Western world is undeniably a strong testimony to the personal capacities of individual artists and artisans, but it is also the vivid record of the hopes, dreams, convictions, and desires that all men and women have shared.

This book seeks to demonstrate that, although subjects and styles in Western painting, sculpture, and architecture have undergone radical transformations, the human impulses and emotions that art expresses have remained the same. The book is intended to bridge the gap between the modern audience and works of art from a distant past by allowing the people of other ages to explain, in their own words, their social and moral codes, their scientific and intellectual endeavors, their personal beliefs and public practices.

In this volume, source documents and readings have been selected to cover the period of Western history from the ancient Near East to the end of the Middle Ages. These selections have been drawn from many areas of intellectual and social history, including religion, philosophy, literature, science, economics, and law. They are intended to reveal the relationship between works of art and the most important ethical, social, political, and religious issues of the various periods of Western history. Each selection has been chosen to correspond to a specific work of art illustrated in H. W. Janson's *History of Art*[1] and Horst de la Croix and Richard G. Tansey's *Gardner's Art Through the Ages.*[2] Each selection is prefaced by a brief essay which discusses the reading in terms of its subject and theme, its source and usage, and its relevance to the study of a specific work of art. The essays are designed to introduce the student to social, political, economic, and aesthetic issues in as direct and accessible a way as possible. Thus the essays avoid discussion of secondary sources and modern questions of interpretation. Whenever possible, modern, easily readable translations have been selected. In some readings, punctuation and spelling have been changed for clarity and consistency. Unfamiliar names and terms have been explained in footnotes to the text. A bibliography of sources for additional study has also been included.

This anthology is intended primarily as a supplementary text for courses in the history of Western art. But as a collection of primary sources which relates works of art to the important themes in Western social and cultural history, it should also prove useful in courses in Western civilization and the humanities.

1. H. W. Janson, *History of Art,* 3rd ed., revised and expanded by Anthony F. Janson (New York: Harry N. Abrams, Inc., 1986). Cited in the text as Janson.

2. H. de la Croix and R. G. Tansey, *Gardner's Art Through the Ages,* 8th ed. (San Diego: Harcourt Brace Jovanovich, 1986). Cited in the text as Gardner.

I

The Art of the Ancient Near East

THE BEGINNINGS

Proto-Neolithic Fortifications, Jericho, 8000–7000 B.C.[1] (Gardner, p. 41, ill. 2:1; Janson, p. 31, ill. 23)
Plastered Human Skull, Jericho, 7000–6000 B.C. (Gardner, p. 41, ill. 2:2; Janson, p. 31, ill. 22)
Old Testament, Joshua 6: 1–16, 20–21, 24: "The Fall of Jericho," c. 586 B.C.

The ancient site of Jericho is located on the west side of the Jordan valley north of the Dead Sea. Jericho is famous in biblical literature because it is associated with the Exodus of the Jews from Egypt. According to biblical accounts, Joshua had assumed leadership of the Israelite tribes after the death of Moses. Under his leadership, the Israelites crossed the Jordan and began the conquest of the Promised Land of Canaan with the attack on Jericho. The conquest can be dated by archaeological evidence to approximately 1300 B.C., although at Jericho most evidence of occupation during this period has disappeared, including the circuit of fortification walls.

The conquest of Jericho is described in the Book of Joshua. The text gives no indication of authorship, but modern scholars attribute it to an unknown individual in Judea. Drawing upon many sources of various ages, the author is believed to have written the Book of Joshua after the destruction of Jerusalem in 586 B.C. as part of a unified history of Israel. A selection from the Book of Joshua, "The Fall of Jericho," is presented here.

However, Jericho is also important because it represents one of the oldest continual settlements yet discovered. Archaeological excavation has revealed that Jericho was first settled around 9000 B.C. By 8000 B.C. the town covered an area

1. Dynasties and the reigns of individual rulers are dated here in accordance with the chronology of *The Cambridge Ancient History,* 3rd ed. (Cambridge: Cambridge University Press, 1971). References to periods or dynasties are followed wherever possible by absolute dates that are more specific.

of ten square acres and included a population of 2,000 to 3,000 persons. Massive stone walls, strengthened at one place by a stone tower, surrounded the settlement.

In approximately 7000 B.C. Jericho was abandoned by its original occupants and was reoccupied by a different cultural group, possibly immigrants from northern Syria. The plastered human skulls found at the site are associated with these settlers.

Between 6000 and 3500 B.C. occupation was intermittent, but by 3000 B.C. urban culture had reappeared. Jericho became a walled town again, with its walls rebuilt many times.

In approximately 1900 B.C., Jericho was occupied by the Canaanites. Excavations have recovered evidence of Canaanite houses and tombs. These discoveries indicate the nature of the culture the Israelites found when they entered Palestine, a culture which they largely adopted.

Joshua 6: 1–16, 20–21, 24[2]

The Fall of Jericho

Now Jericho was shut up from within and from without because of the people of Israel; none went out, and none came in. And the LORD said to Joshua, "See, I have given into your hand Jericho, with its king and mighty men of valor. You shall march around the city, all the men of war going around the city once. Thus shall you do for six days. And seven priests shall bear seven trumpets of rams' horns before the ark; and on the seventh day you shall march around the city seven times, the priests blowing the trumpets. And when they make a long blast with the ram's horn, as soon as you hear the sound of the trumpet, then all the people shall shout with a great shout; and the wall of the city will fall down flat, and the people shall go up every man straight before him." So Joshua the son of Nun called the priests and said to them, "Take up the ark of the covenant, and let seven priests bear seven trumpets of rams' horns before the ark of the LORD." And he said to the people, "Go forward; march around the city, and let the armed men pass on before the ark of the LORD."

And as Joshua had commanded the people, the seven priests bearing the seven trumpets of rams' horns before the LORD went forward, blowing the trumpets, with the ark of the covenant of the LORD following them. And the armed men went before the priests who blew the trumpets, and the rear guard came after the ark, while the trumpets blew continually. But Joshua commanded the people, "You shall not shout or let your voice be heard, neither shall any word go out of your mouth, until the day I bid

2. Reprinted from *The Holy Bible* (Revised Standard Version), *Old Testament* (New York: Thomas Nelson & Son, 1952), by permission of the Division of Education and Ministry of the National Council of Churches of Christ in the USA.

you shout; then you shall shout." So he caused the ark of the LORD to compass the city, going about it once; and they came into the camp, and spent the night in the camp.

Then Joshua rose early in the morning, and the priests took up the ark of the LORD. And the seven priests bearing the seven trumpets of rams' horns before the ark of the LORD passed on, blowing the trumpets continually; and the armed men went before them, and the rear guard came after the ark of the LORD, while the trumpets blew continually. And the second day they marched around the city once, and returned into the camp. So they did for six days.

On the seventh day they rose early at the dawn of day, and marched around the city in the same manner seven times: it was only on that day that they marched around the city seven times. And at the seventh time, when the priests had blown the trumpets, Joshua said to the people, "Shout; for the LORD has given you the city. . . ."[3] So the people shouted, and the trumpets were blown. As soon as the people heard the sound of the trumpet, the people raised a great shout, and the wall fell down flat, so that the people went up into the city, every man straight before him, and they took the city. Then they utterly destroyed all in the city, both men and women, young and old, oxen, sheep, and asses, with the edge of the sword. . . . And they burned the city with fire, and all within it; only the silver and gold, and the vessels of bronze and of iron, they put into the treasury of the house of the LORD.

SUMER

Statuettes from the Abu Temple, Tell Asmar, c. 2700–2500 B.C. (Gardner, p. 49, ill. 2:13; Janson, p. 73, ill. 91)
The Epic of Gilgamesh: "The Slaying of the Bull of Heaven," "Gilgamesh's Protest," and "The Ale-wife's Advice," c. 2000 B.C.

The Epic of Gilgamesh is one of the most important literary compositions from the ancient Near East. The story originated with tales about the exploits of the Sumerian[4] king Gilgamesh, who ruled the city of Uruk[5] on the north bank of the Euphrates. These tales were fully formulated into a continuous epic about 2000

3. Passages that have been omitted by the editor are indicated by points of ellipsis. Passages that are missing from the original are indicated by [. . .].

4. Sumer was the southern part of ancient Mesopotamia, the area of modern Iraq between the Tigris and Euphrates rivers. It was the site of an important civilization from about 3000 B.C. to 1950 B.C..

5. Uruk (or Erech) was the largest Sumerian city. It was an important religious center and dates from the sixth millennium B.C.

B.C. and were discovered at Nineveh in the library of the Assyrian king, Ashurbanipal, whose reign is dated 668–627 B.C. The tales were recorded in the Akkadian language on twelve clay tablets.

Unlike other Sumerian myths, which are theological creations, this epic is focused on human characters, reflecting upon the nature of man and his relationship to the gods. It recounts Gilgamesh's quest for immortality after the death of his friend Enkidu, and it includes the Babylonian version of a great flood, a story analogous to the biblical account of the Flood.

Three selections from *The Epic of Gilgamesh* are presented here. In the first, "The Slaying of the Bull of Heaven," Ishtar, the goddess of love, sends a ferocious beast to attack Gilgamesh after he has rejected her proposal of marriage. In the second selection, "Gilgamesh's Protest," Gilgamesh laments the death of his friend Enkidu and questions man's mortality. In the third selection, "The Ale-wife's Advice," the alewife urges Gilgamesh not to flee from his mortal nature but instead to enjoy the pleasures allotted to humans by the gods.

The question of the relationship between humans and the gods is addressed in ancient Near Eastern sculpture as well as in literature. Almost all Mesopotamian statuary, including the statuettes from Tell Asmar, was intended for temples. In sculptures such as these, the human form was translated into stone for the express purpose of confronting the gods. A statue was regarded as an active presence possessing a life of its own and capable of interceding between mortals and divine beings.

The Epic of Gilgamesh[6]

The Slaying of the Bull of Heaven

With his third snort [the Bull of Heaven][7] sprang at Enkidu.
Enkidu parried his onslaught.
Up leaped Enkidu, seizing the Bull of Heaven by the horns.
The Bull of Heaven hurled his foam in his face,
Brushed him with the thick of his tail.
Enkidu opened his mouth to speak,
Saying to Gilgamesh:
"My friend, we have gloried [. . .]."
(Lines 137–51 mutilated, but the course of the battle is made plain by the following:)
Between neck and horns he thrust his sword.
When they had slain the Bull, they tore out his heart,

6. Reprinted from James B. Pritchard, ed., *Ancient Near Eastern Texts: Relating to the Old Testament,* 3rd ed. with Supplement. Copyright © 1969 by Princeton University Press. Excerpts, pp. 85, 90, 91–2, reprinted by permission of Princeton University Press.

7. Material in brackets [ ] has been inserted by the editor to clarify the text.

Placing it before Shamash.[8]
They drew back and did homage before Shamash.
The two brothers sat down.
Then Ishtar mounted the wall of ramparted Uruk,
Sprang on the battlements, uttering a curse:
"Woe unto Gilgamesh because he insulted me
  By slaying the Bull of Heaven!"
When Enkidu heard this speech of Ishtar,
He tore loose the right thigh of the Bull of Heaven
  And tossed it in her face:
"Could I but get thee, like unto him
I would do unto thee.
His entrails I would hang at thy side!"
Thereupon Ishtar assembled the votaries,
The pleasure-lasses and the temple-harlots.
Over the right thigh of the Bull of Heaven she set up a wail.

Gilgamesh's Protest

Urshanabi said to him, to Gilgamesh:
"Why are thy cheeks wasted, is sunken thy face,
Is so sad thy heart, are worn thy features?
Why should there be woe in thy belly,
Thy face be like that of a wayfarer from afar,
With cold and heat be seared thy countenance,
As in quest of a wind-puff thou roamest over the steppe?"
Gilgamesh said to him, to Urshanabi:
"Urshanabi, why should my cheeks not be so wasted,
  So sunken my face,
So sad my heart, so worn my features?
Why should there not be woe in my belly,
My face not be like that of a wayfarer from afar,
Not be so seared my countenance with cold and heat,
And in quest of a wind-puff should I not roam over the steppe?
My younger friend,
  Who chased the wild ass of the hills, the panther of
  the steppe,
Enkidu, my younger friend,
  Who chased the wild ass of the hills, the panther of
  the steppe,

8. A solar deity who represented order and justice.

We who conquered all things, scaled the mountains,
Who seized the Bull of Heaven and slew him,
Brought affliction on Humbaba who dwelled in the Cedar Forest—
My friend, whom I loved so dearly,
  Who underwent with me all hardships,
Enkidu, my friend, whom I loved so dearly,
  Who underwent with me all hardships
Him has overtaken the fate of mankind!
Six days and seven nights I wept over him,
Until the worm fell out of his nose.
Fearing death, I roam over the steppe,
The matter of my friend rests heavy upon me.
On faraway paths I roam over the steppe,
On distant roads I roam over the steppe;
  The matter of my friend rests heavy upon me.
How can I be silent? How can I be still?
My friend, whom I loved, has turned to clay!
Must I too, like him, lay me down,
  Not to rise again forever and ever?"

The Ale-wife's Advice

"Gilgamesh, whither rovest thou?
The life thou pursuest thou shalt not find.
When the gods created mankind,
Death for mankind they set aside,
Life in their own hands retaining.
Thou, Gilgamesh, let full be thy belly,
Make thou merry by day and by night.
Of each day make thou a feast of rejoicing,
Day and night dance thou and play!
Let thy garments be sparkling fresh;
Thy head be washed; bathe thou in water.
Pay heed to the little one that holds on to thy hand,
Let thy spouse delight in thy bosom!
For this is the task of mankind!"

AKKAD

Victory Stele of Naram-Sin, c. 2300–2200 B.C. (Gardner, p. 54, ill. 2:21; Janson, p. 75, ill. 95)
The King List: "When the Kingship Was Lowered from Heaven," c. 2100 B.C.

The transition from prehistory to protohistory can be defined by the invention of writing and the consequent ability to record contemporary events for posterity. The oldest written documents, still undeciphered, come from Mesopotamia and date from approximately 3100 B.C. However, sources from a somewhat later period recall earlier events and conditions. One of the most important of these sources is *The King List.*

A literary composition dating from c. 2100 B.C., *The King List* recalls the kings of Sumer, Akkad, and Babylonia. Some caution must be used in reading *The King List* as a historical document. Several dynasties listed as reigning in succession are now known to have ruled simultaneously in different cities. Moreover, the exceedingly long reigns assigned to some of the earliest rulers are clearly legendary. A selection from *The King List,* "When the Kingship Was Lowered from Heaven," is presented here.

The King List, like other ancient Near Eastern sources, including *The Epic of Gilgamesh* and the Bible, incorporates a description of a flood caused by divine displeasure with human behavior. After the flood, kingship, described as a divine gift, was rotated among eleven different cities.

Among the many kings recorded in *The King List* are Gilgamesh, Sargon, and Naram-Sin. Gilgamesh was the Sumerian king of Uruk, whose deeds were immortalized in *The Epic of Gilgamesh.* Sargon, who reigned from c. 2340 to 2305 B.C., was a king of Akkad[9] and founder of the Akkadian empire. He was the son of a gardener whose identity was unknown even to Sargon. According to tradition, he was chosen by the god Enlil[10] to assume the kingship. Perhaps because he wished to compensate for his humble origins, Sargon is described in *The King List* by the title "Sharrum-kin," which means "the king is legitimate." Naram-Sin, Sargon's grandson, was addressed as "god of Akkad." The conception of divine kingship also found expression in the *Victory Stele of Naram-Sin,* in which the king wears the horned crown of divinity.

Despite his many victories abroad, Naram-Sin ended his reign in disgrace. According to tradition, Naram-Sin sacked the time-hallowed sanctuary of the god Enlil at Nippur.[11] Akkad fell in an act of divine retribution for this sacrilege.

Soon afterward, the Akkadian kingdom began to shrink in size and influence.

9. Akkad was the name for the northern part of ancient Mesopotamia, inhabited by a Semitic-speaking people.

10. Enlil was an earth god who was responsible for both the order in the universe and the destruction caused by storms.

11. Nippur was a Sumerian settlement and religious center on the Euphrates.

A three-year period of anarchy ensued, expressed tellingly by the phrase in *The King List,* "Who was king, who was not king." Although the kingship was reestablished, the great Akkadian empire had disintegrated.

The King List[12]

When the Kingship Was Lowered from Heaven

When the kingship was lowered from heaven
the kingship was in Eridu(g).
(In) Eridu(g) A-lumim(ak) (became) king
and reigned 28,800 years;
(In) Shuruppuk Ubar-Tutu(k)
became king and reigned 18,600 years.
The Flood swept thereover.
After the Flood had swept thereover,
when the kingship was lowered from heaven
the kingship was in Kish.
In Kish Ga. . .ur(?)
became king
and reigned 1,200 years; . . .
Kish was smitten with weapons;
its kingship to E-Anna(k)
was carried.
In E-Anna(k)
Mes-kiag-gasher,
son of Utu, became high priest
and king and reigned 324 years. . . .
En-me(r)-kur, son of Mes-kiag-gasher,
king of Uruk, the one who built
Uruk,
became king
and reigned 420 years;
divine Lugal-banda, a shepherd,
reigned 1,200 years;
divine Dumu-zi(d), a . . . —
his city (was) Ku'a(ra)—
reigned 100 years;
divine Gilgamesh—

12. Reprinted, by permission of the Oriental Institute of the University of Chicago, from Thorkild Jacobsen, *The Sumerian King List* (Chicago: University of Chicago Press, The Oriental Institute of the University of Chicago, 1939), pp. 71, 75–77, 85–91, 111–13.

his father (was) a *lillû*-demon—[13]
a high priest of Kullab,
reigned 126 years;
Uruk was smitten with weapons;
its kingship
to Agade was carried.
In Agade Sharru(m)-kîn—
his . . . was a date-grower—
cupbearer of Ur-Zababa(k),
king of Agade, the one who
built Agade,
became king and reigned 56 years;
Rîmush, son of Sharru(m)-kîn,
reigned 9 years;
Man-ishtushu,
the older brother of Rîmush,
son of Sharru(m)-kîn,
reigned 15 years;
Narâm-Sin,
son of Man-ishtushu,
reigned 37(?) years;

Who was king? Who was not king?

BABYLONIA

Stele of Hammurabi (upper part), Susa, c. 1760 B.C. (Gardner, p. 56, ill. 2:23; Janson, p. 77, ill. 98)
The Code of Hammurabi: "The Laws of the King," c. 1760 B.C.

In 1900 B.C., Babylon constituted a minor province in the Mesopotamian mosaic of city-states. Its swift and spectacular rise to power over a single century can be attributed, in part, to the intense struggles waged among the other major powers of the period. It was, however, more the personal genius of its greatest ruler, Hammurabi, that resulted in Babylon's ascendancy.

Hammurabi (c. 1817–1750 B.C.) was approximately twenty-five years old when he became ruler of Babylon. During the first thirty years of his reign (c. 1792–1750 B.C.), Hammurabi waged a series of successful military campaigns against neighboring tribes and city-states. *The Code of Hammurabi,* the most complete and perfect monument of Babylonian law, was issued at the end of the

13. A male vampire demon who visits women by night and fathers children by them.

king's reign. The law code is inscribed on the *Stele of Hammurabi,* a large irregular boulder that is over 7 feet tall and 3 feet in circumference at its base. At the time of the conquest of Babylon in 1158 B.C. this slab was carted off to Susa, Iran, where it was excavated in 1901.

The Code of Hammurabi begins with a prologue. In it the king states that he was ordered by Marduk, the tutelary god of Babylon, to bring justice to his subjects and ensure them good government and also to destroy the wicked and prevent the strong from oppressing the weak. The Code itself consists of approximately 280 clauses dealing with both criminal and civil aspects of everyday life. The clauses include regulations governing criminal acts such as theft, assault, and manslaughter, personal matters such as slander, adoption and divorce, and economic transactions such as land and labor contracts, irrigation rights, and interest rates.

The Code of Hammurabi divided Babylonian subjects into three classes: the upper class, the commoners, and the slaves. Punishments, which were severe, were distinguished by class and were determined according to the principle of "an eye for an eye." Despite the harshness of the penalties, *The Code of Hammurabi* must be viewed as the expression of the king's concern to be a just ruler. A selection from *The Code of Hammurabi,* "The Laws of the King," is presented here.

The reign of Hammurabi marked the climax and the end of the Babylonian civilization. Hammurabi's reunification of Mesopotamia was brief-lived. Under his son, Samsuilana, Babylonia shrank in size and was soon prey to foreign invasion.

The Code of Hammurabi[14]

The Laws of the King

If a man has taken up a field for cultivation and then has not raised corn on the field, they shall convict him of not having done the necessary work on the field, and he shall give corn corresponding to the crops raised by his neighbours to the owner of the field.

If he has not cultivated the field but leaves it waste, he shall give corn corresponding to the crops raised by his neighbours to the owner of the field and shall plough the field, which he has left waste and harrow it, and he shall render it to the owner of the field. . . .

If a man incurs a debt and Adad[15] inundates his field or a flood has carried away the soil or else if corn is not raised on the field through lack of water, in that year he shall not render any corn to his creditor; he shall

14. Reprinted, by permission of Oxford University Press, from Geoffrey R. Driver and John Miles, *The Babylonian Laws,* Vol. 2 (Oxford: Clarendon Press, 1955), pp. 27–31, 51, 55–57, 77–79, 95.

15. A storm god believed to be responsible for floods.

blot out the terms inscribed on his tablet and shall not pay interest for that year. . . .

If a man has opened his trench for irrigation and has been slack and so has let the waters carry away the soil on his neighbour's field, he shall pay corn corresponding to the amount of the crop which his neighbour has raised.

If a man has released the waters and so has let the waters carry away the works on his neighbour's field, he shall pay 10 *gur* of corn for every *bur* [of land]. . . .

If a married lady is caught lying with another man, they shall bind them and cast them into the water; if her husband wishes to let his wife live, then the king shall let his servant live. . . .

If a man wishes to divorce his first wife who has not borne him sons, he shall give her money to the value of her bridal gift and shall make good to her the dowry which she has brought from her father's house and so divorce her. . . .

If a married lady who is dwelling in a man's house sets her face to go out of doors and persists in behaving herself foolishly wasting her house and belittling her husband, they shall convict her and, if her husband then states that he will divorce her, he may divorce her; nothing shall be given to her as her divorce-money on her journey. If her husband states that he will not divorce her, her husband may marry another woman; that woman shall dwell as a slave-girl in the house of her husband.

If a woman has hated her husband and states "Thou shalt not have the natural use of me," the facts of her case shall be determined in her district and, if she has kept herself chaste and has no fault, while her husband is given to going about out of doors and so has greatly belittled her, that woman shall suffer no punishment; she may take her dowry and go to her father's house.

If she has not kept herself chaste but is given to going about out of doors, will waste her house and so belittle her husband, they shall cast that woman into the water. . . .

If a man has put out the eye of a free man, they shall put out his eye.

If he breaks the bone of a free man, they shall break his bone.

If he puts out the eye of a villein or breaks the bone of a villein, he shall pay 1 *maneh* of silver.

If he puts out the eye of a free man's slave or breaks the bone of a free man's slave, he shall pay half his price.

If a man knocks out the tooth of a free man equal in rank to himself, they shall knock out his tooth.

If he knocks out the tooth of a villein, he shall pay ½ *maneh* of silver.

If a man strikes the cheek of a free man who is superior in rank to himself, he shall be beaten with sixty stripes with a whip of ox-hide in the assembly.

If the man strikes the cheek of a free man equal to himself in rank, he shall pay 1 *maneh* of silver.

If a villein strikes the cheek of a villein, he shall pay 10 *shekels* of silver.

If the slave of a free man strikes the cheek of a free man, they shall cut off his ear. . . .

These are the just laws which Hammurabi the able king has established and thereby has enabled the land to enjoy stable governance and good rule.

ASSYRIA

Citadel of Sargon II, Khorsabad, c. 720 B.C. (Gardner, p. 58, ills. 2:25 and 2:26; Janson, p. 78, ills. 100 and 101)
The Great Inscription in the Palace of Khorsabad: "The Deeds of Sargon II," c. 706 B.C.

In c. 900 B.C. Assyria was no more than a small kingdom about seventy-five miles square. Centuries of constant warfare had shaped Assyrians into skilled, hardened warriors. During the ninth century, directed by an intense sense of divine protection by Assur, the most important Assyrian god, and led by a succession of vigorous warlords, Assyria began expanding its territories.

One of the greatest of the Assyrian warlords was Sargon II (?–705 B.C.). Sargon inherited an empire built through the conquests of his predecessors. He bore the double responsibility of extending Assyrian conquests abroad and of improving the internal administration of his rapidly assembled empire.

Sargon's sixteen-year reign (721–705 B.C.) was marked by almost constant warfare. Sargon beat down the Chaldeans in Babylonia, he exiled the leaders of the northern kingdom of the Hebrews, Israel, and he extended Assyrian influence as far as the Mediterranean.

Sargon founded a new capital at Khorsabad, which he called Dur Sharrukin. Wanting his palace to match the vastness of his empire, the king planned it in monumental dimensions. Stone reliefs of winged bulls with human heads flanked the entrance. The walls were decorated with long rows of bas-reliefs showing scenes of war and festive processions.

Although tens of thousands of laborers and hundreds of artisans worked upon the great city, the capital was never completed. In 705, during a military campaign in northwestern Iran, Sargon was ambushed and killed. His corpse remained unburied, its flesh food for birds and animals of prey. His son and successor, Sennacherib, who had quarreled with his father, chose to interpret the death of Sargon as a divine punishment.

At its height, the Assyrian empire was the largest state yet formed in the ancient Near East. In their conquests, the Assyrians demonstrated a ruthless spirit. The annals of the kings, including *The Great Inscription in the Palace of Khorsabad,* inscribed on the walls of Sargon's palace, vividly describe the brutalities inflicted upon defeated peoples and jubilantly enumerate the treasures captured in war. A selection from *The Great Inscription in the Palace of Khorsabad,* "The Deeds of Sargon II," is presented here.

The Great Inscription in the Palace of Khorsabad[16]

The Deeds of Sargon II

Palace of Sargon, the great King, the powerful King, King of the legions, King of Assyria, Viceroy of the gods at Babylon, King of the Sumers and of the Akkads, favorite of the great gods. The gods Assur,[17] Nebo,[18] and Merodach[19] have conferred on me the royalty of the nations, and they have propagated the memory of my fortunate name to the ends of the earth. . . .

This is what I did from the beginning of my reign to my fifteenth year of reign: I defeated Khumbanigas, King of Elam, in the plains of Kalu. I besieged and occupied the town of Samaria, and took 27,280 of its inhabitants captive. I took from them 50 chariots, but left them the rest of their belongings. . . .

I imposed a tribute on Pharaoh, King of Egypt; Samsie, Queen of Arabia; It-amar, the Sabean, of gold, sweet smelling herbs of the land, horses, and camels.

Kiakku of Sinukhta had despised the god Assur, and refused submission to him. I took him prisoner, and seized his 30 chariots and 7,350 of his soldiers. . . .

Merodach-Baladan, son of Iakin, King of Chaldaea, the fallacious, the persistent in enmity, did not respect the memory of the gods, he trusted in the sea, and in the retreat of the marshes; he eluded the precepts of the great gods, and refused to send his tributes. He had supported as an ally Khumbanigas, King of Elam. He had excited all the nomadic tribes of the desert against me. He prepared himself for battle, and advanced. . . . I stretched my combatants all along the river dividing them into bands; they conquered the enemies. By the blood of the rebels the waters of these canals reddened like dyed wool. The nomadic tribes were terrified by this disaster

16. Reprinted from Epiphanius Wilson, ed., *Babylonian and Assyrian Literature* (New York: The Colonial Press, 1901), pp. 295–97, 303–307, 309. Selection translated by Julius Oppert.

17. A war god and patron deity of the Assyrians.

18. A god of knowledge, literature, and agriculture.

19. Another rendering of Marduk, god of light and creator of humanity.

which surprised him and fled; . . . I besieged and occupied the town of Dur-Iakin, I took as spoil and made captive, him, his wife, his sons, his daughters, the gold and silver and all that he possessed, the contents of his palace, whatever it was, with considerable booty from the town. I made each family and every man who had withdrawn himself from my arms, accountable for this sin. I reduced Dur-Iakin the town of his power to ashes. I undermined and destroyed its ancient forts. I dug up the foundation stone; I made it like a thunder-stricken ruin. . . .

And the seven Kings of the country of Iahnagi, of the country of Iatnan . . . had been told of my lofty achievements in Chaldea and Syria, and my glory, which had spread from afar to the midst of the sea. They subdued their pride and humbled themselves; they presented themselves before me at Babylon, bearing metals, gold, silver, vases, ebony wood, and the manufactures of their country; they kissed my feet. . . .

In these days, these nations and these countries that my hand has conquered, and that the gods Assur, Nebo, and Merodach have made bow to my feet, followed the ways of piety. With their help I built at the feet of the *musri,* following the divine will and the wish of my heart, a town that I called Dur Sharrukin to replace Nineveh. . . .

I built in the town some palaces covered with the skin of the sea-calf, and of sandal wood, ebony, the wood of mastic tree, cedar, cypress, wild pistachio nut tree, a palace of incomparable splendor, as the seat of my royalty.

May Assur, the father of the gods, bless these palaces, by giving to his images a spontaneous splendor. May he watch over the issue even to the remote future. May the sculptured bull, the protector and god who imparts perfection, dwell in day and in night-time in his presence, and never stir from this threshold!

With the help of Assur, may the King who has built these palaces, attain an old age, and may his offspring multiply greatly! May these battlements last to the most remote future! May he who dwells there come forth surrounded with the greatest splendor; may he rejoice in his corporal health, in the satisfaction of his heart accomplish his wishes, attain his end, and may he render his magnificence seven times more imposing!

NEO-BABYLONIA

Ishtar Gate, Babylon, c. 575 B.C. (Gardner, p. 63, ill. 2:33; Janson, p. 97, color plate 10)
Inscription of Nebuchadnezzar II: "My City Babylon," c. 575 B.C.

Nebuchadnezzar II (?–562 B.C.) was the son and successor of Nabopolassar, the founder of the Neo-Babylonian empire. The greatest king of his dynasty, Nebuchadnezzar pursued a policy of military expansion, which took Babylon armies into Syria and Palestine and extended the Babylonian empire to the Egyptian border. His conquest of Jerusalem and Judea are described in the Old Testament in the Book of Jeremiah.

Despite his many military triumphs, Nebuchadnezzar evidently preferred to be remembered for his peaceful accomplishments, which clearly matched his foreign conquests. Using the wealth of his empire, which he collected through taxes and tribute, the king financed a series of ambitious building projects and transformed Babylon into one of the wonders of the ancient world. He strengthened the old city walls and built new defensive fortifications. He enlarged the old palace by adding new wings and a museum to house his collection of Mesopotamian art. He constructed terraced gardens, which legend referred to as the Hanging Gardens of Babylon. In addition, Nebuchadnezzar completed a five-storied ziggurat,[20] which rose approximately 300 feet high and which some scholars have connected with the Tower of Babel described in the Old Testament in the Book of Genesis. The Ishtar Gate was erected on the processional way that led to the enclosure of the palace and ziggurat. In the *Inscription of Nebuchadnezzar II,* the ruler enumerates his achievements. A selection from the *Inscription of Nebuchadnezzar II,* "My City Babylon," is presented here.

In the Old Testament in the Book of Daniel, Nebuchadnezzar is described as being punished for his arrogance by suffering from a strange form of madness in which he imagined himself to be a beast. For an interval of four, or perhaps seven, years, Nebuchadnezzar supposedly shunned the splendid city which he had created and led the life of a wild animal.

Inscription of Nebuchadnezzar II[21]

My City Babylon

Nebuchadnezzar . . .
King of Babylon am I. . . .

20. A lofty temple in the shape of a rectangular pyramid.

21. Reprinted from Epiphanius Wilson, ed., op. cit., pp. 251, 254–55, 264–65. Selection translated by J. M. Rodwell.

Wares and ornaments
for the women I brought forth,
silver, molden gold, precious stones,
metal, *umritgana* and cedar woods . . .
beautiful things in abundance,
riches and sources of joy,
for my city Babylon. . . .

Bit-Kua, the shrine
of Merodach, Lord of the house of the gods,
I have made conspicuous with fine linen
and its seats
with splendid gold,
as for royalty and deity,
with lapis lazuli and alabaster blocks
I carefully covered them over;
a gate of passage, the gate Beautiful,
and the gate of Bit-Zida and Bit-Saggatu
I caused to be made brilliant as the sun.
A fullness of the treasures of countries I accumulated;
around the city it was placed as an ornament. . . .
I skillfully completed
and exalted as an abode of Royalty.
  Tall pines, the produce of lofty mountains,
thick *asuhu* wood
  and *surman* wood in choice pillars
for its covered porticos I arranged.
Ikki and *musritkanna* woods
cedar and *surman* woods
I brought forth, and in heaps,
with a surface of silver and gold
and with coverings of copper,
  on domes and arches, and with works of metal
its gates I strongly overlaid
and completely with *zamat*-stone
I finished off its top.
  A strong wall in cement and brick
like a mountain I carried round
  a wall, a brick fortress, a great fortress
with long blocks of stone
  gatherings from great lands I made
  and like hills I upraised its head.
  That house for admiration I caused to build

and for a banner to hosts of men:
with carved work I fitted it;
the strong power of reverence for
the presence of Royalty
environs its walls;
  the least thing not upright enters it not,
that evil may not make head.
The walls of the fortress of Babylon
  its defence in war I raised
and the circuit of the city of Babylon
  I have strengthened skillfully.
To Merodach my Lord
my hand I lifted:
O Merodach the Lord, Chief of the gods,
  a surpassing Prince thou hast made me,
and empire over multitudes of men,
hast intrusted to me as precious lives;
thy power have I extended on high,
  over Babylon thy city, before all mankind.

ACHAEMENID PERSIA

Palace of Darius, Persepolis, c. 500 B.C. (Gardner, pp. 65–67, ills. 2:35, 2:36, 2:38, and 2:39; Janson, pp. 83–84, ills. 109–11)
The Behistun Inscription: "I Am Darius, the Great King," c. 500 B.C.

Darius I (?–486 B.C.) was both a powerful personality and a dynamic ruler. During his thirty-six-year reign (522–486 B.C.) Darius extended the geographical domain of the Persian empire to the Indus River on the east and into Europe on the west. Equally important, he reorganized the empire according to a system of government that continued to function until 330 B.C., when Alexander the Great swept across Persia and its territories.

Darius administered his empire from Susa, where he built an audience hall and a royal residence. However, about 520 B.C., Darius began construction of a new royal palace in his native country of Fars (Persis) at Persepolis. The palace complex was completed by his son and successor, Xerxes I.

Although he was related to the royal family, Darius did not stand in direct line to the throne. Darius' predecessor, Cyrus the Great, the great warrior king who had formed the Persian empire, ruled from 559 to 530 B.C. and was survived by two sons, Bardiya and Cambyses. After the death of Cambyses, Darius apparently assassinated Bardiya, the rightful successor to the kingship. He attempted to justify the assassination by claiming that a usurper named Gaumata had posed as Bardiya and had unlawfully seized the throne. He also accused Cambyses of having secretly ordered the murder of Bardiya. He further claimed that Cambyses, upon hearing the news of Gaumata's coup, committed suicide. Darius described himself as deposing the false claimant and assuming the throne in obedience to the will of the god Ormazd, the supreme deity of the Persians.

Darius' autobiographical, and largely fictional, version of the events that led to his accession is recounted in *The Behistun Inscription,* a trilingual inscription cut on a rock face at the base of the Behistun mountain. A selection from *The Behistun Inscription,* "I Am Darius, the Great King," is presented here.

The Behistun Inscription[22]

I Am Darius, the Great King

I am Darius, the great king, the king of kings, the king of Persia, the king of the provinces, the son of Hystaspes, the grandson of Arsames, the Achaemenian.

Says Darius the king—My father was Hystaspes; the father of Hystaspes was Arsames; the father of Arsames was Ariaramnes; the father of Ariaramnes was Teispes; the father of Teispes was Achaemenes.

Says Darius the king—On that account we have been called Achaemenians; from antiquity we have descended; from antiquity our family have been kings.

Says Darius the king—Ormazd granted me the empire. Ormazd brought help to me, so that I gained this empire. By the grace of Ormazd I hold this empire.

Says Darius the king—This is what was done by me after that I became king. A man named Cambyses, son of Cyrus, of our race, he was here king before me. Of that Cambyses there was a brother, Bardiya was his name; of the same mother, and of the same father with Cambyses. Afterwards Cambyses slew that Bardiya. When Cambyses had slain Bardiya, it was not known to the people that Bardiya had been slain. Afterwards Cambyses proceeded to Egypt. When Cambyses had proceeded to Egypt, then the state became wicked. Then the lie became abounding in the land, both in Persia, and in Media, and in the other provinces.

Says Darius the king—Afterwards there was a certain man, a Magian, named Gaumata. He arose from Pissiachada, the mountain named Aracadres, from thence. On the 14th day of the month Vayakhna, then it

22. Reprinted, by permission of the publisher, from Francis R. B. Godolphin, ed., *The Greek Historians: The Complete and Unabridged Historical Works of Herodotus, Thucydides, Xenophon, Arrian,* Vol. 2, copyright © 1942 (New York: Random House, Inc.), pp. 623–24. Selection translated by Henry Rawlinson.

was that he arose. He thus lied to the state, "I am Bardiya, the son of Cyrus, the brother of Cambyses." Then the whole state became rebellious. From Cambyses it went over to him, both Persia, and Media, and the other provinces. He seized the empire. On the 9th day of the month Garmapada, then it was he so seized the empire. Afterwards Cambyses, unable to endure, died.

Says Darius the king—The empire of which Gaumata, the Magian, dispossessed Cambyses, that empire from the olden time had been in our family. After Gaumata the Magian had dispossessed Cambyses both of Persia and Media and the dependent provinces, he did according to his desire: he became king.

Says Darius the king—There was not a man, neither Persian, nor Median, nor any one of our family, who would dispossess that Gaumata the Magian of the crown. The state feared him exceedingly. He slew many people who had known the old Bardiya; for that reason he slew them. "Lest they should recognise me that I am not Bardiya, the son of Cyrus." No one dared to say anything concerning Gaumata the Magian, until I arrived. Then I prayed to Ormazd; Ormazd brought help to me. On the 10th day of the month Bagayadish, then it was, with my faithful men, I slew that Gaumata the Magian, and those who were his chief followers. The fort named Sictachotes in the district of Media called Nisaea, there I slew him. I dispossessed him of the empire. By the grace of Ormazd I became king: Ormazd granted me the sceptre.

Says Darius the king—The empire which had been taken away from our family, that I recovered. I established it in its place. As it was before, so I made it. The temples which Gaumata the Magian had destroyed, I rebuilt. The sacred offices of the state, both the religious chants and the worship, I restored to the people, which Gaumata the Magian had deprived them of. I established the state in its place, both Persia, and Media, and the other provinces. As it was before, so I restored what had been taken away. By the grace of Ormazd I did this. I arranged it, by the grace of Ormazd, so that Gaumata the Magian should not supersede our family.

II

The Art of Egypt

THE EARLY DYNASTIC PERIOD AND THE OLD KINGDOM

1. *Men, Boats, and Animals,* Hierakonpolis, Predynastic Period, c. 3500 B.C.[1] (Gardner, p. 73, ill. 3:1; Janson, p. 55, ill. 52)
Hymn to the Nile: "Adoration to the Nile!" Nineteenth Dynasty, 1320–1200 B.C.

The Nile was central to ancient Egyptian religious life, and it was addressed as a god by the Egyptian people. In the Egyptian cosmos, the river was the physical and symbolic meeting place of earth and heaven. The elongated river valley, which was the center of the Egyptian world, was in the Egyptian mind likened to a man lying prone on whose back the activities of the day-to-day world took place. The sky was conceived as a sea upon which the sun sailed westward in a bark during the day. Another waterway was connected to the Nile and flowed beneath the earth. During the night, the celestial bark sailed on this subterranean stream to appear in the east at dawn. *Men, Boats, and Animals,* the earliest known Egyptian wall painting, illustrates the cycle of life and death that, in Egypt, was focused on the Nile.

The Nile was essential to Egyptian agriculture and thus to Egyptian life. The river was regarded as the major arena of divine and human interaction. The annual floods deposited a residue of nutrient-rich soil over the fields and made the land fertile. To the Egyptians, therefore, these inundations signified the joy of the gods and their beneficence to humankind. Drought resulted in famine and starvation and was regarded as a sign of the gods' displeasure. *Hymn to the Nile* praises the river for all the blessings that it bestows on humanity. It appears to have been composed for an inundation festival that took place in Thebes. The connection between the great river and the Egyptian gods and people is made clear in the second stanza of the hymn: "If the gods suffer in heaven / Then the faces of men

1. Dynasties and the reigns of individual rulers are dated here in accordance with the chronology of *The Cambridge Ancient History,* 3rd. ed. (Cambridge: Cambridge University Press, 1971). References to periods or dynasties are followed, wherever possible, by absolute dates that are more specific.

waste away." Probably composed two hundred years earlier, the *Hymn to the Nile* is preserved in two manuscripts of the Nineteenth Dynasty. A selection from the *Hymn to the Nile,* "Adoration to the Nile!" is presented here.

Hymn to the Nile[2]

Adoration to the Nile!

Adoration to the Nile!
Hail to thee, O Nile!
Who manifesteth thyself over this land
And comest to give life to Egypt!
Mysterious is thy issuing forth from the darkness,
On this day whereon it is celebrated!
Watering the orchards created by Re[3]
To cause all the cattle to live,
Thou givest the earth to drink, inexhaustible one!
Path that descendest from the sky,
Loving the bread of Geb[4] and the first-fruits of Nepri,[5]
Thou causest the workshops of Ptah[6] to prosper!

Lord of the fish, during the inundation,
No bird alights on the crops.
Thou createst the corn, thou bringest forth the barley,
Assuring perpetuity to the temples.
If thou ceasest thy toil and thy work,
Then all that exists is in anguish.
If the gods suffer in heaven
Then the faces of men waste away.

Then he torments the flocks of Egypt,
And great and small are in agony.
But all is changed for mankind when he comes;
He is endowed with the qualities of Nun.[7]

2. Reprinted from Oliver J. Thatcher, ed., *The Library of Original Sources,* Vol. I (New York: University Research Extension, 1907), pp. 79–80, 82–83.

3. The most important of the solar deities, Re represented the midday sun and, when identified with Atum, was regarded as the progenitor of the eight great gods: Shu, Tefnut, Geb, Nut, Osiris, Isis, Set, and Nephthys.

4. The earth god, the father of Osiris and Isis, the son of Shu and Tefnut.

5. The god of grain, often depicted as a child. Nepri was a form of the god Re.

6. The craftsman god, originally associated with the city of Memphis, who was regarded as the creator of all material things.

7. The god of the primeval waters from which all life, including the gods, emerged.

If he shines, the earth is joyous,
Every stomach is full of rejoicing,
Every spine is happy,
Every jaw-bone crushes its food.

He brings the offerings, as chief of provisioning;
He is the creator of all good things,
As master of energy, full of sweetness in his choice.
If offerings are made it is thanks to him.
He brings forth the herbage for the flocks,
And sees that each god receives his sacrifices.
All that depends on him is a precious incense.
He spreads himself over Egypt,
Filling the granaries, renewing the marts,
Watching over the goods of the unhappy.

O inundation of the Nile,
Offerings are made unto thee,
Oxen are immolated to thee,
Great festivals are instituted for thee.
Birds are sacrificed to thee,
Gazelles are taken for thee in the mountain,
Pure flames are prepared for thee.
Sacrifice is made to every god as it is made to the Nile.
The Nile has made its retreats in Southern Egypt,
Its name is not known beyond the Tuau.[8]
The god manifests not his forms,
He baffles all conception.

Men exalt him like the cycle of the gods,
They dread him who creates the heat,
Even him who has made his son the universal master
In order to give prosperity to Egypt.
Come and prosper! come and prosper!
O Nile, come and prosper!
O thou who makest men to live through his flocks
And his flocks through his orchards!
Come and prosper, come,
O Nile, come and prosper!

8. Possibly a reference to the underworld.

2. *Panel of Hesire (or Hesy-ra),* Saqqara. Third Dynasty, c. 2650 B.C. (Gardner, p. 75, ill. 3:3; Janson, p. 58, ill. 55)
The Autobiography of Weni: "The Career of a Court Official," Sixth Dynasty, c. 2270 B.C.

The *Panel of Hesire* depicts a high government official, Hesire, holding the writing materials that symbolize his profession as a scribe. The career of a palace official is most fully described in a text entitled *The Autobiography of Weni.* This text, which was carved on the wall of Weni's mastaba, is the longest narrative inscription from the Old Kingdom. It describes the career of Weni, the loyal servant of three Egyptian kings.

Weni began his career during the reign of the first king of the Sixth Dynasty, Teti II. His first appointment was at an unimportant level as a lowly undercustodian of the royal domain. Under Pepi I, Weni was appointed judge and given rank at the royal court. At the same time he was made a priest of the pyramid temple, which provided him with an income. He was soon promoted to superior custodian of the royal domains. When a conspiracy against the king was formed in the harem, it was the trusted Weni who was chosen to investigate the matter. In addition, Weni served as a military commander. Finally, during the reign of Pepi's son, Mernere, Weni served as governor of Upper Egypt.

In his account of his career, Weni emphasizes the titles he held. However, so many honorary titles had been granted to nobles who performed no duties whatever that, in order to distinguish themselves from mere title holders, the actual administrators of many offices used the word "true" with their titles. A selection from *The Autobiography of Weni,* "The Career of a Court Official," is presented here.

The Autobiography of Weni[9]

The Career of a Court Official

The Count, Governor of Upper Egypt, Chamberlain, Warden of Nekhen, Mayor of Nekheb, Sole Companion, honored by Osiris[10] Foremost-of-the-Westerners, Weni says: I was a fillet-wearing youth under the majesty of King Teti, my office being that of custodian of the storehouse, when I became inspector of tenants of the palace [. . .]. When I had become overseer of the robing-room under the majesty of King Pepi, his majesty gave me the rank of companion and inspector of priests of his pyramid-town.

9. Reprinted, by permission of the University of California Press, from Miriam Lichtheim, ed., *Ancient Egyptian Literature: A Book of Readings* (Berkeley: University of California Press, 1973–76), Vol. 1, pp. 18–22.

10. The son of Geb and Nut, the sky goddess, Osiris was the ruler of the dead. Through his death and subsequent return to life, Osiris was associated with both death and fertility.

While my office was that of [. . .] his majesty made me senior warden of Nekhen, his heart being filled with me beyond any other servant of his. I heard cases alone with the chief judge and vizier, concerning all kinds of secrets. I acted in the name of the king for the royal harem and for the six great houses, because his majesty's heart was filled with me beyond any official of his, any noble of his, any servant of his. . . .

When there was a secret charge in the royal harem against Queen Weret-yamtes, his majesty made me go in to hear it alone. No chief judge and vizier, no official was there, only I alone; because I was worthy, because I was rooted in his majesty's heart; because his majesty had filled his heart with me. Only I put it in writing together with one other senior warden of Nekhen, while my rank was only that of overseer of royal tenants. Never before had one like me heard a secret of the king's harem; but his majesty made me hear it, because I was worthy in his majesty's heart beyond any official of his, beyond any noble of his, beyond any servant of his.

When his majesty took action against the Asiatic Sand-dwellers, his majesty made an army of many tens of thousands from all of Upper Egypt: . . . His majesty sent me at the head of this army, there being counts, royal seal-bearers, sole companions of the palace, chieftains and mayors of towns of Upper and Lower Egypt,[11] companions, scout-leaders, chief priests of Upper and Lower Egypt, and chief district officials at the head of the troops of Upper and Lower Egypt, from the villages and towns that they governed and from the Nubians of those foreign lands. I was the one who commanded them—while my rank was that of overseer of royal tenants—because of my rectitude, so that no one attacked his fellow, so that no one seized a loaf or sandals from a traveler, so that no one took a cloth from any town, so that no one took a goat from anyone. . . .

When I was chamberlain of the palace and sandal-bearer, King Mernere, my lord who lives forever, made me Count and Governor of Upper Egypt, from Yebu in the south to Medenyt in the north, because I was worthy in his majesty's heart, because I was rooted in his majesty's heart, because his majesty's heart was filled with me. When I was chamberlain and sandal-bearer, his majesty praised me for the watch and guard duty which I did at court, more than any official of his, more than any noble of his, more than any servant of his. Never before had this office been held by any servant. . . .

11. Egypt was composed of two kingdoms united into a single state. Lower Egypt, located on the lower reaches of the Nile, was the northern kingdom and Upper Egypt, the southern kingdom. Much of the imagery of the rulers dramatized this dual kingship. Rulers are often portrayed wearing two crowns, the cobra crown of Lower Egypt and the high conical crown of Upper Egypt. Another symbol of Lower Egypt was papyrus, whereas the lotus represented Upper Egypt.

I was one beloved of his father, praised by his mother, gracious to his brothers. The count, true governor of Upper Egypt, honored by Osiris, Weni.

3. Imhotep, Stepped Pyramid of King Zoser, Saqqara. Third Dynasty, c. 2650 B.C. (Gardner, p. 77, ill. 3:6; Janson p. 59, ills. 57–60)
The Pyramid Texts: "Be Not Unaware of Me, O God," "The Reed-Floats of the Sky Are Set Down for Horus," and "If I Be Cursed," Fifth and Sixth Dynasties, c. 2375–2125 B.C.

The Stepped Pyramid of King Zoser, designed by Imhotep, testifies to the overwhelming importance, in Egyptian religion, of the belief in the afterlife. The ancient Egyptians believed that the west, where the sun god Re descended into his grave every night, was the land of the dead. There was also a netherworld where the dead waited in order to join the sun god on his nightly course. The destination of the journey made by the dead was the Field of Rushes, a field where the grain was always abundant and where the dead dwelt in security and plenty. But the Field of Rushes, also known as the Field of the Blessed or the Field of Food Offerings, was surrounded by water. The most common way to cross over the water was to ride in a ferryboat operated by a mysterious ferryman, named Face-behind or Look-behind, because he always faced the rear as he poled his craft. Not everyone succeeded in making the passage. Only those who had led just and honorable lives were allowed to pass over the water and enter the Field of Rushes.

The Pyramid Texts were inscribed on the inner walls and passageways of pyramids constructed during the Fifth and Sixth Dynasties. The texts, which were probably recited by the priests on the day of a king's burial, include funerary rituals, magical incantations, religious hymns, and fragments of ancient myths. They give details of daily life in Egypt, but above all, they insist that the destiny of the king is to join the gods in the sky.

Three selections from *The Pyramid Texts* are presented here. In the first, "Be Not Unaware of Me, O God," the dead king beseeches the gods not to forget him. In the second selection, "The Reed-Floats of the Sky Are Set Down for Horus," the king petitions the ferryman to carry him to his destination. In the third selection, "If I Be Cursed," the king warns the gods not to curse or hinder him on his journey to the sacred realm.

The Egyptian attitude toward death combined fear of the unknown with the audacious insistence that at least one man, the king, would raise himself above the earth, confront the gods, and claim the celestial realm as his kingdom.

The Pyramid Texts[12]

Be Not Unaware of Me, O God

Be not unaware of me, O God;
If you know me, I will know you.
Be not unaware of me, O God;
Of me it is said: "He who has perished."
Be not unaware of me, O Re;
If you know me, I will know you.
Be not unaware of me, O Re;
Of me it is said: "Greatest of all who have been completely destroyed."
Be not unaware of me, O Thoth;[13]
If you know me, I will know you.
Be not unaware of me, O Thoth;
Of me it is said: "He who rests alone."
Be not unaware of me, O Har-Sopd;[14]
If you know me, I will know you.
Be not unaware of me, O Har-Sopd;
Of me it is said: "Miserable One."
Be not unaware of me, O Dweller in the Netherworld;
If you know me, I will know you.
Be not unaware of me, O Dweller in the Netherworld;
Of me it is said: "He who wakes healthy."
Be not unaware of me, O Bull of the sky;
If you know me, I will know you.
Be not unaware of me, O Bull of the sky;
Of me it is said: "This star of the Lower Sky."

The Reed-Floats of the Sky Are Set Down for Horus

The reed-floats of the sky are set down for Horus,[15]
That he may cross on them to the horizon, to Harakhte.[16]
The reed-floats of the sky are set down for me,
That I may cross on them to the horizon, to Harakhte.
The reed-floats of the sky are set down for Shezemte,[17]

12. Reprinted, by permission of Oxford University Press, from *The Ancient Egyptian Pyramid Texts,* trans. by R. O. Faulkner (Oxford: The Clarendon Press, 1969), pp. 70–71, 73–74, 96–97.

13. The moon god and the patron of writing, learning, and the sciences.

14. Possibly a reference to the solar deity Soped.

15. The son of Isis and Osiris, Horus was god of the sky and the sun. He was also associated with kingship.

16. Or "Horus of the Horizon"; Harakhte represented the sun god in his daytime form.

17. God of the East.

That he may cross on them to the horizon, to Harakhte.
The reed-floats of the sky are set down for me,
That I may cross on them to the horizon, to Harakhte.
The Nurse-canal[18] is opened.
The Winding Waterway[19] is flooded,
The Fields of Rushes[20] are filled with water,
And I am ferried over
To yonder eastern side of the sky,
To the place where the gods fashioned me,
Wherein I was born, new and young.

If I Be Cursed

If I be cursed, then will Atum[21] be cursed;
If I be reviled, then will Atum be reviled;
If I be smitten, then will Atum be smitten;
If I be hindered on this road, then will Atum be hindered,
For I am Horus,
I have come following my father,
I have come following Osiris.

4. *Khafre (Chefren),* Fourth Dynasty, c. 2525 B.C. (Gardner, p. 81, ill. 3:13; Janson, p. 61, ill. 65)
The Book of the Dead: "Preserving the Heart," Eighteenth Dynasty, 1567–1320 B.C.

To the ancient Egyptians, the tomb was the place where the crisis of death was faced and where a process of transfiguration occurred. One important function of the tomb was to ensure the continued existence of the physical aspect of the individual's being. In order to accomplish this, the tomb not only preserved the actual physical body of the deceased in the form of a mummy, it also provided the deceased with a substitute for his or her body in the form of portrait statues. An example of this kind of statue is the seated figure *Khafre,* one of a group of seven statues carved for the valley temple of the king at Gizeh.

According to Egyptian beliefs, the physical body was not the only important aspect of human nature. Physical existence was animated by a vital force called the ka, which acted as a guardian spirit to the individual in this world and had a common life with the deceased in the next world. Another nonphysical aspect of the individual's existence was the ba, or "soul," a term which refers to the animated existence of the individual after death.

18–20. These are references to various parts of the heavens.

21. The primeval god and creator of the universe, from whom the other gods were descended. Atum later became associated with the sun and identified with Horus and Re. He was particularly linked with the evening sun.

Thus, according to Egyptian thought, the person consisted of both a visible body and an invisible force, which was believed to reside in the "belly" or the "heart." *The Book of the Dead* includes many hymns that express the importance of ensuring the eternal survival of that animating force.

The texts of *The Book of the Dead* are found in tombs of the New Kingdom. These texts were written on papyrus rolls by priests. The rolls were sold, and the name of the owner was inscribed in a blank space in the roll; the roll was subsequently placed in the tomb to assist the deceased on the hazardous journey to the afterlife. Many copies of these texts have been found, and their numbers indicate that, in the New Kingdom, the possibility of the afterlife was no longer restricted to the kings and important nobles as in earlier periods, but was widely distributed through the upper and middle classes. A selection from *The Book of the Dead,* "Preserving the Heart," is presented here.

The Book of the Dead[22]

Preserving the Heart

Osiris Auf-ankh, triumphant, born of Sheret-Amsu, triumphant saith:

"My heart, my mother; my heart, my mother!
My heart of my existence upon earth.
May naught stand up to oppose me in judgement;
May there be no opposition to me in the presence of the sovereign princes;
May no evil be wrought against me in the presence of the gods.
May there be no parting of thee from me in the presence of the great god, the lord of Amentet.
Homage to thee, O thou heart of Osiris-khent-Amentet!
Homage to you, O my reins![23]
Homage to you, O ye gods who dwell in the divine clouds,
And who are exalted (or holy) by reason of your sceptres!
Speak ye fair words for the Osiris Auf-ankh,
And make ye him to prosper before Nehebka.
And behold, though I be joined unto the earth,
And am in the mighty innermost part of heaven,
Let me remain on the earth and not die in Amentet,
And let me be a *khu*[24] therein forever and ever."

22. Reprinted from *Egyptian Literature: The Book of the Dead,* trans. by E. A. Wallis Budge (London: The Colonial Press, 1901), pp. 23–24.

23. The kidneys.

24. The immortal soul, the seat of intelligence.

5. *Hippopotamus Hunt,* Tomb of Ti, Saqqara, Fifth Dynasty, c. 2400 B.C. (Gardner, p. 83, ill. 3:16; Janson, p. 63, ill. 70)
The Triumph of Horus: "The Harpoon Ritual," "Horus Is Crowned" and "Set Is Butchered," Ptolemaic Period, c. 110 B.C.

The Triumph of Horus describes the mythological contest between the two gods Horus and Set. This contest, as it can be constructed from Egyptian legends, was the result of the murder of Osiris, a good and beneficent king of Egypt, by his brother Set. Osiris was mourned by his sisters, Isis and Nephthys. Isis recovered the body of her slain brother, temporarily restored him to life, and conceived a child by him, Horus. When Horus reached manhood, he, with the assistance of his mother, Isis, battled and defeated Set.

In Egyptian thought, the victory of Horus over Set not only avenged the death of the deified Osiris but also affirmed the right of the living monarch to rule his kingdom. Set, the god of deserts and foreign lands, was often identified with the enemies of Egypt. Horus, the god of the midday sun and the lord of heaven, was identified with the royal lineage. From the beginning of the First Dynasty, every Egyptian ruler was addressed with the name of Horus as the first of his five official names, and every ruler was considered to be the living Horus.

The Triumph of Horus was associated with the annual Festival of Victory celebrated by the king, priests, and people in the second month of winter. Three selections from *The Triumph of Horus* are presented here. In the first, "The Harpoon Ritual," Horus appears as a harpooner and Set as a hippopotamus. Horus, representing Upper and Lower Egypt, thrusts his harpoons into the body of the hippopotamus. In the second selection, "Horus Is Crowned," the victorious Horus is crowned as ruler of Egypt. In the third selection, "Set Is Butchered," the hippopotamus is dismembered and the severed portions of the body are distributed among the gods. Finally, the triumph of Horus and of the king over their enemies is declared. In this translation, the text has been presented in the form of a ritual enacted as a drama.

The Triumph of Horus was inscribed on the walls of the Temple of Edfu during the Ptolemaic Period about 110 B.C. It is thought to be a slightly different version of a text from the later New Kingdom. Although it is considerably later in date than the *Hippopotamus Hunt* from the Tomb of Ti, *The Triumph of Horus* is apparently based on much earlier prototypes. The theme of the harpooning of the hippopotamus is described in the Coffin Texts of the Middle Kingdom and the Pyramid Texts of the Old Kingdom and is depicted on the Palermo Stone of the First Dynasty. Thus, the *Hippopotamus Hunt,* which illustrates Ti hunting the hippopotamus, may well not only depict an actual hunting scene, but may also represent the mythological contest between Horus and Set.

The Triumph of Horus[25]

The Harpoon Ritual

Chorus

Praise to thee, praise to thy name,
Horus the Behdetite, great god, lord of the sky,
Goodly wall of copper round about Egypt.

Demon

I am Chief-of-the-Two-Lands-when-he-rises.
I guard thee from him who is hostile to thee;
I protect Thy Majesty with my charms.
I rage against thy foes as a savage baboon.
I lay low thine enemies in thy path.
I am the Guard of Thy Majesty every day
I protect Thy Majesty every day
I am the first demon of thy crew.

King

The first of the weapons which rushed after him who assailed Horus
And took the breath from the snout of the Hippopotamus.

Horus Lord of Mesen

The first harpoon is stuck fast in his snout and has severed his nostrils.
The blade takes hold in the head of the Hippopotamus in the Place of Confidence.

Chorus

O Horus, fair are thy trappings of giraffe's hair,
Thy net which is Min's,[26]
And thy shaft which belongs to the spear of Onuris.

25. Reprinted, by permission of the University of California Press, from Herbert W. Fairman, *The Triumph of Horus* (Berkeley: University of California Press, 1974), pp. 84–86, 105–106, 113–14, 117.

26. A fertility god who possessed the double form of father and son and who symbolized procreation.

Thy arm was the first to cast the harpoon.
Those upon the banks rejoice at the sight of thee,
As at the rising of Sothis[27] at the year's beginning,
When they behold thy weapons raining down in midstream
Like the moon-beams when the sky is peaceful.
Horus is in his bark like Wenty,
Having overthrown the hippopotami from his war-galley.

Chorus and Onlookers

Hold fast, Horus, hold fast!

Demon

I am the Offeror-who-apportions-his-offerings
I am with thee in the melee
That I may punish the transgressions of thine enemy.
I break his bones, I smash his vertebrae,
I crunch his flesh, I swallow his gore.

King

Thy lance which brought in the Caitiff though he was afar;
It has cleft the crown of the head of the Hippopotamus.

Horus the Behdetite

The second harpoon is stuck fast in his forehead;
It has cleft the crown of the head of the enemy.

Chorus

Grasp firmly the harpoon, breathe the air in Khemmis,
O lord of Mesen,
Captor of the Hippopotamus, Creator of Joy,
Goodly Falcon[28] who boards his boat
And takes to the river in his war-galley;
Prototype man, Battling Horus!
Those who are in the water are afraid of him,
Awe of him fills those who are on the bank.
Thou subjugator of every one,
Thou whose thews are strong,

27. The star Sirius, whose helical rising signaled the beginning of the Egyptian civil year.
28. Horus.

The Perverse One[29] in the water fears thee.
Thou smitest and woundest as if it were Horus who cast the harpoon,
Even the Victorious Bull, Lord of Prowess.
The Son of Re has done for Horus even as Horus himself did,
Yea, the Son of Re has done likewise.
Let thy talons grip the second harpoon.

Chorus and Onlookers

Hold fast, Horus, hold fast!

Horus Is Crowned

Chorus

How happy is thy countenance, now that thou hast appeared gloriously in thy bark,
O Horus the Behdetite, great god, lord of the sky,
Like Re in the Bark of the Morning,
When thou hast received thine office with crook and flail,[30]
And art crowned with the Double Diadem of Horus,
Sekhmet[31] prevailing over him that is rebellious toward thee,
Thoth the Great protecting thee.
Thine inheritance is thine, great god, son of Osiris,
Now that thou hast smitten the Lower Egyptian Bull.
Be glad of heart, ye inhabitants of the Great Seat,
Horus has taken possession of the throne of his father.

Chorus and Onlookers

Horus has taken possession of the throne of his father.

Horus

I am Horus the Behdetite, great god, lord of the sky, lord of Mesen;
Wenty who pierces the Unsuccessful One, his foe;
Him-with-the-Upraised-Arm who wields the three-barbed harpoon in order to slay his enemies.

29. Set in the form of the hippopotamus.

30. Symbols of the two kingdoms of Upper and Lower Egypt.

31. A lion-headed goddess, the wife of Ptah, associated with the destructive powers of the sun's rays and the underworld.

I cast my thirty-barbed harpoon at the snout of the
Hippopotamus,
I wound the foeman of Him-who-is-on-the-Mound. . . .
I am Horus the Behdetite, great god, lord of the sky,
Lord of the Upper Egyptian crown,
Prince of the Lower Egyptian crown,
King of the Kings of Upper Egypt,
King of the Kings of Lower Egypt,
Beneficent Prince, the Prince of princes.
I receive the crook and the whip,
For I am the lord of this land.
I take possession of the Two Lands
In assuming the Double Diadem.
I overthrow the foe of my father Osiris
As King of Upper and Lower Egypt for ever.

Set Is Butchered

Isis

Thou seizest thy harpoon and doest what thou wilt with it,
My son Horus, thou lovable one.

Reader

The King of Upper and Lower Egypt, Heir-of-the-Beneficient-Gods, Chosen-of-Ptah, Justiciar-of-Re, Living-Image-of-Amen, the son of Re, Lord of Diadems, Ptolemaeus-may-he-live-forever, Beloved-of-Ptah, is triumphant in the Broad Hall.
He has overthrown the Beduin of all the countries of Asia.
Lo, he is triumphant in the Broad Hall,
He has suppressed his enemies,
He has taken hold of their backs,
He has clutched the foe by their forelocks.
Bring in the hippopotamus in the form of a cake into the presence of Him-with-the-Upraised-Arm.

Butcher

I am the skilled butcher of the Majesty of Re,
Who cuts up the Hippopotamus, dismembered upon his hide.

Reader

Be thou annihilated, O Set, be thou annihiliated!
Thou shalt not exist and thy soul shall not exist.
Thou shalt not exist and thy body shall not exist.
Thou shalt not exist and thy children shall not exist.
Thou shalt not exist and thy flesh shall not exist.
Thou shalt not exist and thy bones shall not exist.
Thou shalt not exist and thy magic shall not exist.
Thou shalt not exist and no place where thou art shall
exist.
Thou shalt die, . . .
Horus in his strength has united the Two Lands;
Set is overthrown in the form of a hippopotamus.

THE MIDDLE KINGDOM

Sesostris III, Twelfth Dynasty, c. 1850 B.C. (Gardner, p. 86, ill. 3:22)
Portrait of Sesostris III, Twelfth Dynasty, c. 1850 B.C. (Janson, p. 64, ill. 72)
The Man Who Was Tired of Life: "Troubled Times," Twelfth Dynasty, 1991–1786 B.C.

The portraits of Sesostris III present the king, a ruler of the Middle Kingdom, in a strikingly different manner from sculptures of the Old Kingdom rulers. During the First Intermediate Period, Egypt had suffered from internal dissension. After almost one hundred years of unrest, the monarchs of the Middle Kingdom were able to reassert their power and to reestablish prosperity. The furrowed brows and anxious expression of Sesostris contrast strongly with the serene, untroubled countenances depicted in the portrait sculptures of an earlier age.

The anarchy that resulted from this temporary collapse of the Egyptian state is reflected in the literature of the Middle Kingdom, which makes frequent reference to the violence, hunger, and misery that pervaded Egyptian life. The distress felt is especially evident in the treatise known as *The Man Who Was Tired of Life.* The prevailing mood of despair and disillusionment conveys the same feelings as the portraits of Sesostris III. A man, weary of the chaotic conditions, complains that the social order which had given value to an individual's life has been destroyed. He argues with his soul whether he sould continue to live, and he tries to persuade his soul that they should abandon this world and seek a better existence in the next. The soul replies, however, that if the man commits suicide, the soul will be forever parted from the body, whereas if the man dies a natural death, the soul will be able to return and make its home with the man's body. A selection from *The Man Who Was Tired of Life,* "Troubled Times," is presented here.

The Man Who Was Tired of Life[32]

Troubled Times

Lo, my name reeks
Lo, more than carrion smell
On summer days of burning sky.

Lo, my name reeks
Lo, more than a catch of fish
On fishing days of burning sky. . . .

Lo, my name reeks
Lo, more than that of a wife
About whom lies are told to the husband. . . .

To whom shall I speak today?
Brothers are mean,
The friends of today do not love.

To whom shall I speak today?
Hearts are greedy,
Everyone robs his comrade's goods. . . .

To whom shall I speak today?
None are righteous,
The land is left to evildoers. . . .

Death is before me today
Like a sick man's recovery,
Like going outdoors after confinement.

Death is before me today
Like the fragrance of myrrh,
Like sitting under sail on a breezy day.

Death is before me today
Like the fragrance of lotus,
Like sitting on the shore of drunkenness. . . .

Death is before me today
Like a man's longing to see his home
When he has spent many years in captivity.

Truly, he who is yonder will be a living god,
Punishing the evildoer's crime.

32. Reprinted, by permission of the University of California Press, from Lichtheim, op. cit., Vol. 1, pp. 166–69.

Truly, he who is yonder will stand in the sun-bark,
Making its bounty flow to the temples.

Truly, he who is yonder will be a wise man,
Not barred from appealing to Re when he speaks.

What my *ba* said to me: "Now throw complaint on the wood-pile, you my comrade, my brother! Whether you offer on the brazier, whether you bear down on life, as you say, love me here when you have set aside the West! But when it is wished that you attain the West, that your body joins the earth, I shall alight after you have become weary, and then we shall dwell together!"

THE HYKSOS AND THE NEW KINGDOM

1. Mortuary Temple of Queen Hatshepsut, Deir-el-Bahari, Eighteenth Dynasty, c. 1485 B.C. (Gardner, p. 87, ill. 3:23; Janson, p. 65, ills. 74–75)

The Royal Account of the Life of Queen Hatshepsut: "The Conception of Hatshepsut" and "The Coronation of Hatshepsut," Eighteenth Dynasty, c. 1485 B.C.

Hatshepsut, the descendant of a line of influential queens, attained an unprecedented position for a woman. Between 1503 and 1482 B.C. she was recognized as pharaoh of Egypt.

Hatshepsut was the daughter of King Thutmose I and Queen Ahmose. She was married to her half-brother, Thutmose II, and upon the death of her father, she and her husband came to the throne. Thutmose II ruled only eight years. When he died, Thutmose III, the young son of Thutmose II and an obscure concubine, became pharaoh, and Hatshepsut became regent.

Surrounded by a loyal and powerful group of government officials, Hatshepsut soon arranged to be crowned as pharaoh, whereas Thutmose III was made a priest of the god Amen.[33] Hatshepsut exercised direct control over Egypt for twenty-one years. During that time she adopted the titles and regalia of the pharaoh, including the false beard traditionally worn by Egyptian kings.

Hatshepsut emphasized administrative reforms and commercial development. Of the many monuments that she constructed, the most impressive is the mortuary temple intended for herself and her father at Deir-el-Bahari. Its inscriptions, known as *The Royal Account of the Life of Queen Hatshepsut,* describe the birth, coronation, and remarkable deeds of the queen. The accompanying reliefs

33. The most important deity of the New Kingdom, Amen was a sun god who was associated with the powers that created and sustained the world.

follow the tradition that the Egyptian sovereign should be the son of Amen so closely that the infant Hatshepsut is shown as a boy.

Two selections from *The Royal Account* are presented here. In the first, "The Conception of Hatshepsut," the queen is described as being conceived through the divine union of Queen Ahmose and the sun god Amen. In the second selection, "The Coronation of Hatshepsut," Hatshepsut is acknowledged by Thutmose I as the daughter of Amen and the rightful successor to the throne of Egypt.

It is not known whether Hatshepsut died naturally or by violence. However, as she grew older and Thutmose III grew stronger, her power declined. At the end of Thutmose III's reign, a campaign of defacement was directed against the memorials of Hatshepsut.

The Royal Account of the Life of Queen Hatshepsut[34]

The Conception of Hatshepsut

The Scene in the Reliefs

Amen, the sun-god, and Queen Ahmose, the mother of Hatshepsut, are seated facing each other: the god extends to the queen .the symbols of life.

The Interview

Utterance of Amen-Re, lord of Thebes, presider over Karnak. He made his form like the majesty of this husband, the King Okheperkere. He found her as she slept in the beauty of her palace. She waked at the fragrance of the god, which she smelled in the presence of his majesty. He went to her immediately, [he had intercourse with her],[35] he imposed his desire upon her, he caused that she should see him in his form of a god. When he came before her, she rejoiced at the sight of his beauty, his love passed into her limbs, which the fragrance of the god flooded; all his odors were from Punt.

Words of the Queen

Utterance by the king's-wife and king's-mother Ahmose, in the presence of the majesty of this august god, Amen, Lord of Thebes: "How great is thy fame! It is splendid to see thy front; thou hast united my majesty with thy favors, thy dew is in all my limbs." After this, the majesty of this god did all that he desired with her.

Words of Amen

Utterance of Amen, Lord of the Two Lands, before her: "Khnemet-Amen-Hatshepsut shall be the name of this my daughter, whom I have

34. Reprinted from James Henry Breasted, ed. and trans., *Ancient Records of Egypt,* Vol. II (Chicago: University of Chicago Press, 1906), pp. 80–81, 96–97.

35. In Breasted's translation, this is rendered in Latin in the interests of delicacy.

placed in thy body, this saying which comes out of thy mouth. She shall exercise the excellent kingship in this whole land. My soul is hers, my bounty is hers, my crown is hers, that she may rule the Two Lands, that she may lead all the living [. . .]"

The Coronation of Hatshepsut

The Scene in the Reliefs

The coronation of the queen is represented as taking place before the court, at the command of Thutmose I, the father of Hatshepsut, who retires from the throne in his daughter's form. Thutmose I is depicted with his daughter and three rows of courtiers standing in front of him.

Thutmose I Summons His Daughter to Be Crowned

There saw her the majesty of her father, this Horus; how divine is her great fashioner! Her heart is glad, for great is her crown; she advocates her cause in truth, exalter of her royal dignity, and of that which her *ka* does. The living were set before her in his palace of [. . .] Said his majesty to her: "Come, glorious one, I have placed thee before me; that thou mayest see thy administration in the palace, and the excellent deeds of thy *ka* that thou mayest assume thy royal dignity, glorious in thy magic, mighty in thy strength. Thou shalt be powerful in the Two Lands; thou shalt seize the rebellious; thou shalt appear in the palace, thy forehead shall be adorned with the double diadem, resting upon the head of the heiress of Horus, whom I begat, daughter of the white crown, beloved of Buto. The diadems are given to thee by him who presides over the thrones of the gods."

Thutmose I's Address to the Court

Said his majesty before them: "This is my daughter, Khnemet-Amen, Hatshepsut, who liveth, I have appointed her [. . .]; she is my successor upon my throne, she it assuredly is who shall sit upon my wonderful seat. She shall command the people in every place of the palace; she it is who shall lead you; ye shall proclaim her word, ye shall be united at her command. He who shall do her homage shall live, he who shall speak evil in blasphemy of her majesty shall die. Whosoever proclaims with unanimity the name of her majesty, shall enter immediately into the royal chamber, just as it was done by the name of this Horus. For thou art divine, O daughter of a god, for whom even the gods fight; behind whom they exert their protection every day according to the command of her father, the lord of the gods."

2. *Akhenaten,* from a pillar statue in the Temple of Amen-Re, Karnak, Eighteenth Dynasty, c. 1375 B.C. (Gardner, p. 94, ill. 3:36)
Akhenaten, limestone relief portrait, Eighteenth Dynasty, c. 1365 B.C. (Janson, p. 67, ill. 80)
Hymn to Aten: "Splendid You Rise in Heaven's Lightland," Eighteenth Dynasty, c. 1365 B.C.
Correspondence of Rib-Addi to King Akhenaten: "Why Will You Neglect Your Land?" and "Rescue Me out of the Hands of My Enemies," Eighteenth Dynasty, c. 1365 B.C.

Egyptian religion was static and traditional, reinforcing the belief that the natural world was divinely ordered by the gods and that humans should conform to that order. During the Amarna Period of the Eighteenth Dynasty, radical religious changes were introduced by the young and idealistic pharaoh, Akhenaten (Amenhotep IV).

Akhenaten (?–1362 B.C.) is depicted in many portrait statues and reliefs. Physically weak but strong in faith and courage, Akhenaten introduced the worship of the god Aten as the supreme god and declared himself to be the god's high priest. Until the Amarna Period, Aten had been a little-known deity. But under the impress of Akhenaten's convictions, Aten came to be identified with the life-giving and life-sustaining force of the sun. Aten was symbolized by the sun disk, with rays of warmth extending earthward and terminating in hands holding the symbol of life.

To provide for the worship of Aten, Akhenaten immediately constructed a new temple at Thebes. Although Akhenaten did not initially suppress the worship of the older gods, the powerful priesthoods resented the diminution of the stature of the gods whom they served. In response, Akhenaten embarked upon a radical program of religious reform that defied Egyptian traditions. He disbanded the priesthoods of all the gods except Aten; he halted the worship in their temples; and he tried to annihilate their memory by erasing their names and defacing their images wherever they were to be found. Even the king's original name, Amenhotep, was altered because it contained the name of Amen, the god most strongly reviled by the young monarch, and it was changed to Akhenaten, which meant "He who serves Aten."

Perhaps because Thebes was associated with the worship of other gods and with their powerful priesthoods, Akhenaten left the capital city of his fathers and founded a new capital over two hundred miles away. This city, known today as Tell el-Amarna, was named Akhetaten, or "Horizon of Aten," by the king. New temples to Aten arose within the boundaries of the city; tombs for the monarch and his family and for the nobles of his court were excavated nearby in the eastern cliffs of the Nile.

Hymn to Aten is one of the hymns which the king composed to his god and which his nobles inscribed on the walls of their tombs. From this hymn emerges a strong sense of the faith that impelled Akhenaten to such a violent break with tradition. Akhenaten describes Aten as a world creator whose beneficence is everywhere evident in nature and as the radiant source of bounty and beauty. A selection from the *Hymn to Aten,* "Splendid You Rise in Heaven's Lightland," is presented here.

At the time that Akhenaten succeeded his father, Egypt ruled an empire in Africa and Asia Minor. Apparently because he devoted his energy completely to his religious reforms, Akhenaten did not recognize the signs of trouble in his eastern provinces and did not respond to the erosion of his foreign dominions. The Hittites of Asia Minor proved to be formidable enemies, and during Akhenaten's reign the Hittite forces relentlessly swallowed the Egyptian vassal provinces in Syria and Palestine.

The turmoil of the Egyptian empire and the neglect of foreign affairs by the Egyptian king are revealed in a series of documents called the Tell el-Amarna letters. These letters, which number over three hundred, were found in 1888 in the archive chamber of Akhenaten's foreign office in the capital city of Akhetaten. Written on clay tablets in Babylonian cuneiform, they consist of the correspondence between two Egyptian kings, Akhenaten and his father, Amenhotep III, and the rulers of Asia Minor. Rib-Addi was the ruler of Byblos and the loyal vassal of Akhenaten. Over sixty letters are included in the correspondence of Rib-Addi to King Akhenaten.

Two selections from the correspondence are presented here. In "Why Will You Neglect Your Land?" Rib-Addi describes the threats to Egypt's foreign dominions. Earlier, he had asked for help for his sister cities but without avail. As the Hittites steadily advanced, Rib-Addi's pleas became more and more desperate. But still they went unanswered. His own city, Byblos, was now threatened, but the Egyptian king ignored Rib-Addi's peril.

In subsequent letters, it becomes clear that the king had badly misunderstood the situation. He sent an army which attacked Rib-Addi instead of supporting him. In retaliation for the Egyptian action, an insurrection was raised against Rib-Addi in Byblos. Rib-Addi was forced to flee to Beirut to muster aid, while in Byblos his brother grabbed control of the city and delivered his children, perhaps as hostages, to his enemy, Aziru. When Beirut fell, Rib-Addi returned to Byblos and somehow managed to regain control of the city. Although begged by his wife and children to break with Akhenaten and join Aziru, Rib-Addi remained loyal. In the second selection, "Rescue Me out of the Hands of My Enemies," Rib-Addi's growing distress is evident as he beseeches the king to send aid. Finally, the Hittites ravaged his lands and swept over the walls of his city, and the letters of Rib-Addi to Akhenaten ceased.

Hymn to Aten[36]

Splendid You Rise in Heaven's Lightland

Splendid you rise in heaven's lightland,
O living Aten, creator of life!
When you have dawned in eastern lightland,

36. Reprinted, by permission of the University of California Press, from Lichtheim, op. cit., Vol. II, pp. 96–99.

You fill every land with your beauty.
You are beauteous, great, radiant,
High over every land;
Your rays embrace the lands,
To the limit of all that you made.
Being Re, you reach their limits,
You bend them for the son whom you love;
Though you are far, your rays are on earth,
Though one sees you, your strides are unseen.

Earth brightens when you dawn in lightland,
When you shine as Aten of daytime;
As you dispel the dark,
As you cast your rays,
The Two Lands are in festivity.
Awake they stand on their feet,
You have roused them;
Bodies cleansed, clothed,
Their arms adore your appearance.
The entire land sets out to work,
All beasts browse on their herbs;
Trees, herbs are sprouting,
Birds fly from their nests,
Their wings greeting your *ka*
All flocks frisk on their feet,
All that fly up and alight,
They live when you dawn for them.
Ships fare north, fare south as well,
Roads lie open when you rise;
The fish in the river dart before you,
Your rays are in the midst of the sea.

Who makes seed grow in women,
Who creates people from sperm;
Who feeds the son in his mother's womb,
Who soothes him to still his tears.
Nurse in the womb,
Giver of breath,
To nourish all that he made.
When he comes from the womb to breathe,
On the day of his birth,
You open wide his mouth,
You supply his needs.
When the chick in the egg speaks in the shell,

You give him breath within to sustain him;
When you have made him complete,
To break out from the egg,
He comes out from the egg,
To announce his completion,
Walking on his legs he comes from it. . . .

You are in my heart,
There is no other who knows you,
Only your son, *Neferkheprure, Sole-one-of-Re*
Whom you have taught your ways and your might.
Those on earth come from your hand as you made them,
When you have dawned they live,
When you set they die;
You yourself are lifetime, one lives by you.
All eyes are on your beauty until you set,
All labor ceases when you rest in the west;
When you rise you stir everyone for the King,
Every leg is on the move since you founded the earth.
You rouse them for your son who came from your body,
The King who lives by Maat, the Lord of the Two Lands,
Neferkheprure, Sole-one-of-Re,
The Son of Re who lives by Maat, the Lord of crowns,
Akhenaten, great in his lifetime;
And the great Queen whom he loves, the Lady of the Two Lands,
Nefer-nefru-Aten Nefertiti, living forever.

Correspondence of Rib-Addi to King Akhenaten[37]

Why Will You Neglect Your Land?

Rib-Addi speaks to the lord of the lands, the king of the lands, the great king, king of battle: Baalat[38] of Gebal grant power to the king, my lord. At the feet of my lord, my sun, seven and seven times, I fall. Let my lord, the king, know that all is well with Gebal, the faithful handmaid of the king, from the time of his fathers; but behold, at this time, the king has let his faithful city go out of his hand. Let my lord, the king, look upon the lands, which belong to the territory of the king, and see if the man, who is in Gebal, is not a faithful servant. That you need not some day complain

37. Reprinted from *The Tell el-Amarna Letters,* trans. by Hugo Winckler (New York: Lemcke and Buechner, 1896), pp. 127–31, 175–77.

38. Ancient Semitic honorific for a goddess. *Ba'al* means "Lord," and was applied to a god as a term of adoration. *At* is the feminine form.

about your servant, if the hostility of the Habiri[39] powerful against him, and against the gods of your land! Our sons and daughters and our [. . .] will be no more, because we will have to give them to Jarimuta for our sustenance. My fields produce no grain, because there is no sowing. All my cities, which are situated in the mountains and on the sea shore, have come into the hands of the Habiri. Only Gebal and two cities remain to me. And now behold, Abd-asirta has appropriated to himself Sigata, and has said to the people of Ammia, "Kill your lord, and do as we do, and you will then have rest." And they have done according to his words, and have become like the Habiri. And verily, Abd-asirta has now written to the people of Bit-Ninib: "Assemble yourselves, and we will fall upon Gebal." If there were a man to rescue us out of their hands, and [. . .] the chieftains of the lands, and if all the lands should unite with the [. . .], then you could be judge over all the lands, and the boys and girls would be calm to eternity. And moreover, if the king himself should march forth, though all the lands were in rebellion against him, what could they then do to us? In this case they the people would all together do good, but I am very greatly afraid that there is no man to rescue me out of their hands; like a bird, which is caught in a net, so shall I be in Gebal. Why will you neglect your land? Behold I wrote thus to the king's palace, but they paid no attention to my message. Verily, Amanappa is with you; ask him, he knows about it, and has seen the distress, which has come upon me. May the king hear the words of his servant, and give life to his servant, that his servant may live. Then I will defend his faithful city until [. . .] our gods [. . .] and let the king look upon his land and [. . .] upon [. . .] may it seem good to my lord, the king, to send his [. . .], and that I should keep my place, and should come before the lord, the king. And may it be clear to you, what I am doing in my [. . .]. Verily, I am thus mindful, day and night.

Rescue Me out of the Hands of My Enemy

Rib-Addi speaks to the lord of the lands, the king of the lands, the great king, the king of battle: May Baalat of Gebal give power to my lord, the king. At the feet of my lord, my sun, seven and seven times, I fall. May my lord, the king, know that Aziru is hostile to me, and has seized twelve of my people, and has laid upon us, as ransom, 50 minas of silver. Also, the people, whom I had sent to Simyra, he has seized in the city of Jibulia. The ships and people of Simyra, Berut and Sidon, all of them that are in Amurru, are pressing me hard, and behold now, Japa-Addi and Aziri have attacked me, and verily, he has seized one of my ships. And behold, they have thus sailed forth into the ocean, in order to capture my ships. And therefore, let the king care for his city and his servant. For my subjects are

39. The Hittites.

intending to desert. If you are not strong enough to rescue me out of the hand of my enemies, send me word, in order that I may know what to do. . . .

Again, care for me; I love my lord, the king. . . .

3. *Musicians and Dancers,* wall painting from the Tomb of Nebamun, Thebes, Eighteenth Dynasty, c. 1430 B.C. (Gardner, p. 93, ill. 3:35)
The Daughters of Akhenaten, fragment of wall painting from Tell el-Amarna, Eighteenth Dynasty, c. 1365 B.C. (Janson, p. 46, color plate 7)
Love Songs "The Cairo Love Songs" and "The Songs of the City of Memphis," Nineteenth Dynasty, c. 1320–1200 B.C.

The literature of the New Kingdom[40] includes poetry that celebrates physical beauty and sensual pleasure. The same enjoyment of the grace of the human form and its sensuousness is evident in the paintings of the New Kingdom, such as *Musicians and Dancers* and *The Daughters of Akhenaten.*

Four Egyptian manuscripts containing love poems have survived. In some cases, the poems were composed in clearly integrated cycles, whereas in other cases, the poems were loosely grouped together under introductory titles but remained essentially independent. Fresh and immediate in style, the poems conform to a basic pattern. Each is written in the first person as if a man or woman were speaking directly to his or her lover. The lovers frequently use the terms "brother" and "sister" as expressions of endearment.

Two selections of love poems are presented here. The first, "The Cairo Love Songs," consists of a set of eight songs, the first of which is recited by a woman and the following seven of which are recited by her lover. The second selection, "The Songs of the City of Memphis," consist of two poems, the first recited by a woman expressing her longings and the second recited by a man voicing his desire.

Love Songs[41]

The Cairo Love Songs

1

My god, my lover,
it is pleasant to go to the canal
and to bathe in your presence.

I shall let you see . . . my perfection
in a garment of royal linen, wet and clinging.

40. The period of Egyptian history from 1567 to 332 B.C.

41. Reprinted, by permission of Yale University Press, from William Kelly Simpson, ed., *The Literature of Ancient Egypt: An Anthology of Stories, Instructions and Poetry* (New Haven: Yale University Press, 1973), pp. 309–11, 297–99. Selections translated by W. K. Simpson.

Then I'll go into the water at your bidding,
and I'll come out to you with a red fish
who will be happy in my fingers . . .
So come and look me over.

2

The love of my sister lies on yonder side,
and the river is between us;
a crocodile waits on the sandbank.

Yet I'll go down to the water,
I'll head into the waves;
my heart is brave on the water,
and the waves like land to my legs.

3

It is love of her which strengthens me,
as if for me she made a water spell.

I'll watch the lady love return.
My heart rejoices and my arms spread out to clasp her,
my heart is giddy in its seat,
as if this were not fated forever.

Do not keep away, but come to me, my lady.

4

I embrace her,
and her arms open wide,
I am like a man in Punt,
like someone overwhelmed with drugs.

I kiss her,
her lips open,
and I am drunk
without a beer.

5

What is the last thing for preparing her bed?
I tell you, boy,
set fine linen between her limbs,
draw not the covers with royal sheets,
but care for her with simple white stuffs,
sprinkled with fine scented oils.

6

I wish I were her Negro maid
who follows at her feet;
then the skin of all her limbs
would be revealed to me.

7

I wish I were her washerman,
if only for a single month,
then I would be entranced,
washing out the Moringa oils
in her diaphanous garments. . . .

8

I wish I were the seal ring,
the guardian of her fingers,
then [. . .]

The Songs of the City of Memphis

1

If I am not with you, where will you set your heart?
If you do not embrace me, where will you go?
If good fortune comes your way, you still cannot find happiness.
But if you try to touch my thighs and breasts,
Then you'll be satisfied.
Because you remember you are hungry
  would you then leave?
Are you a man
  thinking only of his stomach?
Would you walk off from me
  concerned with your stylish clothes
and leave me the sheet?
Because of hunger
  would you then leave me?
  or because you are thirsty?
Take then my breast:
  for you its gift overflows
Better indeed is one day in your arms . . .
  than a hundred thousand anywhere on earth.

2

Distracting is the foliage of my pasture:
the mouth of my girl is a lotus bud,

her breasts are mandrake apples,
her arms are vines,
her eyes are fixed like berries,
her brow a snare of willow,
and I the wild goose!
My beak snips her hair for bait,
as worms for bait in the trap.

4. Painted Chest, Tomb of Tutankhamen, Eighteenth Dynasty, c. 1355 B.C. (Gardner, p. 99, ill. 3:41; Janson, p. 69, ill. 85)
The Tomb Robberies of Kings Seti I and Ramses II: "The Trial and Testimony of the Tomb Robbers," Twentieth Dynasty, 1126 B.C.

Tutankhaten was the son-in-law of Akhenaten. He was young when he ascended the throne in 1361 B.C. and he was unable to continue the changes initiated by Akhenaten. Akhetaten, the city of Aten, was soon abandoned; Tutankhaten's name, which meant "Living Image of Aten," was changed to Tutankhamen; and the worship of Amen was restored.

Tutankhamen died in 1352 B.C. after only a few short years of rule. The tomb in which he was interred in the Valley of the Kings is the only tomb of an Egyptian ruler to be discovered unrobbed. When Howard Carter and George Herbert, fifth Earl of Caernarvon, entered the chambers of Tutankhamen's resting place in 1922, they found treasures of great value and exquisite beauty. One such treasure is the wooden chest painted with a scene of Tutankhamen hunting.

Evidence from modern excavations of the royal pyramids and tombs suggests that looting began in ancient times. Judging from the value of the objects deposited in the tomb of Tutankhamen, a relatively unimportant king, the treasures of the other kings must have been an irresistible source of wealth to the unscrupulous. In 1111 B.C. two officials, Pewero, mayor of the west side of Thebes, and Peser, mayor of the east side of Thebes, began to investigate rumors that royal tombs were being plundered. Several groups of tomb robbers were apprehended. In 1108 B.C. six persons were convicted of looting the tombs of Seti I and Ramses II, kings of the Nineteenth Dynasty. *The Tomb Robberies of Kings Seti I and Ramses II* consist of a set of documents that record the court proceedings that led to the conviction of the looters. A selection from *The Tomb Robberies,* "The Trial and Testimony of the Tomb Robbers," is presented here.

The Tomb Robberies of Kings Seti I and Ramses II[42]

The Trial and Testimony of the Tomb Robbers

Year 1, of Uhem-mesut, fourth month of the third season, day 15. On this day occurred the examination of the thieves of the tomb of King Usermare-

42. Reprinted from Breasted, op. cit., Vol. IV, pp. 268–71.

Setepnere, the great god; and the tomb of King Menmare, Seti I, which are recorded in the treasury of "The-House-of-King-Usermare-Meriamon," concerning whom the chief of police, Nesuamon, had reported, in this roll of names; for he was there, standing with the thieves, when they laid their hands upon the tombs; who were tortured at the examination on their feet and their hands, to make them tell the way they had done exactly. . . .

Examination. Paykamen, under charge of the overseer of the cattle of Amen, was brought in; the oath of the king was administered to him, not to tell a lie. He was asked: "What was the manner of thy going with the people who were with thee, when ye robbed the tombs of the kings which are recorded in the treasury of 'The-House-of-King-Usermare-Meriamon'?" He said: "I went with the priest Teshere, son of the divine father, Zedi, of 'The House'; Beki, son of Nesuamon, of this house; Nesumontu of the house of Montu, lord of Erment; Paynehsi of the vizier, formerly prophet of Sobek of Peronekh; Teti who belonged to Paynehsi, of the vizier, formerly prophet of Sobek of Peronekh; in all six. . . ."

The watchman of the house of Amen, Karu, was brought in; he was examined with the rod, the bastinade was applied to his feet and his hands; the oath of the king was administered to him, that he might be executed if he told a lie. He was asked: "What was the manner of thy going with the companions when ye robbed in the tomb?" He said: "The thief, Pehenui, he made me take some grain. I seized a sack of grain, and when I began to go down, I heard the voice of the men who were in this storehouse. I put my eye to the passage, and I saw Paybek and Teshere, who were within. I called to him, saying, 'Come!' and he came out to me, having two pieces of copper in his hand. He gave them to me, and I gave him 1 ½ measures of spelt[43] to pay for them. I took one of them, and I gave the other to Enefsu.

The priest, Nesuamon, son of Paybek, was brought in, because of his father. He was examined by beating with the rod. They said to him: "Tell the manner of thy father's going with the men who were with him." He said: "My father was truly there. I was only a little child, and I know not how he did it." On being further examined, he said: "I saw the workman, Ehatinofer, while he was in the place where the tomb is, with the watchman, Nofer, son of Merwer, and the artisan, [. . .] in all three men. They are the ones I saw distinctly. Indeed, gold was taken, and they are the ones whom I know." On being further examined with a rod, he said: "These three men are the ones I saw distinctly. . . ."

A Theban woman, Enroy, the mistress of the priest, Teshere, son of Zedi, was brought in. She was examined by beating with a rod; the bastinade was applied to her feet and her hands. The oath of the king not to

43. A hard-grained wheat.

tell a lie was administered to her; she was asked: "What was the manner of thy husband's going when he broke into the tomb and carried away the copper from it?" She said: "He carried away some copper belonging to this tomb; we sold it and devoured it."

5. Temple of Ramses II, Abu Simbel, Nineteenth Dynasty, c. 1260 B.C. (Gardner, p. 77, ill. 3:22)
Brick Storehouses, Mortuary Temple of Ramesses II (Ramses II), Thebes, c. 1260 B.C. (Janson p. 64, ill. 73)
The Kadesh Inscriptions: "The Battle at Kadesh," Nineteenth Dynasty, c. 1260 B.C.

Ramses II has been called the last great warrior king of Egypt. At the death of his father, King Seti I, the ambitious Ramses thrust aside his elder brother, who had been named crown prince, and gained the throne for himself. Soon after his accession, he turned his attention to the recovery of the Egyptian empire in Asia, an empire that had been greatly diminished during the reign of Akhenaten.

In his first campaign, to regain the coast of Phoenicia, Ramses met with success. But in his second campaign, intended to regain the lands of Syria, Ramses barely averted disaster. With an army of twenty thousand men, Ramses marched against the Hittite army, led by King Metella. As he neared the city of Kadesh, Ramses led one of the four divisions of his army in advance of the others. Then, tricked into believing that the Hittite army had retreated to the north, Ramses took only a small guard of his household troops and advanced closer. At the same time, Metella was maneuvering his troops to cut the king off from his divisions in the rear. If it had not been for the Egyptian capture of two of Metella's spies, who revealed Metella's position, the Hittite strategy would almost certainly have resulted in the total destruction of Ramses' forces. As Ramses and his commanders frantically sought for a way to salvage the situation, Metella attacked one Egyptian infantry division with his chariots and cut them to shreds. As the division fled, the Hittite army followed and soon the division commanded by Ramses was also in flight. In desperation, Ramses charged a weak point in the Hittite line and succeeded in driving the troops back into a river. Then for three hours, the frantic king charged the line again and again, keeping the Hittite army at bay until a division from the rear appeared and forced the Hittites to retreat.

The battle at Kadesh, although it apparently did not result in the actual capture of the city, was an exploit in which Ramses later took great pride. By his actions, Ramses had averted a disaster for the Egyptian army and had demonstrated his personal courage. These military exploits were extolled in an extended literary work called *The Kadesh Inscriptions.* The text and the accompanying reliefs were inscribed on the walls of the Temple of Ramses II at Abu Simbel and of the Ramesseum, Ramses II's mortuary temple, at Thebes. A selection from *The Kadesh Inscriptions,* "The Battle at Kadesh," is presented here.

The Kadesh Inscriptions[44]

The Battle at Kadesh

Now while his majesty sat speaking with the chiefs, the vile Foe from Khatti[45] came with his infantry and his chariotry and the many countries that were with him. Crossing the ford to the south of Kadesh they charged into his majesty's army as it marched unaware. Then the infantry and chariotry of his majesty weakened before them on their way northward to where his majesty was. Thereupon the forces of the Foe from Khatti surrounded the followers of his majesty who were by his side. When his majesty caught sight of them he rose quickly, enraged at them like his father Mont.[46] Taking up weapons and donning his armor he was like Set in the moment of his power. He mounted Victory-in-Thebes, his great horse, and started out quickly alone by himself. His majesty was mighty, his heart stout, one could not stand before him.

All his ground was ablaze with fire; he burned all the countries with his blast. His eyes were savage as he beheld them; his power flared like fire against them. He heeded not the foreign multitude; he regarded them as chaff. His majesty charged into the force of the Foe from Khatti and the many countries with him. His majesty was like Set, great-of-strength, like Sakhmet in the moment of her rage. His majesty slew the entire force of the Foe from Khatti, together with his great chiefs and all his brothers, as well as all the chiefs of all the countries that had come with him, their infantry and their chariotry falling on their faces one upon the other. His majesty slaughtered them in their places; they sprawled before his horses; and his majesty was alone, none other with him. . . .

[*Ramses II speaks*]

No officer was with me, no charioteer,
No soldier of the army, no shield-bearer;
My infantry, my chariotry yielded before them,
Not one of them stood firm to fight with them.
His majesty spoke: "What is this, father Amen?
Is it right for a father to ignore his son?
Are my deeds a matter for you to ignore?
Do I not walk and stand at your work?
I have not neglected an order you gave.
Too great is he, the great lord of Egypt,

44. Reprinted, by permission of the University of California Press, from Lichtheim, op. cit., Vol. II, pp. 61–62, 65–66.
45. The Hittites.
46. A falcon god, worshiped in Thebes, who was associated with Re.

To allow aliens to step on his path!
What are these Asiatics to you, O Amen,
The wretches ignorant of god? . . ."

Now though I prayed in the distant land,
My voice resounded in Southern On.
I found Amen came when I called to him,
He gave me his hand and I rejoiced.
He called from behind as if near by:
"Forward, I am with you,
I, your father, my hand is with you,
I prevail over a hundred thousand men,
I am lord of victory, lover of valor!"
I found my heart stout, my breast in joy,
All I did succeeded, I was like Mont.
I shot on my right, grasped with my left,
I was before them like Set in his moment.
I found the mass of chariots in whose midst I was
Scattering before my horses;
Not one of them found his hand to fight,
Their hearts failed in their bodies through fear of me.
Their arms all slackened, they could not shoot,
They had no heart to grasp their spears;
I made them plunge into the water as crocodiles plunge,
They fell on their faces one on the other.
I slaughtered among them at my will,
Not one looked behind him,
Not one turned around,
Whoever fell down did not rise.

III

The Art of the Aegean

MINOAN ART

1. Palace of Knossos, Crete, c. 1600–1400 B.C. (Gardner, pp. 107–10, ills. 4:5 to 4:9; Janson, pp. 88–89, ills. 117–18)
Diodorus of Sicily, *Library of History:* "King Minos," c. 60–30 B.C.

The civilization of Crete is known by the name "Minoan," after the fabled King Minos of Greek legend. In Greek mythology, Minos was the son of Zeus, the most powerful of the gods, and Europa, a beautiful Phoenician princess. Zeus fell in love with Europa and determined upon her seduction. Appearing to Europa in the form of a white bull with golden horns, he lured her to the seashore. Enchanted by the apparent gentleness of the bull, Europa decked his horns with flower wreaths and sat upon his back. Instantly, Zeus plunged into the sea and carried Europa to Crete. There she bore him three sons: Minos, Rhadamanthys, and Sarpedon. When Zeus left Europa, she married Asterius, the king of Crete. Because he was childless, Asterius adopted Europa's sons and made them his heirs.

According to the Greek accounts, Minos, who became king at Asterius' death, was a powerful and just ruler. He established laws which he received from Zeus, rid the Mediterranean Sea of pirates, and gained control over the Aegean Islands. After the death of his son, Androgeos, at the hands of the Athenians, Minos warred against Athens and brought the Greek city under the control of Crete. He was killed in Sicily by the daughters of King Cocalus, who poured boiling water over him as he was taking a bath. After his death, he became a judge in Hades.

Minos is discussed by many Greek authors, including Plato and Thucydides. An extended account of Minos is provided by the Greek historian Diodorus of Sicily (active first century B.C.), who wrote a forty-volume book, *Library of History,* between c. 60 and 30 B.C. A selection from the *Library of History,* "King Minos," is presented here.

Modern excavations in Crete and elsewhere have recovered a great deal of historical information about the ancient Minoan civilization, and have corroborated some aspects of the Greek legends about Minos. Crete, as is evidenced by the palace at Knossos, was a well-ordered society administered by kings and nobles. Overseas trade, which was the basis of Cretan prosperity, linked the Greek mainland and Crete closely together and extended to Egypt, Asia Minor, Syria, and the Aegean Islands. Although King Minos is clearly a legendary figure, many scholars now consider that the name Minos was a royal or dynastic title for the priestly rulers of Minoan Knossos.

Diodorus of Sicily, *Library of History*[1]

King Minos

Many generations after the birth of the gods, the Cretans go on to say, not a few heroes were to be found in Crete, the most renowned of whom were Minos and Rhadamanthys and Sarpedon. These men, their myth states, were born of Zeus and Europa, the daughter of Agenor, who, men say, was brought across to Crete upon the back of a bull by the design of the gods. Now Minos, by virtue of his being the eldest, became king of the island, and he founded on it not a few cities, the most renowned of which were the three, Knossos in those parts of the island which look toward Asia, Phaestus on the seashore to the south, and Cydonia in the regions to the west facing the Peloponnesus. And Minos established not a few laws for the Cretans, claiming that he had received them from his father, Zeus, when conversing with him in a certain cave. Furthermore, he came to possess a great naval power, and he subdued the majority of the islands and was the first man among the Greeks to be master of the sea.

2. *The Toreador Fresco,* Knossos, c. 1500 B.C. (Gardner, p. 111, ill. 4:12; Janson, p. 99, color plate 12)
Apollodorus, *The Library:* "Pasiphaë and the Bull," second century B.C.

Because there are no decipherable written records that describe Minoan religion, it is difficult to generalize about the basic beliefs of the people of Crete. However, it appears that worship consisted of ecstatic rites conducted at shrines which were located on the tops of mountains, in sacred caves, and at small altars in houses. The practice of bull jumping, in which young men and women seized the horns of trained bulls and vaulted over their backs, was probably one of those rites. Bull jumping is depicted in *The Toreador Fresco* from the palace of Knossos.

The importance of the bull in Minoan religious ceremonies is reflected by the prominence of the animal in Greek legends about Crete. Minos had been fathered by Zeus, who had appeared in the form of a bull to Minos' mother, Europa. Minos' wife, Pasiphaë, conceived the Minotaur through her union with the bull sent to Minos by Poseidon, the god of the sea. The capture of this magnificent bull, which was loosed on the Greek mainland when Poseidon was enraged by Minos' refusal

1. Reprinted, by permission of the publisher and The Loeb Classical Library, from *Library of History* by Diodorus Siculus, trans. by C.H. Oldfather (Cambridge, Mass.: Harvard University Press, 1939), Vol. III, Book V, p. 311.

to sacrifice it to him, was the seventh labor of Heracles. The slaying of the monstrous Minotaur, which was imprisoned by Minos in the labyrinth and was offered seven young men and seven young women of Athens every nine years, was accomplished by Theseus.

Many of the myths about the Minotaur were recorded by Apollodorus of Athens (active second century B.C.). A scholar of great learning, Apollodorus wrote on history, geography, theology, and mythology. The work entitled *The Library* is an important source of mythological material covering the gods and the heroes of Crete and early Greece. A selection from the *The Library,* "Pasiphaë and the Bull," is presented here.

Apollodorus, *The Library*[2]

Pasiphaë and the Bull

When Asterius died childless, Minos sought to rule over Crete but was opposed. He then claimed that he received the kingship from the gods and, in order to prove it, said that whatever he prayed for would occur. While sacrificing to Poseidon he prayed for a bull to appear from the sea and promised to sacrifice it. When Poseidon sent to him a handsome bull he received the kingship, but sent the bull to his herds and sacrificed another. He was the first to control the sea and ruled over almost all the islands. Because he had not sacrificed the bull Poseidon in anger made it wild and aroused desire for it in Pasiphaë. In love with the bull, Pasiphaë asked help from Daedalus, a master craftsman banished from Athens for murder. He built a wooden cow on wheels, hollow on the inside and covered with the hide of a cow. He placed it in the meadow where the bull usually grazed and instructed Pasiphaë to get inside it. The bull came and mounted it as though it were a real cow. She gave birth to Asterius who was called the Minotaur. He had the face of a bull but a human body. Minos, in accordance with certain oracles, kept him shut up in the labyrinth. Constructed by Daedalus, the labyrinth was a large chamber with "a complex set of turns concealing the exit."

2. Reprinted from *Gods and Heroes of the Greeks: The Library of Apollodorus,* trans. by Michael Simpson, copyright © 1976 by the University of Massachusetts Press, p. 139.

MYCENAEAN ART

1. Citadel at Tiryns, Greece, c. 1400–1200 B.C. (Gardner, pp. 118–19, ills. 4:22 to 4:24)
Linear B Texts: "Land Ownership and Use" and "Tribute and Ritual Offerings," c. 1400–1200 B.C.

Both Minoan and Mycenaean civilizations were literate societies. Two linear systems of writing, called Linear A and Linear B, were developed and were used to serve the administrative needs of the palaces. Linear A, which was of Cretan origin, was developed around 1650 B.C. and later spread to the Greek mainland. Linear A has never been deciphered. Linear B was developed around 1400 B.C. Thousands of clay tablets written in Linear B have been found at the sites of Pylos, Mycenae, and Thebes on the Greek mainland and at the site of Knossos in Crete. Although approximately two thirds of the signs in Linear B are similar to Linear A, the two scripts appear to record different languages. In 1952, Michael Ventris deciphered Linear B and demonstrated that this script recorded the Greek language.

Linear B inscriptions consist almost entirely of short lists or inventories. No evidence of a written literary tradition or of historical accounts has survived. Instead, writing was confined chiefly to the palaces, where it was used by the bureaucracy to record matters of daily business. Many inscriptions record lists of individuals who were allotted plots of land either through private ownership or communal possession and who returned agricultural goods such as wheat, barley, olive oil, and figs to the palace. Other inscriptions include lists of persons who were employed in specialized occupations such as spinning, weaving, or metalworking and who received provisions in exchange for their labor. Still other inscriptions inventory palace possessions such as textiles, vessels, and furniture. At Pylos, a site in the western Peloponnese, an inscription on a large tablet records offerings of gold vessels made to a pantheon of deities. In addition, the tablet records that a man was offered to male deities and a woman to female deities. It has been suggested that these human beings were being dedicated to the service of the gods, but the possibility that they were human sacrifices has also been raised.

Two selections from Linear B texts are presented here. The first, "Land Ownership and Use," deals with matters of obvious concern to an agricultural society. The second selection, "Tribute and Ritual Offerings," is from the tablet recovered at Pylos and suggests aspects of Mycenaean religious practices.

From the Linear B tablets a picture emerges of the palace life at sites such as Tiryns and of the hundreds of men, women, and children who were employed in administrative and domestic duties. The palace controlled everything and served as the main channel of economic distribution. The territory of the palace was regarded as the estate of the king, and he apportioned the land to his subjects in exchange for the agricultural produce, the domestic labor, and the military services that he required.

Linear B Texts[3]

Land Ownership and Use

The private plot of Pikreus, so much seed: 312 1. wheat.

Now this is how the tenants hold plots belonging to Pikreus: Aiwaia, servant of the god, holds a lease, so much seed: 12 1. wheat,
P., the king's fuller, holds a lease, so much seed: 24 1. wheat, Korinsia, servant of the god, holds a lease, so much seed: 60 1. wheat . . .

Communal plots not leased, so much seed: 132? 1. wheat.

Aithioq^{u}s holds the lease of a communal plot from the village being himself a plot-owner: so much seed: 174 1. wheat . . .

Huamia, servant of the god, and she holds as a lease a *geras* of the priestess; so much seed: 28 1. wheat,

Eritha the priestess holds the lease of a communal plot from the village; so much seed: 48 1. wheat . . .

So-and-so the cook both holds a *kama* and renders the services; so much seed: 144 1. wheat.

So-and-so the sacrificing priest holds a lease as a *kama*-holder and renders the services; so much seed: 120 1. wheat . . .

Tribute and Ritual Offerings

Pylos: perform a certain action at the shrine of Poseidon and [. . .] the town, and bring the gifts and bring those to carry them.

One gold cup, two women . . .

Pylos: perform a certain action at the shrines of the Dove-goddess and of Iphemedeia and of Diwja, and bring the gifts and bring those to carry them.

To the Dove-goddess: one gold bowl, one woman.

To Iphemedeia: one gold bowl.

To Diwja: one gold bowl, one woman.

To Hermes [. . .]: one gold cup, one man.

Pylos: perform a certain action at the shrine of Zeus, and bring the gifts and bring those to carry them.

To Zeus: one gold bowl, one man.

To Hera: one gold bowl, one woman.

To Drimios the priest of Zeus: one gold bowl, one man . . .

3. Reprinted, by permission of the publisher, from Michael Ventris and John Chadwick, *Documents in Mycenaean Greek,* 2nd ed. (Cambridge: Cambridge University Press, 1973), pp. 244, 251–53, 262, 287.

2. The Lion Gate, Mycenae, 1300 B.C. (Gardner, p. 119, ill. 4:25; Janson, p. 94, ill. 131)
Aeschylus, *Agamemnon:* "The Thing Is Done," c. 458 B.C.

The Lion Gate forms the imposing entrance to the Bronze Age city of Mycenae. Although the Linear B tablets do not record the names or exploits of the kings who conquered, ruled, died, and were buried in the great Mycenaean cities, a rich body of legends and traditions preserved the memories of these kings and became part of the cultural inheritance of the later Greeks. Although often confused in details and distorted by time, these ancient legends suggest the rough outline of Mycenaean history.

Centuries later, Classical Greeks, such as the Athenian playwright Aeschylus, recalled the Mycenaean period with nostalgic pride as the age of heroes and drew upon its figures for dramatic examples of human frailty and human achievement. Aeschylus (525–456 B.C.) has been called the father of Greek drama and the first tragedian. He wrote approximately ninety plays, seven of which survive in their entirety. His greatest achievement was the Oresteia, a set of three plays that deals with the curse on the House of Atreus, the royal family of Argos.[4] In 458 B.C., Aeschylus won first prize for the Oresteia in the annual Athenian competition for tragic drama.

Agamemnon, the first drama in the Oresteia, recounts the murder of Agamemnon, the king of Argos, by his wife, Clytemnestra. The play is set outside Agamemnon's palace, where Clytemnestra is watching for her husband's return from Troy and planning her revenge. Earlier, Agamemnon had led the Greeks to Troy to recapture Helen and had sacrificed his and Clytemnestra's daughter, Iphigenia, to assure good winds for his fleet. In the king's absence, Clytemnestra has shared the throne of Argos with her lover, Aegisthus, a lifelong enemy of Agamemnon and the murderer of Atreus, Agamemnon's father. At last Agamemnon arrives, accompanied by the captive Trojan priestess Cassandra. Clytemnestra greets the king with an extravagant welcome and leads him into the palace, but Cassandra prophesies their doom. Suddenly Agamemnon's cry for help is heard. The doors of the palace are flung open to reveal Clytemnestra standing triumphant over the bloody corpses of Agamemnon and Cassandra.

A selection from *Agamemnon,* "The Thing Is Done," is presented here. In this selection, Clytemnestra exults as she describes to a chorus of elders how she trapped Agamemnon in a netlike robe as he stepped from his bath and stabbed him three times. Clytemnestra offers no apologies for her deed. But the chorus responds ominously that the person who kills today will die tomorrow and that the penalty for blood is blood.

4. In the version of the story in Homer, Agamemnon is identified as the king of Mycenae. Aeschylus moved the location to Argos to satisfy the political demands of his day.

Aeschylus, *Agamemnon*[5]

The Thing Is Done

Clytemnestra

Much have I said before to serve necessity,
but I will take no shame now to unsay it all.
How else could I, arming hate against hateful men
disguised in seeming tenderness, fence high the nets
of ruin beyond overleaping? Thus to me
the conflict born of ancient bitterness is not
a thing new thought upon, but pondered deep in time.
I stand now where I struck him down. The thing is done.
Thus have I wrought, and I will not deny it now.
That he might not escape nor beat aside his death,
as fishermen cast their huge circling nets, I spread
deadly abundance of rich robes, and caught him fast.
I struck him twice. In two great cries of agony
he buckled at the knees and fell. When he was down
I struck him the third blow, in thanks and reverence
to Zeus the lord of dead men underneath the ground.
Thus he went down, and the life struggled out of him;
and as he died he spattered me with the dark red
and violent driven rain of bitter savored blood
to make me glad, as gardens stand among the showers
of God in glory at the birthtime of the buds.
These being the facts, elders of Argos assembled here,
be glad, if it be your pleasure; but for me, I glory.
Were it religion to pour wine above the slain,
this man deserved, more than deserved, such sacrament.
He filled our cup with evil things unspeakable
and now himself come home has drunk it to the dregs.

Chorus

We stand here stunned. How can you speak this way, with mouth
so arrogant, to vaunt above your fallen lord?

5. Reprinted, by permission of the publisher, from Donald Greene and Richmond Lattimore, eds., *The Complete Greek Tragedies* (Chicago: University of Chicago Press, 1953), pp. 80–82. Copyright © 1953 by the University of Chicago. Selection translated by Richmond Lattimore.

Clytemnestra

You try me out as if I were a woman and vain;
but my heart is not fluttered as I speak before you.
You know it. You can praise or blame me as you wish;
it is all one to me. That man is Agamemnon,
my husband; he is dead; the work of this right hand
that struck in strength of righteousness. And that is that.

Chorus

Woman, what evil thing planted upon the earth
or dragged from the running salt sea could you have tasted now
to wear such brutality and walk in the people's hate?
You have cast away, you have cut away. You shall go homeless
now,
crushed with men's bitterness.

Clytemnestra

Now it is I you doom to be cast out from my city
with men's hate heaped and curses roaring in my ears.
Yet look upon this dead man; you would not cross him once
when with no thought more than as if a beast had died,
when his ranged pastures swarmed with the deep fleece of flocks,
he slaughtered like a victim his own child, my pain
grown into love, to charm away the winds of Thrace.
Were you not bound to hunt him then clear of this soil
for the guilt stained upon him? Yet you hear what I
have done, and lo, you are a stern judge. But I say to you:
go on and threaten me, but know that I am ready,
if fairly you can beat me down beneath your hand,
for you to rule; but if the god grant otherwise,
you shall be taught—too late, for sure—to keep your place.

Chorus

Great your design, your speech is a clamor of pride.
Swung to the red act drives the fury within your brain
signed clear in the splash of blood over your eyes.
Yet to come is stroke given for stroke
vengeless, forlorn of friends.

Clytemnestra

Now hear you this, the right behind my sacrament:
By my child's Justice driven to fulfilment, by
her Wrath and Fury, to whom I sacrificed this man,
the hope that walks my chambers is not traced with fear
while yet Aegisthus makes the fire shine on my hearth,
my good friend, now as always, who shall be for us
the shield of our defiance, no weak thing; while he,
this other, is fallen, stained with this woman you behold,
plaything of all the golden girls at Ilium;[6]
and here lies she, the captive of his spear, who saw
wonders, who shared his bed, the wise in revelations
and loving mistress, who yet knew the feel as well
of the men's rowing benches. Their reward is not
unworthy. He lies there; and she who swanlike cried
aloud her lyric mortal lamentation out
is laid against his fond heart, and to me has given
a delicate excitement to my bed's delight.

6. Troy.

IV

The Art of Greece

THE GEOMETRIC AND ARCHAIC PERIODS

1. Dipylon Vase, eighth century B.C. (Gardner, p. 129, ill. 5:3; Janson, p. 105, ill. 135)
Homer, *The Iliad:* "The Death of Patroclus," eighth century B.C.

Greek vases of the Geometric period such as the Dipylon vase were frequently intended to accompany the dead or to stand on top of their funeral mounds. Thus, scenes painted on the vases commonly show corpses on biers attended by mourners, funeral corteges accompanied by warriors, or battles waged on land or sea. The surfaces of the vessels are organized in series of interrelated bands built up from simple, repeated patterns that are subtly varied and balanced. The same qualities of balance, repetition, and variety within overall unity characterize the great Homeric epics, *The Iliad* and *The Odyssey.*

Little is known about the poet Homer. Some scholars have questioned whether the Homeric epics were composed by a single individual or whether they represent compilations of the works of many poets. However, most modern scholars agree that there was a poet called Homer, that he lived during the eighth century B.C., that he was the creator of *The Iliad,* and that he was at least the inspirer and, possibly, the composer of *The Odyssey.*

Although later preserved by the Greeks in written form, the Homeric epics originated as poems of oral literature. For centuries following the collapse of the Mycenaean civilization, no script was employed on the Greek mainland. Literature was created in oral form by singers who composed their verses by relying heavily on stock phrases and repeated lines, and who performed their songs to the accompaniment of the lyre. Homer's contribution was to transform the short poems of the oral tradition into monumental literary works capable of describing many-sided characters and of conveying complex emotions.

Like many poems in the Greek oral tradition, *The Iliad* is concerned with the events of the Trojan War. However, *The Iliad* is also an exploration of the heroic ideal and of its mixed motives of human pride, vanity, and loyalty. The plot is set in a short, six-week period during the tenth year of the Trojan War. It centers on the wrath of Achilles, who is the son of King Peleus and the goddess Thetis. Achilles is insulted when Briseis, a captive whom he covets as his mistress, is claimed instead by Agamemnon. Angered, Achilles withdraws from the battlefield and leaves the Greek forces in disarray. As the Trojans drive the Greeks back to their ships, Patroclus, Achilles' closest friend, prevents a Greek rout by donning Achilles' armor and rallying his countrymen. As he fights in the hero's stead, Patroclus is slain by the great Trojan warrior Hector.

A selection from *The Iliad,* "The Death of Patroclus," is presented here. In this selection Achilles laments the death of Patroclus and repents the folly of his blind anger. When he returns to the battlefield, the death of Hector and the eventual defeat of the Trojans are assured.

Homer, *The Iliad*[1]

The Death of Patroclus

Meanwhile the Achaians[2]
mourned all night in lamentation over Patroclus.
Peleus' son led the thronging chant of their lamentation,
and laid his manslaughtering hands over the chest of his dear friend
with outbursts of incessant grief. As some great bearded lion
when some man, a deer hunter, has stolen his cubs away from him
out of the close wood; the lion comes back too late, and is anguished,
and turns into many valleys quartering after the man's trail
on the chance of finding him, and taken with bitter anger;
so he, groaning heavily, spoke out to the Myrmidons:[3]
"Ah me. It was an empty word I cast forth on that day
when in his halls I tried to comfort the hero Menoetius.
I told him I would bring back his son in glory to Opoeis
with Ilium sacked, and bringing his share of war spoils allotted.
But Zeus does not bring to accomplishment all thoughts in men's minds.
Thus it is destiny for us both to stain the same soil
here in Troy; since I shall never come home, and my father,
Peleus the aged rider, will not welcome me in his great house,
nor Thetis my mother, but in this place the earth will receive me.
But seeing that it is I, Patroclus, who follow you underground,
I will not bury you till I bring to this place the armour
and the head of Hector, since he was your great-hearted murderer.

1. Reprinted, by permission of the publishers, from Homer, *The Iliad,* trans. by Richmond Lattimore (Chicago: University of Chicago Press, 1951), pp. 383–85. Copyright © 1951 by the University of Chicago.
2. A Greek-speaking people who ruled at Mycenae from about 1600 to 1100 B.C. In Homer, "Achaian" is synonymous with "Greek."
3. The warriors from Thessaly who accompanied their king, Achilles, to Troy.

Before your burning pyre I shall behead twelve glorious
children of the Trojans, for my anger over your slaying.
Until then, you shall lie where you are in front of my curved ships
and beside you women of Troy and deep-girdled Dardanian women
shall sorrow for you night and day and shed tears for you, those whom
you and I worked hard to capture by force and the long spear
in days when we were storming the rich cities of mortals."

So speaking brilliant Achilles gave orders to his companions
to set a great cauldron across the fire, so that with all speed
they could wash away the clotted blood from Patroclus.
They set up over the blaze of the fire a bath-water cauldron
and poured water into it and put logs underneath and kindled them.
The fire worked on the swell of the cauldron, and the water heated.
But when the water had come to a boil in the shining bronze, then
they washed the body and anointed it softly with olive oil
and stopped the gashes in his body with stored-up unguents
and laid him on a bed, and shrouded him in a thin sheet
from head to foot, and covered that over with a white mantle.

Then all night long, gathered about Achilles of the swift feet,
the Myrmidons mourned for Patroclus and lamented over him.
But Zeus spoke to Hera, who was his wife and his sister:
"So you have acted, then, lady Hera of the ox eyes.
You have roused up Achilles of the swift feet. It must be then
that the flowing-haired Achaians are born of your own generation."

Then the goddess the ox-eyed lady Hera answered him:
"Majesty, son of Kronos, what sort of thing have you spoken?
Even one who is mortal will try to accomplish his purpose
for another, though he be a man and knows not such wisdom as we do.
As for me then, who claim I am highest of all the goddesses,
both ways, since I am eldest born and am called your consort,
yours, and you in turn are lord over all the immortals,
how could I not weave sorrows for the men of Troy, when I hate
them?"

2. *The Blinding of Polyphemus,* Proto-Attic amphora, c. 675–650 B.C. (Gardner, p. 129, ill. 5:4; Janson, p. 106, ill. 137)
Homer, *The Odyssey:* "The Blinding of Polyphemus," eighth century B.C.

The second great epic of the early Greek literature is *The Odyssey.* A companion piece to *The Iliad, The Odyssey* recounts the ten years of wanderings and trials endured by Odysseus as he journeyed home to Ithaca after the fall of Troy. Interwoven in this are the adventures of his son, Telemachus, who struggled to preserve his inheritance from the grasp of the arrogant suitors of his mother, Penelope.

One of the most famous tales of *The Odyssey* concerns Odysseus' encounter with the one-eyed giant Polyphemus. As Odysseus later related the story, he and his men had been battered by storms at sea and had stopped at an island near the land of the Cyclopes. Discovering a vast cave stocked with wine and cheese, they had waited for the return of the cave-dweller whose identity was unknown to them. At dusk, Polyphemus appeared with his flocks of sheep and barred the entrance to the cave with an enormous boulder. On finding his guests, he responded not by extending the customary Greek offer of hospitality but by seizing and eating two of Odysseus' companions. The alarmed Odysseus and his men realized that they faced a double peril: if they did not kill the giant, Polyphemus would surely eat all of them; but if they did slay the giant, they would all be trapped in the cave. At morning, Polyphemus breakfasted on two more Greeks, drove his flocks from the cave, and left Odysseus and his men imprisoned. That evening, Odysseus, whom Homer repeatedly describes as wily or cunning, feted Polyphemus with wine until the giant fell into a drunken stupor. Then the Greeks poked out his one eye with a stick sharpened in the fire for this purpose. The following morning, when Polyphemus rolled the stone away to let his flocks out of the cave, Odysseus and his men escaped by clinging to the thick fleece of the sheeps' bellies.

A selection from *The Odyssey,* "The Blinding of Polyphemus," is presented here. The Homeric tale is also illustrated in the proto-Attic amphora from Eleusis.

In addition to being one of the world's greatest poets, Homer was also one of the world's most influential artists. *The Odyssey* and *The Iliad* provided the basis of Greek education and culture throughout the Classical age. Greeks regarded the Homeric epics as something more than works of literature; they valued them both as recollections of a heroic time when Greeks were united in a single cause, and, even more important, as sources of practical and moral education for their own age.

Homer, *The Odyssey*[4]

The Blinding of Polyphemus

[Polyphemus] spoke and slumped away and fell on his back, and lay there
with his thick neck crooked over on one side, and sleep who subdues all
came on and captured him, and the wine gurgled up from his gullet
with gobs of human meat. This was his drunken vomiting.

4. Reprinted, by permission of Harper & Row, Publishers, Inc., from *The Odyssey of Homer,* trans. by Richmond Lattimore (New York, 1967), pp. 146–47. Copyright © 1965, 1967 by Richmond Lattimore.

Then I shoved the beam underneath a deep bed of cinders,
waiting for it to heat, and I spoke to all my companions
in words of courage, so none should be in a panic, and back out;
but when the beam of olive, green as it was, was nearly
at the point of catching fire and glowed, terribly incandescent,
then I brought it close up from the fire and my friends about me
stood fast. Some great divinity breathed courage into us.
They seized the beam of olive, sharp at the end, and leaned on it
into the eye, while I from above leaning my weight on it
twirled it, like a man with a brace-and-bit who bores into
a ship timber, and his men from underneath, grasping
the strap on either side whirl it, and it bites resolutely deeper.
So seizing the fire-point-hardened timber we twirled it
in his eye, and the blood boiled around the hot point, so that
the blast and scorch of the burning ball singed all his eyebrows
and eyelids, and the fire made the roots of his eye crackle.
As when a man who works as a blacksmith plunges a screaming
great ax blade or plane into cold water, treating it
for temper, since this is the way steel is made strong, even
so Cyclops' eye sizzled about the beam of the olive.
He gave a giant horrible cry and the rocks rattled
to the sound, and we scuttled away in fear. He pulled the timber
out of his eye, and it blubbered with plenty of blood. . . .

3. *Kroisos (Kouros from Anavysos),* c. 540–515 B.C. (Gardner, p. 135, ill. 5:16; Janson, p. 112, ill. 146)
Sappho, *Ode:* "He Seems to Be a God," mid- to late sixth century B.C.

During the Archaic period, both art and literature showed the growing Greek awareness of the individual as a subject deserving study. In sculpture, such as the *Kroisos,* and in poetry, such as that by Sappho, the physical and emotional aspects of human nature are explored.

Sappho (c. 610–580 B.C.) is one of the most admired of all Greek poets, because of the intensely personal quality of her subjects and the melodious grace of her language. Sappho lived on the island of Lesbos, off the coast of Asia Minor. The wife of a wealthy man named Kerkylas and the mother of at least one child, a daughter named Kleïs, Sappho was also the center of a literary society in which women gathered to compose and recite poetry.

Writing for herself and her friends, Sappho chose personal subjects for her poetry. She gave candid accounts of the love, jealousy, and enmity that flourished within her own and rival circles. Throughout her work Sappho expressed her feelings for other women in terms that ranged from gentle affection to passionate love. Phrased in the vernacular Aeolic dialect spoken by her neighbors rather than in the literary language of the day, Sappho's poetry possesses an unequaled directness and power.

Sappho wrote nine books of lyric poems, but only two odes and a number of fragments have survived. One ode, "He Seems to Be a God," is presented here. In this ode, Sappho addresses a female friend and poignantly describes her own misery as she observes the response of her friend to a man.

Sappho, *Ode*[5]

He Seems to Be a God

He seems to be a god, that man
Facing you, who leans to be close,
Smiles, and, alert and glad, listens
To your mellow voice

And quickens in love at your laughter
That stings my breasts, jolts my heart
If I dare the shock of a glance.
I cannot speak,

My tongue sticks to my dry mouth,
Thin fire spreads beneath my skin,
My eyes cannot see and my aching ears
Roar in their labyrinths.

Chill sweat slides down my body,
I shake, I turn greener than grass.
I am neither living nor dead and cry
From the narrow between.
But endure, even this grief of love.

4. "Basilica," Paestum, Italy, c. 550 B.C. (Gardner, pp. 141–42, ill. 5:22 and 5:23; Janson, p. 121, ills. 161–162)
Temple of Hera ("Temple of Poseidon"), Paestum, Italy, c. 460 B.C. (Gardner, p. 143, ills. 5:25 and 5:26; Janson, p. 122, ills. 163–65)
Aristotle, *Metaphysics:* "On the Pythagoreans," mid-fourth century B.C.

In the sixth century B.C., Greek intellectuals began to investigate the natural world and to study men and women and their place in that world. They asserted that the sphere of nature and of humanity was governed by comprehensible laws, which

5. Reprinted, by permission of the publisher, from Guy Davenport, trans., *Archilochus, Sappho, Alkman* (Berkeley: University of California Press, 1980), pp. 84–85.

could be discovered through the use of human reason. Their study, which united all branches of learning into a single endeavor, was called philosophy, or "the love of wisdom."

Foremost among the Greek philosophers of this period was Pythagoras of Samos. Forced by his political views to leave Samos, Pythagoras settled in southern Italy at Croton between approximately 530 and 510 B.C. Here he founded a religious society which had the political purpose of supporting aristocracies against tyrannies and democracies and which had the moral and religious aim of reforming humanity. Basic to the tenets of Pythagoras and his followers was the belief in the reincarnation of the soul and in the possibility of its purification and its union with the divine through abstinence and intellectual reflection.

Pythagoras is famous for his demonstration that the sum of the squares on two sides of a right-angled triangle is equal to the square of the hypotenuse. However, for Pythagoras the study of mathematics was united with metaphysics —that is, the attempt to understand the fundamental nature of all existence. To Pythagoras all things were numerable and could be expressed numerically. Not only were physical things measurable or proportional in terms of number but abstract things also "had" their number; for example, "justice" was associated with the number 4, and "marriage" with the number 5. Moreover, the connection between two related things could be expressed according to numerical proportion. The number 10, which the Pythagoreans symbolized in the form of 1 + 2 + 3 + 4, had a special significance.

Pythagoreans were especially impressed with the discovery that the musical intervals between the notes on the lyre could be expressed numerically. Pitch may be said to depend upon number, and the intervals on the scale may be expressed by numerical ratios. Just as musical harmony is dependent on number, so Pythagoreans argued that the harmony of the cosmic spheres depended upon number. Pythagoras referred to the "music of the heavens" and later Pythagoreans postulated that the distances of heavenly bodies from the earth corresponded to musical intervals.

The Pythagorean belief in the relationship between cosmic harmony, on the one hand, and mathematical number, ratio, and form, on the other hand, was of paramount importance to Classical Greek culture in the areas of philosophy, science, and art. The comparison between the "Basilica" at Paestum and later Greek temples, such as the Temple of Hera ("The Temple of Poseidon"), also at Paestum, shows the Greek concern for proportion and their experimentation with the ratios of similar forms.

Pythagoras left no writings. His ideas survive only in the commentaries of other writers, such as Aristotle. A selection from Aristotle's *Metaphysics,* "On the Pythagoreans," is presented here.

Aristotle, *Metaphysics*[6]

On the Pythagoreans

The Pythagoreans, as they are called, devoted themselves to mathematics; they were the first to advance this study, and having been brought up in it they thought its principles were the principles of all things. Since of these principles numbers are by nature the first, and in numbers they seemed to see many resemblances to the things that exist and come into being—more than in fire and earth and water (such and such a modification of numbers being justice, another being soul and reason, another being opportunity—and similarly almost all other things being numerically expressible); since, again, they say that the attributes and ratios of the musical scales were expressible in numbers; since, then, all other things seemed in their whole nature to be modelled after numbers, and numbers seemed to be the first things in the whole of nature, they supposed the elements of numbers to be the elements of all things, and the whole heaven to be a musical scale and a number. And all the properties of numbers and scales which they could show to agree with the attributes and parts and the whole arrangement of the heavens, they collected and fitted into their scheme; and if there was a gap anywhere, they readily made additions so as to make their whole theory coherent. E.g. as the number 10 is thought to be perfect and to comprise the whole nature of numbers, they say that the bodies which move through the heavens are ten, but as the visible bodies are only nine, to meet this they invent a tenth—the "counter-earth." . . .

Evidently, then, these thinkers also consider that number is the principle both as matter for things and as forming their modifications and their permanent states, and hold that the elements of number are the even and the odd, and of these the former is unlimited, and the latter limited; and the 1 proceeds from both of these (for it is both even and odd), and number from the 1; and the whole heaven, as has been said, is numbers.

Other members of this same school say there are ten principles, which they arrange in two columns of cognates—limit and unlimited, odd and even, one and plurality, right and left, male and female, resting and moving, straight and crooked, light and darkness, good and bad, square and oblong.

6. Reprinted, by permission of the publisher, from Aristotle, *Metaphysics,* trans. by W. D. Ross (Oxford: Oxford University Press, 1908).

5. Treasury of the Siphnians, Sanctuary of Apollo at Delphi, c. 530 B.C. (Gardner, p. 144, ill. 5:27; Janson, p. 116, ill. 154)
Herodotus, *The Persian Wars:* "The Delphic Oracle," c. 443–424 B.C.

Delphi was the seat of the most famous oracle of antiquity. In earliest times the oracle belonged to the earth goddess Gaea, who sent the serpent Python to guard the chasm from which the prophetic vapors emanated. Apollo seized control of the oracle by slaying the serpent, an act for which the god was required to seek purification and to perform penance for eight years. The penance and purification of Apollo were commemorated in a sacred drama that was enacted at Delphi at first every eight years and later every three years. These Panhellenic ceremonies, which included musical competitions and athletic events, were called the Pythian Games; the priestess who received the oracle from Apollo was called the Pythia.

The influence of the oracle of Delphi was felt throughout the Mediterranean world. Persons seeking advice from the oracle came to Delphi as suppliants. They purified themselves, made sacrifices, and sought permission to ask a question of the oracle. If permission was granted, they approached the priestess in her shrine. In preparation for delivering the oracle, the priestess drank the waters of a sacred spring, chewed laurel leaves, and seated herself on a tripod over the chasm from which the vapors issued. A priest, the only other person present, interpreted the responses of the priestess.

Pilgrims came to Delphi from all regions of the Classical world and consulted the oracle about both public and personal matters. A famous oracle is recounted by the Greek historian Herodotus in *The Persian Wars.* Herodotus (c. 484–424 B.C.) was born in Halicarnassus, a Greek city in southwest Asia Minor. He fought against the Persians, who controlled Halicarnassus, and at a later date left his native city and went to Athens. He became a friend of Sophocles and possibly also of Pericles. Ultimately, he settled in Thurii, a colony founded by Athens in 443 B.C., where he wrote his history and where he died.

Herodotus had traveled widely in Persia and Greece. He had not only a fascination for the legends, customs, and history of the peoples whom he visited but also a gift for storytelling. In *The Persian Wars* Herodotus includes myths, folktales, and anecdotes along with straightforward historical accounts and sometimes repeats stories which he frankly admits he does not believe himself. Above all, he demonstrates a tolerance of and compassion for both the Greek and non-Greek peoples about whom he writes.

The principle theme of *The Persian Wars* is the war between Greece and Persia during the years 480–479 B.C. Greece and Persia had long been engaged in conflict. In the spring of 480 B.C., Xerxes had led an immense Persian army, supported by a large fleet, against the Greek city-states. According to Herodotus, the Athenians sent ambassadors to consult the Delphic oracle about how to defend themselves. The initial reply of the priestess was gloomy but the messengers refused to leave until they heard a more encouraging response. The priestess answered with an obscure recommendation that the Athenians would find safety behind a wooden wall. Themistocles, leader of the Athenians, interpreted the ambiguously phrased reference to a wooden wall to mean a naval force. He persuaded the Athenians to prepare a great fleet, which subsequently won a decisive victory over the Persians at Salamis. A selection from *The Persian Wars,* "The Delphic Oracle," is presented here.

Herodotus, *The Persian Wars*[7]

The Delphic Oracle

When the Athenians, anxious to consult the oracle, sent their messengers to Delphi, hardly had the envoys completed the customary rites about the sacred precinct, and taken their seats inside the sanctuary of the god, when the Pythia, Aristonice by name, thus prophesied:

Wretches, why sit ye here? Fly, fly to the ends of creation,
Quitting your homes, and the crags which your city crowns
with her circlet.
Neither the head, nor the body is firm in its place, nor at bottom
Firm the feet, nor the hands, nor resteth the middle uninjur'd.
All—all ruined and lost. Since fire, and impetuous Ares,[8]
Speeding along in a Syrian chariot, hastes to destroy her.
Not alone shalt thou suffer; full many the towers he will level,
Many the shrines of the gods he will give to a fiery destruction.
Even now they stand with dark sweat horribly dripping,
Trembling and quaking for fear, and lo! from the high roofs trickleth
Black blood, sign prophetic of hard distresses impending.
Get ye away from the temple, and brood on the ills that await ye!

When the Athenian messengers heard this reply, they were filled with the deepest affliction: whereupon Timon, the son of Androbulus, one of the men of most mark among the Delphians, seeing how utterly cast down they were at the gloomy prophecy, advised them to take an olive branch, and entering the sanctuary again, consult the oracle as suppliants. The Athenians followed this advice, and going in once more, said—"O Lord, we pray thee reverence these boughs of supplication which we bear in our hands, and deliver to us something more comforting concerning our country. Else we will not leave thy sanctuary, but will stay here till we die." Upon this the priestess gave them a second answer, which was the following:

7. Reprinted from Herodotus, *The Persian Wars,* trans. by George Rawlinson, in Francis R. B. Godolphin, ed., *The Greek Historians: The Complete and Unabridged Historical Works of Herodotus, Thucydides, Xenophon, Arrian,* Vol. 1 (New York: Random House, Inc., 1942), pp. 433–34.

8. The god of war, the son of Zeus and Hera.

Pallas[9] has not been able to soften the lord of Olympus,
Though she has often prayed him, and urged him with excellent counsel.
Yet once more I address thee in words than adamant firmer.
When the foe shall have taken whatever the limit of Cecrops[10]
Holds within it, and all which divine Cithaeron[11] shelters,
Then far-seeing Zeus grants this to the prayers of Athena;
Safe shall the wooden wall continue for thee and thy children.
Wait not the tramp of the horse, nor the footmen mightily moving
Over the land, but turn your back to the foe, and retire ye.
Yet shall a day arrive when ye shall meet him in battle.
Holy Salamis, thou shalt destroy the offspring of women,
When men scatter the seed, or when they gather the harvest.

THE FIFTH CENTURY

1. *Charioteer,* from the Sanctuary of Apollo at Delphi, c. 470 B.C. (Gardner, p. 148, ill. 5:37; Janson, p. 130, ill. 180)
Parmenides, *The Way of Truth:* "The Chariot Journey," mid-fifth century B.C.
Plato, *Phaedrus:* "The Charioteer," early to mid-fourth century B.C.

During the fifth century B.C., Greek philosophers and artists shared the quest to comprehend the universe in rational and logical terms as an orderly structure and to understand the nature of humanity and its role in the universe. The image of the charioteer appears both in fifth-century sculpture and in contemporaneous philosophical writings.

Parmenides (c. 515 B.C.–?) was an influential Greek philosopher. Born in Elea on the southern coast of Italy, Parmenides was for a time a member of the Pythagorean brotherhood that had its center at Croton. He is believed to have arrived in Athens at the age of sixty-five, where, according to some accounts, he became acquainted with his younger contemporary, Socrates.

Parmenides' ideas are expressed in a didactic poem, *The Way of Truth,* written in hexameters. The poem opens with an allegory describing a chariot journey in which the nature of reality is revealed to Parmenides. Guided by the daughters of the Sun, who are described as "immortal charioteers," the poet is led

9. Another name of Athena, the patron goddess of Athens.

10. The "limit of Cecrops" refers to that part of Athenian territory that was held under its legendary first king, Cecrops, the founder of the city. Cecrops was half man and half serpent and established laws for the city, which, among other things, abolished human sacrifice.

11. A mountain range in central Greece to the north of Athens.

from darkness into light. He arrives at a temple sacred to the goddess Wisdom, who welcomes him and advises him that he must be prepared to reject illusion and learn the truth.

Through the voice of the goddess, Parmenides outlines his belief in the single, unchangeable state of being. Sensory experience suggests that the universe is in constant flux, and popular opinion describes the world in terms of pairs of opposites such as light and dark, hot and cold, male and female. But reason rejects the illusions of the senses and apprehends reality. The universe, for Parmenides, is whole, motionless, timeless, indivisible, and imperishable. A selection from *The Way of Truth,* "The Chariot Journey," is presented here.

The allegory of the charioteer was also used by the fourth-century Greek philosopher Plato (c. 429–347 B.C.). In *Phaedrus,* Plato explained his doctrine of the tripartite nature of the soul. The soul, according to Plato, consists of three elements—reason, spirit, and appetite. Reason is what distinguishes man from the brute and is the highest element of the soul. Reason has a natural affinity for the invisible and intelligible world. Akin to the divine, reason achieves immortality. Spirit and appetite are bound up essentially with the body. Both are perishable, but of the two, spirit is the nobler. Related to moral courage, it is the natural ally of reason. Appetite refers to bodily desires.

Plato compares the rational element of the soul to a charioteer and the spirit and appetite elements to two horses. The one horse, the spirit element, is allied to reason, honor, temperance, and modesty, and is good; the other horse, the appetite element, is allied to passion, chaos, arrogance, and insolence, and is bad. While the good horse is easily driven according to the directions of the charioteer, the bad horse is unruly and tends to obey the voice of sensual passion and therefore must be restrained with the whip. Plato thus explains the conflict that individuals feel within themselves. At the same time he unequivocally insists on the right of the rational element to rule and to act as the charioteer. A selection from *Phaedrus,* "The Charioteer," is presented here.

Parmenides, *The Way of Truth*[12]

The Chariot Journey

The steeds that carry me took me as far as my heart could desire, when once they had brought me and set me on the renowned way of the goddess, which leads the man who knows through every town. On that way I was conveyed; for on it did the wise steeds convey me, drawing my chariot, and maidens led the way. And the axle glowing in the socket—for it was urged round by well-turned wheels at each end—was making the holes of the

12. Reprinted, by permission of the publisher, from G. S. Kirk, J. E. Raven, and M. Schofield, eds. and trans., *The Pre-Socratic Philosophers* (Cambridge: Cambridge University Press, 1957; 2nd ed., 1984), pp. 266–67.

naves sing, while the daughters of the Sun, hastening to convey me into the light, threw back the veils from off their faces and left the abode of night. There are the gates of Night and Day, fitted above with a lintel and below with a threshold of stone. They themselves, high in the air, are closed by mighty doors, and avenging Justice controls the double bolts. Her did the maidens entreat with gentle words and cunningly persuade to unfasten without demur the bolted bar from the gates. Then, when the doors were thrown back, they disclosed a wide opening, when their brazen posts fitted with rivets and nails swung in turn on their hinges. Straight through them, on the broad way, did the maidens guide the horses and the car. And the goddess greeted me kindly, and took my right hand in hers, and spoke to me these words: "Welcome, O youth, that comest to my abode on the car that bears thee, tended by immortal charioteers. It is no ill chance, but right and justice, that has sent thee forth to travel on this way. Far indeed does it lie from the beaten track of men. Meet it is that thou shouldst learn all things, as well as the unshaken heart of well-rounded truth, as the opinions of mortals in which is no true belief at all. Yet none the less shalt thou learn these things also—how, passing right through all things, one should judge the things that seem to be."

Plato, *Phaedrus*[13]

The Charioteer

As to soul's immortality then we have said enough, but as to its nature there is this that must be said: what manner of thing it is would be a long tale to tell, and most assuredly a god alone could tell it; but what it resembles, that a man might tell in briefer compass: let this therefore be our manner of discourse. Let it be likened to the union of powers in a team of winged steeds and their winged charioteer. Now all the gods' steeds and all their charioteers are good, and of good stock; but with other beings it is not wholly so. With us men, in the first place, it is a pair of steeds that the charioteer controls; moreover one of them is noble and good, and of good stock, while the other has the opposite character, and his stock is opposite. Hence the task of our charioteer is difficult and troublesome.

And now we must essay to tell how it is that living beings are called mortal and immortal. All soul has the care of all that is inanimate, and traverses the whole universe, though in ever-changing forms. Thus when

13. Reprinted, by permission of the publisher, from *Plato's Phaedrus,* trans. by R. Hackforth (Cambridge: Cambridge University Press, 1972), pp. 69–71.

it is perfect and winged it journeys on high and controls the whole world; but one that has shed its wings sinks down until it can fasten on something solid, and settling there it takes to itself an earthy body which seems by reason of the soul's power to move itself. This composite structure of soul and body is called a living being, and is further termed "mortal": "immortal" is a term applied on no basis of reasoned argument at all, but our fancy pictures the god whom we have never seen, nor fully conceived, as an immortal living being, possessed of a soul and a body united for all time. Howbeit let these matters, and our account thereof, be as god pleases; what we must understand is the reason why the soul's wings fall from it, and are lost. It is on this wise.

The natural property of a wing is to raise that which is heavy and carry it aloft to the region where the gods dwell; and more than any other bodily part it shares in the divine nature, which is fair, wise and good, and possessed of all other such excellences. Now by these excellences especially is the soul's plumage nourished and fostered, while by their opposites, even by ugliness and evil, it is wasted and destroyed. And behold, there in the heaven Zeus, mighty leader, drives his winged team: first of the host of gods and daemons he proceeds, ordering all things and caring therefore: and the host follows after him, marshalled in eleven companies. For Hestia[14] abides alone in the gods' dwelling-place; but for the rest, all such as are ranked in the number of the twelve as ruler gods lead their several companies, each according to his rank.

Now within the heavens are many spectacles of bliss upon the highways whereon the blessed gods pass to and fro, each doing his own work; and with them are all such as will and can follow them: for jealousy has no place in the choir divine. But at such times as they go to their feasting and banquet, behold they climb the steep ascent even unto the summit of the arch that supports the heavens; and easy is that ascent for the chariots of the gods, for that they are well-balanced and readily guided; but for the others it is hard, by reason of the heaviness of the steed of wickedness, which pulls down his driver with his weight, except that driver have schooled him well.

And now there awaits the soul the extreme of her toil and struggling. For the souls that are called immortal, so soon as they are at the summit, come forth and stand upon the back of the world: and straightway the revolving heaven carries them round, and they look upon the regions without.

14. The goddess of the hearth, fire, and domestic life, Hestia was the daughter of Cronus and Rhea.

2. Myron, *Discobolos,* c. 450 B.C. (Gardner, p. 148, ill. 5:38; Janson, p. 132, ill. 184)

Hippocratic Writings, *Precepts:* "Time Is That Wherein There Is Opportunity," undated; *Aphorisms:* "Life Is Short, the Art Long," undated; *Nature of Man:* "The Elements of Man's Body," undated

Modern science, as well as philosophy, is indebted to Greek thought. Hippocrates, a Greek physician of the late fifth and early fourth centuries B.C., is today considered the father of medicine. Very little is known about his life. According to tradition, Hippocrates (c. 469–377 B.C.) was the son of a physician. Throughout his life he traveled widely in Greece and Asia Minor, practicing his profession and teaching his pupils.

Shortly after his death, references were made to writings by Hippocrates. The number of medical treatises "by Hippocrates" known to the Classical world was seventy; the number now surviving is about sixty. These works apparently represent the library of a medical school, probably that on the island of Cos, where Hippocrates was born. It is likely that many of the works attributed to Hippocrates were not actually written by the physician but by his students and later followers.

Selections from three of the Hippocratic writings are presented here. In the first, from the *Precepts,* "Time Is That Wherein There Is Opportunity," the author discards traditional approaches to medicine. He insists that sickness is caused by natural rather than supernatural factors, and he recommends the simple, reasonable treatment of an illness based upon observation and experience rather than accepted custom and belief. In the selection from the *Aphorisms,* "Life Is Short, the Art Long," the author defines medicine as a rational study which, like art, outlasts the span of an individual's life, and he offers specific advice on the diagnosis and treatment of illnesses. In the selection from the *Nature of Man,* "The Elements of Man's Body," the author explains the theory then prevalent in the ancient world that man's physical constitution consists of four essences, or "humors": yellow bile, black bile, blood, and phlegm. It was believed that, in order to maintain good health, these humors had to be kept in balance by a proper diet and a regulated conduct of life. Although the descriptions of many illnesses in the Hippocratic writings are extremely accurate, contemporary religious belief did not allow vivisection, and Greek doctors therefore had only a rudimentary knowledge of anatomy. This misconception about man's physical nature underlay medical concepts in the West until the eighteenth century.

According to Plato, Hippocrates was as well known to Greeks as a physician as Polykleitos and Phidias were as sculptors. Plato credited Hippocrates with a philosophical approach to medicine because Hippocrates claimed that one cannot understand the workings of the individual parts of the body without understanding the nature of the body as a whole. A similar concern for understanding man's body as an organism, and for investigating its internal workings as well as its outward appearance, is evident in examples of Greek sculpture, such as the *Discobolos* by Myron.

Hippocratic Writings, *Precepts*[15]

Time Is That Wherein There Is Opportunity

Time is that wherein there is opportunity, and opportunity is that wherein there is no great time. Healing is a matter of time, but it is sometimes also a matter of opportunity. However, knowing this, one must attend in medical practice not primarily to plausible theories, but to experience combined with reason. For a theory is a composite memory of things apprehended with sense-perception. For the sense-perception, coming first in experience and conveying to the intellect the things subjected to it, is clearly imaged, and the intellect, receiving these things many times, noting the occasion, the time and the manner, stores them up in itself and remembers. Now I approve of theorising also if it lays its foundation in incident, and deduces its conclusions in accordance with phenomena. For if theorising lays its foundation in clear fact, it is found to exist in the domain of intellect, which itself receives from other sources each of its impressions. So we must conceive of our nature as being stirred and instructed under compulsion by the great variety of things; and the intellect, as I have said, taking over from nature the impressions, leads us afterwards into truth. But if it begins, not from a clear impression, but from a plausible fiction, it often induces a grievous and troublesome condition. All who so act are lost in a blind alley. Now no harm would be done if bad practitioners received their due wages. But as it is their innocent patients suffer, for whom the violence of their disorder did not appear sufficient without the addition of their physician's inexperience.

Hippocratic Writings, *Aphorisms*[16]

Life Is Short, the Art Long

Life is short, the Art long, opportunity fleeting, experiment treacherous, judgment difficult. The physician must be ready, not only to do his duty himself, but also to secure the co-operation of the patient, of the attendants and of externals. . . .

A restricted and rigid regimen is treacherous, in chronic diseases always, in acute, where it is not called for. Again, a regimen carried to the

15. Reprinted, by permission of the publisher and The Loeb Classical Library, from Hippocrates, *Works,* trans. by W.H.S. Jones (Cambridge, Mass.: Harvard University Press, 1967), Vol. 1, pp. 313–15.

16. Reprinted, by permission of the publisher and The Loeb Classical Library, from Hippocrates, *Works,* trans. by W.H.S. Jones (Cambridge, Mass.: Harvard University Press, 1967), Vol. 4, pp. 99–101, 105–107, 111, 115–17, 121.

extreme of restriction is perilous; and in fact repletion too, carried to extremes, is perilous. . . .

Exacerbations and constitutions will be made plain by the diseases, by the seasons of the year, and by the correspondence of periods to one another, whether they come every day, every other day, or at a longer interval. Moreover, there are supervening symptoms; for example, in pleurisy, if expectoration supervene immediately on the commencement of the disease, it means a shorter illness, if afterwards a longer one. Urine, stools, sweats, by the manner in which they supervene, show whether the disease will have a difficult crisis or an easy one, whether it will be short or long. . . .

Do not disturb a patient either during or just after a crisis, and try no experiments, neither with purges nor with other irritants, but leave him alone. . . .

Bodies that have wasted away slowly should be slowly restored; those that have wasted quickly should be quickly restored. . . .

One must not trust improvements that are irregular, nor yet fear overmuch bad symptoms that occur irregularly; for such are generally uncertain and are not at all wont to last or grow chronic. . . .

At the beginning of diseases, if strong medicines seem called for, use them; when they are at their height it is better to let the patient rest.

At the beginning and at the end all symptoms are weaker, at the height they are stronger. . . .

In every disease it is a good sign when the patient's intellect is sound and he enjoys his food; the opposite is a bad sign. . . .

When acting in all things according to rule, do not, when results are not according to rule, change to another course of treatment if the original opinion remains.

Hippocratic Writings, *Nature of Man*[17]

The Elements of Man's Body

He who is accustomed to hear speakers discuss the nature of man beyond its relations to medicine will not find the present account of any interest. For I do not say at all that a man is air, or fire, or water, or earth, or anything else that is not an obvious constituent of a man; such accounts I leave to those that care to give them. Those, however, who give them have not in my opinion correct knowledge. For while adopting the same idea

17. Reprinted, by permission of the publisher and The Loeb Classical Library, from Hippocrates, *Works,* trans. by W.H.S. Jones (Cambridge, Mass.: Harvard University Press, 1967), Vol. 4, pp. 3–7, 11–13.

they do not give the same account. Though they add the same appendix to their idea—saying that "what is" is a unity, and that this is both unity and the all—yet they are not agreed as to its name. One of them asserts that this one and the all is air, another calls it fire, another, water, and another, earth; while each appends to his own account evidence and proofs that amount to nothing. The fact that, while adopting the same idea, they do not give the same account, shows that their knowledge too is at fault. . . .

Now about these men I have said enough, and I will turn to physicians. Some of them say that a man is blood, others that he is bile, a few that he is phlegm. Physicians, like the metaphysicians, all add the same appendix. For they say that a man is a unity, giving it the name that severally they wish to give it; this changes its form and its power, being constrained by the hot and the cold, and becomes sweet, bitter, white, black and so on. But in my opinion these views are incorrect. Most physicians then maintain views like these, if not identical with them; but I hold that if man were a unity he would never feel pain, as there would be nothing from which a unity could suffer pain. And even if he were to suffer, the cure too would have to be one. But as a matter of fact cures are many. . . .

The body of man has in itself blood, phlegm, yellow bile and black bile; these make up the nature of his body, and through these he feels pain or enjoys health. Now he enjoys the most perfect health when these elements are duly proportioned to one another in respect of compounding, power and bulk, and when they are perfectly mingled. Pain is felt when one of these elements is in defect or excess, or is isolated in the body without being compounded with all the others. For when an element is isolated and stands by itself, not only must the place which it left become diseased, but the place where it stands in a flood must, because of the excess, cause pain and distress. In fact when more of an element flows out of the body than is necessary to get rid of superfluity, the emptying causes pain. If, on the other hand, it be to an inward part that there takes place the emptying, the shifting and the separation from other elements, the man certainly must, according to what has been said, suffer from a double pain, one in the place left, and another in the place flooded.

3. Polykleitos, *Doryphoros,* c. 450–440 B.C. (Gardner, p. 160, ill. 5:61; Janson, p. 130, ill. 179)
Sophocles, *Antigone:* "Many Are the Wonders But Nothing Walks Stranger Than Man," c. 441 B.C.

Classical civilization in fifth-century Greece produced an extraordinary many-sided outburst of human genius. The brilliant achievements of Greek civilization during this brief period rested upon the harmonious fusion of old and new forces.

From the past, the Greeks inherited a deep religious faith in the power of basically benevolent, just gods, a patriotic devotion to the cause of the city-state, and a belief in the personal ideals of dignity, courage, and dedication. To this they added an ever-greater sense of the importance of the individual, a rational and questioning attitude of mind, and an exaltation of spirit.

Athenian drama, especially tragedy, conveys the most essential qualities of the Classical period in Greece. Commissioned by the state and presented at religious festivals in honor of the god Dionysus, Greek drama employed a chorus, which consisted of twelve to fifteen men and which voiced the inner thoughts of the central characters and the audience. In addition to the chorus, a play might have any number of individual characters, but no more than three actors appeared on the stage at once. Since actors wore masks, they could assume several roles. All feminine parts were played by men. Music accompanied the drama.

The dramatist Sophocles (c. 496–406 B.C.) gave profound form to the complex dilemmas of experience in fifth-century Greece. A friend of the statesman Pericles, Sophocles lived in Athens during the period of its greatest cultural, political, and economic development. To his contemporaries, Sophocles appeared genial in character, serene in temperament, and orthodox in viewpoint. At the same time, his plays demonstrate that he understood the complexity of human nature.

Antigone was written by Sophocles c. 441 B.C. The tragedy focuses on the conflict between Antigone, the daughter of Oedipus, and her uncle, Creon, who, after the deaths of Antigone's two brothers, had become ruler of Thebes. Antigone has defied Creon's order that the body of the traitorous brother Polynices be denied an honorable burial. Antigone's defiance, which pits the dictates of divine law and family honor against the man-made law of the king, leads to her doom and to the death of her lover, Haemon, who is also Creon's son.

In *Antigone,* Sophocles describes the intense passions, deep sufferings, and terrible despair that are part of human existence, and at the same time radiantly proclaims the faith of his generation in humanity and its affinity with the divine. The same faith in the intellectual and spiritual capacities of the individual, as well as admiration for the physical beauty of the human form, are also evident in contemporary Greek sculpture, such as the *Doryphoros* by Polykleitos. A selection from *Antigone,* "Many Are the Wonders But Nothing Walks Stranger Than Man," is presented here.

Sophocles, *Antigone*[18]

Many Are the Wonders But Nothing Walks Stranger Than Man

Chorus

Many are the wonders but nothing walks stranger than man.
This thing crosses the sea in the winter's storm,

18. Reprinted, by permission of the publisher, from Donald Greene and Richmond Lattimore, eds., *The Complete Greek Tragedies* (Chicago: University of Chicago Press, 1959), Vol. 2, pp. 170–71. Copyright © 1959 by the University of Chicago. Selection translated by Elizabeth Wyckoff.

making his path through the roaring waves.
And she, the greatest of gods, the earth—
ageless she is, and unwearied—he wears her away
as the ploughs go up and down from year to year
and his mules turn up the soil.

Gay nations of birds he snares and leads,
wild beast tribes and the salty brood of the sea,
with the twisted mesh of his nets, this clever man.
He controls with craft the beasts of the open air,
walkers on hills. The horse with his shaggy mane
he holds and harnesses, yoked about the neck,
and the strong bull of the mountain.

Language, and thought like the wind
and the feelings that make the town,
he has taught himself, and shelter against the cold,
refuge from rain. He can always help himself.
He faces no future helpless. There's only death
that he cannot find an escape from. He has contrived
refuge from illnesses once beyond all cure.

Clever beyond all dreams
the inventive craft that he has
which may drive him one time or another to well or ill.
When he honors the laws of the land and the gods' sworn right
high indeed in his city; but stateless the man
who dares to dwell with dishonor. Not by my fire,
never to share my thoughts, who does these things.

4. Iktinos and Kallikrates, The Parthenon, Acropolis, Athens, 448–432 B.C. (Gardner, pp. 151, 153, ills. 5:44 to 5:46; Janson, p. 123, ill. 166)

Mnesikles, The Propylaea, Acropolis, Athens, c. 437–432 B.C. (Gardner, p. 156, ill. 5:53; Janson, pp. 125–26, ills. 169–71)

Thucydides, *History of the Peloponnesian War:* "Pericles' Funeral Oration," c. 431 B.C.

From the modern point of view, Athens was a small, simply organized city-state. However, in the Mediterranean world of the fifth century B.C., the city was an important naval and commercial power. At the same time that it controlled an overseas empire, Athens developed a democratic pattern of government at home.

Pericles, the greatest statesman of ancient Athens, brought Athenian democracy to its zenith, established Athens as the undisputed intellectual leader of Greece, and built two of the most magnificent buildings on the Acropolis, the Parthenon and the Propylaea.

Pericles (c. 495–429 B.C.) was a member of a powerful and influential Athenian family. After receiving an excellent education in philosophy, politics, and music, he became prominent in public life. The leader of the democratic party, he won the support and respect of the masses by initiating democratic reforms.

Simultaneously, Pericles pursued a policy of increasing Athenian power and influence abroad. In order to arrest this growing power, Sparta sought a pretext to embark on war with Athens. The result was the Peloponnesian War, which was to embroil the Greek city-states in a protracted struggle that lasted from 431 B.C. to 404 B.C.

The Peloponnesian War was described by the Greek historian Thucydides (c. 460–400 B.C.). A native of Athens, Thucydides was an ardent admirer of Pericles, who, in his view, combined caution in action with daring in imagination and intellect. Thucydides served as a general in the war, but his failure in 424 B.C. to defend the city of Amphipolis against Brasidas, the brilliant Spartan general, resulted in his being exiled from Athens for twenty years.

His direct involvement with the war ended, Thucydides turned to writing a contemporary account of the struggle between Athens and Sparta, known as the *History of the Peloponnesian War.* His intention, he stated, was not only to recount the chronological sequence of events but also to study the human mind and character in times of turmoil.

Throughout his *History,* Thucydides uses the dramatic device of putting speeches into the mouths of his main figures in order to reveal the motives and ambitions of the leading protagonists in his narrative. Thucydides' account of the oration which Pericles delivered at the public ceremony to honor the Athenians killed in the first year of the war is an example of the historian's method. The speech records the ideals of Athenian democracy. A selection from the *History of the Peloponnesian War,* "Pericles' Funeral Oration," is presented here.

Thucydides, *History of the Peloponnesian War*[19]

Pericles' Funeral Oration

I have no wish to make a long speech on subjects familiar to you all: so I shall say nothing about the warlike deeds by which we acquired our power or the battles in which we or our fathers gallantly resisted our enemies, Greek or foreign. What I want to do is, in the first place, to discuss the spirit in which we faced our trials and also our constitution and the

19. Reprinted, by permission of the publisher, from Thucydides, *History of the Peloponnesian War,* trans. by Rex Warner (London: Penguin Classics, 1954), pp. 117–20. Copyright © by Rex Warner, 1954.

way of life which has made us great. After that I shall speak in praise of the dead, believing that this kind of speech is not inappropriate to the present occasion, and that this whole assembly, of citizens and foreigners, may listen to it with advantage.

Let me say that our system of government does not copy the institutions of our neighbours. It is more the case of our being a model to others, than of our imitating anyone else. Our constitution is called a democracy because power is in the hands not of a minority but of the whole people. When it is a question of settling private disputes, everyone is equal before the law; when it is a question of putting one person before another in positions of public responsibility, what counts is not membership of a particular class, but the actual ability which the man possesses. No one, so long as he has it in him to be of service to the state, is kept in political obscurity because of poverty. And, just as our political life is free and open, so is our day-to-day life in our relations with each other. We do not get into a state with our next-door neighbour if he enjoys himself in his own way, nor do we give him the kind of black looks which, though they do no real harm, still do hurt people's feelings. We are free and tolerant in our private lives; but in public affairs we keep to the law. This is because it commands our deep respect.

We give our obedience to those whom we put in positions of authority, and we obey the laws themselves, especially those which are for the protection of the oppressed, and those unwritten laws which it is an acknowledged shame to break.

And here is another point. When our work is over, we are in a position to enjoy all kinds of recreation for our spirits. There are various kinds of contests and sacrifices regularly throughout the year; in our own homes we find a beauty and a good taste which delight us every day and which drive away our cares. Then the greatness of our city brings it about that all the good things from all over the world flow in to us, so that to us it seems just as natural to enjoy foreign goods as our own local products. . . .

Our love of what is beautiful does not lead to extravagance; our love of the things of the mind does not make us soft. We regard wealth as something to be properly used, rather than as something to boast about. As for poverty, no one need be ashamed to admit it: the real shame is in not taking practical measures to escape from it. Here each individual is interested not only in his own affairs but in the affairs of the state as well: even those who are mostly occupied with their own business are extremely well-informed on general politics—this is a peculiarity of ours: we do not say that a man who takes no interest in politics is a man who minds his own business; we say that he has no business here at all. We Athenians, in our own persons, take our decisions on policy or submit them to proper discussions: for we do not think that there is an incompatibility between words and deeds; the worst thing is to rush into action before the consequences have been properly debated. And this is another point where we differ from other people. We are capable at the same time of taking risks and of estimating them beforehand. Others are brave out of ignorance; and, when they stop to think, they begin to fear. But the man who can most truly be accounted brave is he who best knows the meaning of what is sweet in life and of what is terrible, and then goes out undeterred to meet what is to come. . . .

Taking everything together then, I declare that our city is an education to Greece, and I declare that in my opinion each single one of our citizens, in all the manifold aspects of life, is able to show himself the rightful lord and owner of his own person, and do this, moreover, with exceptional grace and exceptional versatility. And to show that this is no empty boasting for the present occasion, but real tangible fact, you have only to consider the power which our city possesses and which has been won by those very qualities which I have mentioned. Athens, alone of the states we know, comes to her testing time in a greatness that surpasses what was imagined of her. In her case, and in her case alone, no invading enemy is ashamed at being defeated, and no subject can complain of being governed by people unfit for their responsibilities. Mighty indeed are the marks and monuments of our empire which we have left. Future ages will wonder at us, as the present age wonders at us now. We do not need the praises of a Homer, or of anyone else whose words may delight us for the moment, but whose estimation of facts will fall short of what is really true. For our adventurous spirit has forced an entry into every sea and into every land; and everywhere we have left behind us everlasting memorials of good done to our friends or suffering inflicted on our enemies.

This, then, is the kind of city for which these men, who could not bear the thought of losing her, nobly fought and nobly died.

5. *Horsemen,* from the west frieze of the Parthenon, c. 440 B.C. (Gardner, p. 155, ill. 5:51; Janson, p. 135, ill. 188)
Aeschylus, *The Eumenides:* "The Ordinance of Athena" and "The Procession of the Furies," 458 B.C.

The subject of a Greek tragedy was usually the story of a heroic legend or, less often, the description of a historic event. Narration of a story or event, however, was only the vehicle by which the author might explore the nature of humanity. For this purpose, the Greek dramatist considered the realistic depiction of average citizens inadequate. Instead, he aimed at depicting heroic men and women who moved on an ideal plane where they shared the stage with the gods.

Aeschylus (c. 525–456 B.C.) is considered one of the greatest of the Greek tragedians. Born in Eleusis, the nearby city to which Athenians went to celebrate the solemn rites of the Eleusis Mysteries, Aeschylus was profoundly concerned with religious questions. A member of the Athenian army during the Persian Wars, he was also deeply attached to democratic values. He wrote over eighty plays, of which only seven survive.

The Oresteia of 458 B.C. is a trilogy that traces the life of Orestes. At the same time it deals with the abstract problem of justice and the supremacy of communal life over kinship ties. In *Agamemnon,* the first of the plays, Orestes' father is murdered by his mother, Clytemnestra, and her lover, Aegisthus. In *The Libation Bearers,* the second play, Orestes is directed by the god Apollo to avenge his father's murder by killing Clytemnestra and Aegisthus. In *The Eumenides,* the final play, Orestes, now guilty of matricide, must be brought to trial for his bloody deed.

As the play unfolds, Orestes takes refuge in Athens, where he is discovered on the Acropolis clinging to the statue of Athena, guardian of the city. Around him circle the Furies, the ancient spirits of retribution, who insist that blood vengeance must be exacted for blood crimes. Athena appears, hears the dispute, and decrees that the issue must be decided by a court of Athenian citizens. Enraged that mercy is shown to Orestes by the jury and by Athena, the Furies threaten destruction on Athens and Attica. But Athena persuades them to make their home in the city, where they will henceforth be honored as the "Eumenides," or "Kindly Ones." Athenian women lead the Furies in a torchlight procession to their new shrine on the Acropolis.

Two selections from *The Eumenides* are presented here. In the first, "The Ordinance of Athena," the goddess exhorts the jury to judge Orestes' case on the basis of the high ideals of social order and impartial justice which, to the Athenians, were the qualities that distinguished them from all other people. In the second selection, "The Procession of the Furies," a display of pageantry in honor of the Furies concludes the trilogy.

The final scene in *The Eumenides* is based upon the Panathenaic procession, which was part of the annual festival, called the Panathenaea, honoring Athena. The procession of youths, maidens, and citizens was familiar to both Aeschylus and the contemporary sculptor Phidias. In scenes such as *Horsemen,* in the Panathenaic frieze, Phidias depicts this event.

Aeschylus, *The Eumenides*[20]

The Ordinance of Athena

Athena

If it please you, men of Attica, hear my decree
now, on this first case of bloodletting I have judged.
For Aegeus'[21] population, this forevermore
shall be the ground where justices deliberate.
Here is the Hill of Ares, here the Amazons[22]
encamped and built their shelters when they came in arms
for spite of Theseus,[23] here they piled their rival towers
to rise, new city, and date his city long ago,
and slew their beasts for Ares. So this rock is named
from then the Hill of Ares. Here the reverence
of citizens, their fear and kindred do-no-wrong
shall hold by day and in the blessing of night alike
all while the people do not muddy their own laws
with foul infusions. But if bright water you stain
with mud, you nevermore will find it fit to drink.

No anarchy, no rule of a single master. Thus
I advise my citizens to govern and to grace,
and not to cast fear utterly from your city. What
man who fears nothing at all is ever righteous? Such
be your just terrors, and you may deserve and have
salvation for your citadel, your land's defence,
such as is nowhere else found among men, neither
among the Scythians,[24] nor the land that Pelops[25] held.

20. Reprinted, by permission of the publishers, from Donald Greene and Richmond Lattimore, eds., *The Complete Greek Tragedies* (Chicago: University of Chicago Press, 1953), Vol. 1, pp. 159–60, 171. Copyright © 1953 by the University of Chicago. Selection translated by Richmond Lattimore.

21. Aegeus was a king of Athens and the supposed father of Theseus. Mistakenly thinking his son had been killed by the Minotaur in Crete, Aegeus committed suicide by leaping into the sea—henceforth named for him the Aegean Sea.

22. The Amazons were a mythological race of female warriors believed by the Greeks to have lived near the Black Sea.

23. Theseus was an Athenian hero. Either the son of Poseidon, the god of the sea, or of King Aegeus of Athens, he insisted on being one of the seven young men offered to the Minotaur and, with the help of Ariadne, the daughter of King Minos, he succeeded in killing the monster.

24. A people living to the north of the Black Sea who were frequently hired by the Greeks as mercenaries.

25. Pelops was the son of Tantalus, the King of Lydia and a son of Zeus. Through his marriage to Hippodamia, he was the father of Atreus and Thyestes, whose deadly rivalry set the tragic destiny of the royal house of Mycenae. The Peloponnese, the southern peninsula of Greece, takes its name from Pelops.

I establish this tribunal. It shall be untouched
by money-making, grave but quick to wrath, watchful
to protect those who sleep, a sentry on the land.

These words I have unreeled are for my citizens,
advice into the future. All must stand upright
now, take each man his ballot in his hand, think on
his oath, and make his judgment. For my word is said.

The Procession of the Furies

Athena

Well said, I assent to all the burden of your prayers,
and by the light of flaring torches now attend
your passage to the deep and subterranean hold,
as by us walk those women whose high privilege
it is to guard my image. Flower of all the land
of Theseus, let them issue now, grave companies,
maidens, wives, elder women, in processional.
In the investiture of purple stained robes
dignify them, and let the torchlight go before
so that the kindly company of these within
our ground may shine in the future of strong men to come.

Chorus (by the women who have been forming for processional)

Home, home, o high, o aspiring
Daughters of Night,[26] aged children, in blithe processional.
Bless them, all here, with silence.

In the primeval dark of earth-hollows
held in high veneration with rights sacrificial
bless them, all people, with silence.

Gracious be, wish what the land wishes,
follow, grave goddesses, flushed in the flamesprung
torchlight gay on your journey.
Singing all follow our footsteps.

There shall be peace forever between these people
of Pallas and their guests. Zeus the all seeing
met with Destiny to confirm it.
Singing all follow our footsteps.

26. The Furies.

6. The Erechtheum, Acropolis, Athens, 421–405 B.C. (Gardner, pp. 157–58, ills. 5:55 to 5:57; Janson, p. 127, ill. 174)
Euripides, *Andromache:* "Where's There a Man That Doesn't Find You Odious," c. 425 B.C.; *The Trojan Women:* "O Darling Child I Loved Too Well for Happiness," 415 B.C.

The Erechtheum was planned by Pericles but was built after the death of the Athenian statesman during the Peloponnesian War. It has been suggested that the economic impact of the war affected the construction of the Erechtheum and caused alterations in the original plan. The moral impact of the long war on the Athenian spirit was traced by the third of Athens' greatest tragic dramatists, Euripides.

Euripides was born in a village of Attica about 494 B.C. A serious student of philosophy and rhetoric, he was a lifelong friend of Socrates. Like the Athenian philosopher, Euripides, too, constantly questioned inherited religious beliefs and social practices.

Euripides wrote over ninety plays, of which eighteen survive. Deeply troubled by the Peloponnesian War, he wrote many plays that depicted legends from the Trojan War and simultaneously referred to contemporary situations. In his earlier wartime plays, Euripides displays a patriotic zeal for the Athenian cause. One such play is *Andromache,* written around 425 B.C. In it Euripides alludes to the Athenian part in the Peloponnesian War as an idealistic undertaking intended to defend the oppressed, and he vilifies the Spartan enemy in strong, propagandistic language. A selection from *Andromache,* "Where's There a Man That Doesn't Find You Odious," is presented here.

Ten years later, however, when he wrote *The Trojan Women,* Euripides had become disillusioned by the indiscriminate bloodshed and meaningless suffering caused by war. The previous year Athens had committed one of the worst atrocities of the war when it attacked the neutral island of Melos, slaughtered all its men, and enslaved its women and children. Euripides' response was *The Trojan Women,* one of the most powerful pleas for peace ever written.

This play centers on the hopeless yet dignified women of Troy, who have survived the Trojan defeat. As they await their enslavement as menial servants or as concubines to the Greek conquerors, the women mourn the fall of their city, the deaths of their husbands, and the murder of their children. In one harrowing scene, Andromache, wife of the Trojan hero Hector, learns that she has been chosen as a prize by Achilles' son. Her humiliation at her own fate, however, turns to horror when she discovers that her young son, Astyanax, is to be hurled to his death from the walls of Troy. Andromache's farewell speech to her child from *The Trojan Women,* "O Darling Child I Loved Too Well for Happiness," is presented here.

Euripides' view of humankind was grim and despairing. Human passion constantly overwhelmed reason; chance thwarted order; the gods proved indifferent to morality. In 408 B.C. Euripides left Athens. He died in Macedonia in 406 B.C. before the final defeat of his city by Sparta in the Peloponnesian War.

Euripides, *Andromache*[27]

Where's There a Man That Doesn't Find You Odious

Andromache

Where's there a man that doesn't find you odious,
You citizens of Sparta, devious schemers,
Masters of falsehood, specialists in evil,
Your minds all warped and putrid, serpentine?
How iniquitous your prosperity in Greece!
Name any foulness and it's yours: assassins:
Your palms a tetter of itchiness; your tongues
Off scavenging one way and your minds another.
Damn your Spartan souls!

Euripides, *The Trojan Women*[28]

O Darling Child I Loved Too Well for Happiness.

Andromache

O darling child I loved too well for happiness,
your enemies will kill you and leave your mother forlorn.
Your own father's nobility, where others found
protection, means your murder now. The memory
of his valor comes ill-timed for you. O bridal bed,
O marriage rites that brought me home to Hector's house
a bride, you were unhappy in the end. I lived
never thinking the baby I had was born for butchery
by Greeks, but for lordship over all Asia's pride of earth.

Poor child, are you crying too? Do you know what they
will do to you? Your fingers clutch my dress. What use,
to nestle like a young bird under the mother's wing?
Hector cannot come back, not burst from underground

27. Reprinted, by permission of the publisher, from Donald Greene and Richmond Lattimore, eds., *The Complete Greek Tragedies* (Chicago: University of Chicago Press, 1959), Vol. 3, p. 576. Copyright © 1959 by the University of Chicago. Selection translated by John Frederick Nims.

28. Reprinted, by permission of the publisher, from Donald Greene and Richmond Lattimore, eds., *The Complete Greek Tragedies* (Chicago: University of Chicago Press, 1959), Vol. 3, pp. 640–41. Copyright © 1959 by the University of Chicago. Selection translated by Richmond Lattimore.

to save you, that spear of glory caught in the quick hand,
nor Hector's kin, nor any strength of Phrygian arms.
Yours the sick leap head downward from the height, the fall
where none have pity, and the spirit smashed out in death.
O last and loveliest embrace of all, O child's
sweet fragrant body. Vanity in the end. I nursed
for nothing the swaddled baby at his mother's breast;
in vain the wrack of the labor pains and the long sickness.
Now once again, and never after this, come close
to your mother, lean against my breast and wind your arms
around my neck, and put your lips against my lips.

7. *Nike Fastening Her Sandal,* Temple of Athena Nike, Acropolis, Athens, c. 410 B.C. (Gardner, p. 159, ill. 5:59; Janson, p. 136, ill. 189)
Aristophanes, *Lysistrata:* "War Is the Care of the Women," 411 B.C.

The winged figure of victory from the parapet of the Temple of Athena Nike, *Nike Fastening Her Sandal,* is dated about 410 B.C. Ironically, the sculpture was created at the time that Athens was facing defeat in the Peloponnesian War. In 415 B.C. Athens had launched a major expedition against the state of Syracuse in Sicily. After a two-year stalemate, the expedition suffered a disastrous defeat, and Sparta seized the opportunity to close with its enemy. Fortified by Persian money, Sparta built a fleet that strangled the Athenian empire. In 405 B.C. Sparta lay siege to Athens by land and sea; in the spring of 404 B.C., after starving through the winter, the proud Athenians surrendered.

Aristophanes (c. 450–c. 385 B.C.) was the most famous comic dramatist of Greece. An Athenian citizen, he wrote about forty plays, of which eleven survive. Many of his plays are concerned with the social, literary, and philosophical life of Athens, but many also deal with themes provoked by the Peloponnesian War. A pacifist, tried in 426 B.C. on charges of treasonable action for his denunciation of Athenian cruelty to its enemies, Aristophanes boldly attacked the political leaders of Athens who had embroiled Greece in a protracted war; a democrat who had no sympathy with the oligarchic reaction that followed the Athenian defeat of 413 B.C., he censured the public for its poor judgment. Although the attacks on war in Euripides' plays have a clear connection with contemporary conditions, Athenian tragedy never engaged in such topical references as did Aristophanes' comedies.

Lysistrata was written in 411 B.C. The play describes a stratagem devised by the Greek women to obtain peace. Led by Lysistrata, the women of Athens have confiscated the city treasury and seized the Acropolis, where they have been joined in their efforts by women from all over Greece. Reluctant but determined, they have declared a sex strike until such time as the Greek men will make peace. In the selection from *Lysistrata* presented here, "War Is the Care of the Women," Lysistrata scolds the men for their constant fighting and suggests that the women will have to save Greece.

In the comedies of Aristophanes such as *Lysistrata,* improbable, even slapstick plots are enlivened by a wealth of imagination, freshness of wit, and bawdy burlesque as well as by bursts of pure lyric poetry. Through his comic gifts, Aristophanes turned his misgivings about Athenian democracy, imperialism, and materialism into ribald mockery.

Aristophanes, *Lysistrata*[29]

War Is the Care of the Women

Chorus of Men:

Monsters, enough!—our patience now is gone.
   It's time for you to tell
Why you are barricaded here upon
   Our hallowed citadel.

Leader [*to Magistrate*]: Now question her, and test her out, and never own she's right:
It's shameful to surrender to a girl without a fight.

Magistrate [*to Lysistrata*]: Well, the first thing I want to know is—what in Zeus' name do you mean by shutting and barring the gates of our own Acropolis against us?

Lysistrata: We want to keep the money safe and stop you from waging war.

Magistrate: The war has nothing to do with money—

Lysistrata: Hasn't it? Why are Peisander and the other office-seekers always stirring things up? Isn't it so they can take a few more dips in the public purse? Well, as far as we're concerned they can do what they like; only they're not going to lay their hands on the money in there.

Magistrate: Why, what are you going to do?

Lysistrata: Do? Why, we'll be in charge of it.

Magistrate: *You* in charge of *our* finances.

29. Reprinted, by permission of the publisher, from Aristophanes, *Lysistrata and Other Plays,* trans. by Alan H. Sommerstein (London: Penguin Classics, 1973), pp. 198–202. Copyright © by Alan H. Sommerstein, 1973.

Lysistrata: Well, what's so strange about that? We've been in charge of all your housekeeping finances for years.

Magistrate: But that's not the same thing.

Lysistrata: Why not?

Magistrate: Because the money here is needed for the war!

Lysistrata: Ah, but the war itself isn't necessary.

Magistrate: Not necessary! How is the City going to be saved then?

Lysistrata: We'll save it for you.

Magistrate: You!!!

Lysistrata: Us.

Magistrate: This is intolerable!

Lysistrata: It may be, but it's what's going to happen.

Magistrate: But Demeter!—I mean, it's against nature!

Lysistrata [*very sweetly*]: We've got to save you, after all, Sir.

Magistrate: Even against my will?

Lysistrata: That only makes it all the more essential.

Magistrate: Anyway, what business are war and peace of yours?

Lysistrata: I'll tell you.

Magistrate [*restraining himself with difficulty*]: You'd better or else.

Lysistrata: I will if you'll listen and keep those hands of yours under control.

Magistrate: I can't—I'm too livid.

Stratyllis [*interrupting*]: It'll be you that regrets it.

Magistrate: I hope it's you, you superannuated crow! [*To Lysistrata*] Say what you have to say.

Lysistrata: In the last war we were too modest to object to anything you men did—and in any case you wouldn't let us say a word. But don't think we approved! We knew everything that was going on. Many times we'd hear at home about some major blunder of yours, and then when you came home we'd be burning inside but we'd have to put on a smile and ask what it was you'd decided to inscribe on the pillar underneath the Peace Treaty. —And what did my husband always say?—"Shut up and mind your own business!" And I did.

Stratyllis: I wouldn't have done!

Magistrate [*ignoring her—to Lysistrata*]: He'd have given you one if you hadn't!

Lysistrata: Exactly—so I kept quiet. But sure enough, next thing we knew you'd take an even sillier decision. And if I so much as said, "Darling, why are you carrying on with this silly policy?" he would glare at me and say, "Back to your weaving, woman, or you'll have a headache for a month. 'Go and attend to your work; let war be the care of the menfolk.' "[30]

Magistrate: Quite right too, by Zeus.

Lysistrata: Right? That we should not be allowed to make the least little suggestion to you, no matter how much you mismanage the City's affairs? And now, look, every time two people meet in the street, what do they say? "Isn't there a man in the country?" and the answer comes, "Not one." That's why we women got together and decided we were going to save Greece. What was the point of waiting any longer, we asked ourselves. Well now, we'll make a deal. You listen to us—and we'll talk sense, not like you used to—listen to us and keep quiet, as we've had to do up to now, and we'll clear up the mess you've made.

Magistrate: Insufferable effrontery! I will not stand for it!

Lysistrata [*magisterially*]: Silence!

Magistrate: You, confound you, a woman with your face veiled, dare to order me to be silent! Gods, let me die!

30. A quotation from Hector's speech to Andromache in Book Six of Homer's *Iliad.*

Lysistrata: Well, if that's what's bothering you—
[*During the ensuing trio the women put a veil on the Magistrate's head, and give him a sewing-basket and some uncarded wool.*]

Lysistrata:

With veiling bedeck
Your head and your neck,
And then, it may be, you'll be quiet.

Myrrhine: This basket fill full—

Calonice: By carding this wool—

Lysistrata:

Munching beans—they're an excellent diet.
So hitch up your gown
And really get down
To the job—you could do with some
slimmin'
And keep this refrain
Fixed firm in your brain—

All: That war is the care of the women!

THE FOURTH CENTURY AND THE HELLENISTIC PERIOD

1. *Mausolus,* from the Mausoleum at Halicarnassus, c. 355 B.C. (Gardner, p. 165, ill. 5:69; Janson, p. 140, ill. 195)
Plato, *Republic:* "The Philosopher-King," early to mid-fourth century B.C.

The colossal statue of Mausolus combines Greek and Eastern characteristics and suggests the cosmopolitan nature of fourth-century Greek culture. At the same time that the sculptor, evidently familiar with Greek artistic traditions, created this portrait-likeness of the actual ruler of Caria, a kingdom in southwest Asia Minor, the Athenian philosopher Plato described the qualities that should be possessed by the ideal ruler, whom he called the philosopher-king.

Plato (c. 429–347 B.C.) was both an influential teacher and a prolific writer. He was the student of the philosopher Socrates. Socrates (c. 469–399 B.C.) practiced philosophy by feigning ignorance and posing a sequence of questions in the apparent hope of receiving enlightenment—a technique which has since become known as the Socratic method. Throughout his life, he questioned the ethical beliefs and moral standards of his fellow Athenians. In 399 B.C. he was accused of impiety and of corrupting the youth. Tried and found guilty, Socrates accepted the death penalty imposed by the court and ended his own life by drinking hemlock.

Socrates left no writings. Plato, however, wrote twenty-six major philosophical treatises, all of which survive. Almost all are written in the form of a dialogue in which several characters discuss a subject on a high moral plane. In the *Republic,* written by Plato in the early to mid-fourth century, Socrates is the main figure. The conversation between Socrates and several friends seems at first to be simple and homely, but gradually, through the device of the Socratic dialogue, Plato expounds his own political views and integrates them into his wider metaphysical and moral beliefs.

Plato held the view that the basic entities of the world are abstract universals, or "forms" (often called "ideas"), such as justice, beauty, and—highest of all—the good. In the *Republic,* Plato is especially concerned with the issue of justice. He outlines a society in which justice holds sway, and he argues that the great moral principles that should govern private life are identical with those that must regulate public life. In his political system, Plato distinguishes three categories of individuals: (1) the person devoted to philosophy, (2) the person seeking enjoyment, (3) the person qualified for action. The first person attains wisdom, the second gratification, the third distinction. The ideal society is structured into three classes corresponding to the three types of individuals: (1) the philosopher-kings, who understand the system of absolute values embodied in the structure of the universe, (2) the general civilian population, which provides for the material requirements of the community, and (3) the army, whose members respond to the martial needs of the state. In the just state, each class understands its own function and behaves according to its limits. Such a society is a true aristocracy (rule of the best). A selection from the *Republic,* "The Philosopher-King," is presented here.

In 387 B.C. Plato founded the Academy, on the outskirts of the city of Athens, as an institute for the pursuit of philosophical and scientific research. He presided over it for the rest of his life, and it survived after his death until as late as the sixth century.

On one occasion, Plato tried to realize his goal of creating a state ruled by a philosopher-king. In 364 B.C., at the death of the ruler Dionysius I, Plato was invited to Syracuse to educate his successor, Dionysius II, as a constitutional king. Plato was unsuccessful in his short-lived effort, but the *Republic* remains, without question, the most important work of political philosophy in the Western tradition.

Plato, *Republic*[31]

The Philosopher-King

Socrates:
Unless either philosophers become kings in their countries or those who are now called kings and rulers come to be sufficiently inspired with a genuine desire for wisdom; unless, that is to say, political power and philosophy meet together, while the many natures who now go their several ways in the one or the other direction are forcibly debarred from doing so, there can be no rest from troubles, my dear Glaucon, for states, nor yet, as I believe, for all mankind; nor can this commonwealth which we have imagined ever till then see the light of day and grow to its full stature. This it was that I have so long hung back from saying: I knew what a paradox it would be, because it is hard to see that there is no other way of happiness either for the state or for the individual. . . .

Glaucon:
And whom do you mean by the genuine philosophers?

Socrates:
Those whose passion it is to see the truth.

Glaucon:
That must be so; but will you explain?

Socrates:
It would not be easy to explain to everyone; but you, I believe will grant my premiss.

Glaucon:
Which is—?

Socrates:
That since beauty and ugliness are opposite, they are two things; and consequently each of them is one. The same holds of justice and injustice, good and bad, and all the essential Forms: each in itself is one; but they manifest themselves in a great variety of combinations, with actions, with material things, and with one another, and so each seems to be many.

31. Reprinted, by permission of the publisher, from *The Republic of Plato,* trans. by Francis M. Cornford (Oxford: Oxford University Press, 1941), pp. 178–79, 183–84, 189.

Glaucon:

That is true.

Socrates:

On the strength of this premiss, then, I can distinguish your amateurs of the arts and men of action from the philosophers we are concerned with, who are alone worthy of the name.

Glaucon:

What is your distinction?

Socrates:

Your lovers of sights and sounds delight in beautiful tones and colours and shapes and in all the works of art into which these enter; but they have not the power of thought to behold and to take delight in the nature of Beauty itself. That power to approach Beauty and behold it as it is in itself, is rare indeed.

Glaucon:

Quite true.

Socrates:

Now if a man believes in the existence of beautiful things, but not of Beauty itself, and cannot follow a guide who would lead him to a knowledge of it, is he not living in a dream? Consider: does not dreaming, whether one is awake or asleep, consist in mistaking a semblance for the reality it resembles?

Glaucon:

I should certainly call that dreaming.

Socrates:

Contrast with him the man who holds that there is such a thing as Beauty itself and can discern that essence as well as the things that partake of its character, without ever confusing the one with the other—is he a dreamer or living in a waking state?

Glaucon:

He is very much awake.

Socrates:

So may we say that he knows, while the other has only a belief in appearances; and might we call their states of mind knowledge and belief?

Glaucon:

Certainly.

Socrates:

The name of philosopher, then, will be reserved for those whose affections are set, in every case, on the reality.

Glaucon:

By all means.

2. Lysippos, *Apoxyomenos,* c. 330 B.C. (Gardner, p. 166, ill. 5:70; Janson, p. 143, ill. 200)
Aristotle, *Nicomachean Ethics:* "The Pursuit of Happiness," mid- to late fourth century B.C.

Aristotle (384–322 B.C.) was, with Socrates and Plato, one of the three philosophers of ancient Greece who among them laid the philosophical foundations of Western culture. The son of a Macedonian court physician, Aristotle came to Athens when he was seventeen years old. He joined Plato's Academy, where he remained for twenty years, until Plato's death. In 343–42 B.C., Aristotle was chosen by Philip of Macedonia to be the tutor of his son Alexander (later known as Alexander the Great). In 335 B.C., at Philip's death, Aristotle returned to Athens and founded his own school, the Lyceum. A year before his death, he was accused of impiety, the same charge leveled earlier against Socrates, and Aristotle was forced to flee Athens.

Aristotle believed that knowledge could be divided into three branches: (1) theoretical, which was pursued for its own sake; (2) practical, which was pursued in order to control man's social environment; (3) productive, which was necessary in order to make useful or beautiful things. The Lyceum was a research institute that encompassed all branches of learning.

Because of his deep interest in the natural world, Aristotle made important contributions to the history of science. He carried on extensive botanical, zoological, and anatomical investigations. One of the originators of the inductive method, Aristotle sought to collect and test all available information relevant to his studies, to form his hypotheses, and then to apply these hypotheses.

In addition to studying the phenomena of the natural world, Aristotle also addressed a broad range of philosophical issues. He wrote about politics and law, poetry and rhetoric, ethics and morality, physical existence and the metaphysical realm. One of the most important of Aristotle's works is the *Nicomachean Ethics.* In it, he investigates the purpose of human conduct.

According to Aristotle, happiness is the goal for which every individual strives and the aim of all his actions. Happiness is defined by Aristotle as an activity of the rational soul carried out in accordance with virtue. There are, in Aristotle's view, two kinds of virtue, moral and intellectual. The first, moral virtue, is the product of habit, of pursuing a moderate course of action that avoids extremes. The second, intellectual virtue, is acquired with time and experience and requires instruction and discipline. The happiness that ensues from moral goodness is highly desirable but purely human, whereas the happiness that ensues from intellectual excellence approximates the divine. A selection from the *Nicomachean Ethics,* "The Pursuit of Happiness," is presented here.

Aristotle's philosophy examined the meaning of human experience from all possible viewpoints. Concurrently the sculptor Lysippos, who served in the court of Alexander the Great, reexamined the human body. The *Apoxyomenos* exemplifies many of the changes in proportion and pose introduced by Lysippos in the depiction of the human figure.

Aristotle, *Nicomachean Ethics*[32]

The Pursuit of Happiness

If happiness is activity in accordance with virtue, it is reasonable that it should be in accordance with the highest virtue; and this will be that of the best thing in us. Whether it be reason or something else that is the element which is thought to be our natural ruler and guide and to take thought of things noble and divine, whether it be itself also divine or only the most divine element in us, the activity of this in accordance with its proper virtue will be perfect happiness. That this activity is contemplative we have already said.

Now this would seem to be in agreement both with what we said before and with the truth. For, firstly, this activity is the best (since not only is reason the best thing in us, but the objects of reason are the best of knowable objects); and, secondly, it is the most continuous, since we can contemplate truth more continuously than we can do anything. And we think happiness ought to have pleasure mingled with it, but the activity of philosophic wisdom is admittedly the pleasantest of virtuous activities: at all events philosophy is thought to offer pleasures marvellous for their purity and their enduringness, and it is to be expected that those who know will pass their time more pleasantly than those who inquire. And the self-sufficiency that is spoken of must belong most to the contemplative activity. For while a philosopher, as well as a just man or one possessing any other virtue, needs the necessaries of life, when they are sufficiently equipped with things of that sort the just man needs people towards whom and with whom he shall act justly, and the temperate man, the brave man, and each of the others is in the same case but the philosopher, even when by himself, can contemplate truth, and the better the wiser he is; he can

32. Reprinted, by permission of the publisher, from Aristotle, *Nicomachean Ethics,* trans. by W. D. Ross and revised by J. L. Ackrill and J. O. Urmson (Oxford: Oxford University Press, 1980), pp. 263–66.

perhaps do so better if he has fellow workers, but still he is the most self-sufficient. And this activity alone would seem to be loved for its own sake; for nothing arises from it apart from the contemplating, while from practical activities we gain more or less apart from the action. And happiness is thought to depend on leisure, for we are busy that we may have leisure, and make war that we may live in peace. Now the activity of the practical virtues is exhibited in political or military affairs, but the actions concerned with these seem to be unleisurely. Warlike actions are completely so (for no one chooses to be at war, or provokes war, for the sake of being at war; any one would seem absolutely murderous if he were to make enemies of his friends in order to bring about battle and slaughter); but the action of the statesman is also unleisurely, and aims—apart from the political action itself—at despotic power and honours, or at all events happiness, for him and his fellow citizens—a happiness different from political action, and evidently sought as being different. So if among virtuous actions political and military actions are distinguished by nobility and greatness, and these are unleisurely and aim at an end and are not desirable for their own sake, but the activity of reason, which is contemplative, seems both to be superior in worth and to aim at no end beyond itself, and to have its pleasure proper to itself (and this augments the activity), and the self-sufficiency, leisureliness, unweariedness (so far as this is possible for man), and all the other attributes ascribed to the supremely happy man are evidently those connected with this activity, it follows that this will be the complete happiness of man, if it be allowed a complete term of life (for none of the attributes of happiness is incomplete).

But such a life would be too high for man; for it is not in so far as he is man that he will live so, but in so far as something divine is present in him; and by so much as this is superior to our composite nature is its activity superior to that which is the exercise of the other kind of virtue. If reason is divine, then, in comparison with man, the life according to it is divine in comparison with human life. But we must not follow those who advise us, being men, to think of human things, and, being mortal, of mortal things, but must, so far as we can, make ourselves immortal, and strain every nerve to live in accordance with the best thing in us; for even if it be small in bulk, much more does it in power and worth surpass everything. And this would seem actually to be each man, since it is the authoritative and better part of him. It would be strange, then, if he were to choose not the life of himself but that of something else. And what we said before will apply now; that which is proper to each thing is by nature best and most pleasant for each thing; for man, therefore, the life according to reason is best and pleasantest, since reason more than anything else is man. This life therefore is also the happiest.

3. Praxiteles, *Aphrodite of the Cnidians,* c. 330 B.C. (Janson, p. 141, ill. 197)
Aphrodite of Melos, c. 150–100 B.C. (Gardner, p. 174, ill. 5:83)
Neo-Pythagorean text: "On Chastity," c. 200 B.C.

Although the goddess Athena was revered by the citizens of Athens, women in Athens had a low social status. With the notable exception of Sparta, women in almost the whole of Greece during the Classical period had few legal rights and were severely restricted in their right to own property, to arrange their own marriages, or to represent their own interests in court. Women in the lower economic classes did work outside the home in order to help maintain their families, but prosperous women were secluded in their houses. The women's quarters, which were separated from men's quarters, were mostly kept shut up and seldom entered by men. There young girls grew up in the society of their nurses and mothers and had no access to the education and training encouraged in their brothers. A respectable married woman went out of her quarters as rarely as possible, since it was a disgrace for her to be seen frequently in the streets. Excluded from the public assemblies, Panhellenic games, and perhaps from the theater, the woman stayed dutifully at home. It was only on the occasions of public holidays and family festivals that it was appropriate for a woman to leave the house. The authority of the master over all aspects of a woman's life was virtually absolute.

During the Hellenistic period, the gap in privileges between men and women became much narrower. The Hellenistic world was dramatically different from that of the preceding period. Loss of political autonomy on the part of the city-states resulted in a diminution of the importance of men's political activities and their popular assemblies. This change, in turn, affected the position of women. In many parts of the Hellenistic world, although not in Athens, women gained more influence in political, economic, and legal affairs; had greater access to education; and acquired more control over the conduct of their personal lives.

Confronted by the fluctuating mores of the Hellenistic period, the Neo-Pythagoreans—that is, the later followers of Pythagoras—were concerned with the proper behavior of respectable women and wrote several texts on the subject. A selection from a Neo-Pythagorean text written around 200 B.C., "On Chastity," is presented here.

At the same time that chastity was regarded as a woman's greatest virtue, prostitution was flourishing in the Greek cities. In Athens, state-owned brothels staffed by female slaves were one of the attractions of the city. Two types of prostitutes were especially distinctive, the *hetairai* and the *hierodules.*

The *hetairai,* or "companions to men," were often women who, in addition to physical beauty, had intellectual training and possessed intellectual gifts. These women were accepted in the society of rulers, philosophers, scholars, and artists, and were admired for their intelligence and accomplishments. The *Aphrodite of the Cnidians* by Praxiteles was said to be modeled on the sculptor's mistress, the *hetaira* Phryne.

The *hierodules,* or "sacred slaves," were women who served Aphrodite, the goddess of love. The *Aphrodite of Melos* celebrates the goddess of love and her sensuous beauty in a style that is derived from Praxiteles. As the property of the sanctuary, the *hierodules* gave themselves to strangers to win the favor of Aphrodite for the nation, the temple, or themselves.

Neo-Pythagorean Text[33]

On Chastity

In general a woman must be good and orderly—and this no one can become without virtue. . . . A woman's greatest virtue is chastity. Because of this quality she is able to honor and to cherish her own particular husband.

Now some people think it is not appropriate for a woman to be a philosopher, just as a woman should not be a cavalry officer or a politician. . . . I agree that men should be generals and city officials and politicians, and women should keep house and stay inside and receive and take care of their husbands. But I believe that courage, justice, and intelligence are qualities that men and women have in common. . . . Courage and intelligence are more appropriately male qualities because of the strength of men's bodies and the power of their minds. Chastity is more appropriately female.

Accordingly a woman must learn about chastity and realize what she must do quantitatively and qualitatively to be able to obtain this womanly virtue. I believe that there are five qualifications (1) the sanctity of her marriage bed (2) the cleanliness of her body (3) the manner in which she chooses to leave her house (4) her refusal to participate in secret cults or Cybeline rituals (5) her readiness and moderation in sacrificing to the gods.

4. *Dying Gaul,* Pergamum, c. 240 B.C. (Gardner, p. 170, ill. 5:77; Janson, p. 144, ill. 201)
Diogenes Laertius, *Lives of Eminent Philosophers:* "Epicurean Principles" and "Stoic Doctrine," early third century A.D.

The *Dying Gaul* from Pergamum reflects concerns prominent in the Hellenistic age. In the heroic proportions of the Gaul, the sculpture reflects the breakdown of the earlier distinction between Greek and barbarian peoples; in the tensed musculature of the body and the expression of the face, the sculpture explores physical pain and human mortality. Both the awareness of the dignity of the non-Greek peoples and the desire to escape from pain and from the fear of death are reflected in the thought of Hellenistic philosophers.

33. Reprinted, by permission of the publisher, from Mary R. Lefkowitz and Maureen B. Fant, eds. *Women's Life in Greece and Rome* (Baltimore: The Johns Hopkins University Press, 1982), pp. 104–105. Copyright © 1982 by M. B. Fant and M. R. Lefkowitz. Selection translated by Mary R. Lefkowitz.

The Hellenistic age was a period of transition. As social and political disorder increased and traditional values eroded, Hellenistic philosophers furnished guides to the personal conduct of the individual's daily life. Two of the most influential schools of thought, Epicureanism and Stoicism, arose in Athens during the end of the Classical period and flourished during the Hellenistic age.

The Athenian philosopher Epicurus (342–271 B.C.) was the founder of Epicureanism. Epicurus established his school in Athens in his garden. Philosophy was, for Epicurus, the art of living, and its aim was to achieve happiness. Epicurus defined happiness as freedom from trouble in the mind and pain in the body.

In order to realize the goal of a happy life, in Epicurus' view a person must do two things. First, the dread of divine interference and death must be overcome. This can be done only by understanding that the universe is governed by mechanistic principles rather than by the will of the gods. Second, Epicurus argued that we must seek pleasure and avoid pain. However, Epicurus did not advocate a hedonistic search for sensual experiences, but instead held that true and lasting pleasure is to be found by reducing one's wants to a minimum, leading a simple life free of desires, and forming enduring friendships. Prudence, honor, and justice are the qualities considered essential to our lives by Epicurus.

The founder of Stoicism was Zeno of Citium in Cyprus (335–263 B.C.). Zeno had come to Athens on business as a young man and remained in the city the rest of his life. The name of Zeno's school came from the place where he taught—the Painted Stoa, which overlooked the marketplace of Athens.

Stoicism postulated that the world is divinely governed on rational principles. Humans, too, are endowed with divine reason and have the capacity to act in accordance with it. Their goal should be to live according to nature, in agreement with the design of the world.

Stoic moral theory is based on the view that the world, as one great city, is a unity. While the followers of Epicurus were encouraged to withdraw from the public arena of competition and strife, the disciples of Stoicism viewed themselves as world citizens with an obligation and loyalty to all things in that city. Individuals must play an active role in world affairs and display the virtue and right action exemplified in nature. Thus, moral worth and duty were emphasized by the Stoics.

Two selections related to Hellenistic philosophy are presented here. The first, "Epicurean Principles," is from a letter written by Epicurus to Menoeceus, in which Epicurus outlines the major principles of his thought, including his understanding of the nature of pleasure and pain. The second selection, "Stoic Doctrine," describes the teachings of Zeno and his most prominent followers. Both selections are preserved in the *Lives of Eminent Philosophers,* written by Diogenes Laertius in the first half of the third century.

Diogenes Laertius, *Lives of Eminent Philosophers*[34]

Epicurean Principles

Pleasure is our first and kindred good. It is the starting point of every choice and of every aversion, and to it we come back, inasmuch as we make feeling the rule by which to judge of every good thing. And since pleasure is our first and native good, for that reason we do not choose every pleasure whatsoever, but ofttimes pass over many pleasures when a greater annoyance ensues from them. And ofttimes we consider pains superior to pleasures when submission to the pains for a long time brings us as a consequence a greater pleasure. . . .

And again, we regard independence of outward things as a great good, not so as in all cases to use little, but so as to be contented with little if we have not much, being honestly persuaded that they have the sweetest enjoyment of luxury who stand least in need of it, and that whatever is natural is easily procured and only the vain and worthless hard to win. . . .

When we say, then, that pleasure is the end and aim, we do not mean the pleasures of the prodigal or the pleasures of sensuality, as we are understood to do by some through ignorance, prejudice, or wilful misrepresentation. By pleasure we mean the absence of pain in the body and of trouble in the soul. It is not an unbroken succession of drinking-bouts and of revelry, not sexual love, not the enjoyment of the fish and other delicacies of a luxurious table, which produce a pleasant life; it is sober reasoning, searching out the grounds of every choice and avoidance, and banishing those beliefs through which the greatest tumults take possession of the soul. Of all this the beginning and the greatest good is prudence. Wherefore prudence is a more precious thing even than philosophy; from it spring all the other virtues, for it teaches that we cannot lead a life of pleasure which is not also a life of prudence, honour, and justice; nor lead a life of prudence, honour, and justice, which is not also a life of pleasure. For the virtues have grown into one with a pleasant life, and a pleasant life is inseparable from them.

Stoic Doctrine

This is why Zeno was the first . . . to designate as the end "life in agreement with nature" (or living agreeably to nature), which is the same as a virtuous life, virtue being the goal towards which nature guides us. . . .

Again, living virtuously is equivalent to living in accordance with

34. Reprinted, by permission of the publisher and The Loeb Classical Library, from Diogenes Laertius, *Lives of Eminent Philosophers,* trans. by R. D. Hicks (Cambridge, Mass.: Harvard University Press, 1950), Vol. 2, pp. 655–57, 195–97, 239–43.

experience of the actual course of nature, . . . for our individual natures are parts of the nature of the whole universe. And this is why the end may be defined as life in accordance with nature, or, in other words, in accordance with our own human nature as well as that of the universe, a life in which we refrain from every action forbidden by the law common to all things, that is to say, the right reason which pervades all things, and is identical with this Zeus, lord and ruler of all that is. And this very thing constitutes the virtue of the happy man and the smooth current of life, when all actions promote the harmony of the spirit dwelling in the individual man with the will of him who orders the universe. . . .

[The Stoics] hold that there are two principles in the universe, the active principle and the passive. The passive principle, then, is a substance without quality, i.e. matter, whereas the active is the reason inherent in this substance, that is God. For he is everlasting and is the artificer of each several thing throughout the whole extent of matter. . . .

God is one and the same with Reason, Fate, and Zeus; he is also called by many other names. In the beginning he was by himself; he transformed the whole of substance through air into water, and just as in animal generation the seed has a moist vehicle, so in cosmic moisture God, who is the seminal reason of the universe, remains behind in the moisture as such an agent, adapting matter to himself with a view to the next stage of creation. Thereupon he created first of all the four elements, fire, water, air, earth. . . .

The world, in their view, is ordered by reason and providence . . . inasmuch as reason pervades every part of it, just as does the soul in us. . . . Thus, then, the whole world is a living being, endowed with soul and reason. . . .

5. *Laocoön Group,* early first century B.C. (Gardner, p. 172, ill. 5:80; Janson, p. 146, ill. 207)
Virgil, *The Aeneid:* "The Wooden Horse" and "The Death of Laocoön," 30–19 B.C.

Laocoön was a figure in the Greek legends about the Trojan War. A priest at Troy, he had offended Apollo by marrying and becoming the father of children and by profaning the image of the god. In the last year of the war, Laocoön was chosen by the Trojans to make offerings to Poseidon, the god of the sea (called Neptune by Virgil). When the wooden horse in which the Greek soldiers were hiding was seen on the beach before Troy, Laocoön denounced it as a Greek trick. He hurled his spear at its side and urged the Trojans not to take it inside the walls. But as the Trojans hesitated, Apollo sent two huge sea serpents to punish Laocoön for his earlier offenses. Grasping the priest and his two sons in their coils, the serpents crushed them to death and slithered off with their bodies to the shrine of Athena.

Mistakenly thinking that the sea serpents had been sent to punish Laocoön for doubting that the wooden horse had been sent as a divine gift, the Trojans welcomed the horse within their walled city and thereby ensured their doom.

The story of Laocoön is commemorated in one of the most famous examples of ancient sculpture, the *Laocoön Group,* sometimes attributed to the Greek sculptors Agesander, Athanadoros, and Polydoros of Rhodes. In literature, Virgil, the greatest Roman poet, also captured the dramatic pathos of the legend.

Virgil (70–19 B.C.) was born in northern Italy. He received a good education and might have remained a gentleman farmer all his life. However, his family land was expropriated by the state for the use of veteran soldiers. Virgil's earliest poetry praises the beauty of the Italian countryside and the joys of country life. But it is upon *The Aeneid,* Virgil's epic poem of the origin of Rome, that the poet's fame chiefly rests.

Composed between 30 and 19 B.C., *The Aeneid* tells the story of Aeneas, the exiled Trojan prince who founds the city of Rome after the Greek destruction of Troy. Aeneas is briefly mentioned by Homer in *The Iliad* as a man who would one day found a dynasty of kings. In *The Aeneid,* Virgil remodels Homeric characters and stories and relates them to the contemporary Roman world and to the emperor at that time, Augustus. Aeneas becomes the exemplar of the traditional Roman way of life and the precursor of the new hero, Augustus. By celebrating the past, Virgil hoped to do for Rome what Homer had done for the Greeks—to unite a people divided by a recent civil war into a single nation dedicated to pursuing its exalted destiny. Two selections from *The Aeneid,* "The Wooden Horse" and "The Death of Laocoön," are presented here. Ulysses (the Roman name for Odysseus, the cunning Greek hero) is the narrator in both passages.

Virgil, *The Aeneid*[35]

The Wooden Horse

Laocoön came running,
With a great throng at his heels, down from the hilltop
As fast as ever he could, and before he reached us,
Cried in alarm: "Are you crazy, wretched people?
Do you think they have gone, the foe? Do you think that any
Gifts of the Greeks lack treachery? Ulysses,—
What was his reputation? Let me tell you,
Either the Greeks are hiding in this monster,
Or it's some trick of war, a spy, or engine,
To come down on the city. Tricky business
Is hiding in it. Do not trust it, Trojans,
Do not believe this horse. Whatever it may be,
I fear the Greeks, even when bringing presents."

35. Reprinted, by permission of the publisher, from *The Aeneid of Virgil,* trans. by Rolfe Humphries (New York: Charles Scribner's Sons, 1951), pp. 32–33, 38–40.

With that, he hurled the great spear at the side
With all the strength he had. It fastened, trembling
And the struck womb rang hollow, a moaning sound.
He had driven us, almost, to let the light in
With the point of the steel, to probe, to tear, but something
Got in his way, the gods, or fate, or counsel,
Ill-omened, in our hearts; or Troy would be standing
And Priam's[36] lofty citadel unshaken. . . .

The Death of Laocoön

Then something else,
Much greater and more terrible, was forced
Upon us, troubling our unseeing spirits.
Laocoön, allotted priest of Neptune,
Was slaying a great bull beside the altars,
When suddenly, over the tranquil deep
From Tenedos,[37]—I shudder even now,
Recalling it—there came a pair of serpents
With monstrous coils breasting the sea, and aiming
Together for the shore. Their heads and shoulders
Rose over the waves, upright, with bloody crests,
The rest of them trailing along the water,
Looping in giant spirals; the foaming sea
Hissed under their motion. And they reached the land,
Their burning eyes suffused with blood and fire,
Their darting tongues licking the hissing mouths.
Pale at the sight, we fled. But they went on
Straight toward Laocoön, and first each serpent
Seized in its coils his two young sons, and fastened
The fangs in those poor bodies. And the priest
Struggled to help them, weapons in his hand.
They seized him, bound him with their mighty coils,
Twice round his waist, twice round his neck, they squeezed
With scaly pressure, and still towered above him.
Straining his hands to tear the knots apart,
His chaplets stained with blood and the black poison,
He uttered horrible cries, not even human,
More like the bellowing of a bull, when wounded
It flees the altar, shaking from the shoulder

36. King of Troy.
37. An island in the Aegean Sea, used by the Greeks as a base for their fleet. The main Greek force had withdrawn there while waiting to see if the Trojans fell for their ruse.

The ill-aimed axe. And on the pair went gliding
To the highest shrine, the citadel of Pallas,
and vanished underneath the feet of the goddess
And the circle of her shield.
            The people trembled
Again; they said Laocoön deserved it,
Having, with spear, profaned the sacred image.
It must be brought to its place, they cried, the goddess
Must be appeased.

V

Etruscan Art

1. *Apollo,* from Veii, c. 510 B.C. (Gardner, p. 189, ill. 6:8; Janson, p. 170, color plate 19)
Livy, *The History of Rome from Its Foundation:* "The Conquest of Veii," late first century B.C.

Pre-Roman Italy was inhabited by many peoples, who differed in their origins, languages, and cultural traditions. The region of central Italy between the valley of the Tiber, the valley of the Arno, and the Apennines, called Etruria, was inhabited by the Etruscans.

Knowledge about the Etruscans is limited by the scarcity and incompleteness of our sources. Most Etruscan literature has been lost; most of the inscriptions that have survived are short and only partially decipherable. Greek and Roman authors recorded some information about Etruria, but they were chiefly interested in the region as it related to the Greek and Roman worlds. Modern archaeological excavations have uncovered Etruscan tombs, paintings, and ceramics, as well as other artifacts.

Between the eighth and sixth centuries B.C. the Etruscan cities constituted the most important political, economic, and cultural centers established by the Italic peoples. The wealth of the Etruscan cities, which were loosely united in a religious and economic league, was based upon rich mines which produced copper, iron, and silver. By the commercial exploitation of these mineral resources, Etruria developed lucrative trade routes throughout the Mediterranean world. At the same time, Etruria expanded its territorial control over most of central and northern Italy.

However, the Etruscan power was eventually challenged by Rome. Although distinct in language and culture, Rome had been heavily influenced by nearby Etruscan cities such as Caere and Veii. Indeed, Etruscan monarchs had ruled Rome for over a century. But during the fifth century B.C., Rome initiated a century-long period of continuous border conflicts with Veii that ended in the defeat and destruction of the Etruscan city in 396 B.C. Eventually, all Etruria was controlled by Rome. By the time of the Roman empire, the Etruscan language was discarded and the last vestige of Etruscan autonomy had disappeared.

The Roman historian Livy (c. 59 B.C.–A.D. 17) described the capture of Veii in his *History of Rome from Its Foundation.* One element in the Roman conquest was the *evocatio,* or the invitation, to the gods of the besieged city to desert their temples and to join the attackers, who promised them richer temples and greater honors. During the attack on Veii, the Roman army, led by Camillus, called upon the god Apollo for his assistance and urged the goddess Juno[1] to give her allegiance to the Romans. After their victory, the Romans removed the cult statue of Juno to Rome, where it was installed in a temple as a symbol of Roman supremacy. The statue of Juno which figures so prominently in Livy's account has been lost, but an earlier Etruscan temple image from Veii, *Apollo,* has survived. A selection from *The History of Rome from Its Foundation,* "The Conquest of Veii," is presented here.

Livy, *The History of Rome from Its Foundation*[2]

The Conquest of Veii

The crisis in the long campaign had now come. Camillus left his headquarters and took the auspices; then he ordered all troops to stand to. "Pythian Apollo," he prayed, "led by you and inspired by your holy breath, I go forward to the destruction of Veii, and I vow to you a tenth part of the spoils. Queen Juno, to you too I pray, that you may leave this town where now you dwell and follow our victorious arms into our City of Rome, your future home, which will receive you in a temple worthy of your greatness."

From every direction and with overwhelming numbers Roman troops moved forward to the assault . . . in an instant of time the defenders were flung from the walls and the town gates opened; Roman troops came pouring through, or climbed the now defenceless walls; everything was overrun, in every street the battle raged. After terrible slaughter resistance began to slacken, and Camillus gave the order to spare all who were not carrying arms. No more blood was shed, the unarmed began to give themselves up and the Roman troops with Camillus's leave, dispersed to sack the town. . . .

When all property of value belonging to men had been taken from Veii, work began on the removal of what belonged to the gods—the temple treasures and the divine images themselves. It was done with the deepest reverence; young soldiers were specially chosen for the task of conveying Queen Juno to Rome; having washed their bodies and dressed themselves in white, they entered her temple in awe, and shrank at first from what seemed the sacrilege of laying hands upon an image, which the Etruscan religion forbade anyone except the holder of a certain hereditary priesthood to touch. Suddenly one of them said: "Juno, do you want to go to

1. Juno was the wife and sister of Jupiter and was identified with the Greek goddess Hera. She eventually became the most important goddess of the Roman state.

2. Reprinted, by permission of the publisher, from Livy, *The Early History of Rome.* Books I–V of *The History of Rome from Its Foundation,* trans. by Aubrey de Sélincourt (London: Penguin Classics, 1960), pp. 364–66. Copyright © by the Estate of Aubrey de Sélincourt, 1960.

Rome?" Whether the question was divinely inspired or merely a young man's joke, who knows? but his companions all declared that the statue nodded its head in reply. We are told, too, that words were uttered, signifying assent. In any case—fables apart—she was moved from her place with only the slightest application of mechanical power, and was light and easy to transport—almost as if she came of her own free will—and was taken undamaged to her eternal dwelling-place on the Aventine,[3] whither the Dictator had called her in his prayer. And there Camillus afterwards dedicated to her the temple he had vowed.

Such was the fall of Veii, the wealthiest city of Etruria.

2. Engraved Back of a Mirror, c. 400 B.C. (Gardner, p. 191, ill. 6:12; Janson, p. 156, ill. 225)
Sophocles, *Antigone:* "Auguries," c. 441 B.C.
Cicero, *On Divination:* "The Science of Divination," c. 44 B.C.

The back of an Etruscan mirror is engraved with a scene representing a winged figure named Calchas practicing divination. The Etruscans were especially famous in the ancient world for the art of divination. Divination was the search to discover the will of the gods in order to interpret the past and predict the future. The most important divinatory technique was the reading and interpretation of the entrails of sacrificed animals, especially the liver. Second in importance was the observation of lightning and other celestial phenomena, such as the numbers, flights, and cries of birds. Finally, priests interpreted the future by the appearances of powerful signs such as thunderbolts and comets and inexplicable prodigies, such as the birth of a two-headed dog. All private and public actions were undertaken only after consulting the auguries. If the omen was unfavorable, complex ceremonies were undertaken in order to propitiate divine wrath and restore favor. Scrupulous attention was paid to the rigid observance of ritual detail in performing divinatory practices.

Divination can be traced back to the ancient civilizations of the Near East, especially to Mesopotamia. Divinatory rites were practiced throughout the Mediterranean world, including Greece. The Romans held the Etruscans in highest respect as the most expert practitioners of the art and adopted many of their practices. A college of augurs, or priests who practiced augury, was established in Rome, where advice might be sought by petitioners or where unsolicited advice might be offered.

Two selections related to divination are presented here. The first, "Auguries," is from the play *Antigone* by the Greek playwright Sophocles (c. 496–406 B.C.); in it, Teiresias, a blind prophet, explains his attempt to understand the will of the gods through the auguries. The second selection, "The Science of Divination," is from *On Divination,* an extended treatise by the Roman writer Cicero (106–43 B.C.), who was himself an augur.

3. One of the seven hills of ancient Rome.

Sophocles, *Antigone*[4]

Auguries

Teiresias

You'll know, when you hear the signs that I have marked
I sat where every bird of heaven comes
in my old place of augury, and heard
bird-cries I'd never known. They screeched about
goaded by madness, inarticulate.
I marked that they were tearing one another
with claws of murder. I could hear the wing-beats.
I was afraid, so straight away I tried
burnt sacrifice upon the flaming altar.
No fire caught my offerings. Slimy ooze
dripped on the ashes, smoked and sputtered there.
Gall burst its bladder, vanished into vapor;
the fat dripped from the bones and would not burn.
These are the omens of the rites that failed,
as my boy here has told me. He's my guide
as I am guide to others.

Cicero, *On Divination*[5]

The Science of Divination

There is an ancient belief, handed down to us even from mythical times and firmly established by the general agreement of the Roman people and of all nations, that divination of some kind exists among men; this the Greeks call *mantike*—that is, the foresight and knowledge of future events. A really splendid and helpful thing it is—if only such a faculty exists—since by its means men may approach very near to the power of gods. . . .

Now I am aware of no people, however refined and learned or however savage and ignorant, which does not think that signs are given of

4. Reprinted, by permission of the publisher, from Donald Greene and Richmond Lattimore, eds., *The Complete Greek Tragedies* (Chicago: University of Chicago Press, 1959), Vol. 2, pp. 192–93. Copyright © 1959 by the University of Chicago. Selection translated by Elizabeth Wyckoff.

5. Reprinted, by permission of the publisher and The Loeb Classical Library from Cicero, *De Devinatione,* trans. by William A. Falconer (Cambridge, Mass.: Harvard University Press, 1971), pp. 223–27.

future events, and that certain persons can recognize those signs and foretell events before they occur. . . .

Nor is it only one single mode of divination that has been employed in public and in private. For, to say nothing of other nations, how many of our own people have embraced it! In the first place, according to tradition, Romulus, the father of this City, not only founded it in obedience to the auspices, but was himself a most skilful augur. Next, the other Roman kings employed augurs; and, again, after the expulsion of the kings, no public business was ever transacted at home or abroad without first taking the auspices. Furthermore, since our forefathers believed that the soothsayers' art had great efficacy in seeking for omens and advice, as well as in cases where prodigies were to be interpreted and their effects averted, they gradually introduced that art in its entirety from Etruria, lest it should appear that any kind of divination had been disregarded by them.

VI

Roman Art

THE REPUBLICAN PERIOD

1. Temple of "Fortuna Virilis," Rome, late second century B.C. (Gardner, p. 196, ill. 6:16; Janson, p. 159, ill. 227)
Livy, *The History of Rome from Its Foundation:* "The Establishment of Religion in Rome," late first century B.C.

Recent excavations have increased our knowledge about the early history of Rome. However, the construction of the modern city of Rome above the ancient city limits the extent of archaeological excavation that is possible. Almost no structures built between the initial settlement of Rome in the eighth century B.C. and the third century B.C. are visible today. However, the existence of temples and other buildings has been identified in Rome from c. 575 B.C. onward. The Temple of "Fortuna Virilis," a well-preserved example of Roman architecture from the Republican period, dates from the late second century B.C. This temple is now thought to have been dedicated to Fortunus, the god of the harbor, rather than to Fortuna Virilis, the goddess of fortune and good luck and the bringer of virility to men.

Early Rome was a religious community. The Romans borrowed religious elements, such as the rites of divination and the religious calendar, from the Etruscans. At the same time, the Romans cherished a powerful and distinctive religion. Chief among the Roman gods were Jupiter, Mars, and Quirinus. Jupiter was worshiped as the god of the sky, Mars as the god of war, and Quirinus as the deified Romulus, the legendary first king of Rome (753–716 B.C.). Each of these gods was served by one of the three senior Roman priests, or *flamines maiores,* who wore a distinctive dress including a white conical cap and who observed an elaborate system of taboos in order to keep themselves free from any defilement.

Two other religious forces were Janus and Vesta. Janus was the god of doorways and the special god of all undertakings. His temple in the Forum had two doors, which were kept open in times of war and closed only in the rare event of universal peace. The opened doors indicated the sanctified route by which the Roman army marched to battle.

Vesta was worshiped as the hearth goddess. She presided over both the family hearth or altar and the central altar of the state. Her symbol was a sacred fire reputed by legend to have been brought by Aeneas from Troy and preserved in

Rome in the sanctuary of the goddess in the Forum. The fire was watched by six virgins. The vestal virgins were consecrated to the goddess as young girls and remained in her service for thirty years. They were treated with the highest degree of reverence. Any offense against a vestal virgin was punishable by death; any violation of the vow of chastity by a vestal virgin was punishable by being buried alive in an underground vault.

The early traditions of Roman religion are described by the Roman historian Livy (59 B.C.–A.D. 17) in his *History of Rome from Its Foundation.* Born in Padua in northern Italy, Livy spent most of his life in Rome, where he wrote the comprehensive survey of early Rome. His history covered the period from the legendary founding of the city in 753 B.C. until the death of Drusus, Augustus' stepson, in 9 B.C. As a historian, Livy was less concerned with literal accuracy and less critical of his sources than other ancient historians, such as Thucydides. His object was to revive the patriotism of his contemporaries by recalling their great heritage.

Livy attributed the origin of Roman religion to Numa, who was the legendary second king of Rome (715–673 B.C.). According to Roman mythology, Egeria, one of the nymphs of the springs as well as a birth goddess and a prophetess, instructed Numa on the religious rites which he should establish in Rome. A selection from *The History of Rome from Its Foundation,* "The Establishment of Religion in Rome," is presented here.

Livy, *The History of Rome from Its Foundation*[1]

The Establishment of Religion in Rome

Rome had originally been founded by force of arms; the new king now prepared to give the community a second beginning, this time on the solid basis of law and religious observance. These lessons, however, could never be learned while his people were constantly fighting; war, he well knew, was no civilizing influence, and the proud spirit of his people could be tamed only if they learned to lay aside their swords. Accordingly, at the foot of the Argiletum he built the temple of Janus, to serve as a visible sign of the alternations of peace and war: open, it was to signify that the city was in arms; closed, that war against all neighboring peoples had been brought to a successful conclusion. . . .

Rome was now at peace; there was no immediate prospect of attack from outside and the tight rein of constant military discipline was relaxed. In these novel circumstances there was an obvious danger of a general relaxation of the nation's moral fibre, so to prevent its occurrence Numa decided upon a step which he felt would prove more effective than anything else with a mob as rough and ignorant as the Romans were in those days.

1. Reprinted, by permission of the publisher, from Livy, *The Early History of Rome.* Books I–V of *The History of Rome from Its Foundation,* trans. by Aubrey de Sélincourt (London: Penguin Classics, 1960), pp. 38–40.

This was to inspire them with the fear of the gods. Such a sentiment was unlikely to touch them unless he first prepared them by inventing some sort of marvellous tale; he pretended, therefore, that he was in the habit of meeting the goddess Egeria by night, and that it was her authority which guided him in the establishment of such rites as were most acceptable to the gods and in the appointment of priests to serve each particular duty.

His first act was to divide the year into twelve lunar months; and because twelve lunar months come a few days short of the fall solar year, he inserted intercalary months, so that every twenty years the cycle should be completed, the days coming round again to correspond with the position of the sun from which they had started. Secondly, he fixed what came to be known as "lawful" and "unlawful" days—days, that is, when public business might, or might not, be transacted—as he foresaw that it would be convenient to have certain specified times when no measures should be brought before the people. Next he turned his attention to the appointment of priests; most of the religious ceremonies, especially those which are now in the hands of the *Flamen Dialis,* or priest of Jupiter, he was in the habit of presiding over himself, but he foresaw that in a martial community like Rome future kings were likely to resemble Romulus rather than himself and to be often, in consequence, away from home on active service, and for the reason appointed a Priest of Jupiter on a permanent basis, marking the importance of the office by the grant of special robes and the use of the royal curule chair. This step ensured that the religious duties attached to the royal office should never be allowed to lapse. At the same time two other priesthoods, to Mars and Quirinus, were created.

He further appointed virgin priestesses for the service of Vesta, a cult which originated in Alba and was therefore not foreign to Numa who brought it to Rome. The priestesses were paid out of public funds to enable them to devote their whole time to the temple service, and were invested with special sanctity by the imposition of various observances of which the chief was virginity. The twelve *Salii,* or Leaping Priests, were given the uniform of an embroidered tunic and bronze breastplate, and their special duty was to carry the ancilia, or sacred shields, one of which was fabled to have fallen from heaven, as they moved through the city chanting their hymns to the triple beat of their ritual dance.

Numa's next act was to appoint as pontifex the senator Numa Marcius, son of Marcus. He gave him full written instructions for all religious observances, specifying for the various sacrifices the place, the time, and the nature of the victim, and how money was to be raised to meet the cost. He also gave the pontifex the right of decision in all other matters connected with both public and private observances, so that ordinary people might have someone to consult if they needed advice, and to prevent the confusion which might result from neglect of national religious rites or the adoption of foreign ones. It was the further duty of the pontifex to teach the proper forms for the burial of the dead and the propitiation of the spirits of the departed, and to establish what portents manifested by lightning or other visible signs were to be recognized and acted upon. To elicit information on this subject from a divine source, Numa consecrated on the Aventine an altar to Jupiter Elicius, whom he consulted by augury as to what signs from heaven it should be proper to regard.

By these means the whole population of Rome was given a great many new things to think about and attend to, with the result that everybody was diverted from military preoccupations. They now had serious matters to consider; and believing, as they now did, that the heavenly powers took part in human affairs, they became so much absorbed in the cultivation of religion and so deeply imbued with the sense of their religious duties, that the sanctity of an oath had more power to control their lives than the fear of punishment for lawbreaking. Men of all classes took Numa as their unique example and modelled themselves upon him, until the effect of this change of heart was felt even beyond the borders of Roman territory. Once, Rome's neighbours had considered her not so much as a city as an armed camp in their midst threatening the general peace; now they came to revere her so profoundly as a community dedicated wholly to worship, that the mere thought of offering her violence seemed to them like sacrilege.

2. Temple of the "Sibyl," Tivoli, early first century B.C. (Gardner, p. 196, ill. 6:17; Janson, p. 159, ills. 228–29)
Cato, *On Agriculture:* "The Harvest Sacrifice," c. 160 B.C.

By the beginning of the third century B.C. Rome had become the master of Italy and was rapidly becoming a Mediterranean power. Contact with the Greek world, which had been conquered by Rome in 147 B.C., had a strong impact upon Roman civilization. Children of upper-class Roman families were tutored by Greeks and thus learned to speak Greek at an early age, and to appreciate Greek learning. Greek literature was emulated by Roman playwrights such as Plautus, who wrote comedies, and by poets such as Livius, who published a Latin version of Homer's *Odyssey.* Greek art was imported into Rome, and Greek models of architecture were adapted to Roman buildings. The Temple of the "Sibyl" at Tivoli is an example of the integration of Greek elements with Roman forms.

Romans were startled by, and attracted to, aspects of Greek religion. Unlike the Romans, the Greeks attributed human attributes to their gods and goddesses and depicted them in art in the images of men and women. At the same time the skeptical attitudes of contemporary Greeks toward religion shocked the fundamental piety of the Romans.

Faced with the growing popularity of Greek ideas, Roman conservatives feared that the firm stability of Roman traditional life was being undermined by the new taste for Greek art and Greek thought. They were especially alarmed by the sharp logic of Greek philosophers, who used reason to destroy belief. Among the defenders of Roman religious traditions was Cato (234–149 B.C.).

Born of peasant stock, Marcus Porcius Cato served his country as a general and a statesman. He was one of the two censors—that is, the magistrates charged with the responsibility for the financial control of the state revenues and for the supervision of the citizenry's manners and morals. He was determined to restore the integrity of morals and the simplicity of manners that had prevailed in the early days of the Republic, and he sought to stem the corrupting influences from the East. When three distinguished Greek philosophers arrived in Rome in 155 B.C. on a diplomatic mission, Cato had them bundled out of the city.

Cato wrote voluminously, but his only surviving work is the treatise *On Agriculture.* A practical handbook designed to aid farmers, it contains details of old religious rites, customs, and beliefs, and it indicates the close connection between early Roman religion and agriculture. A selection from *On Agriculture,* "The Harvest Sacrifice," is presented here.

Cato, *On Agriculture*[2]

The Harvest Sacrifice

Before harvest the sacrifice of the [sacrificial hog] should be offered in this manner: Offer a sow as [sacrificial hog] to Ceres before harvesting spelt, wheat, barley, beans, and rape seed; and address a prayer, with incense and wine, to Janus, Jupiter, and Juno, before offering the sow. Make an offering of cakes to Janus, with these words: "Father Janus, in offering these cakes, I humbly beg that thou wilt be gracious and merciful to me and my children, my house and my household." Then make an offering of cake to Jupiter with these words: "In offering this cake, O Jupiter, I humbly beg that thou, pleased by this offering, wilt be gracious and merciful to me and my children, my house and my household." Then present the wine to Janus, saying: "Father Janus, as I prayed humbly in offering the cakes, so wilt thou to the same end be honoured by this wine placed before thee." And then pray to Jupiter thus: "Jupiter, wilt thou deign to accept the cake; wilt thou deign to accept the wine placed before thee." Then offer up the [sacrificial hog]. When the entrails have been removed, make an offering of cakes to Janus, with a prayer as before; and an offering of a cake to Jupiter, with a prayer as before. After the same manner, also, offer wine to Janus and offer wine to Jupiter, as was directed before for the offering of the cakes, and the consecration of the cake. Afterwards offer entrails and wine to Ceres.[3]

2. Reprinted, by permission of the publisher and The Loeb Classical Library, from Marcus Porcius Cato, *On Agriculture,* trans. by W. D. Hooper (Cambridge, Mass.: Harvard University Press, 1967), p. 115.

3. The goddess of agriculture, identified with the Greek goddess Demeter.

3. *Portrait of a Roman,* c. 80 B.C. (Gardner, p. 195, ill. 6:14; Janson, p. 178, ill. 254)
Cicero, *Cato the Elder on Old Age:* "Old Age and Its Rewards," 44 B.C.

Reverence for the dead and respect for the elderly were two values deeply embedded in Roman tradition. To Romans, the family was of paramount importance. The eldest male served as the head of the family and exercised total authority over the members of his household, including his wife and adult sons. So long as he was alive, his word was law.

After death, the dead man's memory was revered by his descendants. Speeches in praise of the paterfamilias and his ancestors were given at his funeral. A wax mask or portrait bust, like the *Portrait of a Roman,* was kept in the family shrine, where it, along with images of other ancestors, was honored in religious ceremonies. These ancestral portraits were displayed in funeral processions in order to evoke memories of the illustrious dead and to buttress the prestige of their descendants.

An understanding of the values and traditions cherished by the Romans of the late Republican period emerges from the writings of Cicero (106–43 B.C.). Marcus Tullius Cicero was born in a wealthy but nonaristocratic family in Arpino, a town southeast of Rome. Educated in Rome and Greece, Cicero started his public career as a lawyer. He entered politics and, in 63 B.C., was elected consul with the support of the aristocratic party.

The years that followed were turbulent. During the civil wars that ended the Roman republic and established the empire, Cicero supported Pompey against Caesar. After Caesar's assassination, Cicero hoped to influence Caesar's heir, Octavian (who later became known as Augustus), to restore the republic and to induce the Senate to declare Antony a public enemy. When Octavian and Antony, together with Lepidus, formed an alliance, called the Second Triumvirate, Cicero realized his danger and attempted to flee. He was seized by Antony's soldiers and put to death on December 7, 43 B.C. His head and right hand were cut off and sent to Rome, where Antony ordered that they be nailed to the public speaker's platform.

Despite his political activities, Cicero could not shape the time in which he lived. His fame rests on the literary contributions he made as one of the greatest prose stylists in the Latin language. His output of essays and letters was enormous.

Among Cicero's works, most of which were written in periods of enforced political inactivity, is the essay *Cato the Elder on Old Age,* written in 44 B.C. The essay is set at the fictive date of 150 B.C. and presented in the form of an imaginary conversation between Cato, who would then have been eighty-four, and two younger friends. Cicero greatly admired the stern morality and conservative values exemplified by Cato, part of whose writings from *On Agriculture* have been included here earlier. In this essay, Cato describes to his audience the advantages of old age and the respect and authority accorded the elderly. A selection from *Cato the Elder on Old Age,* "Old Age and Its Rewards," is presented here.

Cicero, *Cato the Elder on Old Age*[4]

Old Age and Its Rewards

When I think about old age I can find four reasons why this is regarded as an unhappy time. First, because it takes us away from active work. Secondly, because it weakens the body. Thirdly, because it deprives us of practically all physical pleasures. And fourthly, because it is not far from the death. If you like we will go over the reasons one by one, and see how much truth there is in each of them. "Old age takes us away from active work." From what sort of work? Presumably from the sort which needs youth and strength. But surely there are also occupations fitted for old men's minds and brains even when their bodies are infirm. . . .

[Second] people who declare that there are no activities for old age are speaking beside the point. It is like saying that the pilot has nothing to do with sailing a ship because he leaves others to climb the masts and run along the gangways and work the pumps, while he himself sits quietly in the stern holding the rudder. He may not be doing what the younger men are doing, but his contribution is much more significant and valuable than theirs. Great deeds are not done by strength or speed or physique: they are the products of thought, and character, and judgment. And far from diminishing, such qualities actually increase with age. . . . Nowadays I do not miss the powers of youth—that was the second point about the failings of old age—any more than when I was young, I felt the lack of a bull's strength or an elephant's. A man should use what he has and in all his doings accommodate himself to his strength. . . .

Next we come to the third allegation against old age. This was its deficiency in sensual pleasures. But if age really frees us from youth's most dangerous failing, then we are receiving a most blessed gift. . . .

Now we must consider the fourth objection to being old; one which might be thought well calculated to worry and distress a man of my years. I refer to the nearness of death. When a man is old, there can obviously be no doubt that it is near. Yet if, during his long life, he has failed to grasp that death is of no account he is unfortunate indeed. There are two alternatives: either death completely destroys human souls, in which case it is negligible; or it removes the soul to some place of eternal life—in which case its coming is greatly to be desired. There can be no third possibility. If, then, after death I shall either lack unhappiness or even be positively happy, I have nothing whatever to fear.

To be respected is the crowning glory of old age . . . and the authority

4. Reprinted, by permission of the publisher, from Cicero, *Selected Works,* trans. by Michael Grant (London: Penguin Classics, 1965, 1971), pp. 219–20, 223–24, 228, 240, 238. Copyright © by Michael Grant, 1960, 1965, 1971.

which belongs to old age, especially when enhanced by a distinguished record, is more precious than all the pleasures of youth.

4. Sanctuary of Fortuna Primigenia, Praeneste (Palestrina), c. 80 B.C. (Gardner, pp. 197–98, ill. 6:18 to 6:20; Janson, p. 160, ills. 230–32)
Appian, *The Civil Wars:* "Sulla's Victories," mid-second century B.C.

During the final decades of the Roman republic, Roman politics was filled with suspicion, intrigue, and violence. The struggle between competing factions to control Rome led to the outbreak of civil wars and to the rise of military rulers. In 88 B.C. Sulla, a Roman general who had quelled a revolt against Rome by her Italian allies, marched on Rome and occupied the city. Shortly afterward, however, Sulla left Rome to direct a military campaign in Greece and Asia Minor, and during his absence his enemies declared him to be a public enemy. In 83 B.C. Sulla returned to Rome to face his opponents. His victories the following year at the Colline gate in the northern district of Rome and at Praeneste—a town about twenty miles east of Rome, where his chief rival, Marius, was encamped—ended all opposition.

Now master of the Roman state, Sulla established himself in the office of dictator. He began a reign of terror, in which he executed hundreds of enemies and confiscated their property. Previously impoverished, Sulla became a lavish sponsor of vast building programs. At Praeneste he built the great Sanctuary of Fortuna Primigenia.

Fortuna, the goddess of fortune and good luck, was a potent goddess associated with the bountifulness of the earth and the fertility of men and women. At Praeneste, where she was called Primigenia[5] because she was regarded as the eldest daughter of Jupiter, Fortuna had an ancient oracular shrine. Sulla, who took the surname Felix[6] as an indication of his own good fortune, built the impressive sanctuary at Praeneste to acknowledge his debt to the goddess.

Sulla's military occupation of Rome in 88 B.C. was the first time that a Roman citizen had led a Roman army against his own city. Sulla tried to prevent the rise of any other military ruler. In 80 B.C. he abdicated his dictatorship and became consul; the following year he returned to private life. Nonetheless, other ambitious men followed Sulla's example. Bloody wars were fought between Pompey and Caesar and between Octavian and Antony for control of Rome. This turbulent period was chronicled by the historian Appian in the second century A.D.

Born in Alexandria, Egypt, Appian obtained Roman citizenship and moved to Rome. He wrote, in Greek, a twenty-four-volume history of the Roman empire from its beginnings until the time of the emperor Trajan (A.D. 53–117). *The Civil Wars* formed part of Appian's history and included a description of the battle at the Colline gate and the surrender of Praeneste to Sulla and his lieutenant, Lucretius. A selection from *The Civil Wars,* "Sulla's Victories," is presented here.

5. "First Born."
6. "The Lucky One."

Appian, *The Civil Wars*[7]

Sulla's Victories

Sulla feared for the safety of the city, and sent his cavalry forward with all speed to hinder their march, and then hastened in person with his whole army and encamped beside the Colline gate near the temple of Venus about noon, the enemy being already encamped around the city. A battle was fought at once, late in the afternoon. On the right wing Sulla was victorious, but his left was vanquished and fled to the gates. The old soldiers on the walls, when they saw the enemy rushing in with their own men, dropped the portcullis, which fell upon and killed many soldiers and many senators. But the majority, impelled by fear and necessity, turned and fought the enemy. The fighting continued through the night and a great many were slain. The generals, Telesinus and Albinus, were slain also and their camp was taken. Lamponius the Lucanian, Marcius, and Carinas, and the other generals of the faction of Carbo, fled. It was estimated that 50,000 men on both sides lost their lives in this engagement. . . .

When the Praenestians saw them and knew that Carbo's army was completely destroyed, and that Norbanus himself had fled from Italy, and that Rome and all the rest of Italy were entirely in the power of Sulla, they surrendered their city to Lucretius. Marius hid himself in an underground tunnel and shortly afterward committed suicide. . . .

When Lucretius took Praeneste he seized the senators who had held commands under Marius, and put some of them to death and cast the others into prison. The latter were put to death by Sulla when he came that way. All the others who were taken in Praeneste he ordered to march out to the plain without arms, and when they had done so he chose out a very few who had been in any way serviceable to him. The remainder he ordered to be divided into three sections, consisting of Romans, Samnites, and Praenestians respectively. When this had been done he announced to the Romans by herald that they had merited death, but nevertheless he would pardon them. The others he shot down to the last man, but their wives and children he allowed to go unharmed. The town, which was extremely rich at that time, he gave over to plunder.

In this way was Praeneste taken.

7. Reprinted, by permission of the publisher and The Loeb Classical Library, from *Appian's Roman History,* trans. by Horace White (Cambridge, Mass.: Harvard University Press, 1968), pp. 169–71.

THE EMPIRE

1. Ara Pacis Augustae, Rome, 13–9 B.C. (Gardner, p. 226, ill. 6:58; Janson, p. 180, ill. 258)
Augustus, *Res Gestae Divi Augusti:* "To Serve Rome with Courage, Clemency, Justice, and Piety," A.D. 13

The Roman empire was created by Augustus (63 B.C.–A.D. 14), who, after his military success against Antony and Cleopatra, claimed that he wanted to establish the best civilian government possible. The system of government which he devised endured with no major changes for the next three centuries.

Augustus was originally named Gaius Octavius, or Octavian. He was only seventeen when Caesar, his great-uncle, was assassinated. By Caesar's will, Octavian, whose natural father had died when he was four years old, was named as Caesar's heir and son. Although he was opposed by much more powerful and influential men, Octavian was determined to avenge Caesar and to claim his inheritance. He fought and defeated Antony in Mutina in northern Italy in 43 B.C. Shortly afterward he joined forces with Antony and Antony's ally, Lepidus, to form the Second Triumvirate.[8] In 42 B.C. Octavian and Antony won the battle of Philippi against Caesar's assassins, Brutus and Cassius. Antony took control of the eastern provinces of the Roman state and Octavian of the western provinces. Octavian was then able to use Antony's entanglement with Cleopatra as a pretext for arousing public opinion and for declaring war on his rival.

After the defeat of Antony in the naval battle of Actium, Octavian became the sole ruler of the Roman world. In 27 B.C., he assumed the title Augustus. During the next forty-four years of his rule, Augustus exercised unprecedented powers, while preserving, in form, the republican institutions of government. He died universally respected and admired. His body was burned, and the ashes placed in a mausoleum by the Tiber, the river that runs through Rome. By a decree of the Senate, Augustus was named one of the gods to be worshiped by the Romans.

An important source of information about Augustus' life is his autobiography, *Res Gestae Divi Augusti,* written the year before his death. The *Res Gestae* was inscribed on two bronze tablets on Augustus' mausoleum and on stone tablets throughout the empire. The document details the public honors awarded Augustus, such as the dedication by the Senate of the Ara Pacis Augustae in recognition of his role in establishing peace. It also describes his victorious military campaigns and successful foreign negotiations, such as the return of the Roman spoils and standards lost by Crassus and Antony in their unsuccessful campaigns against the Parthians of Asia in 53, 40 and 36 B.C. The relief carved on Augustus' breastplate in the emperor's portrait, *Augustus of Primaporta,* records the same event. Augustus concluded his autobiography by acknowledging his undisputed authority in the imperial government and by simultaneously expressing his respect for republican liberty. A selection from the *Res Gestae Divi Augusti,* "To Serve Rome with Courage, Clemency, Justice, and Piety," is presented here.

8. A ruling coalition of three men.

Augustus, *Res Gestae Divi Augusti*[9]

To Serve Rome with Courage, Clemency, Justice, and Piety

At the age of nineteen on my own responsibility and at my own expense I raised an army, with which I successfully championed the liberty of the republic when it was oppressed by the tyranny of a faction.[10] On that account the senate passed decrees in my honour enrolling me in its order in the consulship of Gaius Pansa and Aulus Hirtius, assigning me the right to give my opinion among the consulars and giving me imperium.[11] It ordered me as a propraetor[12] to provide in concert with the consuls that the republic should come to no harm. In the same year, when both consuls had fallen in battle, the people appointed me consul and triumvir for the organization of the republic.

I drove into exile the murderers of my father,[13] avenging their crime through tribunals established by law; and afterwards, when they made war on the republic, I twice defeated them in battle.

I undertook many civil and foreign wars by land and sea throughout the world, and as victor I spared the lives of all citizens who asked for mercy. When foreign peoples could safely be pardoned I preferred to preserve rather than to exterminate them. . . . On my return from Spain and Gaul in the consulship of Tiberius Nero and Publius Quintillius after successfully arranging affairs in those provinces, the senate resolved that an altar of the Augustan Peace should be consecrated next to the Campus Martius[14] in honour of my return, and ordered that the magistrates, priests and Vestal virgins should perform an annual sacrifice there.

It was the will of our ancestors that the gateway of Janus Quirinus should be shut when victories had secured peace by land and sea throughout the whole empire of the Roman people; from the foundation of the city down to my birth, tradition records that it was shut only twice, but while I was the leading citizen the senate resolved that it should be shut on three occasions. . . .

I extended the territory of all those provinces of the Roman people on whose borders lay peoples not subject to our government. I brought

9. Reprinted, by permission of the publisher, from Augustus, *Res Gestae Divi Augusti,* ed. by P. A. Brunt and J. M. Moore (Oxford: Oxford University Press, 1981), pp. 19, 25, 31–33, 35–37.

10. Antony and his army.

11. Supreme administrative and judicial authority usually granted for a specific location and a limited time.

12. A praetor was a judge who served for a year. If his office was extended by the Senate, he was termed a propraetor. Usually this was done in order that a praetor might take office as a provincial governor.

13. Julius Caesar.

14. A district of Rome on the banks of the Tiber, which was originally set aside for military drills. It later became a park.

peace to the Gallic and Spanish provinces as well as to Germany, throughout the area bordering on the Ocean from Cadiz to the mouth of the Elbe. I secured the pacification of the Alps from the district nearest the Adriatic to the Tuscan sea, yet without waging an unjust war on any people. My fleet sailed through the Ocean eastwards from the mouth of the Rhine to the territory of the Cimbri,[15] a country which no Roman had visited before either by land or sea, and the Cimbri, Charydes, Semnones and other German peoples of that region sent ambassadors and sought my friendship and that of the Roman people. At my command and under my auspices two armies were led almost at the same time into Ethiopia and Arabia Felix; vast enemy forces of both peoples were cut down in battle and many towns captured. Ethiopia was penetrated as far as the town of Nabata, which adjoins Meroe; in Arabia the army advanced into the territory of the Sabaeans to the town of Mariba.

I added Egypt to the empire of the Roman people. . . . By victories over enemies I recovered in Spain and in Gaul, and from the Dalmatians several standards lost by other commanders. I compelled the Parthians[16] to restore to me the spoils and standards of three Roman armies and to ask as suppliants for the friendship of the Roman people. Those standards I deposited in the innermost shrine of the temple of Mars the Avenger.

In my sixth and seventh consulships, after I had extinguished civil wars, and at a time when with universal consent I was in complete control of affairs, I transferred the republic from my power to the dominion of the senate and people of Rome. For this service of mine I was named Augustus by decree of the senate, and the door-posts of my house were publicly wreathed with bay leaves and a civic crown was fixed over my door and a golden shield was set in the Curia Julia, which, as attested by the inscription thereon was given me by the senate and people of Rome on account of my courage, clemency, justice and piety. After this time I excelled all in influence, although I possessed no more official power than others who were my colleagues in the several magistracies.

In my thirteenth consulship the senate, the equestrian order and the whole people of Rome gave me the title of Father of my Country, and resolved that this should be inscribed in the porch of my house and in the Curia Julia and in the Forum Augustum below the chariot which had been set there in my honour by decree of the senate. At the time of writing I am in my seventy-sixth year.

15. Modern Jutland.

16. Parthia was located in Asia to the southeast of the Caspian Sea in modern Iran. The Parthian empire reached its height in the first century B.C. and for a time threatened Roman Asia Minor.

2. *"Tellus" Relief,* panel from the Ara Pacis Augustae, 13–9 B.C. (Gardner, p. 226, ill. 6:59; Janson, p. 182, ill. 261)
Virgil, *Georgic I:* "What Makes the Crops Rejoice," c. 37–29 B.C.
Horace, *Epode II:* "The Family Farm," c. 30 B.C.

The Augustan age was the greatest period of Roman civilization. Augustus was not only a skillful politician but also a genuine connoisseur of art and literature, who encouraged artists and poets with both financial subsidies and his own deft criticisms. Under his aegis, the arts expressed the Roman peoples' enjoyment of the newly established conditions of peace and prosperity, and their resurgence of patriotism.

The greatest poet of the age, and of all Roman history, was Virgil (70–19 B.C.). The son of a landowner, Virgil was deeply devoted to the Italian countryside, and he celebrated its glories in verse. Virgil wrote four books, called *The Georgics,* on the practices and pleasures of Italian agriculture. Composed between c. 37 and 29 B.C., *The Georgics* are dedicated to Maecenas, one of Augustus' chief ministers and the leading patron of the arts. Crops and weather, the cultivation of fruit-trees, the care of farm animals, and the techniques of beekeeping are Virgil's principal subjects. A selection from *Georgic I,* "What Makes the Crops Rejoice," is presented here.

The second great poet of the age was Horace (65–68 B.C.). Born in southeast Italy, Horace was the son of a former slave. Through his father's determined efforts, Horace received a good education in Rome and Athens. As a young man he supported the republican cause and in 42 B.C. he fought in the army of Brutus at Philippi against Antony and Augustus. Despite his early opposition, Horace later became an admirer and friend of Augustus. Virgil introduced Horace to Maecenas, who provided him with a farm in the Sabine hills near Rome. Horace divided the year between his house in Rome, where he lived modestly, and his farm, where he enjoyed the quiet delights of the countryside.

In c. 30 B.C., Horace published *The Epodes,* consisting of seventeen poems. *The Epodes* deal with a variety of topics including political and social problems, love and friendship, and nature. A selection from *Epode II,* "The Family Farm," is presented here.

Both Virgil and Horace praised Augustus for ending the nightmare epoch of the civil wars. A similar expression of gratitude for the age of peace established by Augustus and of appreciation for the pastoral world which he safeguarded is seen in the *"Tellus" Relief* of the Ara Pacis Augustae. The imagery of the *"Tellus" Relief,* which apparently depicts the Roman earth mother, Tellus, flanked by personifications of the winds, links the interrelated themes of the fertility of the earth, the bounties of nature, and the blessings of peace.

Virgil, *Georgic I*[17]

What Makes the Crops Rejoice

What makes the crops rejoice, beneath what star
To plough, and when to wed the vines to elms,
the care of cattle, how to rear a flock,
How much experience thrifty bees require:
Of these, Maecenas, I begin to sing.
You, sun and moon, our world's resplendent lights,
Who lead the year revolving through the skies;
And Bacchus[18] and kind Ceres,[19] by whose grace
Earth exchanged acorns for fertile grain
And mingled rivers' waters with new wine;
You, Fauns,[20] the country's ever-present spirits,
(Come, oh Fauns, and dance with the Dryad[21] maids!):
Your gifts I sing. And Neptune,[22] whose great fork
Struck earth and first produced the neighing steeds;
And Aristaeus,[23] guardian of groves,
Whose herds in hundreds graze Aegean lands;
And Pan,[24] good shepherd, leave your native groves
And vales, to bless us in Arcadia[25] here;
Come, Minerva,[26] patron of the olive,
Triptolemus,[27] the hero of the plough,
Silvanus[28] with a young and slender cypress:

17. Reprinted, by permission of the publisher, from *Virgil's Georgics,* trans. by Smith Palmer Bovie (Chicago: University of Chicago Press, 1956), pp. 3–5. Copyright © by the University of Chicago, 1956.

18. The god of wine, identified with the Greek Dionysus.

19. The goddess of agriculture, identified with the Greek Demeter.

20. Creatures that were half man and half goat, the fauns were minor rural deities who were the attendants of Pan.

21. Wood nymphs.

22. The god of the sea, the Greek Poseidon.

23. The son of Apollo and the nymph Cyrene, Aristaeus was honored as the inventor of beekeeping and olive culture.

24. A rural god of ancient Greece whose worship was centered in Arcadia. Pan was represented with the horns, ears, tail, and rear legs of a goat and was believed, on occasion, to inspire unreasoned fear—hence, panic.

25. A region in the central mountains of the Peloponnese, noted for the simple, happy life of its inhabitants.

26. Identified with the Greek Athena, Minerva was a patron of learning and crafts and the goddess of peace. One of her symbols was the olive branch. She also taught humans the use of horses.

27. A figure associated with the mystery cult of Demeter (Ceres) at Eleusis in Greece, Triptolemus was given by Demeter a chariot, drawn by winged dragons, from which to sow corn. He was honored as the figure by which the knowledge of agriculture was spread.

28. The god of uncultivated land, Silvanus had to be propitiated before any land was brought under the plow.

All gods and goddesses who guard the fields,
Protecting random fruit and showering rain
On seedling plants: be with us now.
You also we would hail, oh godlike man,
Octavian Caesar: you will be a god,
But in what form the gods do not reveal;
You may become a deity of land
Protecting towns and fields, a great provider,
Lord of seasons, crowned with Venus' myrtle. . . .
Whatever form, O Caesar, you assume,
Smooth my path, condone this enterprise
Of bold experiment in verse, and share
Concern with me for uninstructed farmers:
Grow used to prayers appealing to your name.

Horace, *Epode II*[29]

The Family Farm

A man is happy when, far from the business world,
  like the earliest tribe of men
he cultivates the family farm with his team,
  and is free from usury's ties
(not as a soldier, stirred by the trumpet's wild cry,
  nor quaking in an angry sea),
when he keeps away from the Forum and the proud
  doorways of influential men.
This is his life: when the shoots of his vines mature,
  he marries them to tall poplars,
or, in a secluded valley, he looks over
  his lowing cattle as they graze,
and pruning away useless branches with his hook,
  grafts more fruitful ones to the trees,
or he puts up pressed honey in his well-scrubbed jars
  or shears the struggling, helpless sheep;
above all, when through his lands Autumn lifts his head
  with a crown of ripening fruit,
how delighted he is, plucking the grafted pears
  and the purple cluster of grapes

29. Reprinted, by permission of the publisher, from *The Odes and Epodes of Horace,* trans. by Joseph P. Clancy (Chicago: University of Chicago Press, 1960), p. 202. Copyright © by the University of Chicago, 1960.

as your offering, Priapus,[30] and Silvanus,
  protector of boundary lines.
How pleasant to rest, sometimes beneath an old oak,
  sometimes on a carpet of grass;
all the while the brook glides by between its high banks,
  the birds are trilling in the trees,
and the splashing waters of springs play counterpoint,
  a summons to easy slumber.

3. *Augustus of Primaporta,* c. 20 B.C. (Gardner, p. 225, ill. 6:57; Janson, p. 180, ills. 256–257)
Ovid, *The Art of Love:* "Love Is Never a Thing to Be Hurried," c. 1 B.C.
Ovid, *Metamorphoses:* "We Cannot Think Him Mortal, Our Augustus," c. A.D. 8

The statue *Augustus of Primaporta,* which includes a figure of Cupid riding a dolphin, represents the divine descent of the Roman emperor. In Roman mythology, Cupid was the divine son of Venus, the goddess of love, and in Roman legend, Aeneas, the founder of Rome, was the human son of Venus. Julius Caesar claimed to be the descendant of Iulus, Aeneas' son, and Augustus was recognized as the adoptive son and the political heir of Caesar. Despite his claim of descent from Venus, Augustus was not amused when, in 1 B.C., the Roman poet Ovid published his poem *The Art of Love.*

Ovid (43 B.C.–A.D. 17) was the third great poet of the Augustan age. Born in Sulmo, a town ninety miles east of Rome, Ovid was the son of a wealthy and respectable landowner. His father intended that he enter a career in government, but Ovid decided that public life did not suit him and devoted himself instead to poetry.

Written in three books, *The Art of Love* is a handbook on the art of seduction. The first two books offer instruction to men; the third book gives advice to women. The frankly sensual view of life and love espoused by Ovid in this work ran counter to Augustus' sober moral principles. The previous year, Augustus had banished his only child, Julia, for sexual profligacy, and he was attempting, though with little success, to raise the moral standards of upper-class Roman society. To Augustus, Ovid's poem was shocking and offensive. A selection from *The Art of Love,* "Love Is Never a Thing to Be Hurried," is presented here.

Ovid attempted to placate Augustus with another of his compositions, the *Metamorphoses.* A long poem written in fifteen books, the *Metamorphoses* is a collection of mythological and legendary stories drawn from Greek, Latin, and Eastern sources. All stories share a common element: a miraculous transformation. The stories are told in chronological order, beginning with the Creation, in which Chaos is transformed into the ordered universe of earth, sea, and sky, and cul-

30. A fertility god of Greek origin, later honored as the guardian deity of gardens.

minating with the assassination of Julius Caesar, in which Caesar is transformed into a star. The final transformation of the poem was intended by Ovid to be a tribute to the divinity of Augustus. A selection from the *Metamorphoses,* "We Cannot Think Him Mortal, Our Augustus," is presented here.

In A.D. 8, just as he was finishing the *Metamorphoses,* Ovid was summoned to Rome for a personal interview with the emperor. Ovid was aghast to learn that he was to be banished. One reason given by Augustus for his banishment was his poem *The Art of Love.*

Ovid was ordered to Tomis, a semi-Hellenized port on the Black Sea at the extreme edge of the Roman empire. Tomis, near the modern town of Constantsa, Romania, was subject to periodic attacks by surrounding barbarian peoples. Ovid suffered from personal danger, from the severe climate, and, most of all, from the intellectual isolation of the place. From Tomis, Ovid addressed repeated appeals for clemency, first to Augustus, and later to his successor, Tiberius. Ovid died in exile in A.D. 17.

Ovid, *The Art of Love*[31]

Love Is Never a Thing to Be Hurried

Take my word for it, love is never a thing to be hurried,
  Coax it along, go slow, tease it with proper delay.
When you have found the place where a woman loves to be fondled,
  Let no feeling of shame keep your caresses away.
Then you will see in her eyes a tremulous brightness, a glitter,
  Like the flash of the sun when the water is clear.
She will complain, but not mean it, murmuring words of endearment,
  Sigh in the sweetest way, utter appropriate cries.
Neither go too fast, nor let her get there before you;
  Pleasure is best when both come at one time to the goal.
Slow is the pace to keep when plenty of leisure is given,
  When you can dally at ease, free from the pressure of fear,
But when delay is not safe, it is useful to drive with full power,
  Useful to give your mount spirited prick of the spur.

31. Reprinted, by permission of the publisher, from Ovid, *The Art of Love,* trans. by Rolfe Humphries (Bloomington, Ind.: Indiana University Press, 1957), pp. 151–52.

Ovid, *Metamorphoses*[32]

We Cannot Think Him Mortal, Our Augustus

We cannot think him mortal, our Augustus,
Therefore our Julius must be made a god
To justify his son.
And golden Venus
Saw this, and saw, as well, the murder plotted
Against her priest, the assassins in their armor,
And she grew pale with fear. "Behold," she cried
To all the gods in turn, "Behold, what treason
Threatens me with its heavy weight, what ambush
Is set to take Iulus' last descendant!" . . .
Then Venus beat
Her breast with both her hands, and tried to hide him,
Her Caesar, in a cloud, as she had rescued
Paris[33] from Menelaus, as Aeneas[34]
Fled Diomedes' sword. And Jove spoke to her:
"My daughter, do you think your power alone
Can move the fates no power can ever conquer?

Enter the home of the Three Sisters:[35] there
You will see the records, on bronze and solid iron,
Wrought with tremendous effort, and no crashing
Of sky, no wrath of lightning, no destruction
Shall make them crumble. They are safe, forever.
There you will find engraved on adamant
The destinies of the race, unchangeable.
I have read them, and remembered; I will tell you
So you may know the future. He has finished
The time allotted him, this son you grieve for;
His debt to earth is paid. But he will enter
The Heaven as a god, and have his temples
On earth as well: this you will see fulfilled,

32. Reprinted, by permission of the publisher, from Ovid, *Metamorphoses,* trans. by Rolfe Humphries (Bloomington, Ind.: Indiana University Press, 1955), pp. 388–91.

33. The Trojan prince, the son of Priam and Hecuba, whose elopement with Helen caused the Trojan War. He was rescued by Aphrodite (Venus), the goddess of love, from a duel with Menelaus.

34. A Trojan who escaped the fall of Troy and eventually came to Italy, where his descendants founded the city of Rome. His exploits are the subject of Virgil's *Aeneid.* During the Trojan War, he was saved by Aphrodite from death at the hands of the Greek hero Diomedes, the king of Aetolia.

35. The Three Fates who govern the lives of humans from birth to death.

Will bring about, you and his son together.
He shall inherit both the name of Caesar
And the great burden, and we both shall help him
Avenge his father's murder. Under him
Mutina's conquered walls will sue for mercy,
Pharsalia[36] know his power, and Philippi
Run red with blood again, and one more Pompey
Go down to death in the Sicilian waters.
A Roman general's Egyptian woman[37]
Foolish to trust that liaison, will perish
For all her threats that our own capitol
Would serve Canopus.[38] Need I bring to mind
Barbarian lands that border either ocean?
Whatever lands men live on, the world over,
Shall all be his to rule, and the seas also.
And when peace comes to all the world, his mind
Will turn to law and order, civil justice,
And men will learn from his sublime example,
And he, still looking forward toward the future,
The coming generations, will give order
That his good wife's young son should take his name,
His duty when he lays the burden down,
Though he will live as long as ancient Nestor[39]
Before he comes to Heaven to greet his kinsmen.
Now, in the meantime, from the murdered body
Raise up the spirit, set the soul of Julius
As a new star in Heaven, to watch over
Our market place, our Capitol."

4. *Vespasian,* c. A.D. 75 (Gardner, p. 232, ill. 6:69; Janson, p. 185, ill. 266)
Suetonius, *The Lives of the Twelve Caesars:* "Vespasian's Personality," early second century

When Nero committed suicide in A.D. 68, the Julio-Claudian dynasty of emperors, established by Julius Caesar and Augustus, came to an ignominious end. Nero's

36. Or Pharsalus, the ancient Greek town in Thessaly near modern Larissa, near which Julius Caesar defeated Pompey, a general who was Caesar's rival for power and who had earlier been his co-ruler.

37. Cleopatra, the queen of Egypt.

38. An Egyptian water god who was worshiped as the conqueror of fire.

39. King of Pylos during the Trojan War, he was respected by the other Greeks for his age and experience.

death was followed by a civil war fought among four different factions. Vespasian (A.D. 9–79), once a general of Nero, emerged as the military victor. On December 22, A.D. 69, the Senate obligingly conferred all the imperial powers upon him.

Vespasian proved to be an astute and effective, although unimaginative, ruler. The son of a tax collector in the Sabine region, Vespasian did not come from Rome or its aristocracy. He was known for his plain tastes, simple life-style, coarse humor, and great capacity for hard work. Earlier in his career, he had reputedly been dismissed from Nero's court and had fled for his life when he was caught sleeping during one of the emperor's song recitals. Vespasian's portrait bust captures the emperor's shrewd and earthy qualities.

The same personal qualities emerge in the biography of Vespasian written by the Roman historian Suetonius (c. A.D. 70–c. 122). Suetonius began his career as a teacher of rhetoric and served the emperor Hadrian as his private secretary. After his dismissal from that post, Suetonius turned his attention to writing books on a wide variety of topics. His most famous work is *The Lives of the Twelve Caesars,* a collection of biographical accounts of the first twelve Roman emperors. In the *Lives,* Suetonius recounts the scandalous gossip about the personal lives of the emperors and largely ignores general topics about the empire and its administration. A selection from the *Lives,* "Vespasian's Personality," is presented here.

Suetonius, *The Lives of the Twelve Caesars*[40]

Vespasian's Personality

He was from first to last modest and restrained in his conduct of affairs, and more inclined to parade, than to cast a veil over, his humble origins. Indeed, when a group of antiquaries tried to connect his ancestors with the founders of Reiti, and with one of Hercules's comrades whose tomb is still to be seen on the Salarian Way, Vespasian burst into a roar of laughter. He had anything but a craving for outward show; on the day of his triumph the painful crawl of the procession so wearied him that he said frankly: "What an old fool I was to demand a triumph, as though I owed this honour to my ancestors or had ever made it one of my own ambitions! It serves me right!" . . .

Vespasian was square-shouldered, with strong, well-formed limbs, but always wore a strained expression on his face; so that once, when he asked a well-known wit who always used to make jokes about people: "Why not make one about me?" the answer came: "I will, when you have at last finished relieving yourself." He enjoyed perfect health and took no medical precautions for preserving it, except to have his throat and body massaged regularly in the ball-alley, and to fast one whole day every month.

40. Reprinted, by permission of A. P. Watt Ltd. on behalf of the Executors of the Estate of Robert Graves, from Suetonius, *The Lives of the Twelve Caesars,* trans. by Robert Graves (London: Penguin Classics, 1957), pp. 281, 284–85.

Here follows a general description of his habits. After becoming Emperor he would rise early, before daylight even, to deal with his private correspondence and official reports. Next, he would invite his friends to wish him good-morning while he put on his shoes and dressed for the day. Having attended to any urgent business he would first take a drive and then return to bed for a nap—with one of the several mistresses whom he had engaged after Caenis's[41] death. Finally, he took a bath and went to dinner, where he would be in such a cheerful mood that members of his household usually chose this time to ask favours of him.

Yet Vespasian was nearly always just as good-natured, cracking frequent jokes; and, though he had a low form of humour and often used obscene expressions, some of his sayings are still remembered. . . .

With his knack of apt quotation from the Greek Classics, he once described a very tall man whose genitals were grotesquely overdeveloped as:

"Striding along with a lance which casts a preposterous shadow,"—a line out of the *Iliad*. . . .

Titus[42] complained of the tax which Vespasian had imposed on the contents of the City urinals (used by the fullers to clean woollens). Vespasian handed him a coin which had been part of the first day's proceeds: "Does it smell bad, my son?" he asked. "No, Father!" "That's odd: it comes straight from the urinal!" When a deputation from the Senate reported that a huge and expensive statue had been voted him at public expense, Vespasian held out his hand, with: "The pedestal is waiting."

Nothing could stop this flow of humour, even the fear of imminent death. . . . His death-bed joke was: "Dear me! I must be turning into a god."

5. *Spoils from the Temple in Jerusalem* and *Triumph of Titus,* Arch of Titus, Rome, A.D. 81 (Gardner, pp. 227–28, ills. 6:61 to 6:63; Janson, p. 183, ills. 263–64)

Josephus, *The Jewish War:* "The Destruction of the Temple" and "The Triumph of Titus," c. A.D. 78

After securing the imperial throne, Vespasian turned his attention to ending the Jewish rebellion. Judea had been a Roman province since A.D. 6. Although Jews had been granted certain privileges, including exemption from military service and from participation in the imperial cult, there was deep unrest in Judea. Jews resented the rule of foreigners as an offense to their religion. Open revolt flared in A.D. 66, when rebels drove a Roman garrison from Jerusalem. Fighting spread quickly through Judea and spilled over to Syria and Egypt.

In A.D. 67 Vespasian was appointed by Nero to direct the reconquest of Judea.

41. Vespasian's favorite mistress.
42. Vespasian's son and eventual successor.

His military campaign, however, was interrupted, first by the outbreak of civil war after the suicide of Nero and then by his need to consolidate his position as emperor. In A.D. 70 Vespasian, as emperor, sent his eldest son, Titus, to Judea to finish putting down the rebellion. Faced by the strong walls and towers that defended Jerusalem, Titus laid siege to the city. The population was weakened by famine but resisted with desperate courage. Finally unable to withstand the Roman assaults, Jerusalem was conquered. The city was destroyed, the temple was burned, and the Jewish rebellion was smashed.

Titus succeeded his father as emperor in A.D. 79. He commemorated his victory in Jerusalem by the arch that still stands near the Roman Forum. The arch is decorated by two reliefs which illustrate events in the Jewish war, *Spoils from the Temple in Jerusalem* and *Triumph of Titus.*

The same events are described by the Jewish historian Josephus. Josephus (c. A.D. 37–c. 93) was a soldier, a statesman, a historian, and a priest. Born in Jerusalem in an aristocratic family, he was educated in the Jewish religious law and became a Pharisee. In A.D. 64 he visited Rome on a diplomatic mission to obtain the release of Jewish prisoners. Upon his return from Rome, he was appointed governor of Galilee by the Sanhedrin, the great council of Jews in Jerusalem. In A.D. 66 he joined the Jewish revolt and organized the defense of the city of Jotapata. Captured by the Romans, Josephus won the favor of Vespasian by prophesying that he would one day become emperor; when the prediction proved true, Josephus was released. During the siege of Jerusalem, he changed sides and served Titus as an interpreter. Hated by the Jews as a traitor, Josephus accompanied Titus to Rome, where he became a Roman citizen and received a pension.

In c. A.D. 78 Josephus published an official account of the Jewish rebellion, entitled *The Jewish War,* based upon his own observations and recollections. Two selections from *The Jewish War* are presented here. The first, "The Destruction of the Temple," describes the burning of the temple in Jerusalem. The second selection, "The Triumph of Titus," describes the pageant in Rome that honored Titus' victory by a display of prisoners and loot captured in the Jewish war.

Josephus, *The Jewish War*[43]

The Destruction of the Temple

Titus retired . . . intending at stand-to next day to launch a full-scale attack and surround the Sanctuary[44] completely. . . . But it was the Jews themselves who caused and started this conflagration. When Titus had retired the partisans remained quiet for a time, then again attacked the Romans, the garrison of the Sanctuary clashing with those who were putting out the fire in the Inner Temple, and who routed the Jews and chased them as far

43. Reprinted, by permission of the publisher, from Josephus, *The Jewish War,* trans. by G. A. Williamson, revised by E. Mary Smallwood (London: Penguin Classics, 1959; revised edition 1969, 1981), pp. 323–24, 348–50. Copyright © by G. A. Williamson, 1959, 1969; copyright © by E. M. Smallwood, 1981.

44. The Temple.

as the Sanctuary. Then one of the soldiers, without waiting for orders and without a qualm for the terrible consequences of his action but urged on by some unseen force, snatched up a blazing piece of wood and climbing on another soldier's back hurled the brand through a golden aperture giving access to the chambers built round the Sanctuary. As the flames shot into the air the Jews sent up a cry that matched the calamity and dashed to the rescue, with no thought now of saving their lives or husbanding their strength; for that which hitherto they had guarded so devotedly was disappearing before their eyes. . . .

As the legions charged in, neither persuasion nor threat could check their impetuosity: passion alone was in command. Crowded together round the entrances many were trampled by their friends, many fell among the still hot and smoking ruins of the colonnades and died as miserably as the defeated. . . .

Most of the victims were peaceful citizens, weak, and unarmed, butchered wherever they were caught. Round the Altar the heap of corpses grew higher and higher, while down the Sanctuary steps poured a river of blood and the bodies of those killed at the top slithered to the bottom. The soldiers were like men possessed and there was no holding them, nor was there any arguing with the fire.

The Triumph of Titus

Resuming his interrupted journey to Egypt, Titus crossed the desert by the shortest route and arrived at Alexandria. . . . Of the prisoners he ordered the leaders, Simon and John, with 700 of the rank and file picked out for their exceptional stature and physique, to be conveyed to Italy without a moment's delay, intending to display them in his triumphal procession. The voyage went according to plan, and Rome gave him as warm a welcome as it had given his father; but it was a more glorious occasion for Titus because his father himself came out to welcome him. The throng of citizens could not contain their joy when they saw all three together.[45] A few days later they decided to celebrate a single triumph in common in honour of their exploits, though the Senate had decreed a separate triumph for each. Notice was given in advance of the day appointed for the victory procession, and not one person stayed at home out of the immense population of the City: everyone came out and, although there was only standing-room, found a place somewhere, so that there was barely enough room left for the procession itself to pass. . . . It is impossible to give a satisfactory account of the innumerable spectacles, so magnificent in every way one could think of, whether as works of art or varieties of wealth or rarities

45. Vespasian, Titus, and Titus' brother, Domitian.

of nature; almost all the treasures that have ever come one at a time into the hands of fortune's favourites—the priceless marvels of many different peoples—were brought together on that day, showing forth the greatness of the Roman Empire. Masses of silver and gold and ivory in every shape known to the craftsman's art could be seen, not as if carried in procession but like a flowing river. There were hangings borne along, some in the rarest shades of crimson, others embroidered with life-like portraits by Babylonian artists; transparent stones, some set in golden crowns, some in other mounts, were carried past in such numbers that we could see how foolish we had been to suppose any of them rare. In the procession too were images of the Roman gods wonderful in size and of true artistic merit, every one of them made from costly materials; and animals of many kinds were led past, all decked with the proper trappings. Every item in the procession was escorted by a large group of men arrayed in garments of true scarlet dye interwoven with gold; those chosen to take part in the procession itself had about them the choicest and most astonishing wealth of ornament. Furthermore, not even the host of captives went unadorned: under their elaborate and beautiful garments any disfigurement due to physical sufferings was hidden from view.

But what caused the greatest wonder was the structure of the traveling stages; indeed their immense size caused alarm through mistrust of their stability, as many of them were three or even four storeys high, while their lavish equipment was viewed with delighted surprise. Many were hung with curtains interwoven with gold, and all were framed in wrought ivory and gold. Numbers of tableaux showed the successive stages of the war most vividly portrayed. Here was to be seen a smiling countryside laid waste, there whole formations of the enemy put to the sword; men in flight and men led off to captivity; walls of enormous size thrown down by engines, great strongholds stormed, cities whose battlements were lined with defenders utterly overwhelmed, an army streaming inside the ramparts, the whole place reeking of slaughter, those unable to resist raising their hands in supplication, temples set on fire and houses torn down over the heads of their occupants, and after utter desolation and misery rivers flowing, not over tilled fields, supplying drink to men and animals, but through a countryside still blazing on every hand. . . . Placed on each stage was the commander of a captured town just as he had been when captured. A number of ships followed.

Most of the spoils that were carried were heaped up indiscriminately, but more prominent than all the rest were those captured in the Temple at Jerusalem—a golden table weighing several hundredweight, and a lampstand similarly made of gold but differently constructed from those we normally use. The central shaft was fixed to a base, and from it extended slender branches placed like the prongs of a trident, and with the end of each one forged into a lamp: these numbered seven, signifying the honour paid to that number by the Jews. After these was carried the Jewish Law,[46] the last of the spoils. Next came a large group carrying images of Victory, all fashioned of ivory and gold. Behind them drove Vespasian first with Titus behind him: Domitian rode alongside, magnificently adorned himself, and with his horse a splendid sight.

6. Column of Trajan, Rome, 113 (Gardner, p. 229, ill. 6:64 and 6:65; Janson, p. 184, ill. 265)
Tacitus, *Germania:* "Political Customs and Private Life," A.D. 98

The internal security of the Roman empire depended in large part upon the ability of the army to protect its borders. In his effort to establish easily defensible borders at natural boundaries, Augustus had annexed more territory than any Roman ruler before him. At the time of his death in A.D. 14, the Euphrates River formed the eastern frontier; the Sahara Desert provided a formidable barrier along part of the southern frontier; Roman control reached to the Atlantic in the west; and the Rhine and Danube rivers defined the northern border.

The defense of the Rhine-Danube frontier proved a formidable military task. Restless tribes along the northern border maintained constant pressure on the Roman garrisons. The Column of Trajan depicts the Roman campaigns against the Dacians (in modern Romania) between 101 and 106.

The most complete description of the peoples on the northern frontier of the empire is to be found in the writings of Tacitus, the greatest of the Roman historians. Although little is known about his early life, it appears that Cornelius Tacitus (c. A.D. 4–117) was born in the Roman provinces of northern Italy or southern Gaul, grew up in a prosperous family, and received a good education. He entered a public career as an administrator, which culminated with his appointment by Trajan as proconsul of Asia (that is, the Middle East).

In 98, Tacitus wrote *Germania,* a description of the Germanic tribes on the Rhine River. Familiar with the imperial system through firsthand experience, Tacitus looked back longingly to the freedom of the Roman republic and condemned the tyranny of the emperors. In *Germania,* Tacitus emphasizes the simple life-style, moral virtues, and personal freedom of the Germanic tribes and laments the disappearance of these qualities in imperial Roman life. A selection from *Germania,* "Political Customs and Private Life," is presented here.

46. The sacred scrolls of the Torah from the Temple.

Tacitus, *Germania*[47]

Political Customs and Private Life

They take their kings on the ground of birth, their generals on the basis of courage: the authority of their kings is not unlimited or arbitrary; their generals control the people by example rather than command, and by means of the admiration which attends upon energy and a conspicuous place in front of the line. But anything beyond this—capital punishment, imprisonment, even flogging—is permitted only to the priests, and then not as a penalty or under the general's orders, but as an inspiration from the god whom they suppose to accompany them on campaign: certain totems also and emblems are fetched from groves and carried into battle. The strongest incentive to courage lies in this, that neither chance nor casual grouping makes the squadron or the wedge, but family and kinship: close at hand, too, are their dearest, whence is heard the wailing voice of woman and the child's cry: here are the witnesses who are in each man's eyes most precious; here the praise he covets most: they take their wounds to mother and wife, who do not shrink from counting the hurts or demanding a sight of them: they minister to the combatants food and exhortation. . . .

So their life is one of fenced-in chastity. There is no arena with its seductions, no dinner-tables with their provocations to corrupt them. Of the exchange of secret letters men and women alike are innocent; adulteries are very few for the number of the people. Punishment is prompt and is the husband's prerogative: her hair close-cropped, stripped of her clothes, her husband drives her from his house in presence of his relatives and pursues her with a lash through the length of the village. For prostituted chastity there is no pardon; beauty nor youth nor wealth will find her a husband. No one laughs at vice there; no one calls seduction, suffered or wrought, the spirit of the age. Better still are those tribes where only maids marry, and where a woman makes a pact, once for all, in the hopes and vows of a wife; so they take one husband only, just as one body and one life, in order that there may be no second thoughts, no belated fancies: in order that their desire may not be for the man, but for marriage, so to speak; to limit the number of their children, to make away with any of the later children is held abominable, and good habits have more force with them than good laws elsewhere.

47. Reprinted, by permission of the publisher and The Loeb Classical Library, from *Tacitus*, Vol. 1, trans. by M. Hutton, rev. and ed. by E. H. Warmington (Cambridge, Mass.: Harvard University Press, 1970), pp. 141–43, 159–61.

7. *Equestrian Statue of Marcus Aurelius,* c. 165 (Gardner, p. 233, ill. 6:72; Janson, p. 187, ill. 269)
Marcus Aurelius, *Meditations:* "Rules for Living," mid-second century

Marcus Aurelius (121–180) has been called the Roman philosopher-king. The nephew and adopted son of the emperor Antoninus Pius, Marcus Aurelius and his adoptive brother Verus shared the rulership of the Roman empire from the time of Antoninus Pius' death in 161 until Verus' death in 169. Between 169 and 180 Marcus Aurelius ruled alone.

Marcus Aurelius was serious and contemplative, with no genuine relish for power and little personal ambition. He undertook the government of the empire as a duty and devoted himself unstintingly to its service. Drawn to philosophy, he found in Stoicism his chief intellectual interest and his spiritual creed. His writings, called the *Meditations,* reveal that Marcus Aurelius tried to carry out in daily practice the moral precepts of Stoic philosophy.

Written in Greek, the *Meditations* are Marcus Aurelius' thoughts and reflections jotted down in the midst of his military campaigns and his administrative chores and intended for his personal guidance. Sometimes criticized for their lack of originality, the *Meditations* nonetheless restate the Stoic moral creed with a new intensity of feeling. A selection from the *Meditations,* "Rules for Living," is presented here.

The *Equestrian Statue of Marcus Aurelius* represents the emperor as the commander of the legions. It is an irony that the reign of Marcus Aurelius was consumed by matters of war rather than peace. From 161 to 165, Rome was embroiled in war in Syria, and from 167 to 180 in Germany. As emperor, Marcus Aurelius vigorously led his troops to battle while, at the same time, he was introspectively measuring his character against irreproachable standards of conduct.

Marcus Aurelius, *Meditations*[48]

Rules for Living

Begin each day by telling yourself: Today I shall be meeting with interference, ingratitude, insolence, disloyalty, ill will, and selfishness—all of them due to the offenders' ignorance of what is good or evil. But for my part I have long perceived the nature of good and its nobility, the nature of evil and its meanness, and also the nature of the culprit himself, who is my brother (not in the physical sense, but as a fellow-creature similarly endowed with reason and a share of the divine); therefore none of those things can injure me, for nobody can implicate me in what is degrading. Neither

48. Reprinted, by permission of the publisher, from Marcus Aurelius, *Meditations,* trans. by Maxwell Staniforth (London: Penguin Classics, 1964), pp. 45–47, 51. Copyright © by Maxwell Staniforth, 1964.

can I be angry with my brother or fall foul of him; for he and I were born to work together, like a man's two hands, feet, or eyelids, or like the upper and lower rows of his teeth. To obstruct each other is against Nature's law —and what is irritation or aversion but a form of obstruction? . . .

Hour by hour resolve firmly, like a Roman and a man, to do what comes to hand with correct and natural dignity, and with humanity, independence, and justice. Allow your mind freedom from all other considerations. This you can do, if you will approach each action as though it were your last, dismissing the wayward thought, the emotional recoil from the commands of reason, the desire to create an impression, the admiration of self, the discontent with your lot. See how little a man needs to master, for his days to flow on in quietness and piety: he has but to observe these few counsels, and the gods will ask nothing more. . . .

Are you distracted by outward care? Then allow yourself a space of quiet, wherein you can add to your knowledge of the Good and learn to curb your restlessness. Guard also against another kind of error: the folly of those who weary their days in much business, but lack any aim on which their whole effort, nay, their whole thought, is focussed. . . .

In the life of a man, his time is but a moment, his being an incessant flux, his senses a dim rushlight, his body a prey of worms, his soul an unquiet eddy, his fortune dark, and his fame doubtful. In short, all that is of the body is as coursing waters, all that is of the soul as dreams and vapours; life a warfare, a brief sojourning in an alien land; and after repute, oblivion. Where, then, can man find the power to guide and guard his steps? In one thing and one alone: Philosophy.

8. Wall Painting, Villa of the Mysteries, Pompeii, c. A.D. 50 (Gardner, p. 204, ill. 6:28; Janson, p. 174, color plate 24, p. 194, ill. 283)
Apuleius, *The Golden Ass:* "Orgiastic Frenzy," second century

To the growing urban populations of the Roman empire, the ancient agricultural gods of Roman religion became increasingly remote and irrelevant. Although the official cults, and especially the imperial cult, were useful in reinforcing patriotic ties to the state, they failed to provide individuals with a sense of personal involvement and spiritual satisfaction. Romans turned, in ever-increasing numbers, to the mystery religions.

Mystery religions attracted adherents for a variety of reasons. In contrast to the formal ceremonies of traditional Roman cults, the mystery cults emphasized elaborate rituals, which appealed both to the physical senses and to the emotions of the worshipers. Through secret rites, which often included rituals of initiation, self-mortification, and communion with the gods, the believer was cleansed of earthly defilements and roused to spiritual ecstasy. Moreover, the promise of eternal life consoled the believer for the burdens of his present existence.

The mystery religions can be traced back to early Greece, to the elaborate secret ceremonies of Demeter, the Greek earth goddess, and to the disturbing, frenzied worship of Dionysus, god of wine, who was known in Italy as Bacchus. The Dionysiac cult had become widespread in the Mediterranean world during the Hellenistic period. In 186 B.C. reports of the orgiastic rites practiced by cult members alarmed the Senate into passing sharp measures aimed at suppressing the cult. However, the cult continued to attract innumerable adherents.

Other mystery cults entered the Roman world from the Near East. These included those of Cybele, the earth mother, and her consort, Attis, from Asia Minor; of Isis, the mother goddess, and her consort, Osiris, from Egypt; and of Mithra, god of light and truth, from Persia. The allure of the mystery cult is evidenced in Apuleius' novel *The Golden Ass.*

Lucius Apuleius (124–c. 180) was born in the African colony of Madauros (M'Daourouch in modern Algeria). The son of an important and well-to-do local official, Apuleius was educated in Carthage and Athens. He traveled extensively in the East, where he was initiated into the mysteries of Isis and Osiris. After practicing rhetoric in Rome, he returned to Africa and settled in Carthage.

Apuleius wrote a number of philosophical treatises, but his most famous work is *The Golden Ass,* the only Latin novel that has survived intact. Its hero, Lucius, who narrates the story, is accidentally transformed into a jackass and undergoes a variety of adventures, which reveal to him the debauched nature of humankind. He is saved by Isis, through whose aid he resumes his human shape. In gratitude, Lucius devotes himself to the worship of the goddess and experiences her sacred rites.

The selection from *The Golden Ass* presented here, "Orgiastic Frenzy," describes the worship of Atargatis, the Syrian fertility goddess. The ritual performed by the eunuch priests of Atargatis suggests close similarities to the imagery seen in the wall paintings of the Villa of the Mysteries at Pompeii. Both *The Golden Ass* and the murals suggest the ecstatic experiences of the believers of the mystery rites.

Apuleius, *The Golden Ass*[49]

Orgiastic Frenzy

The next morning the eunuch priests prepared to go out on their rounds, all dressed in different colours and looking absolutely hideous, their faces daubed with rouge and their eye-sockets painted to ring out the brightness of their eyes. They wore mitre-shaped birettas, saffron-coloured chasubles, silk surplices, girdles and yellow shoes. . . . They covered the Goddess with a silk mantle and set her on my back, the horn-player struck up and they

49. Reprinted, by permission of A. P. Watt Ltd. on behalf of the Executors of the Estate of Robert Graves, from Apuleius, *The Golden Ass,* trans. by Robert Graves (London: Penguin Classics, 1976), pp. 169–71.

started brandishing enormous swords and maces, and leaping about like maniacs, with their arms bared to the shoulders.

After passing through several hamlets we reached a large country-house where, raising a yell at the gate, they rushed frantically in and danced again. They would throw their heads forward so that their long hair fell down over their faces, then rotate them so rapidly that it wheeled around in a circle. Every now and then they would bite themselves savagely and as a climax cut their arms with the sharp knives that they carried. One of them let himself go more ecstatically than the rest. Heaving deep sighs from the very bottom of his lungs, as if filled with the spirit of the Goddess, he pretended to go stark-mad. . . . He began by making a bogus confession of guilt, crying out in prophetic tones that he had in some way offended against the holy laws of his religion. Then he called on his own hands to inflict the necessary punishment and snatching up one of the whips that these half-men always carry . . . gave himself a terrific flogging. The ground was slippery with the blood that oozed from the knife-cuts and the wounds made by the flying bones. . . . At last they grew tired, or thought that they had cut themselves about enough for the day; so they stopped. The crowd that had gathered competed for the pleasure of dropping money into the open pockets of their robes, and not only small change, but silver, too. They also gave them a barrel of wine, cheese, milk, barley and wheat flour.

9. Colosseum, Rome, A.D. 70–82 (Gardner, p. 217, ills. 6:45 and 6:46; Janson, p. 163, ills. 235–37)
Seneca, *Moral Epistles:* "On the Games," c. A.D. 62–65

Latin literature after the Augustan age frequently expressed the themes of disillusionment and cynicism. To writers and intellectuals, the luxury of imperial Rome appeared to have bred the vices of greed and dissipation, whereas memories of republican Rome recalled the vanished moral virtues of selfless patriotism and steadfast duty. The Roman author Seneca exemplifies this view.

Seneca (4 B.C.–A.D. 65) was the leading intellectual in Rome in the middle of the first century A.D. Orator, tragedian, philosopher, and statesman, Seneca came from a wealthy family in Spain. He entered Roman politics and law. His career was turbulent, but in A.D. 49 he was appointed by the emperor Claudius tutor to his adoptive son and heir, Nero. At Claudius' death in A.D. 54, Nero was only sixteen years old, and Seneca, as his adviser, became one of the most powerful people in Rome.

However, as Nero grew older, he became less content to permit the empire to be governed by others. Sensing that his position was becoming increasingly precarious, Seneca retired in A.D. 62. Three years later, he was accused of involvement in a conspiracy against Nero and was ordered to commit suicide. He did so with dignity and composure.

During his retirement, Seneca wrote a group of 124 letters, called the *Moral*

Epistles, which dealt with a wide range of current topics. Among the subjects of Seneca's pen were the gladiatorial games, a popular form of entertainment subsidized by wealthy patrons. Although they had originated as solemn funeral ceremonies for important individuals, by the time of the Roman empire the games had become bloody, large-scale shows. The dedication of the Colosseum in A.D. 80 by the emperor Titus was marked by one hundred days of gladiatorial events. Even this extravaganza of blood and gore was to be surpassed in the later Roman empire as promoters devised increasingly brutal and bloody shows to satisfy jaded appetites. Seneca vehemently opposed all such gladiatorial contests. A selection from the *Moral Epistles,* "On the Games," is presented here.

Seneca, *Moral Epistles*[50]

On the Games

But nothing is as ruinous to the character as sitting away one's time at a show—for it is then, through the medium of entertainment, that vices creep into one with more than usual ease. What do you take me to mean? That I go home more selfish, more self-seeking and more self-indulgent? Yes, and what is more, a person crueller and less humane through having been in contact with human beings. I happened to go to one of these shows at the time of the lunch-hour interlude, expecting there to be some light and witty entertainment then, some respite for the purpose of affording people's eyes a rest from human blood. Far from it. All the earlier contests were charity in comparison. The nonsense is dispensed with now: what we have now is murder pure and simple. The combatants have nothing to protect them; their whole bodies are exposed to the blows; every thrust they launch gets home. A great many spectators prefer this to the ordinary matches and even to the special, popular demand ones. And quite naturally. There are no helmets and no shields repelling the weapons. What is the point of armour? Or of skill? All that sort of thing just makes the death slower in coming. In the morning men are thrown to the lions and the bears: but it is the spectators they are thrown to in the lunch hour. The spectators insist that each on killing his man shall be thrown against another to be killed in his turn; and the eventual victor is reserved by them for some other form of butchery; the only exit for the contestants is death. Fire and steel keep the slaughter going. And all this happens while the arena is virtually empty.

"But he was a highway robber, he killed a man." And what of it? Granted that as a murderer he deserved this punishment, what have you

50. Reprinted, by permission of the publisher, from Seneca, *Letters from a Stoic,* trans. by Robin Campbell (London: Penguin Classics, 1969), pp. 41–42. Copyright © by Robin Alexander Campbell, 1969.

done, you wretched fellow, to deserve to watch it? "Kill him! Flog him! Burn him! Why does he run at the other man's weapon in such a cowardly way? Why isn't he less half-hearted about killing? Why isn't he a bit more enthusiastic about dying? Whip him forward to get his wounds! Make them each offer the other a bare breast and trade blow for blow on them." And then there is an interval in the show: "Let's have some throats cut in the meantime, so that there's something happening!"

10. *Portrait of a Lady,* c. A.D. 90 (Gardner, p. 232, ill. 6:70; Janson, p. 185, ill. 267)
Juvenal, *Satires:* "Hateful Wives," c. 116
Pliny, *Letters:* "An Admirable Bride," c. 105

Women were relegated to a secondary position in Rome as well as in Greece. During the republican period, the male head of the family was the undisputed master of the household. Before her marriage, a woman was almost completely subordinate to her father or brother; after her marriage her husband took the father's place, and in the case of his death, she became subject to her son. Women could not represent their interests in court, nor could they hold public office. However, the breakdown of the patriarchal system during the imperial period liberated women to some extent. Women achieved a higher legal status and gained greater economic rights.

In literature of the republican period, the Roman matron is praised for her nobility of character, steadfastness of purpose, and willingness to sacrifice her personal interests to the good of her husband and family. In literature of the imperial age, a new ideal for women emerges. Women are praised for their beauty, their knowledge of literature, their wit in conversation, and their accomplishments in fields such as singing, dancing, and poetry.

The elegance and sophistication that were admired by imperial society are reflected in the sculpture *Portrait of a Lady* and in the writings of Juvenal and Pliny.

Juvenal (c. A.D. 60–c. 128) was one of the greatest Roman satirists. According to tradition, Juvenal was born in Aquinum in central Italy. He spent much of his life in Rome, where at times he endured terrible poverty. Late in his life, he published sixteen long satirical poems, in which he bitterly attacked contemporary Roman society. Satire VI is a vicious denunciation of women. In the selection from Satire VI presented here, "Hateful Wives," Juvenal ridicules the physical appearance and personal morals of fashionable women.

Pliny the Younger (A.D. 62–113) was the nephew and adoptive son of the elder Pliny, himself a prolific author. The younger Pliny pursued a career as a civil administrator and held posts both in Rome and in the provinces. Between 100 and 109 he published nine books of literary letters, known as the *Letters.* A tenth book consists of Pliny's official correspondence with the emperor Trajan.

Pliny's letters, which were written with great attention to style, paint a picture of private and public life in the Roman empire. In Book IV of the *Letters,* Pliny writes to his aunt and praises the personal virtues and graceful accomplishments of his young wife, Calpurnia. He assures his aunt that she played so significant a role in raising the orphaned Calpurnia that she might be considered the young woman's father. A selection from the *Letters,* "An Admirable Bride," is presented here.

Juvenal, *Satires*[51]

Hateful Wives

There's nothing a woman won't do, nothing she thinks is disgraceful
With the green gems at her neck, or pearls distending her ear lobes.
Nothing is worse to endure than your Mrs. Richbitch, whose visage
Is padded and plastered with dough, in the most ridiculous manner.
Furthermore, she reeks of unguents, so God help her husband
With his wretched face stunk up with these, smeared by her lipstick
To her lovers she comes with her skin washed clean. But at home
Why does she need to look pretty? Nard[52] is assumed for the lover,
For the lover she buys all the Arabian perfumes.

It takes her some time to strip down to her face, removing the layers
One by one, till at last she is recognizable, almost,
Then she uses a lotion, she-asses' milk; she'd need herds
Of these creatures to keep her supplied on her northernmost journeys.
But when she's given herself the treatment in full, from the ground base
Through the last layer of mud pack, from the first wash to a poultice,
What lies under all this—a human face, or an ulcer? . . .
No Sicilian court is more unjust than her household
If she has made a decision, and wants to appear more becoming
Than her usual style, in a hurry to get to the gardens
Where her somebody waits, or to get to the temple of Isis
(Brothel would be more like it), her hair is put up by a handmaid,
Psecas by name, with her own hair a mess, and naked of shoulder,
Naked of breasts. "Why won't this curl lie flat?" And the cowhide
Takes it out on the maid because of the lack of a cowlick.
Why was that Psecas' fault? Or how in the world could she help it
If the lady found the shape of her own nose disgusting?
Another maid needs both hands to comb her hair and to coil it,
Then there's one more on the staff, who used to work for her mother,
Now more or less retired, but first to express her opinion

51. Reprinted, by permission of the publisher, from Juvenal, *The Satires of Juvenal,* trans. by Rolfe Humphries (Bloomington, Ind: Indiana University Press, 1958), pp. 82–84.

52. A perfumed ointment made from the roots of plants.

By seniority's right; let the younger or awkwarder follow
Taking the floor in due course, as if we had here great questions
Of church or of state, of life or death, not merely the problem
Of the build-up of beauty, hair skyscraper-high on the head.
Look at her from the front—that must be Andromache, surely!
But from the rear she seems a good deal more like a midget.
What can she do if the luck of the draw has assigned her dimensions,
Given her half-pint size, which even high heels can't correct,
So that she has to jump straight up in the air for her kisses?
Meanwhile, she takes no thought for her husband, or what she must cost him,
More like a neighbor than wife, and intimate only in hating
Both his friends and his slaves, and in running up bills.

Pliny, *Letters*[53]

An Admirable Bride

You show us all how we should love our own family. Your brother was a fine man. You loved him as much as he loved you. You now love his daughter as if she were your own. You are not only an aunt to her but also a father.

You will be pleased to know that she is a credit to her father, to you and to her grandfather. She is very sharp and very careful. I am the only man she loves and that shows you what sort of girl she is. She also likes reading literature. She has got this from me. She has all my books which she reads. She has also learnt them by heart.

You should see her when I am about to go to court. How worried she is! When I have finished speaking there, how pleased she is. She sends slaves out into the city. They fly back and tell her how I have got on. She wants to know how often I was clapped and how I won the day.

If I invite my friends to a reading, she sits and listens behind a curtain. When they clap me, she laps up the applause. She has even set some of my poems to music and plays them on the lyre. Love, which is the best teacher in the world, has made her do this. No one else has forced her.

This is why I am sure our happiness will grow as the days go by and last for ever. She is not in love with me as I am nor with my body. This will grow old and weak as time goes by. She loves me for what I stand for. This is just what I would expect from someone who has been educated by

53. Reprinted, by permission of the publisher, from *Pliny: A Selection of his Letters,* trans. by Clarence Greig (Cambridge: Cambridge University Press, 1978), p. 16.

your hands. She has been trained in your camp and she sees only what is holy and honest.

No wonder she has come to love me as you said she would. For you always looked upon my mother as your mother. Even when I was small, it was you who guided me. It was you who praised me. You knew the sort of person I would be. So each of us fall over each other to thank you. I, because you gave her to me, and she because you gave me to her. You would think we had chosen each other.

11. The Pantheon, Rome, 118–125 (Gardner, pp. 221–23, ills. 6:51 to 6:53; Janson, p. 164, ills. 238–41)
Minucius Felix, *Octavius:* "Atrocities of the Christians" and "Superstitions of the Romans," early third century

The Pantheon was built by the emperor Hadrian as a temple to the seven planetary gods—the sun, the moon, Mercury, Venus, Mars, Jupiter, and Saturn. Despite the repeated efforts of the emperors to strengthen the state religion of Rome, its vitality steadily diminished. In 112 Pliny the Younger, who at the time was serving as a provincial governor in Asia Minor, complained to the emperor Trajan that until recently the Roman temples were deserted and that sacrificial animals could not be purchased anywhere.

During the second and third centuries, Christianity, which was identified by the Romans as a mystery cult, spread rapidly. As the new religion gained in numbers and strength, popular hostility mounted. Christians were accused of performing criminal acts such as child murder and cannibalism, and they were suspected of indulging in immoral practices such as sexual orgies and incest. Christian writers responded to the attacks against their faith by defending their beliefs and by criticizing the Roman state religion. One such writer was Minucius Felix.

Although little is known about his life, it appears that Minucius was born in North Africa in the late second century. As a young man, he received an excellent education. He became a lawyer in Rome and took a role in the trials against the Christians. Impressed by the courage of the Christians and the sincerity of their belief, he became a convert. In his book *Octavius* he presents a defense of the faith, which he had embraced.

Octavius is written in the form of a dialogue between two of Minucius' friends, Caecilius and Octavius. Caecilius, a pagan, charges the Christians with a litany of lurid crimes. Octavius, a Christian, replies by characterizing the Roman religion as a collection of superstitions and folktales. The dialogue concludes with Caecilius' recognition of his errors and his acceptance of the Christian faith.

Two selections from *Octavius* are presented here. In the first, "Atrocities of the Christians," Caecilius is the speaker. In the second selection, "Superstitions of the Romans," Octavius offers his reply.

Minucius Felix, *Octavius*[54]

Atrocities of the Christians

Is it not deplorable, then, that fellows . . . belonging to an incorrigible, outlawed, and desperate gang, riot against the gods? Fellows who gather together ignoramuses from the lowest dregs of society, and credulous women, an easy prey because of the instability of their sex, and thus organize an unholy mob of conspirators who become leagued together in nocturnal gatherings, by solemn fasts and atrocious repasts, not by any rite, but by an inexpiable crime—a furtive race which shuns the light, mute in the open but garrulous in the corners. They despise the temples as no better than sepulchres, abominate the gods, sneer at our sacred rites. Pitiable themselves, they pity . . . the priests; half-naked themselves, they spurn positions of honor and purple robes. What strange folly! What incredible insolence! They do not care about present tortures, but dread those of an uncertain future; while they fear death after death, they are not afraid of death here on earth. Thus, deceptive hope soothes their fear with the comforting idea of a future life.

And now—for the evil grows apace—the corruption of morals gains ground from day to day, and throughout the entire world those abominable shrines of this evil confederacy increase in number. This conspiracy must be radically rooted out and execrated. They recognize each other by secret marks and signs and fall in love before they scarcely know each other. Everywhere they practice among themselves, a kind of cult of lust, so to speak, and indiscriminately call each other brothers and sisters, so that even ordinary fornication, under the cloak of a hallowed name, becomes incest. Thus, their vain and insane superstition actually boasts of its crimes.

Concerning the latter, if there were no truth at their base, keen sighted public opinion would not mention such terribly abominable acts which need to be prefaced by an apology. I am told that, because of I know not what foolish belief, they consecrate and worship the head of an ass, the meanest of all animals—a religion worthy of and sprung from such morals. Others tell that they reverence even the genital organs of their bishop and priest, and adore, as it were, the creative power of their parent. This suspicion may be false, but, at any rate, it has been attached to their secret and nocturnal rites. And anyone who says that the objects of their worship are a man who suffered the death penalty for his crime, and the deadly wood of the cross, assigns them altars appropriate for incorrigibly wicked men, so that they actually worship what they deserve.

54. Reprinted, by permission of the publisher, from Minucius Felix, *Octavius,* in *The Fathers of the Church,* Vol. 10 (Washington, D.C.: Catholic University of America Press, 1977), pp. 334–38, 359–60. Selection translated by Rudolph Arbesmann.

And, now, the stories told about the initiation of their novices: they are as detestable as they are notorious. An infant covered with a dough crust to deceive the unsuspecting is placed beside the person to be initiated into their sacred rites. This infant is killed at the hands of the novice by wounds inflicted unintentionally and hidden from his eyes, since he has been urged on as if to harmless blows upon the surface of the dough. The infant's blood—oh, horrible—they sip up eagerly; its limbs they tear to pieces, trying to outdo each other; by this victim they are leagued together; by being privy to this crime they pledge themselves to mutual silence. These sacred rites are more shocking than any sacrilege.

Their form of banqueting is notorious; far and wide everyone speaks of it, . . . On the appointed day, they assemble for their banquets with all their children, sisters, and mothers—people of both sexes and every age. After many sumptuous dishes, when the company at table has grown warm and the passion of incestuous lust has been fired by drunkenness, a dog which has been tied to a lamp stand is tempted by throwing a morsel beyond the length of the leash by which it is bound. It makes a dash, and jumps for the catch. Thus, when the witnessing light has been overturned and extinguished, in the ensuing darkness which favors shamelessness, they unite in whatever revoltingly lustful embraces the hazard of chance will permit. Thus, they are all equally guilty of incest, . . .

Superstitions of the Romans

But, if the universe is governed by Providence and guided by the will of one God, our unsophisticated forefathers, delighted, or rather ensnared by their pet fables, ought not to rush us into agreeing with them. For, they are refuted by the teachings of their own philosophers, bolstered by the authority of reason and tradition. Our ancestors were so ready to believe in any product of imagination that, without critical judgment, they accepted even such monstrous and marvellous wonders as Scylla[55] with many bodies, Chimaera[56] of many shapes, Hydra[57] being reborn from its life-giving wounds, and the Centaurs, beings with the dual nature of horse and man. In short, whatever popular imagination could invent they were eager to hear. What about those old women's tales of human beings turned into birds and wild beasts, and of people transformed into trees and flowers?

55. A sea monster with six heads and twelve feet who lived in a cave on the straits between Italy and Sicily opposite the whirlpool Charybdis. Scylla would devour six sailors from any ship passing too close to her while trying to pass through the straits. Some legends held that at one time she possessed human form.

56. A monster who was part lion, part goat, and part serpent. It was slain by Bellerophon with the aid of the winged horse Pegasus.

57. A hundred-headed serpent monster who was finally slain by Hercules. When one of Hydra's heads was cut off, a new one grew in its place.

If such things had ever happened, they would still happen today; but, since they cannot happen today, they never happened at all. In a similar way, our ancestors were mistaken about their gods; uncritical, credulous, they formed their faith with naive simplicity.

12. *Constantine the Great,* c. 330 (Gardner, p. 242, ill. 6:87; Janson, ill. 188, p. 272)
Eusebius, *The Life of the Blessed Emperor Constantine:* "The Vision of Constantine," c. 337

When the emperor Diocletian retired in 305, the Roman empire, already weakened by the military, political, and economic crises of the third century, was plunged back into chaos. Constantine (280–337), the son of an army officer and a member of the military governing class of the late Roman empire, was proclaimed emperor by the army troops under his command. In the complex civil war that followed, Constantine emerged as the successor of Diocletian. In 312 Constantine defeated his father-in-law, Maxentius, for control of the Western empire; in 324 Constantine defeated his co-ruler, Licinius, for control of the Eastern empire. From 324 until his death Constantine was the sole master of the Roman empire. The colossal statue *Constantine the Great,* originally 30 feet high, symbolized the emperor's absolute mastery.

Constantine restored order to the empire. Under his guidance two decisive actions were taken with far-reaching consequences. First, Constantine moved the capital of the empire from Rome to the city of Byzantium, which he rebuilt on an impressive scale and renamed Constantinople. Second, Constantine converted to Christianity.

In his early life, Constantine was a worshiper first of Hercules and then of Sol Invictus, the sun god. He had visited the Grand Temple of the Sun in the Vosges Mountains of Gaul, where he had experienced his first vision—a pagan one. During his campaign against Maxentius in 312, he experienced his second vision —a lighted cross in the sky. His subsequent victory proved to him the power of the Christian god. Although he was not baptized until he lay on his deathbed, he never wavered in his support of Christianity.

The Life of the Blessed Emperor Constantine is attributed to the Christian historian Eusebius (260–340). About 314 Eusebius became bishop of Caesarea, the Roman capital of Palestine. Impressed by the personal sincerity of the emperor's faith as well as by the political support offered to the Christian church, Eusebius regarded Constantine's reign as the fulfillment of divine providence. A selection from *The Life of the Blessed Emperor Constantine,* "The Vision of Constantine," is presented here.

Eusebius, *The Life of the Blessed Emperor Constantine*[58]

The Vision of Constantine

As soon then as he [Constantine] was established on the throne, he began to care for the interests of his paternal inheritance, and visited with much considerate kindness all those provinces which had previously been under his father's government. Some tribes of the barbarians who dwelt on the banks of the Rhine, and the shores of the Western ocean, having ventured to revolt, he reduced them all to obedience, and brought them from their savage state to one of gentleness and submission. He contented himself with checking the inroads of others, and drove from his dominions, like untamed and savage beasts, those whom he perceived to be altogether incapable of the settled order of civilized life. Having disposed of these affairs to his satisfaction, he directed his attention to other quarters of the world, and first passed over to the British nations, which lie in the very bosom of the ocean. These he reduced to submission, and then proceeded to consider the state of the remaining portions of the empire, that he might be ready to tender his aid wherever circumstances might require it. . . .

Being convinced, however, that he needed some more powerful aid than his military forces could afford him, on account of the wicked and magical enchantments which were so diligently practised by the tyrant, he began to seek for Divine assistance, . . . Accordingly he called on Him with earnest prayer and supplications that He would reveal to him who He was, and stretch forth His right hand to help him in his present difficulties. And while he was thus praying with fervent entreaty, a most marvellous sign appeared to him from heaven. . . . He said that about mid-day, when the sun was beginning to decline, he saw with his own eyes the trophy of a cross of light in the heavens, above the sun, and bearing the inscription, CONQUER BY THIS. At this sight he himself was struck with amazement, and his whole army also, which happened to be following him on some expedition, and witnessed the miracle.

58. Reprinted, by permission of the publisher, from Eusebius, *The Life of the Blessed Emperor Constantine* (London: Samuel Bagster and Sons, 1845), pp. 23–27.

VII

Early Christian, Byzantine, and Islamic Art

EARLY CHRISTIAN ART

1. Painted Ceiling, Catacomb of Saints Peter and Marcellinus, Rome, fourth century (Gardner, p. 251, ill. 7:3; Janson, p. 199, ill. 287)

New Testament, Luke 11:1–13, 29–30: "Prayer and Salvation," late first century A.D.

Christianity is centered on a historical person, Jesus of Nazareth. Although the exact dates of many events in Jesus' life are not known, an approximate chronology can be reconstructed from New Testament sources. It seems that Jesus was born c. 4 B.C., that he began his ministry c. A.D. 27 or 28, and that he was crucified c. A.D. 33. However, Jesus' importance to his believers transcends the particular events of his life. Jesus Christ offered a message of universal compassion, forgiveness, and eternal salvation, and his self-sacrifice provided a compelling vehicle for faith.

A ceiling painting in the catacomb of Saints Peter and Marcellinus in Rome depicts Christ the Savior as the Good Shepherd. Around Christ are four scenes illustrating the story of Jonah from the Old Testament and four standing figures representing persons in the attitude of prayer.

The themes of prayer, faith, and salvation are emphasized in Luke. One of the four Gospels collected in the New Testament, Luke describes Jesus' life and presents Christ as the human-divine Savior whose words and deeds extend love and forgiveness to everyone in need. Although its authorship is open to question, the gospel is attributed to Luke, who was a Gentile convert and a physician. He was not an eyewitness to the gospel events, but he was a companion of the Apostle Paul. Luke appears to have been written in the late first century A.D.

A selection from Luke, "Prayer and Salvation," is presented here. In this selection, Jesus institutes the Lord's Prayer and links Jonah's deliverance from the whale to the salvation which he offered to all.

Luke 11: 1–13, 29–30[1]

Prayer and Salvation

[Jesus] was praying in a certain place, and when he ceased, one of his disciples said to him, "Lord, teach us to pray, as John taught his disciples." And he said to them, "When you pray, say:

'Father, hallowed be thy name. Thy kingdom come. Give us each day our daily bread; and forgive us our sins, for we ourselves forgive every one who is indebted to us; and lead us not into temptation.' "

And he said to them, "Which of you who has a friend will go to him at midnight and say to him, 'Friend, lend me three loaves; for a friend of mine has arrived on a journey, and I have nothing to set before him'; and he will answer from within, 'Do not bother me; the door is now shut, and my children are with me in bed; I cannot get up and give you anything'? I tell you, though he will not get up and give him anything because he is his friend, yet because of his importunity he will rise and give him whatever he needs. And I tell you, Ask, and it will be given you; seek, and you will find; knock, and it will be opened to you. For everyone who asks receives, and he who seeks finds, and to him who knocks it will be opened. What father among you, if his son asks for a fish, will instead of a fish give him a serpent; or if he asks for an egg, will give him a scorpion? If you then, who are evil, know how to give good gifts to your children, how much more will the heavenly Father give the Holy Spirit to those who ask him!"

When the crowds were increasing, he began to say, "This generation is an evil generation; it seeks a sign, but no sign shall be given to it except the sign of Jonah. For as Jonah became a sign to the men of Nineveh, so will the Son of man be to this generation."

2. Old St. Peter's, Rome, c. 333 (Gardner, pp. 252–53, ills. 7:4 and 7:6; Janson, p. 200, ills. 288–90)
Prudentius, *Crowns of Martyrdom, The Passion of the Apostles Peter and Paul:* "Peter—The Apostle's Martyrdom and the Basilica of His Bones," c. 403
The Martyrdom of Perpetua and Felicitas: "Perpetua's Persecution and Death," third century

Almost from its inception, the Christian church was in conflict with Roman secular power. The Christian rejection of the pagan gods and refusal to participate in the cult of emperor worship was regarded as treason by the Roman state.

1. Reprinted, by permission of the Division of Education and Ministry of the National Council of Churches of Christ in the USA, from *The Holy Bible, Revised Standard Version,* op. cit.

Christians were unpopular both with the Roman leaders and the Roman populace, and persecution of them began in the first century and continued, off and on, until the early fourth century.

A turning point in the history of Christianity was reached in 311, when the emperor Galerius, himself once a persecutor, promulgated the Edict of Toleration. This enactment recognized Christianity as a legal religion. In 313 Constantine, together with Licinius, issued the Edict of Milan, which proclaimed a policy of complete religious freedom for the Roman state. The final step was taken by the emperor Theodosius. In 380 he ordered all his subjects to accept the Christian creed formulated at the Council of Nicaea in 325.

The cult of the martyrs became popular during the early Christian period and continued to increase in popularity throughout the Middle Ages. An important destination for pilgrims was the basilica of Old St. Peter's in Rome. Built by the emperor Constantine, Old St. Peter's was constructed at the site where the relics of the apostle Peter were believed to be entombed.

Early Christian tradition describes Peter as having lived in Rome after the death of Christ, as having served the city as its bishop for twenty-five years, and as having been martyred between A.D. 64 and 67 during the reign of Nero. According to legend, Peter was crucified in a head-downward position in the vicinity of the Vatican. Modern archaeological excavations, however, have not been able to confirm the location of Peter's martyrdom and burial.

The deaths suffered by early Christian martyrs such as Peter are described by various Christian authors to serve as illustrious examples of Christian faith. Prudentius (348–c. 405), the greatest Christian Latin poet, wrote the *Crowns of Martyrdom,* consisting of fourteen lyric poems on martyrs. A selection from *The Passion of the Apostles Peter and Paul,* in the *Crowns of Martyrdom,* "Peter—The Apostle's Martyrdom and the Basilica of His Bones," is presented here.

The dramatic martyrdom of two Christian women, Perpetua and Felicitas, in Tunisia, Africa, in 202 is described in an anonymous document from the third century. Perpetua was a young noblewoman, and Felicitas was her slave girl. At her trial, Perpetua resolutely chose to renounce her parents, relinquish her infant son, and sacrifice her life rather than to renounce her faith. In prison, Perpetua experienced several apocalyptic visions of paradise. She faced her death in the arena of Carthage. A selection from *The Martyrdom of Perpetua and Felicitas,* "Perpetua's Persecution and Death," is presented here. The body of the text is narrated by Perpetua in the first person. The introductory paragraph and concluding description of Perpetua's death are recounted in the third person by the anonymous author of the text.

Prudentius, *Crowns of Martyrdom: The Passion of the Apostles Peter and Paul*[2]

Peter—The Apostle's Martyrdom and the Basilica of His Bones

Sentence fell . . . upon Peter, condemned by the laws of cruel Nero
To die, upon a lofty tree suspended.
Fearing, however, to rival the glory won by his Lord and Master
By death upon a towering wooden gibbet,
He was resolved to be nailed with his feet in the air and head bent downward
So that the crown unto the base extended.
Straightway his hands were then fastened below and his feet turned toward the summit,
His soul more noble as his frame was humbled.
Mindful that heaven is wont to be reached from a lowly place more quickly,
He bowed his head in giving up his spirit.
On the right bank [of the Tiber River] in a golden basilica lie the bones of Peter,
Mid olives gray and near a purling fountain.
Water that trickles from springs on the hilltop sustains this lively streamlet,
Forever fruitful of the holy chrism.
Now through a channel of marble it rushes and moistens all the hillside,
At last emerging in a verdent basin.
Down in the lowermost part of the underground crypt the stream falls loudly
Into a deep and icy pool of water.
Bright-hued mosaics above are reflected upon its glassy surface,
The gold is tinged with green from shining mosses,
While in the shades of the water is mirrored the overhanging purple;
The ceiling seems to dance upon the billows.
There the great Shepherd now laves in this icy cold pool of living waters
The sheep that thirst for Christ's eternal fountains.

2. Reprinted, by permission of the publisher, from Prudentius, *The Poems of Prudentius,* in *The Fathers of the Church,* Vol. 43 (Washington, D.C.: The Catholic University of America Press, 1962), pp. 261–63. Selection translated by M. Clement Eagan.

3. A specially consecrated oil used by Greek and Roman churches in several of the Sacraments.

The Martyrdom of Perpetua and Felicitas[4]

Perpetua's Persecution and Death

[*Narrator:*]

A number of young catechumens[5] were arrested, Revocatus and his fellow slave Felicitas, Saturninus and Secundulus, and with them Vibia Perpetua, a newly married woman of good family and upbringing. Her mother and father were still alive and one of her two brothers was a catechumen like herself. She was about twenty-two years old and had an infant son at the breast. (Now from this point on the entire account of her ordeal is her own, according to her own ideas and in the way that she herself wrote it down.)

[*Perpetua:*]

While we were still under arrest (she said) my father out of love for me was trying to persuade me and shake my resolution. "Father," said I, "do you see this vase here, for example, or waterpot or whatever?"

"Yes, I do," said he.

And I told him: "Could it be called by any other name than what it is?"

And he said: "No."

"Well, so too I cannot be called anything other than what I am, a Christian."

At this my father was so angered by the word "Christian" that he moved towards me as though he would pluck my eyes out. But he left it at that and departed, vanquished along with his diabolical arguments.

For a few days afterwards I gave thanks to the Lord that I was separated from my father, and I was comforted by his absence. During these few days I was baptized, and I was inspired by the Spirit not to ask for any other favour after the water but simply the perseverance of the flesh. A few days later we were lodged in the prison; and I was terrified, as I had never before been in such a dark hole. What a difficult time it was! With the crowd the heat was stifling; then there was the extortion of the soldiers; and to crown all, I was tortured with worry for my baby there.

Then Tertius and Pomponius, those blessed deacons[6] who tried to take care of us, bribed the soldiers to allow us to go to a better part of the prison

4. Reprinted, by permission of Oxford University Press, from Herbert Musurillo, ed., *The Acts of the Christian Martyrs* (Oxford: Clarendon Press, 1972), pp. 109–11, 125–26, 129, 131.

5. The name given in the early Christian church to those undergoing instruction prior to baptism.

6. The rank in the Christian ministry below priest (presbyter). Their responsibilities included care for the physical well-being of those in need.

to refresh ourselves for a few hours. Everyone then left that dungeon and shifted for himself. I nursed my baby, who was faint from hunger. In my anxiety I spoke to my mother about the child, I tried to comfort my brother, and I gave the child in their charge. I was in pain because I saw them suffering out of pity for me. These were the trials I had to endure for many days. Then I got permission for my baby to stay with me in prison. At once I recovered my health, relieved as I was of my worry and anxiety over the child. My prison had suddenly become a palace, so that I wanted to be there rather than anywhere else.

Then my brother said to me: "Dear sister, you are greatly privileged; surely you might ask for a vision to discover whether you are to be condemned or freed."

Faithfully I promised that I would, for I knew that I could speak with the Lord, whose great blessings I had come to experience. And so I said: "I shall tell you tomorrow." Then I made my request and this was the vision I had.

I saw a ladder of tremendous height made of bronze, reaching all the way to the heavens, but it was so narrow that only one person could climb up at a time. To the sides of the ladder were attached all sorts of metal weapons: there were swords, spears, hooks, daggers, and spikes; so that if anyone tried to climb up carelessly or without paying attention, he would be mangled and his flesh would adhere to the weapons.

At the foot of the ladder lay a dragon of enormous size, and it would attack those who tried to climb up and try to terrify them from doing so. And Saturus was the first to go up, he who was later to give himself up of his own accord. He had been the builder of our strength, although he was not present when we were arrested. And he arrived at the top of the staircase and he looked back and said to me: "Perpetua, I am waiting for you. But take care; do not let the dragon bite you."

"He will not harm me," I said, "in the name of Christ Jesus." Slowly, as though he were afraid of me, the dragon stuck his head out from underneath the ladder. Then, using it as my first step, I trod on his head and went up.

Then I saw an immense garden, and in it a grey-haired man sat in shepherd's garb; tall he was, and milking sheep. And standing around him were many thousands of people clad in white garments. He raised his head, looked at me, and said: "I am glad you have come, my child."

He called me over to him and gave me, as it were, a mouthful of the milk he was drawing; and I took it into my cupped hands and consumed it. And all those who stood around said: "Amen!" At the sound of this word I came to, with the taste of something sweet still in my mouth. I at once told this to my brother, and we realized that we would have to suffer, and that from now on we would no longer have any hope in this life. . . .

[*Narrator:*]

The day of their victory dawned, and they marched from the prison to the amphitheatre joyfully as though they were going to heaven, with calm faces, trembling, if at all, with joy rather than fear. Perpetua went along with shining countenance and calm step, as the beloved of God, as a wife of Christ, putting down everyone's stare by her own intense gaze. . . .

For the young women, however, the Devil had prepared a mad heifer. This was an unusual animal, but it was chosen that their sex might be matched with that of the beast. So they were stripped naked, placed in nets and thus brought out into the arena. Even the crowd was horrified when they saw that one was a delicate young girl and the other was a woman fresh from childbirth with the milk still dripping from her breasts. And so they were brought back again and dressed in unbelted tunics.

First the heifer tossed Perpetua, and she fell on her back. Then sitting up she pulled down the tunic that was ripped along the side so that it covered her thighs, thinking more of her modesty than of her pain. Next she asked for a pin to fasten her untidy hair: for it was not right that a martyr should die with her hair in disorder, lest she might seem to be mourning in her hour of triumph. . . . But the mob asked that their bodies be brought out into the open that their eyes might be the guilty witnesses of the sword that pierced their flesh. And so the martyrs got up and went to the spot of their own accord as the people wanted them to, and kissing one another they sealed their martyrdom with the ritual kiss of peace. . . .

Perpetua, however, had yet to taste more pain. She screamed as she was struck on the bone; then she took the trembling hand of the young gladiator and guided it to her throat. It was as though so great a woman, feared as she was by the unclean spirit, could not be dispatched unless she herself were willing.

3. *Priestess Celebrating the Rites of Bacchus,* leaf of an ivory diptych of the Nicomachi and the Symmachi, c. 380–400 (Gardner, p. 262, ill. 7:19; Janson, p. 207, ill. 303)

Zosimus, *Modern History:* "The Impiety of Serena and the Romans," c. 498

In spite of the Emperor Theodosius' adoption of Christianity as the state religion and his ban of all forms of pagan worship, paganism persisted. Pagan philosophy continued to be taught in the schools of Athens; Stoicism, with its high ideal of personal conduct, and Neoplatonism, with its abstract formulations of theoretical concepts, appealed to educated people. The mystery cults exercised a strong emotional hold over their followers, and Roman patriotism encouraged loyalty to the

Greco-Roman gods who were believed to have been responsible for the city's greatness. The ivory plaque *Priestess Celebrating the Rites of Bacchus* illustrates the survival of pagan worship as well as of Classical ideals of beauty.

During the fifth century, the Roman armies were no longer able to protect Rome or its empire from the onslaught of barbarian invasions. In 410, the Visigoths, a Germanic tribe, captured and sacked Rome. It was the first time since the Gauls attacked it, in 390 B.C., that Rome had been entered by a foreign army.

The fall of Rome was described by the last of the pagan historians, Zosimus (fifth century). Little is known of his life except that he was an imperial official and that he composed a history of "recent" times. His *Modern History,* which was completed sometime after 498, covered the period of the Roman empire from Augustus to 410.

A selection from the *Modern History,* "The Impiety of Serena and the Romans," is presented here. In this selection, Zosimus relates the final events that preceded Rome's fall. Serena was the niece of the emperor Theodosius, who had died in 395, and was the widow of Stilicho, who had served as regent to the young emperor Honorius until his murder in 408 by his soldiers. Serena was accused of conspiring against Rome with Alaric, the leader of the Visigoths, and was executed. Zosimus notes that, although the charge of treason was false, Serena was guilty of impiety toward the pagan gods and that her death was therefore justified. He further blames the sack of Rome upon the people's desertion of their ancestral religion. Nonetheless, pagan religion virtually disappeared within the Roman empire between the fifth and ninth centuries.

Zosimus, *Modern History*[7]

The Impiety of Serena and the Romans

Alaric was already in the vicinity of Rome and had laid its inhabitants under siege. The Senate began to hold Serena under suspicion as if she had influenced the barbarians to attack the city: unanimously it (together with the Emperor's sister by the same father, Placidia) decided that Serena be put to death as being responsible for the current woes; for, they thought, with Serena out of the way Alaric himself would take leave of the city, there being no one left that he could expect would betray it to him. Now in fact this suspicion was false, for nothing of the sort had entered Serena's head; but she paid the penalty proper to her impiety toward the gods, which impiety I am now going to narrate. When the elder Theodosius had put down the tyranny of Eugenius, he came to Rome and instilled in everyone contempt for the sacred rites by denying the use of public funds for the sacrifices. Priests and priestesses alike

7. Reprinted, by permission of the publisher, from *Zosimus: Historia Nova,* trans. by James J. Buchanan and Harold T. Davis (San Antonio, Texas: Trinity University Press, 1967), pp. 235–38.

were expelled and the shrines were forsaken, deprived of religious ceremonies. At that time, then, Serena, making light of this, desired to see the temple of the Great Mother.[8] Spying the necklace on the image of Rhea, an ornament worthy of her divine cult, she removed it from the image and placed it around her own neck. And when an old woman, the last of the Vestal Virgins,[9] upbraided this impiety to her face, she mocked her and ordered her attendants to eject her. As the woman descended she called down upon the heads of Serena and her husband and her children everything and all things that her impiety deserved. But Serena, taking no notice of this, left the shrine sporting the necklace. Thereafter oftentimes there came a dream by night or a vision by day warning her of her impending death, and several others and visitations very similar to hers. To such an extent did Iustitia,[10] who pursues the impious, prevail in fulfilling her office that even though Serena knew what was coming she took no precautions but placed at the disposal of the noose that very neck around which she had hung the goddess' ornament. . . .

However, not even Serena's death budged Alaric from his siege, but he encircled the city and all its gates and, by occupying the Tiber River, prevented the sending up of supplies from the harbor. . . .

When the envoys reached Alaric they were ashamed of the ignorance which had for so long a time gripped the Romans, but they announced the Senate's business. Alaric listened, above all to the statement that the people were under arms and prepared for battle, and replied, "Thick grass is more easily cut than thin." At this utterance he let loose upon the envoys a big belly-laugh. When they turned to discussions about a peace he employed language that surpassed even a barbarian's insolence, for he said that he would under no circumstances put an end to the siege unless he received all the gold which the city possessed and all the silver, plus all the movables he might find throughout the city as well as the barbarian slaves. When one of the envoys asked, "If you should take all these things, what would be left over for those who are inside the city?" he answered, "Their lives." Upon receipt of this answer the envoys sought permission to consult with those inside the city as to what should be done. Permission granted, they reported back what words had been exchanged in their mission. Then it was that the Romans were convinced that the man who was making war on them was Alaric, and, despairing of all things that pertain to human strength, they recalled the resources which the city had formerly known in times of crisis and of which they were now bereft because they had violated the ancestral rites.

8. Rhea Cybele, identified by the Romans as the earth mother.
9. The servants of the shrine of Vesta, the goddess of the hearth.
10. The goddess of justice.

4. *The Parting of Lot and Abraham,* mosaic from Santa Maria Maggiore, Rome, c. 430 (Gardner, p. 227, ill. 7:12; Janson, p. 204, ill. 298)

Augustine, *The City of God:* "The Two Cities," c. 412–426

Zosimus' claim that the sack of Rome by Alaric in 410 was caused by neglect of the pagan gods was refuted by Augustine in *The City of God.* Together with Jerome, Ambrose, and Gregory the Great (Pope Gregory I), Augustine (354–430) is known as one of the four Fathers of the Christian church. *The City of God,* written between c. 412 and 426, is considered one of the greatest treatises of Christian theology. In it Augustine argued that the fall of Rome was not the result of Rome's neglect of its ancestral religion but the consequence of its ancient crimes, including paganism and its persecution of Christians.

Augustine was born in a small town in North Africa and was raised in a middle-class family. His father was a pagan, and his mother was a devout Christian. When he was sixteen, Augustine was sent to Carthage for an education. There he alternated between frantic indulgence in sensual pleasures and feverish devotion to study, reading the Classical philosophers and poets, as well as the Scriptures. Unpersuaded by the faith of the Christian church, he adopted Manichaeanism, a dualistic system of thought which explained God as light and evil as darkness.

Augustine's conversion to Christianity occurred suddenly one summer day in Milan in 386. Seated alone in a garden he heard a child's voice chant the words "Take up and read." Augustine rushed into the house, opened the Bible at random, and read from Romans 13:14, in which Paul admonished his readers to put aside their physical desires and to accept Christ. Suddenly, Augustine's long years of spiritual torment and personal struggle were ended. The following year Augustine was baptized.

Dismissing the woman who had lived with him for seventeen years and who had borne him a son, Augustine returned to Africa, where he and a few friends led a life of secluded study and contemplation. He was ordained in 391, and in 395 he became bishop of the city of Hippo (near modern Bône in northeast Algeria). He died in 430 during the Vandal siege of that city.

Although most of his time was occupied by his duties as bishop, Augustine was a prolific writer. In *The City of God,* he drew a picture of two communities, which he called, metaphorically, the Earthly City and the Heavenly City (the City of God). The Earthly City is the community of unbelief; its members are moved by a love of self, and they behave according to their physical appetites. The Heavenly City is a community of faith; its members are moved by the love of God, and they behave according to their spiritual aspirations. Although the members of these two communities are intermixed in the present world, they are destined for separate fates. The first will suffer eternal damnation; the second will find eternal peace with God. According to Augustine, history is a drama revolving around the constant struggle between the two. A selection from *The City of God,* "The Two Cities," is presented here.

The division of the world into two spiritual communities is suggested in the church of Santa Maria Maggiore in Rome in the mosaic *The Parting of Lot and Abraham.* To the right, Lot leads his family toward Sodom, the city of sinners, while to the left Abraham, together with his yet unborn son, Isaac, proceeds to Canaan, where he lives in accordance with God's will.

Augustine, *City of God*[11]

The Two Cities

I have already said, in previous Books, that God had two purposes in deriving all men from one man. His first purpose was to give unity to the human race by the likeness of nature. His second purpose was to bind mankind by the bond of peace, through blood relationship, into one harmonious whole. I have said further that no member of this race would ever have died had not the first two—one created from nothing and the second from the first—merited this death by disobedience. The sin which they committed was so great that it impaired all human nature—in this sense, that the nature has been transmitted to posterity with a propensity to sin and a necessity to die. Moreover, the kingdom of death so dominated men that all would have been hurled, by a just punishment, into a second and endless death had not some been saved from this by the gratuitous grace of God. This is the reason why, for all the difference of the many and very great nations throughout the world in religion and morals, language, weapons, and dress, there exist no more than the two kinds of society, which, according to our Scriptures, we have rightly called the two cities. One city is that of men who live according to the flesh. The other is of men who live according to the spirit. Each of them chooses its own kind of peace and, when they attain what they desire, each lives in the peace of its own choosing. . . .

What we see, then, is that two societies have issued from two kinds of love. Worldly society has flowered from a selfish love which dared to despise even God, whereas the communion of saints is rooted in a love of God that is ready to trample on self. In a word, this latter relies on the Lord, whereas the other boasts that it can get along by itself. The city of man seeks the praise of men, whereas the height of glory for the other is to hear God in the witness of conscience. The one lifts up its head in its own boasting; the other says to God: "Thou art my glory, thou liftest up my head."

In the city of the world both the rulers themselves and the people they dominate are dominated by the lust for domination; whereas in the City of God all citizens serve one another in charity, whether they serve by the

11. Reprinted, by permission of the publisher, from Augustine, *The City of God,* in *The Fathers of the Church,* Vol. 7 (Washington, D.C.: Catholic University of America Press, 1952), pp. 347, 410–11. Selection translated by Gerald G. Walsh and Grace Monahan.

responsibilities of office or by the duties of obedience. The one city loves its leaders as symbols of its own strength; the other says to its God: "I love thee, O Lord, my strength." Hence, even the wise men in the city of man live according to man, and their only goal has been the goods of their bodies or of the mind or of both; though some of them have reached a knowledge of God, "they did not glorify him as God or give thanks but became vain in their reasonings, and their senseless minds have been darkened. For while professing to be wise" (that is to say, while glorying in their own wisdom, under the domination of pride), "they have become fools, and they have changed the glory of the incorruptible God for an image made like to corruptible man and to birds and four-footed beasts and creeping things" (meaning that they either led their people, or imitated them, in adoring idols shaped like these things), "and they worshiped and served the creature rather than the Creator who is blessed forever." In the City of God, on the contrary, there is no merely human wisdom, but there is a piety which worships the true God as He should be worshiped and has as its goal that reward of all holiness whether in the society of saints on earth or in that of angels of heaven, which is "that God may be all in all."

BYZANTINE ART

1. *Justinian and Attendants,* apse mosaic from San Vitale, c. 547 (Gardner, p. 274, ill. 7:36; Janson, p. 219, ill. 310)
Corpus Juris Civilis, The Digest of Justinian: "The Authority of the Emperor" and "The Status of Persons," 533

Throughout the fifth century, the Roman empire was subjected to invasion by barbarian tribes. In addition to the Visigoths, the Vandals, Franks, Burgundians, Anglo-Saxons, and Huns moved across the frontiers of the empire in search of land, loot, and food. By the end of the fifth century, control of Italy and Rome had passed to a German king, Theodoric, and his tribe, the Ostrogoths.

But while the Western empire disintegrated, the Eastern empire survived the upheavals. Not only were the Byzantine emperors successful in retaining control of their territories in the East, several also tried to extend their empire to include portions of the West. Between 535 and 540, Italy was conquered by the Byzantine general Belisarius, for the emperor Justinian. The city of Ravenna in northern Italy became the center of government during the brief period of Byzantine domination that followed.

Justinian (483–565) was born near Skopje in southeast Yugoslavia. The nephew and adopted heir of Justin, an illiterate soldier who rose through the ranks of the imperial army to become emperor, Justinian ruled the Byzantine empire for thirty-eight years.

Justinian was a vigorous military campaigner abroad and a methodical administrator at home. His greatest achievement was his codification of law, the *Corpus Juris Civilis,* done at his instigation by a commission of expert jurists. The purpose of this codification was to collect the Roman laws that had accumulated for centuries and to resolve the controversies in the mass of confusing and contradictory legal interpretations that had developed. At the same time, the codification was intended to provide a systematic legal basis for governing an empire that was no longer pagan but Christian.

The *Corpus Juris Civilis* consists of four parts, the most important of which is the *Pandects,* or *The Digest of Justinian,* a collection of abstracts from writings of the most famous Roman jurists, to which Justinian gave the effect of substantive law. Almost every modern nation has developed a legal system based on or influenced by the *Digest.*

Two selections from *The Digest of Justinian* are presented here. In the first, "The Authority of the Emperor," the law of the Byzantine empire is related to divine law. In the second selection, "The Status of Persons," the opinions of several Roman jurists regarding the legal status of different classes of persons are collected and presented systematically. These jurists include Gaius, Hermogenianus, Florentinus, Marcianus, Paulus, Papinianus, and Ulpianus.

Justinian is depicted in an apse mosaic, *Justinian and Attendants,* in the church of San Vitale in Ravenna. The emperor is shown surrounded by twelve representatives of the army, church, and state. The identification of Justinian with Christ, who gathered twelve disciples around him, suggests the divine sanction claimed by the Byzantine emperor to exercise the authority of the law.

Corpus Juris Civilis, The Digest of Justinian[12]

The Authority of the Emperor

Governing under the authority of God our empire, which was delivered to us by His Heavenly Majesty, we prosecute wars with success, we adorn peace, we bear up the frame of the State, and we so lift up our minds in contemplation of the aid of the omnipotent Deity that we do not put our trust in our arms, nor in our soldiers, nor in our leaders in war, nor in our own skill, but we rest all our hopes in the providence of the Supreme Trinity alone, from whence proceeded the elements of the whole universe, and their disposition throughout the orb of the world was derived. Whereas then there is in all things nothing found so worthy of respect as the authority of enacted law, which disposes well things both divine and human, and expels all iniquity, and yet we find the whole course of our

12. Reprinted, by permission of the publisher, from *The Digest of Justinian,* Vol. 1, trans. by Charles Henry Munro (Cambridge: Cambridge University Press, 1904), pp. xiii and 24–26.

statutes, such as they come down from the foundation of the city of Rome and from the days of Romulus, to be in a state of such confusion that they reach to an infinite length and surpass the bounds of all human capacity, it was therefore our first desire to make a beginning with the most sacred Emperors of old times, to amend their statutes, and to put them in a clear order, so that they might be collected together in one book, and being divested of all superfluous repetition and most inequitable disagreement, might afford to all mankind the ready resource of their unalloyed character.

The Status of Persons

1. Gaius (*Institutes* 1) All law in force amongst us deals with either persons, or things, or actions.

2. Hermogenianus (*Epitomes of law* 1) Seeing then that all law has been established for the sake of mankind, we will discuss first personal status, then the remaining subjects, following the arrangement of the *Edictum perpetuum,*[13] and joining to the above the titles next in order and connected therewith, so far as the nature of the subject allows.

3. Gaius (*Institutes* 1) Now the main division of the law of persons is this, that all human beings are either free or slaves.

4. Florentinus (*Institutes* 9) Liberty is the natural power of doing what anyone is disposed to do, save so far as a person is prevented by force or by law. 1. Slavery is a creation of the *jus gentium*[14] by which a man is subjected, contrary to nature, to ownership on the part of another. 2. Slaves are called *servi* because military commanders commonly sell their captives and so *preserve* them instead of killing them; 3. they are called *mancipia*[15] because they are taken by the hands of their enemies.

5. Marcianus (*Institutes* 10) Now all slaves have one and the same legal condition; of free men some are *ingenui,* some are *libertini.* 1. Slaves become subjects of ownership either by the civil law or by the *jus gentium;* by the civil law, a man over twenty years of age becomes a slave by allowing

13. An authoritative edition of all the legal rules decreed by various Roman magistrates. It was composed for the emperor Hadrian by the jurist Salvius Julianus c. 130. After this time, the right of magistrates to decree new edicts was abolished.

14. The law of nations. Initially, the legal rules that governed the relationship between states in war and peace, the *ius gentium* came to include those aspects of Roman law that dealt with foreigners who might be engaged in trade with the empire or who might become its subjects through conquest.

15. Literally, "those taken by the hand." To emancipate is to free someone from this status.

himself to be sold in order to have a share in the purchase-money; by the *jus gentium* people own as slaves those who are captured from their enemies or who are born from their female slaves. 2. Persons are *ingenui* who are born of a free mother; it is enough that the mother should be free at the moment when the child is born, though she should have been a slave at the time of conception. Even in the converse case, where she is free at conception, but a slave at the time of the birth, the law is that the child is born free; and it matters not whether the mother conceived in lawful wedlock or in random intercourse; the mother's ill fortune ought not to prejudice the unborn child. 3. Hence arose this question:—if a slavewoman is manumitted, being with child at the time, and after that is reduced to slavery again, or sent into banishment, and then gives birth to a child, is the child free or a slave? However, the view which has found deserved favour is that the child is born free, and that it is sufficient for the unborn child that the mother was free at some time or other during the period of pregnancy.

6. Gaius (*Institutes* 1) *Libertini* are those who have been manumitted out of lawful slavery.

7. Paulus (on the portions allowed to children of condemned persons). An unborn child is taken care of just as much as if it were in existence, in any case in which the child's own advantage comes in question; though no one else can derive any benefit through the child before its birth.

8. Papinianus (*Questions* 3) The Emperor Titus Antoninus laid down that the position of children is not prejudiced by the terms of a badly drawn instrument.

9. The Same (*ibid.* 31) There are many points in our law in respect of which women are in a worse legal position than men.

10. Ulpianus (*on Sabinus* 1) The question has been asked:—according to which sex are hermaphrodites to be treated? but I should say on the whole that they ought to be treated as having the sex which predominates in them.

11. Paulus (*Responsa* 18) Paulus gave the opinion that where a boy was conceived in the lifetime of the father (of his mother), but without such father being aware of the connexion formed by his daughter, then, even though the boy should be born after the death of such grandfather, he is not to be held to be the lawful son of the man who begot him.

12. The Same (*ibid.* 19) It is now generally admitted on the authority of the very learned physician Hippocrates that a completely formed child may be born in seven months (*septimo mense*); it may be therefore held that a boy who is born in lawful marriage in seven months is a lawful son.

13. Hermogenianus (*Epitomes of law* 1) Where a slave is given up by his owner to the fortune of a trial at law in a capital case, though he should be acquitted, he does not become free.

14. Paulus (*Sentences* 4) We cannot apply the word "children" (*liberi*) to offspring which is born fashioned in some way which is contrary to the normal form of the human species; for instance, where a woman is delivered of something monstrous or portentous. But any offspring which exceeds the natural number of limbs used by man may in a sense be said to be fully formed, and will therefore be reckoned among children.

2. Anthemius of Tralles and Isidorus of Miletus, Hagia Sophia, Constantinople, 532–537 (Gardner, pp. 278–80, ills. 7:41 to 7:44; Janson, pp. 220–21, ills. 312–17)
Procopius, *History of the Wars:* "The Nika Revolt," mid-sixth century

During his long reign, Justinian was almost constantly at war. The greatest threat to his rule, however, was posed by an internal uprising called the Nika revolt.

The internal policies pursued by Justinian alienated a large segment of the population in Constantinople. He attempted to raise public morals by banning all games and spectacles and to save money by eliminating some municipal services. In addition, he alienated members of the bureaucracy by decreeing that officials could not buy or sell government offices or acquire property while in office. In 532, public discontent reached a fever pitch. Two factions in Constantinople, called the Blues and the Greens, attacked police and government officials, freed prisoners from jail, marched on the palace, and proclaimed a rival to Justinian as emperor. Justinian's throne was saved by the determination of his wife, the empress Theodora. As Justinian and his officials discussed a means of escape, Theodora refused to flee. She rallied the court by declaring that she would prefer to die in the imperial palace rather than live in ignominious exile. With the help of their generals, Justinian and Theodora suppressed the insurrection.

The church of Hagia Sophia[16] in Constantinople symbolized the throne where the Byzantine emperor received his divine authority to rule. The original church of Hagia Sophia was burned during the Nika revolt. In order to efface the memory of the rebellion, Justinian lavished funds upon the construction of a magnificent new building to replace it. The result was the impressive structure now called Aya Sofya, which has been used successively as a church, mosque, and museum.

16. "Holy Wisdom."

The Nika revolt is described by the historian Procopius (late fifth to mid-sixth centuries). Between 527 and 540, Procopius accompanied the imperial army on military campaigns to Persia, North Africa, and Italy. He wrote an extended account of the emperor Justinian, his military actions, and his government policies in *History of the Wars.* A selection from *History of the Wars,* "The Nika Revolt," is presented here.

Procopius, *History of the Wars*[17]

The Nika Revolt

At this same time an insurrection broke out unexpectedly in Byzantium among the populace, and, contrary to expectation, it proved to be a very serious affair, . . .

But at this time the officers of the city administration in Byzantium were leading away to death some of the rioters. But the members of the two factions, conspiring together and declaring a truce with each other, seized the prisoners and then straightway entered the prison and released all those who were in confinement there, whether they had been condemned on a charge of stirring up sedition, or for any other unlawful act. And all the attendants in the service of the city government were killed indiscriminately; meanwhile, all of the citizens who were sane-minded were fleeing to the opposite mainland, and fire was applied to the city as if it had fallen under the hand of an enemy. The sanctuary of Sophia and the baths of Zeuxippus, and the portion of the imperial residence from the propylaea as far as the so-called House of Ares were destroyed by fire, and besides these both the great colonnades which extended as far as the market place which bears the name of Constantine, in addition to many houses of wealthy men and a vast amount of treasure. During this time the emperor and his consort with a few members of the senate shut themselves up in the palace and remained quietly there. Now the watchword which the populace passed around to one another was Nika,[18] and the insurrection has been called by this name up to the present time. . . .

Now the emperor and his court were deliberating as to whether it would be better for them if they remained or if they took to flight in the ships. And many opinions were expressed favouring either course. And the Empress Theodora also spoke to the following effect: "As to the belief that a woman ought not to be daring among men or to assert herself boldly among those who are holding back from fear, I consider that the present crisis most certainly does not permit us to discuss whether the matter

17. Reprinted, by permission of the publisher and The Loeb Classical Library, from Procopius, *History of the Wars,* trans. by H. B. Dewing (Cambridge, Mass.: Harvard University Press, 1954), Vol. 1, pp. 219, 221–22, 231–32.

18. "Conquer!"

should be regarded in this or in some other way. For in the case of those whose interests have come into the greatest danger nothing else seems best except to settle the issue immediately before them in the best possible way. My opinion then is that the present time, above all others, is inopportune for flight, even though it bring safety. For while it is impossible for a man who has seen the light not also to die, for one who has been an emperor it is unendurable to be a fugitive. May I never be separated from this purple,[19] and may I not live that day on which those who meet me shall not address me as mistress. If, now, it is your wish to save yourself, O Emperor, there is no difficulty. For we have much money, and there is the sea, here the boats. However consider whether it will not come about after you have been saved that you would gladly exchange that safety for death. For as for myself, I approve a certain ancient saying that royalty is a good burial-shroud." When the queen had spoken thus, all were filled with boldness, and, turning their thoughts towards resistance, they began to consider how they might be able to defend themselves if any hostile force should come against them.

3. *Theodora and Attendants,* apse mosaic from San Vitale, c. 547 (Gardner, p. 274, ill. 7:37; Janson, p. 211, color plate 29)
Procopius, *The Secret History:* "Theodora—A Shameless Woman," mid-sixth century

Praise was replaced by bitter hatred in Procopius' succeeding book, *The Secret History.* Procopius described *The Secret History* as a supplement to *History of the Wars.* In it, Procopius launched vicious attacks upon the emperor Justinian and especially upon his wife, Theodora. He described Theodora as the daughter of a bear keeper in the circus at Constantinople, as a child stage performer, and, later, as a notorious prostitute. He further accused her of continuing to indulge in acts of unbridled moral depravity as empress.

Although Theodora led a reproachless personal life after her marriage to Justinian, some of Procopius' revelations about her early life appear to have had a factual basis. Theodora was a courtesan at the time she met Justinian. In order to marry her, Justinian had to prevail upon his uncle, Justin I, to repeal the law forbidding senators to marry actresses. A selection from *The Secret History,* "Theodora—A Shameless Woman," is presented here.

An apse mosaic from San Vitale in Ravenna, *Theodora and Attendants,* depicts the empress. The embroidered motif of the three Magi carrying gifts to the Virgin Mary and Christ Child on the hem of Theodora's mantle symbolically identifies the empress with the Mother of God.

19. Purple was the color of the imperial robes.

Procopius, *The Secret History*[20]

Theodora—A Shameless Woman

In Byzantium there was a man called Acacius, a keeper of the circus animals, belonging to the Green faction and entitled the Bearward. This man died of sickness while Anastasius occupied the imperial throne, leaving three daughters, Comito, Theodora, and Anastasia, of whom the eldest had not yet completed her seventh year. The widow married again, hoping that her new husband would from then on share with her the management of her house and the care of the animals. . . .

When the children were old enough, they were at once put on the stage there by their mother, as their appearance was very attractive; not all at the same time, however, but as each one seemed to her to be mature enough for this profession. The eldest one, Comito, was already one of the most popular harlots of the day. Theodora, who came next, clad in a little tunic with long sleeves, the usual dress of a slave girl, used to assist her in various ways, . . . For the time being Theodora was still too undeveloped to be capable of sharing a man's bed or having intercourse like a woman; but she acted as a sort of male prostitute to satisfy customers of the lowest type, and slaves at that, who when accompanying their owners to the theatre seized their opportunity to divert themselves in this revolting manner; and for some considerable time she remained in a brothel, given up to this unnatural bodily commerce. But as soon as she was old enough and fully developed, she joined the women on the stage and promptly became a courtesan, of the type our ancestors called "the dregs of the army." For she was not a flautist or harpist; she was not even qualified to join the corps of dancers; but she merely sold her attractions to anyone who came along, putting her whole body at his disposal. . . .

Never was anyone so completely given up to unlimited self-indulgence. Often she would go to a bring-your-own-food dinner-party with ten young men or more, all at the peak of their physical powers and with fornication as their chief object in life, and would lie with all her fellow-diners in turn the whole night long: when she had seduced them all to a state of exhaustion she would go to their menials, as many as thirty on occasions, and copulate with every one of them; but not even so could she satisfy her lust. . . .

As for Theodora, she had an attractive face and a good figure, but was short and pallid, though not in an extreme degree, for there was just a trace of colour. Her glance was invariably fierce and intensely hard. If I were

20. Reprinted, by permission of the publisher, from Procopius, *The Secret History,* trans. by G. A. Williamson (London: Penguin Classics, 1966), pp. 82–84, 91. Copyright © by G. A. Williamson, 1966.

to attempt a detailed account of her life upon the stage, I could go on for the rest of time; but the few incidents picked out for inclusion in the preceding paragraphs should be enough to give a complete picture of this woman's character, for the enlightenment of those yet to come.

4. *David Composing the Psalms,* page from the so-called *Paris Psalter,* c. 900 (Gardner, p. 290, ill. 7:61; Janson, p. 214, color plate 33)
Theophanes Graptos, Ode 1: "David, Thy Forefather, O Lady, Shall Sing to Thee," early ninth century

During the first centuries of the Christian era, a rift developed between the Roman Catholic Church of Western Europe and the Eastern Orthodox Church of the Byzantine empire. This rift continued throughout the Middle Ages and culminated in the Schism of 1054. The Eastern and Western churches were divided by a number of conflicts, including the primacy claimed by the Church of Rome, the differing interpretations over the nature of the Trinity, the use of Greek rather than Latin in the Eastern Orthodox Church, the marriage of the Eastern clergy in contrast to the celibacy of the Western clergy, and the prohibition against the use of religious images by eighth-century Byzantine emperors.

One of the most important factors in the spread and survival of the Eastern Orthodox Church was its distinctive liturgy. In the Eastern church, the liturgy is viewed as a total experience, appealing simultaneously to the emotional, intellectual, and aesthetic faculties of the worshiper. The liturgy includes music, incense, art, and movement as well as formal theological statements.

Throughout the centuries, the Eastern Orthodox liturgy has been enriched by cycles of hymns called *kanons.* The word *kanon* means "rule" or "standard." In music it is applied to a form of counterpoint which strictly follows a rule—the rule being that the voice which begins a melody must be precisely copied, note for note, by a second voice, which begins a few measures later. The Byzantine *kanon* originated in Jerusalem at the end of the seventh century. In the Eastern Orthodox Church, hymns had traditionally been sung only during Lent and between Easter and Pentecost, but by the ninth century they were included throughout the entire ecclesiastical year. Many *kanons* have been adopted into modern Western hymnbooks.

A Byzantine *kanon* consists of nine odes, each of which is sung to a different melody. Dogmatic ideas are expressed in these hymns of praise by means of reiteration and variation. At times the *kanons* employ direct speech and approach the impact of drama. An example is the *kanon* "David, Thy Forefather, O Lady, Shall Sing to Thee." This *kanon* was composed by Theophanes Graptos (759–c. 842) in the form of a dialogue between the angel Gabriel and the Virgin Mary. It is based upon the Gospel passages (Luke 1:26–38) designated to be read on March 25, the feast of the Annunciation of Our Lady. Ode 1 from the *kanon* "David, Thy Forefather, O Lady, Shall Sing to Thee" is presented here.

The manuscript illumination from the *Paris Psalter, David Composing the*

Psalms, represents David, the most famous composer of sacred music in the Bible. Behind David is the town of Bethlehem, the birthplace of Christ. In the New Testament, David is described as the ancestor of Mary.

Theophanes Graptos, Ode 1[21]

David, Thy Forefather, O Lady, Shall Sing to Thee

David, thy forefather, O lady, shall sing to thee, plucking the lyre of the spirit; listen, O daughter, to the joyful voice of the angel, for he announces to thee an inexpressible joy.

The Angel: In joy I cry to thee. Incline thine ear and listen to me announcing the unbegotten conception of god. For thou hast found favour before the Lord as no other has ever found, O immaculate.

The Mother of God: Make known to me, O Angel, the meaning of your words, how shall what you have said come to pass. Speak plainly: how am I, being a maid, to conceive, and how am I to become the mother of the Creator?

The Angel: It appears that you believe me to be speaking deceitfully, and yet I rejoice to see your circumspection. Take courage, O lady, for, through the will of God, even the incredible is easily accomplished.

5. St. Mark's, Venice, begun 1063 (Gardner, pp. 283–84, ills. 7:49 to 7:51; Janson, p. 224, ills. 322–23)
Constantine VII, *On the Government of the Empire:* "Venice—Its Origin and History," mid-tenth century
Robert of Clari, *The Conquest of Constantinople:* "The Splendour of Constantinople," early thirteenth century

Byzantine influence can be seen in the plan and construction of St. Mark's in Venice. Begun in 1063, St. Mark's was originally modeled after a Byzantine building, the Church of the Holy Apostles, in Constantinople. The relics of Saint Mark were removed from Alexandria to Venice in the ninth century. The four bronze horses above the entrance to St. Mark's were looted from Constantinople during the Venetian sack of the Byzantine capital in 1204.

The history of Venice is closely linked with events in the Byzantine empire. Venice was founded in the sixth century by refugees from the Lombard invasion of Italy. It fell under control of the Exarchate of Ravenna, the Byzantine military

21. Reprinted, by permission of Oxford University Press, from Egon Wellesz, *A History of Byzantine Music and Hymnography* (Oxford: Clarendon Press, 1949), p. 171.

government established at Ravenna. In the middle of the eighth century the Ravenna exarchate was conquered by the Franks and was turned over by Pepin, the first Carolingian king, to Pope Stephen II. Venice became an independent state.

Situated between the East and the West, Venice was an important trading center in the Mediterranean. Its growing commercial power led the city into conflict with the Byzantine empire. The rivalry between the Venetians and the Byzantines culminated in the early thirteenth century. The ruler of Venice, the doge Enrico Dandalo, diverted the Fourth Crusade from its original objective of recovering Jerusalem from the Muslims. Instead the crusaders were led by the Venetians in an attack upon the Byzantine empire. Constantinople fell in April 1204, and the crusaders indulged themselves in a frenzy of looting and destruction. Venice appropriated the empire's principal harbors and islands on its most desirable trading routes. The other crusaders parceled out Constantinople's European and Asiatic provinces.

The origin and history of Venice are discussed by the Byzantine emperor Constantine VII, also known as Constantine Porphyrogenitus (905–959). A ruler during the age of the Byzantine empire's greatest ascendancy, Constantine was also a scholar well versed in the tradition of Classical antiquity. He wrote three great works on the administration, the court ceremonies, and the provinces of the empire. *On the Government of the Empire* was written as an instruction book on foreign policy for the emperor's son, Romanus II. A selection from *On the Government of the Empire,* "Venice—Its Origin and History," is presented here.

The Venetian sack of Constantinople is described by the French knight Robert of Clari. Little is known about Robert except that he was a man of humble origins who served as a knight in the Fourth Crusade. Robert's chronicle, *The Conquest of Constantinople,* begins with the assembly of the crusaders in Venice in 1202 and traces events through 1205. Like most Westerners, Robert was awed by the wealth of Constantinople, by the beauty of its churches, and by the venerability of its relics. A selection from *The Conquest of Constantinople,* "The Splendour of Constantinople," is presented here.

Constantine VII, *On the Government of the Empire*[22]

Venice—Its Origin and History

When those who are now called Venetians, but were originally called Enetikoi, crossed over, they began by constructing a strongly fortified city, in which the doge of Venice still has his seat today, a city surrounded by some six miles of sea, . . .

Of old, Venice was a desert place, uninhabited and swampy. Those who are now called Venetians were Franks from Aquileia[23] and from the

22. Reprinted from Constantine Porphyrogenitus, *De Administrando Imperio (The Administration of the Empire),* Gy. Moravcsik, ed., trans. by K. J. H. Jenkins (Budapest: Pazmany Peter Tudomanyegyetemi Gorog Filologiai Intezet, 1949), pp. 117, 119, 121.

23. A city in northeast Italy on the Adriatic Sea; it was sacked by Attila in 452.

other places in Francia, and they used to dwell on the mainland opposite Venice. But when Attila, the king of the Avars,[24] came and utterly devastated and depopulated all the parts of Francia, all the Franks from Aquileia and from the other cities of Francia began to take to flight, and to go to the uninhabited islands of Venice and to build huts there, out of their dread of king Attila. Now when this king Attila had devastated all the country of the mainland and had advanced as far as Rome and Calabria[25] and had left Venice far in his wake, those who had fled for refuge to the islands of Venice, having obtained a breathing-space and, as it were, shaken off their faintness of heart, took counsel jointly to settle there, which they did, and have been settled there till this day. But again, many years after the withdrawal of Attila, king Pepin arrived, who at that time was ruling over Papia and other kingdoms. For this Pepin had three brothers, and they were ruling over all the Frank and Slavonic regions. Now when king Pepin came against the Venetians with power and a large army, he blockaded them along the mainland, on the far side of the crossing between it and the islands of Venice, at a place called Aeibolas. Well, when the Venetians saw king Pepin coming against them with his power and preparing to take ship with the horses to the island of Madamaucon (for this is an island near the mainland), they laid down spars and fenced off the whole crossing. The army of king Pepin, being brought to a stand (for it was not possible for them to cross at any other point), blockaded them along the mainland six months, fighting with them daily. The Venetians assailed them with arrows and javelins, and stopped them from crossing over to the island. So then king Pepin, at a loss, said to the Venetians: "You are beneath my hand and my providence, since you are of my country and domain." But the Venetians answered him: "We want to be servants of the emperor of the Romans, and not of you." When, however, they had for long been straitened by the trouble that had come upon them, the Venetians made a treaty of peace with king Pepin, agreeing to pay him a very considerable tribute. But since that time the tribute has gone on diminishing year by year, though it is paid even to this day. For the Venetians pay to him who rules over the kingdom of Italy, that is, Papia, a twopenny fee of 36 pounds of uncoined silver annually. So ended the war between Franks and Venetians. When the folk began to flee away to Venice and to collect there in numbers, they proclaimed as their doge him who surpassed the rest in nobility. The first doge among them had been appointed before king Pepin came against them. At that time the doge's residence was at a place called Civitanova, which means "new city." But

24. Attila the Hun.

25. At this time, the name Calabria referred to the southeastern province of Italy, rather than the present southwestern area known by that name.

because this island aforesaid is close to the mainland, by common consent they moved the doge's residence to another island, where it now is at this present, because it is at a distance from the mainland, as far off as one may see a man on horseback.

Robert of Clari, *The Conquest of Constantinople*[26]

The Splendour of Constantinople

Afterwards it was ordered that all the wealth of the spoils should be brought to a certain church in the city. The wealth was brought there, and they took ten knights, high men, of the pilgrims and ten of the Venetians who were thought to be honorable, and they set them to guard this wealth. So the wealth was brought there. And it was so rich, and there were so many rich vessels of gold and silver and cloth of gold and so many rich jewels, that it was a fair marvel, the great wealth that was brought there. Not since the world was made, was there ever seen or won so great a treasure or so noble or so rich, not in the time of Alexander nor in the time of Charlemagne nor before nor after. Nor do I think, myself, that in the forty richest cities of the world there had been so much wealth as was found in Constantinople. For the Greeks say that two thirds of the wealth of this world is in Constantinople and the other third scattered throughout the world. . . .

And the palace of Boukoleon was very rich and was made in such a way as I shall tell you. Within this palace, which was held by the marquis, there were fully five hundred halls, all connected with one another and all made with gold mosaic. And in it there were fully thirty chapels, great and small, and there was one of them which was called the Holy Chapel, which was so rich and noble that there was not a hinge nor a band nor any other part such as is usually made of iron that was not all of silver, and there was no column that was not of jasper or porphyry or some other rich precious stone. And the pavement of this chapel was of white marble so smooth and clear that it seemed to be of crystal, and this chapel was so rich and so noble that no one could ever tell you its great beauty and nobility. Within this chapel were found many rich relics. One found there two pieces of the True Cross as large as half a *toise*[27] and one found there also the iron of the lance with which Our Lord had His side pierced and two of the nails which were driven through His hands and feet, and one

26. Reprinted, by permission of the publisher, from Robert of Clari, *The Conquest of Constantinople,* trans. by Edgar Holmes McNeal (New York: Columbia University Press, 1936), pp. 101–03, 105–07.

27. A unit of length equaling a fathom, or six feet.

found there in a crystal phial quite a little of His blood, and one found there the tunic which He wore and which was taken from Him when they led Him to the Mount of Calvary, and one found there the blessed crown with which He was crowned, which was made of reeds with thorns as sharp as the points of daggers. And one found there a part of the robe of Our Lady and the head of my lord St. John the Baptist and so many other rich relics that I could not recount them to you or tell you all the truth. . . .

Then the pilgrims regarded the great size of the city, and the palaces and fine abbeys and churches and the great wonders which were in the city, and they marveled at it greatly. And they marveled greatly at the church of Saint Sophia and at the riches which were in it. Now I will tell you about the church of Saint Sophia, how it was made. Saint Sophia in Greek means Sainte Trinité[28] in French. The church of Saint Sophia was entirely round, and within the church there were domes, round all about, which were borne by great and very rich columns, and there was no column which was not of jasper or porphyry or some other precious stone, nor was there one of these columns that did not work cures. There was one that cured sickness of the reins[29] when it was rubbed against, and another that cured sickness of the side, and others that cured other ills. And there was no door in this church and no hinges or bands or other parts such as are usually made of iron that were not all of silver. . . . On the ring of the great door of the church, which was all of silver, there hung a tube, of what material no one knew; it was the size of a pipe such as shepherds play on. This tube had such virtue as I shall tell you. When an infirm man who had some sickness in his body like the bloat, so that he was bloated in his belly, put it in his mouth, however little he put it in, when this tube took hold it sucked out all the sickness and it made the poison run out of his mouth and it held him so fast that it made his eyes roll and turn in his head, and he could not get away until the tube had sucked all of this sickness out of him. And the sicker a man was the longer it held him, and if a man who was not sick put it in his mouth, it would not hold him at all, much or little.

28. "Holy Trinity," but Robert's Greek was rusty, since Sophia is the Greek word for "wisdom."

29. Kidneys or loins.

ISLAMIC ART

1. Great Mosque (Mosque of Mutawakkil), Samarra, Iraq, 848–852 (Gardner, pp. 294–95, ills. 7:66 and 7:67; Janson, p. 244, ills. 336–37)

Koran: "Allah Is the Light of the Heavens and the Earth," c. 650

Ibn Ishaq, *The Life of Mohammed:* "The Raid on the Quraysh Caravan," mid-eighth century

Islam was founded by Mohammed, a person of humble origins whose beliefs and actions were to have an immense impact upon the religious faith, political events, and cultural achievements in Arabia, Africa, Asia, and Europe. Born in Mecca, an important trading center, Mohammed (c. 570–632) was the son of a merchant. Orphaned at an early age, he was raised by an uncle whom he accompanied on trading journeys to Syria. As a young man, he became a traveling merchant but his profound interest in religious questions soon overwhelmed all other concerns.

In 610 an extraordinary event occurred which convinced Mohammed that he had been chosen as a messenger, or prophet, of God. Mohammed had a vision of a majestic being, whom he later identified as the angel Gabriel, and he heard a voice saying to him, "You are the messenger of God." From this time, the angelic voice called to him frequently. The revelations vouchsafed to Mohammed throughout his life were collected and written down c. 650 and form the Koran, the sacred text of Islam.

Sincere in his belief that he was entrusted with the gift of prophecy and a divine mission, Mohammed began to preach publicly. His unequivocal rejection of the pagan gods of Mecca met with little understanding. As he gained more followers, opposition arose. A campaign of persecution caused Mohammed and his followers to leave Mecca in 622. The date of the Prophet's migration, or *hijrah* (hegira), marks the traditional beginning of the Islamic calendar.

Mohammed settled in Medina, an oasis town. He built a house with a large courtyard which, during his lifetime, served as a gathering place for Muslims to hold prayers and, at his death, became a mosque. It is possible that the development of the hypostyle mosque, such as the Great Mosque at Samarra, Iraq, was based in part upon the plan of the Prophet's house in Medina.

The following year, driven by financial necessity, Mohammed began to lead raids against the Meccan caravans that passed near Medina on their way to Syria. Although this was a serious breach of the ancient Arab moral code, Mohammed justified it as a holy war against nonbelievers. An important confrontation occurred in 624. Mohammed and his followers, numbering about three hundred men, were pursuing a rich Meccan caravan owned by the Quraysh tribe and led by Abu Sufyan. Aware of his danger, Abu Sufyan managed to elude Mohammed's raiding party while he awaited the arrival of a supporting force of eight hundred men led by Abu Jahl. Faced by a powerful army that outnumbered his, the Prophet had to summon all his powers of inspiration to persuade his followers to take up the unequal struggle. In the ensuing battle, Mohammed scored a decisive victory, which he interpreted as a divine vindication of his faith.

Although the succeeding years brought some setbacks, Mohammed continued to attract followers. In 630 he led a successful march on Mecca and entered the city with little resistance. By the time of his death, Mohammed was the most powerful man in Arabia, and within a century Muslims had created an Islamic empire that spread from Spain across Central Asia to India.

Two selections related to the life and teachings of Mohammed are presented here. The first, "Allah Is the Light of the Heavens and the Earth," is a section from the Koran. The Koran contains the fundamental religious ideas of Islam. Allah (God) is acknowledged as the only god of the universe and as the creator and sustainer of the world. Humanity is the noblest of Allah's creations; all other parts of nature are subservient. But each person must be willing to surrender to the will of God. The Arabic word for surrender is *islam.*

The second selection presented here, "The Raid on the Quraysh Caravan," is a section from the earliest biography of Mohammed, *The Life of Mohammed,* by Mohammed Ibn Ishaq (c. 707–773). In this selection, Ibn Ishaq describes the raid led by Mohammed against Abu Sufyan and recounts the Prophet's promise that anyone who dies in a holy war will enter Paradise. The concept of the holy war helps to explain the astonishingly rapid spread of Islam.

Koran[30]

Allah Is the Light of the Heavens and the Earth

Allah is the light of the heavens and the earth. His light may be compared to a niche that enshrines a lamp, the lamp within a crystal of star-like brilliance. It is lit from a blessed olive tree neither eastern nor western. Its very oil would almost shine forth, though no fire touched it. Light upon light; Allah guides to His light whom He will.

Allah coins metaphors for men. He has knowledge of all things.

His light is found in temples which Allah has sanctioned to be built for the remembrance of His name. In them morning and evening His praise is sung by men whom neither trade nor profit can divert from remembering Him, from offering prayers, or from giving alms; who dread the day when men's hearts and eyes shall writhe with anguish; who hope that Allah will requite them for their noblest deeds and lavish His grace upon them. Allah gives without measure to whom He will.

As for the unbelievers, their works are like a mirage in a desert. The thirsty traveller thinks it is water, but when he comes near he finds that it is nothing. He finds Allah there, who pays him back in full. Swift is Allah's reckoning.

30. Reprinted, by permission of the publisher, from *The Koran,* trans. by N. J. Dawood (London: Penguin Books, 1956; rev. ed. 1959; second rev. ed. 1966; third rev. ed. 1968; fourth rev. ed. 1974), pp. 217–20. Copyright © by N. J. Dawood, 1956, 1959, 1966, 1968, 1974.

Or like darkness on a bottomless ocean spread with clashing billows and overcast with clouds: darkness upon darkness. If he stretches out his hand he can scarcely see it. Indeed the man from whom Allah withholds His light shall find no light at all.

Do you not see how Allah is praised by those in heaven and earth? The very birds praise him as they wing their flight. He notes the prayers and praises of all His creatures, and has knowledge of all their actions.

To Allah belongs the kingdom of the heavens and the earth. To Him shall all things return.

Do you not see how Allah drives the clouds, then gathers them and piles them up in masses which pour down torrents of rain? From heaven's mountains He sends down hail, pelting with it whom He will and turning it away from whom He pleases. The flash of His lightning almost snatches off men's eyes.

He makes the night succeed the day: surely in this there is a lesson for clear-sighted men.

Allah created every beast from water. Some creep upon their bellies, others walk on two legs, and others on four. Allah creates what He pleases. He has power over all things.

We have sent down revelations showing the truth. Allah guides whom He will to a straight path.

They declare: "We believe in Allah and His apostle and obey them both." But no sooner do they utter these words than some of them turn their backs. Surely these are no believers.

And when they are called to Allah and His apostle that he may judge between them, some turn away. Had justice been on their side they would have come to him in all obedience.

Is there a sickness in their hearts, or are they full of doubt? Do they fear that Allah and His apostle may deny them justice? Surely these are wrongdoers.

But when true believers are called to Allah and His apostle that he may pass judgment upon them, their only reply is "We hear and obey." Such men shall surely prosper.

Those that obey Allah and His apostles, those that revere Allah and fear Him, shall surely triumph.

They solemnly swear by Allah that if you order them to fight they will obey you. Say: "Do not swear: your obedience, not your oaths, will count. Allah is cognizant of all your actions."

Say: "Obey Allah and obey His apostle. If you do not, he is still bound to fulfill his duty, as you yourselves are bound to fulfill yours. If you obey him, you shall be guided. The duty of an apostle is only to give plain warning."

Allah has promised those of you who believe and do good works to make them masters in the land as He had made their ancestors before them, to strengthen the Faith He chose for them, and to change their fears to safety. Let them worship Me and serve no other gods besides Me. Wicked indeed are they who after this deny Me.

Attend to your prayers, pay the alms-tax, and obey the Apostle, so that you may be shown mercy.

Never think that the unbelievers will escape the wrath of Allah in this world. Hell shall be their home. An evil fate awaits them. . . .

To Allah belongs what the heavens and the earth contain. He has knowledge of all your thoughts and actions. On the day when they return to Him He will declare to them all that they have done. He has knowledge of all things.

Ibn Ishaq, *The Life of Mohammed*[31]

The Raid on the Quraysh Caravan

When the apostle heard about Abu Sufyan coming from Syria, he summoned the Muslims and said, "This is the Quraysh caravan containing their property. Go out to attack it, perhaps God will give it as a prey." The people answered his summons, some eagerly, others reluctantly because they had not thought that the apostle would go to war. When he got near to the Hijaz, Abu Sufyan was seeking news, and questioning every rider in his anxiety, until he got news from some riders that Mohammed had called out his companions against him and his caravan. He took alarm at that and hired Damdam b. 'Amr al-Ghifari and sent him to Mecca, ordering him to call out Quraysh in defence of their property, and to tell them that Mohammed was lying in wait for it with his companions. So Damdam left for Mecca at full speed. . . .

Quraysh, having marched forth at daybreak, now came on. When the apostle saw them descending from the hill 'Aqanqal into the valley, he cried, "O God, here come the Quraysh in their vanity and pride, contending with Thee and calling Thy apostle a liar. O God, grant the help which Thou didst promise me. Destroy them this morning!" . . .

Then they advanced and drew near to one another. The apostle had ordered his companions not to attack until he gave the word, and if the enemy should surround them they were to keep them off with showers of arrows. He himself remained in the hut with Abu Bakr. . . . The apostle was beseeching his Lord for the help which He had promised to him, and

31. Reprinted, by permission of the publisher, from Muhammad Ibn Ishaq, *The Life of Muhammad,* trans. by A. Guillaume (Oxford: Oxford University Press, 1974), pp. 289, 297, 299–300.

among his words were these: "O God, if this band perish today Thou wilt be worshiped no more." But Abu Bakr said, "O prophet of God, your constant entreaty will annoy thy Lord, for surely God will fulfill His promise to thee." While the apostle was in the hut he slept a light sleep; then he awoke and said, "Be of good cheer, O Abu Bakr. God's help is come to you. Here is Gabriel holding the rein of a horse and leading it. The dust is upon his front teeth." . . .

Then the apostle went forth to the people and incited them saying, "By God in whose hand is the soul of Mohammed, no man will be slain this day fighting against them with steadfast courage advancing not retreating but God will cause him to enter Paradise." 'Umayr b. al-Humam brother of b. Salima was eating some dates which he had in his hand. "Fine, Fine!" said he, "is there nothing between me and my entering Paradise save to be killed by these men?" He flung the dates from his hand, seized his sword, and fought against them till he was slain, saying the while

In God's service take no food
But piety and deeds of good.
If in God's war you've firmly stood
You need not fear as others should
While you are righteous true and good.

2. Great Mosque, Córdoba, Spain, eighth to tenth centuries (Gardner, pp. 296–97, ills. 7:68 to 7:71; Janson, pp. 245–46, ills. 338–40)
Ibn Abd-el-Hakem: *History of the Conquest of Spain:* "The Muslim Invasion," end of the eighth century

The Arab conquest of Spain began in 711. Spain had been ruled by the Visigoths[32] since 414. A civil war over the succession to the kingship opened the door to the Muslim invasion. In 710 the Visigothic king Witiza died after designating his son Akhila as his successor. When, instead, a powerful group of nobles elected Roderick king, Witiza's family appealed to the Muslims for aid. The Muslim governor of the western provinces, Musa ibn Nasayr, dispatched his general, Tariq ibn Ziyad, to Spain. In 711 Tariq decisively defeated Roderick. Tariq marched to Córdoba, which surrendered quickly, and then proceeded to Toledo, the Visigothic capital, which offered little resistance. The following year Musa led a military force to Spain and took Seville. The capital of Muslim Spain was transferred first to Seville and then, in 717, to Córdoba. In 784 the governor of Spain, Abd-ar-Rahman I, founded the Great Mosque at Córdoba on the site of a Roman temple and a Visigothic church.

The Arabs called their new domain al-Andalus and incorporated it into the

32. A Germanic tribe that, under Alaric, attacked Rome in 410, successfully demanding a substantial ransom. Later it established a kingdom in southern Spain and achieved considerable power.

vast empire that spread from Spain and Morocco to Central Asia and India. The conquest of Spain is recorded by Ibn Abd-el-Hakem, a native of Egypt, in his work *History of the Conquest of Spain.* Abd-el-Hakem (ninth century) attributed the invasion of Spain to the treachery of the Spanish king, Roderick. According to legend, Roderick had been entrusted with the education of the daughter of one of his governors, Ilyan. When his daughter was dishonored by the king, Ilyan was enraged and turned to the Muslims to gain his revenge against Roderick. A selection from the *History of the Conquest of Spain*, "The Muslim Invasion," is presented here.

Ibn Abd-el-Hakem, *History of the Conquest of Spain*[33]

The Muslim Invasion

The governor of the straits between this district and Andalus, was a foreigner called Ilyan, Lord of Septa. He was also the governor of a town called Alchadra, situated on the same side of the straits of Andalus as Tangiers. Ilyan was a subject of Roderick the Lord of Andalus, who used to reside in Toledo. Tariq put himself in communication with Ilyan, and treated him kindly, until they made peace with each other. Ilyan had sent one of his daughters to Roderick, the Lord of Andalus, for her improvement and education; but she became pregnant by him. Ilyan having heard of this, said, I see for him no other punishment or recompense, than that I should bring the Arabs against him. He sent to Tariq, saying I will bring thee to Andalus: Tariq being at that time in Tlemsen, and Musa Han Nosseyr in Cairwan. . . . After that Tariq went to Ilyan who was in Septa on the straits. The latter rejoicing at his coming, said, I will bring thee to Andalus. But there was a mountain called the mountain of Tariq[34] between the two landing places, that is, between Septa and Andalus. When the evening came, Hyan brought him the vessels, in which he made him embark for that landing-place, where he concealed himself during the day, and in the evening sent back the vessels to bring over the rest of his companions. So they embarked for the landing-place, none of them being left behind: whereas the people of Andalus did not observe them, thinking that the vessels crossing and recrossing were similar to the trading vessels which for their benefit plied backwards and forwards. Tariq was in the last division which went across. . . . When Tariq landed, soldiers from Córdoba came to meet him; and seeing the small number of his companions they despised him on that account. They then fought. The battle with Tariq was

33. Reprinted from Ibn Abd-el-Hakem, *History of the Conquest of Spain,* trans. by John Harris Jones (London: Williams & Norgate, 1858), pp. 18–20.

34. In Arabic, the mount of Tariq is Jebel-al-Tariq, from which comes the modern name of his landing, Gibraltar.

severe. They were routed, and he did not cease from the slaughter of them till they reached the town of Córdoba. When Roderick heard of this, he came to their rescue from Toledo. They then fought in a place of the name of Shedunia, in a valley which is called this day the valley of Umm-Hakim. They fought a severe battle; but God, mighty and great, killed Roderick and his companions.

3. Madrasah and attached mausoleum of Sultan Hasan, Cairo, Egypt, 1356–1363. (Gardner, p. 302, ills. 7:80 and 7:81; Janson, p. 247, ill. 343–44)
One Thousand and One Nights: The Tale of Ma'aruf the Cobbler: "Ma'aruf and the Jinnee," fourteenth century

In 639 Egypt was conquered by the Muslims. In a land rich with history, a new culture was formed. By the time of the Mamluk rulers (1250–1517), Arabic was the language of the country and Islam was the religion of the overwhelming majority of Egyptians.

During the Mamluk dynasty, Egypt became a leading center of Arabic culture. In the visual arts, the architectural achievements of the Mamluks are especially evident. The madrasah and mausoleum of Sultan Hasan are among the most impressive monuments built by the Mamluks to enrich their capital city, Cairo.

It was also during the Mamluk period that Islamic literature flourished in Egypt. The present form of the story cycle *One Thousand and One Nights* appeared in Egypt in the fourteenth century.

One Thousand and One Nights is a collection of tales unified by a device of the storyteller. According to the storyteller, Shahrazad is married to King Shahrayr, the lord of India and China. To prevent any woman from dishonoring him through her infidelity, Shahrayr has shared only the wedding night with his previous wives and has executed them in the morning. In order to delay her fate, Shahrazad entertains her husband for a thousand and one nights by telling stories. By the time she has finished her tales, Shahrazad has borne the king three sons and has won his love.

Stories from many different cultures are interwoven into the framework provided by Shahrazad's ruse. The nucleus of the collection is of Indian origin. Translated into Persian, the stories were expanded and gathered into a book called *A Thousand Tales.* These, in turn, were translated into Arabic. Stories and anecdotes were then added from Baghdad. Later, tales from Egypt, including *The Tale of Ma'aruf the Cobbler,* were incorporated.

A selection from *The Tale of Ma'aruf the Cobbler,* "Ma'aruf and the Jinnee," is presented here. In this story Ma'aruf is a poor cobbler who is driven from his native city, Cairo, by his shrewish wife, Fatimah. Entering the city Ikhtiyan al-Khatan, Ma'aruf pretends to be a wealthy merchant. The greedy king marries his daughter, the Princess Dunya, to Ma'aruf. But the king's minister threatens to expose Ma'aruf as a penniless impostor. Ma'aruf flees the city. Cold and hungry, he meets a farmer who offers him a meal. In return, Ma'aruf volunteers to plow the farmer's field and discovers an immense treasure hoard of gold and jewels and, even more miraculously, a jinnee's ring. As Ma'aruf rubs the ring, a jinnee appears and offers to grant the cobbler his wish. A series of adventures unfolds as the ring passes through the hands of many people.

One Thousand and One Nights: The Tale of Ma'aruf the Cobbler[35]

Ma'aruf and the Jinnee

Not wishing to offend the old man, Ma'aruf dismounted and sat down on the grass, while his host hurried away.

As he waited for the peasant's return, Ma'aruf thought; "I am keeping this poor man from his work. I will make up for his lost time by working at the plough myself."

He rose and, going up to the oxen, drove the plough along the furrow. The beasts had not gone far, however, when the share struck against an object in the ground and came to a sudden halt. Ma'aruf goaded the oxen on but, though they strained powerfully against the yoke, the plough remained rooted in the ground. Clearing away the soil about the share, Ma'aruf found that it had caught in a great ring of gold set in a marble slab the size of a large millstone. He exerted all his strength, and when he had moved the slab aside, he saw below it a flight of stairs. Going down the stairs he found himself in a square vault as large as the city baths containing four separate halls. The first was filled with gold from floor to ceiling; the second with pearls, emeralds, and coral; the third with jacinths, rubies, and turquoises; and the fourth with diamonds and other precious stones. At the far side of the vault stood a coffer of clearest crystal and upon it a golden casket no larger than a lemon.

The cobbler marvelled and rejoiced at this discovery. He went up to the little casket and, lifting its lid, found in it a gold signet-ring finely engraved with strange talismanic inscriptions that resembled the legs of creeping insects. He slipped the ring upon his finger and, as he did so, rubbed the seal.

At once a mighty jinnee appeared before him, saying: "I am here, master, I am here! Speak and I will obey! What is your wish? Would you have me build a capital, or lay a town in ruin? Would you have me slay a king, or dig a river-bed? I am your slave, by order of the Sovereign of the Jinn, Creator of the day and night! What is your wish?"

35. Reprinted, by permission of the publisher, from *Tales from the Thousand and One Nights,* trans. by N. J. Dawood (London: Penguin Classics, 1954; rev. ed. 1973), pp. 392–94.

Amazed at the apparition, Ma'aruf cried: "Creature of Allah, who are you?"

"I am Abul-Sa'adah, the slave of the ring," replied the jinnee. "Faithfully I serve my master, and my master is he who rubs the ring. Nothing is beyond my power; for I am lord over seventy-two tribes of jinn, each two-and-seventy thousand strong: each jinnee rules over a thousand giants, each giant over a thousand goblins, each goblin over a thousand demons, and each demon over a thousand imps. All these owe me absolute allegiance; and yet for all my power, I cannot choose but to obey my master. Ask what you will, and it shall be done. Be it on land or sea, by day or night: should you need me you have but to rub the ring, and I will be at hand to do your bidding. Of one thing only I must warn you; if you twice rub the ring I shall be consumed in the fire of the powerful words engraved on the seal, and you will lose me for ever."

VIII

Early Medieval Art

THE MIGRATION PERIOD

1. Purse Cover from the Sutton Hoo Ship Burial, c. 655 (Gardner, p. 318, ill. 8:2; Janson, p. 256, ill. 357)
Beowulf: "The Battle Between Beowulf and Grendel's Mother," c. eighth century

Anglo-Saxon tribes from the coast of the North Sea began to invade Britain during the fifth century. As they settled the land, they forced the native Celts into the mountainous areas of the west and the north and replaced the Roman-British culture of the south with their own Germanic language and customs. The territories controlled by the Anglo-Saxon kingdoms came to be known as England (Angle-land).

Many aspects of the Germanic culture of the Anglo-Saxon tribes are revealed by the epic poem *Beowulf.* The poem, which recounts the exploits of the hero, Beowulf, was composed in Old English most probably during the eighth century.

The story is set against the historical background of sixth-century Scandinavia. Denmark is menaced by the monster Grendel. When the Danish warriors are proved powerless against the monster's nightly attacks, Beowulf, a young nobleman of southern Sweden, offers the Danes his help. As he guards the king's great hall, Heorot, Grendel appears and a ferocious battle ensues. The unarmed Beowulf mortally wounds the monster by ripping off its arm. Denmark rejoices in Beowulf's deed, but Grendel's mother seeks revenge. To subdue her, Beowulf journeys to her lair, a lonely lake in the hills, and dives into the water. The two powerful foes meet, and Grendel's mother is slain. The threat to Denmark overcome, Beowulf returns to his homeland, where he soon becomes king. He rules wisely for fifty years, but at the end of his reign he is slain in combat with a dragon which is ravaging Sweden as it seeks to recover its stolen treasure horde. The fallen hero is cremated and his ashes are buried, together with the dragon's treasure, in a great mound.

A selection from *Beowulf,* "The Battle Between Beowulf and Grendel's Mother," is presented here. The selection begins with Beowulf diving into the lake in search of Grendel's mother.

Just as the epic poem *Beowulf* is the supreme expression of Anglo-Saxon poetic genius, the objects from Sutton Hoo are among the most spectacular examples of Anglo-Saxon metalwork. The rich burial goods found there parallel the description of the magnificent funeral and treasures accorded to Beowulf, and the two ornamental plaques on the purse lid depict the ancient theme of the confrontation between man and beast that formed the basis of the Anglo-Saxon poem.

Beowulf[1]

The Battle Between Beowulf and Grendel's Mother

The waters swallowed [Beowulf].
Part of the day had already passed
before he reached that unfathomed bottom.
At once that ravenous hag who had ruled
those flooding waters for fifty years
discovered, slavering, that some strange human
was diving down to her demon lair.
She grappled with him, gripping him tight
with terrible claws, but she could not harm
his body, for the ring-mail wrapped it around.
Unable to get at the Geat through his sark[2]
or penetrate it with her piercing talons,
the sea-hag, clutching him, swam to the bottom,
dragging that prince to her dismal home
in a manner that, no matter how brave he was,
he could reach no weapon. Harassing him,
many a curious creature of the depths
broke its tusks against his byrnie;[3]
monsters pursued him.
Then the warrior perceived
that now he stood in a strange battle-hall,
where no water was getting him wet
and the swirling tarn[4] could never touch him
because of the roof. He saw ruddy flames,
a blaze of firelight shining brightly.
And then the hero saw that hag,
the incredible mere-witch, and cut a great swathe

1. Reprinted, by permission of the publisher, from *Beowulf,* trans. by Marijane Osborn, with an introduction by Fred. C. Robinson (Berkeley: University of California Press, in association with Robert Springer, Pentangle Press, 1983), pp. 54–58.

2. Shirt.

3. His coat of ring-mail armor.

4. Mountain river or lake.

through the air with his blade, holding nothing back,
so that crashing on her skull the ring-marked sword
sang out greedily. Then her guest found out
that his gleaming blade would not bite
or harm her, no, that heavy sword
failed him at need. Many a fight
had it endured, often driven
through a fated man's helmet; that time was the first
for that gleaming treasure that its glory faded.

Now Hygelac's nephew,[5] keen for renown,
was resolute; and in a rage
he hurled that sword, with its shining marks
and steel blade, so it struck the ground
and lay there, still. He trusted his strength,
the might of his grip. Thus a man shall do
when he hopes to gain some lasting glory
for his deeds in battle: he does not fear death!

Then by the shoulder Beowulf seized
Grendel's mother—the Geat was now
furious, and had few qualms about fighting—
and swung her, hard, so she smashed to the floor!
Promptly she paid him back for that pass,
closing upon him with a clammy embrace,
and, weary, that strongest of warriors stumbled;
catching his foot, he went crashing down.
She straddled her hall-guest and drew her sax,
a gleaming knife; she wanted to get
vengeance for her child. But on his chest
lay the woven sark; that saved his life
with iron rings that blunted both point and blade.
Edgetheow's son would have ended his days
there under the pool, the prince would have perished,
except he was helped by his woven sark,
that hard net of war—and by holy God,
who brought him victory in that battle.
The Ruler of the Skies decided it rightly,
with ease, when Beowulf stood up again.
He saw before him a fabulous blade
among other armor, an ancient sword
worthy of a warrior, the choicest of weapons—

5. Beowulf.

except it was mightier than any other man
could bear into battle but Beowulf,
heavy and ornate, the handwork of giants.
The daring champion of the Shieldings dived
for that radiant hilt, raised it high,
despairing of his life, lunged angrily,
slashing down hard through the skin of her neck,
breaking the vertebrae, the blade vanishing
through her. Fated, she fell to the floor.
The warrior rejoiced, lifting his weapon.

The flame leapt up and light poured out,
shining as bright as the sun in heaven,
the sky's candle. He cast an eye
around him, then walked along the wall,
holding that weapon high by the hilt
with a single purpose. That sword was still useful
to that prince of warriors, for he wished to repay
Grendel for many a remorseless attack
that the demon had made on the men of the Danes,
more often, by far, than that one occasion
when he had slain Hrothgar's hearth companions
asleep in their beds, and eaten, slavering,
fifteen men of the Danish folk,
and carried another such number away—
hideous booty! Beowulf well
had paid him back, to the point that now
he saw Grendel lifeless, lying on his bed
a foul corpse, as the fight at Heorot
had earlier decreed. That corpse sprang apart
when Beowulf dealt it a final blow,
hacking off Grendel's monstrous head.

2. Cross Page, *Lindisfarne Gospels,* late seventh century (Gardner, p. 321, ill. 8:6; Janson, p. 267, color plate 38)
Bede, *Ecclesiastical History of the English People:* "Pagan Customs and Christian Practices" and "The Sparrow's Flight," c. 731

Christianity was introduced into Britain during the Roman occupation. In the southern and western areas of the country, the early Christian church did not survive the collapse of Roman rule, but the faith had been firmly established in Ireland, largely through the efforts of Saint Patrick (c. 373–463).

The Irish Church was independent of Rome. In order to check its spread and to extend the influence of the Roman Church in England, Pope Gregory I (c. 540–604) established missions among the Anglo-Saxon tribes. The mission was led by Gregory's friend Augustine (?–c. 607), who became the first archbishop of Canterbury.

The conversion of the Anglo-Saxons was chronicled by the Venerable Bede (c. 672–735). Except for a trip to York, Bede spent virtually his entire life in Northumbria in northern England. He entered the twin monasteries of Wearmouth and Jarrow at age seven and on one occasion visited Lindisfarne, the Holy Island. Bede's *Ecclesiastical History of the English People* was written around 731 and was based on historical records from churches in England and on documents from the papal archives in Rome.

Two selections from the *Ecclesiastical History of the English People* are presented here. The first, "Pagan Customs and Christian Practices," is a letter written in 601 by Pope Gregory to Abbot Mellitus, an English missionary. In this letter, Gregory urges the churchman and his companions to incorporate pagan elements into Christian practices as a way to win Anglo-Saxon converts. The second selection, "The Sparrow's Flight," is part of an account of the conversion to Christianity of King Edwin of Northumbria,[6] who reigned between 616 and 633. According to Bede, the king held a council to decide whether or not the Northumbrians should accept Christianity. Paulinus, a Christian missionary, and Coifi, the high priest, were both present. At this council one of Edwin's advisers spoke, comparing the life of a person to the flight of a sparrow in a dark winter storm. He observed that the sparrow briefly flies through the warm, brightly lighted banquet hall, and then vanishes into the black stormy night from whence it came. Arguing that Christianity might provide more knowledge about whatever precedes and follows temporal existence, Edwin's adviser urged the acceptance of the new faith. This speech was followed by Coifi's dramatic gesture of repudiation of paganism.

Although all the Anglo-Saxon kingdoms of England accepted the Roman Catholic faith within a hundred years of the arrival of Gregory's missionaries, pagan traditions persisted. In the cross page from the *Lindisfarne Gospels,* the writhing, fantastic monsters of the pagan world are combined with the Christian cross. Even today, the names of northern European gods, such as Tiu, Woden, Thor, and Frigg survive in the English day names Tuesday, Wednesday, Thursday, and Friday.

6. An ancient Saxon kingdom which encompassed all of northern England and much of southeastern Scotland.

Bede, *Ecclesiastical History of the English People*[7]

Gregory I, Letter to Abbot Mellitus: Pagan Customs and Christian Practices

To my most beloved son, Abbot Mellitus, Gregory, servant of the servants of God.

Since the departure of our companions and yourself I have felt much anxiety because we have not happened to hear how your journey has prospered. However, when Almighty God has brought you to our most reverend brother Bishop Augustine, tell him what I have decided after long deliberation about the English people, namely that the idol temples of that race should by no means be destroyed, but only the idols in them. Take holy water and sprinkle it in these shrines, build altars and place relics in them. For if the shrines are well built, it is essential that they should be changed from the worship of devils to the service of the true God. When this people see that their shrines are not destroyed they will be able to banish error from their hearts and be more ready to come to the places they are familiar with, but now recognizing and worshiping the true God. And because they are in the habit of slaughtering much cattle as sacrifices to devils, some solemnity ought to be given them in exchange for this. So on the day of the dedication or the festivals of the holy martyrs, whose relics are deposited there, let them make themselves huts from the branches of trees around the churches which have been converted out of shrines, and let them celebrate the solemnity with religious feasts. Do not let them sacrifice animals to the devil, but let them slaughter animals for their own food to the praise of God, and let them give thanks to the Giver of all things for His bountiful provision. Thus while some outward rejoicings are preserved, they will be able more easily to share in inward rejoicings. It is doubtless impossible to cut out everything at once from their stubborn minds: just as the man who is attempting to climb to the highest place, rises by steps and degrees and not by leaps. Thus the Lord made Himself known to the Israelites in Egypt; yet he preserved in his own worship the forms of sacrifice which they were accustomed to offer to the devil and commanded them to kill animals when sacrificing to him. So with changed hearts, they were to put away one part of the sacrifice and retain the other, even though they were the same animals as they were in the habit of offering, yet since the people were offering them to the true God and not to idols, they were not the same sacrifices. These things then, dearly beloved, you must say to our brother so that in his present position he may

7. Reprinted, by permission of Oxford University Press, from Bertram Colgrave and R.A.B. Mynors, eds., *Bede's Ecclesiastical History of the English People* (Oxford: Clarendon Press, 1969), pp. 107–109, 183–87.

carefully consider how he should order all things. May God keep you in safety, most beloved son.

The Sparrow's Flight

When the king had heard his words, he answered that he was both willing and bound to accept the faith which Paulinus taught. He said, however, that he would confer about this with his loyal chief men and his counsellors so that, if they agreed with him, they might all be consecrated together in the waters of life. Paulinus agreed and the king did as he had said. A meeting of his council was held and each one was asked in turn what he thought of this doctrine hitherto unknown to them and this new worship of God which was being proclaimed.

Coifi, the chief of the priests, answered at once, "Notice carefully, King, this doctrine which is now being expounded to us. I frankly admit that, for my part, I have found that the religion which we have hitherto held has no virtue nor profit in it. None of your followers has devoted himself more earnestly than I have to the worship of our gods, but nevertheless there are many who receive greater benefits and greater honour from you than I do and are more successful in all their undertakings. If the gods had any power they would have helped me more readily, seeing that I have always served them with greater zeal. So it follows that if, on examination, these new doctrines which have now been explained to us are found to be better and more effectual, let us accept them at once without any delay."

Another of the king's chief men agreed with this advice and with these wise words and then added, "This is how the present life of man on earth, King, appears to me in comparison with that time which is unknown to us. You are sitting feasting with your ealdormen and thegns[8] in winter time; the fire is burning on the hearth in the middle of the hall and all inside is warm, while outside the wintry storms of rain and snow are raging; and a sparrow flies swiftly through the hall. It enters in at one door and quickly flies out through the other. For the few moments it is inside, the storm and wintry tempest cannot touch it, but after the briefest moment of calm, it flits from your sight, out of the wintry storm and into it again. So this life of man appears but for a moment; what follows or indeed what went before, we know not at all. If this new doctrine brings us more certain information, it seems right that we should accept it." Other elders and counsellors of the king continued in the same manner, being divinely prompted to do so.

Coifi added that he would like to listen still more carefully to what Paulinus himself had to say about God. The king ordered Paulinus to

8. Two ranks of nobility.

speak, and when he had said his say, Coifi exclaimed, "For a long time now I have realized that our religion is worthless; for the more diligently I sought the truth in our cult, the less I found it. Now I confess openly that the truth shines out clearly in this teaching which can bestow on us the gift of life, salvation, and eternal happiness. Therefore I advise your Majesty that we should promptly abandon and commit to the flames the temples and the altars which we have held sacred without repaying any benefit." Why need I say more? The king publicly accepted the gospel which Paulinus preached, renounced idolatry, and confessed his faith in Christ. When he asked the high priest of their religion which of them should be the first to profane the altars and the shrines of the idols, together with their precincts, Coifi answered, "I will; for through the wisdom the true God has given me no one can more suitably destroy those things which I once foolishly worshiped, and so set an example to all." And at once, casting aside his vain superstitions, he asked the king to provide him with arms and a stallion; and mounting it he set out to destroy the idols. Now a high priest of their religion was not allowed to carry arms or to ride except on a mare. So, girded with a sword, he took a spear in his hand and mounting the king's stallion he set off to where the idols were. The common people who saw him thought he was mad. But as soon as he approached the shrine, without any hesitation he profaned it by casting the spear which he held into it; and greatly rejoicing in the knowledge of the worship of the true God, he ordered his companions to destroy and set fire to the shrine and all the enclosures. The place where the idols once stood is still shown, not far from York, to the east, over the river Derwent. Today it is called Goodmanham, the place where the high priest, through the inspiration of the true God, profaned and destroyed the altars which he himself had consecrated.

3. Animal Head from the Oseberg Ship Burial, c. 825 (Gardner, p. 319, ill. 8:4; Janson, p. 257, ill. 358)
Ahmed Ibn Fadlan, *Account of a Traveler:* "A Viking Ship Burial," 922

The stability of the Anglo-Saxon kingdoms in England and the Celtic communities in Ireland was brutally disrupted by the Scandinavian raiders. Closely related in language and racial stock to the Germanic peoples, the Scandinavians, more commonly called Vikings, inhabited the more remote territories of northern Europe. During the late eighth century, internal pressures, perhaps caused by overpopulation and the decline of agricultural productivity, drove the Vikings to expand outside their homelands. Their superior shipbuilding techniques enabled them to develop seaworthy vessels capable of navigating over the northern seas, along the Russian rivers, and even into the Mediterranean. Using their swift, low-slung, oar-propelled boats, the Vikings brought terror to the coasts. They were able to land at will, pillage, loot, and burn a town, and to depart before a defending army drew near. Between 800 and 1050, they destroyed the Irish monasteries and crushed the Irish tradition of literature, learning, and art; they overwhelmed the Anglo-Saxon kingdom of Northumbria, where Bede and his fellow scholars had lived; and they raided the territories of the Carolingian empire with impunity.

The Vikings were a pagan people. Not until the tenth and eleventh centuries did Christian missionary activities begin to win converts in Scandinavia or alter the customs of Scandinavian society. The Vikings honored their own traditional gods such as Odin (or Wotan), god of war and lord of the heavens, and Thor, god of thunder and guardian of the family.

The animal head carved on the terminal of a post, discovered in a Viking ship burial near Oseberg, Norway, expresses the pagan fierceness of the Scandinavians. This fierceness was also evident in the burial of a Viking chieftain as it was seen and described in 922 by a Muslim traveler, Ahmed Ibn Fadlan.

Ibn Fadlan had been sent as an ambassador and Muslim missionary from the caliph of Baghdad to the king of Bulgaria. Ibn Fadlan's route to Bulgaria was a circuitous one. On the Volga River he encountered a tribe of armed merchants whom he called Northmen or Rus and whom most scholars identify as Swedish Vikings settled in Russia. He wrote an account of a Viking funeral and of the gruesome rituals of sacrifice which preceded it. No parallels for these sacrifices can be found in Viking literature, but other chroniclers of the age, such as Adam of Bremen, describe the Viking practice of human sacrifice in Sweden, Norway, and Denmark and the Viking use of methods such as hanging, spearing, drowning, and burning. A selection from Ibn Fadlan's account, "A Viking Ship Burial," is presented here.

Ahmed Ibn Fadlan, *Account of a Traveler*[9]

A Viking Ship Burial

I was told that the least of what they do for their chiefs when they die, is to consume them with fire. When I was finally informed of the death of one of their magnates, I sought to witness what befell. . . . When one of their chiefs dies, his family asks his girls and pages: "Which one of you will die with him?" Then one of them answers, "I." . . . When the day was now come that the dead man and the girl were to be committed to the flames, I went to the river in which his ship lay, but found that it had already been drawn ashore. . . . [Then] they brought a couch, placed it in the ship, and covered it with Greek cloth of gold, wadded and quilted, with pillows of the same material. There came an old crone, whom they call the angel of death, and spread the articles mentioned on the couch. It was she who

9. Reprinted from Albert Cook, "Ibn Fadlan's Account of Scandinavian Merchants on the Volga in 922," *Journal of English and Germanic Philology,* Vol. 22 (1923), pp. 59–63.

attended to the sewing of the garments, and to all the equipment; it was she, also, who was to slay the girl. I saw her; she was dark . . . thick-set, with a lowering countenance. . . .

They carried [the dead man] into a tent placed in the ship, seated him on the wadded and quilted covering, supported him with the pillows, and, bringing strong drink, fruits, and basil, placed them all beside him. . . .

The girl who had devoted herself to death meanwhile walked to and fro, entering one after another of the tents which they had there. The occupant of each tent lay with her, saying, "Tell your master, 'I [the man] did this only for love of you.' " . . . Then they led her away to the ship.

Here she took off her two bracelets, and gave them to the old woman who was called the angel of death, and who was to murder her. She also drew off her two anklets, and passed them to the two serving-maids, who were the daughters of the so-called angel of death. Then they lifted her into the ship, but did not yet admit her to the tent. Now men came up with shields and staves, and handed her a cup of strong drink. This she took, sang over it, and emptied it. "With this," so the interpreter told me, "she is taking leave of those who are dear to her." Then another cup was handed her, which she also took, and began a lengthy song. The crone admonished her to drain the cup without lingering, and to enter the tent where her master lay. By this time, as it seemed to me, the girl had become dazed; she made as though she would enter the tent, and had brought her head forward between the tent and the ship, when the hag seized her by the head, and dragged her in. At this moment the men began to beat upon their shields with the staves, in order to drown the noise of her outcries, which might have terrified the other girls, and deterred them from seeking death with their masters in the future. Then six men followed into the tent, and each and every one had carnal companionship with her. Then they laid her down by her master's side, while two of the men seized her by the feet, and two by the hands. The old woman known as the angel of death now knotted a rope around her neck, and handed the ends to two of the men to pull. Then with a broad-bladed dagger she smote her between the ribs, and drew the blade forth, while the two men strangled her with the rope till she died.

The next of kin to the dead man now drew near, and, taking a piece of wood, lighted it, and walked backwards toward the ship, holding the stick in one hand, with the other placed upon his buttocks (he being naked), until the wood which had been piled under the ship was ignited. Then the others came up with staves and firewood, each one carrying a stick already lighted at the upper end, and threw it all on the pyre. The pile was soon aflame, then the ship, finally the tent, the man, and the girl, and everything else in the ship. A terrible storm began to blow up, and thus intensified the flames, and gave wings to the blaze.

At my side stood one of the Northmen, and I heard him talking with the interpreter, who stood near him. I asked the interpreter what the Northman had said, and received this answer: "You Arabs," he said, "must be a stupid set! You take him who is to you the most revered and beloved of men, and cast him into the ground, to be devoured by creeping things and worms. We, on the other hand, burn him in a twinkling, so that he instantly, without a moment's delay, enters into Paradise." At this he burst out into uncontrollable laughter, and then continued: "It is the love of the Master [God] that causes the wind to blow and snatch him away in an instant." And, in very truth, before an hour had passed, ship, wood, and girl had, with the man, turned to ashes.

Thereupon they heaped over the place where the ship had stood something like a rounded hill, and, erecting on the centre of it a large birchen post, wrote on it the name of the deceased, along with that of the king of the Northmen. Having done this, they left the spot.

CAROLINGIAN PERIOD

1. Palatine Chapel of Charlemagne, Aachen, 792–805 (Gardner, p. 329, ills. 8:16 and 8:17; Janson, p. 260, ills. 363–65)
Notker the Stammerer, *Charlemagne:* "The Visit of the Byzantine Envoys," 884

Charlemagne (742–814) was the greatest of the Carolingian rulers. In 768, at the death of their father, Pepin III, Charlemagne and his younger brother, Carloman, shared the Frankish kingdom as joint sovereigns. In 771 Carloman died, and Charlemagne became the sole ruler.

Throughout his forty-six-year reign, Charlemagne pursued his ideal of establishing a powerful, unified Christian state. Almost constantly at war, Charlemagne expanded the territories under Frankish rule, until within ten years of his accession he controlled more territory in the West than any ruler since the fourth-century Roman emperors.

At the same time, Charlemagne championed the Christian church. He issued reform directives to the clergy, strengthened the church administration, and protected the papacy. In 800, Charlemagne was crowned Holy Roman Emperor by Pope Leo III during Christmas mass in St. Peter's.

Charlemagne made his capital at Aachen (Aix-la-Chapelle). The palace, which is now incorporated into a fourteenth-century city hall, and the Palatine Chapel, which survives intact, were the first important stone buildings to be constructed in northern Europe since the fall of Rome. Their erection symbolized the recovery of the West during the Carolingian period.

The Palatine Chapel at Aachen is modeled on the church of San Vitale in

Ravenna, which Charlemagne had visited and admired. San Vitale, in turn, is modeled on Hagia Sophia, the imperial church of the Byzantine emperors. In addition, columns and pavement stones from Ravenna were incorporated into the chapel at Aachen. Thus, in its design, decorations, and construction, the chapel reveals the ambitions of Charlemagne to be recognized as the successor of the Roman emperors in the West and as the equal of the Byzantine emperors in the East.

Charlemagne's conscious assumption of the trappings of royal power is also evident in the account of a state visit to Aachen paid by Byzantine envoys in 812. The encounter is described in the anecdotal and highly imaginative biography of Charlemagne written by the Swiss monk Notker the Stammerer, in 884. According to Notker, the envoys mistakenly identified servants in the palace as Charlemagne. When finally admitted into the presence of the emperor himself, they were overwhelmed by Charlemagne's glory, which combined the splendor of worldly power with the radiance of spiritual might.

A selection from Notker's *Charlemagne,* "The Visit of the Byzantine Envoys," is presented here.

Notker the Stammerer, *Charlemagne*[10]

The Visit of the Byzantine Envoys

A short time afterwards the [Byzantine emperor] sent his own envoys to the glorious Charlemagne. By chance it happened that at this very moment the bishop and the count whom I have mentioned were staying with the Emperor. When it was announced that the envoys were about to arrive, these two advised the prudent Charlemagne that [the envoys] should be conducted by a circuitous route through the mountains and pathless wildernesses, until everything which they possessed was worn out and used up. Not until they were reduced to great penury were they to be summoned to the Emperor's presence.

When the envoys finally arrived, the bishop and his fellow conspirator ordered the official in charge of the stables to sit on a lofty throne in the midst of his ostlers, in such pomp that it was impossible to believe that he was anyone else but the Emperor. The moment the envoys saw him, they fell to the ground and wanted to worship him. They were driven back by the court officials and forced to move on again. They came to another spot and there they saw the Count of the Palace in the middle of a group of noblemen who were holding council. Again they thought that it was the Emperor and they threw themselves on the ground. Those who were present said: "That is not the Emperor! That is not the Emperor!" and hit

10. Reprinted, by permission of the publisher, from Einhard and Notker the Stammerer, *Two Lives of Charlemagne,* trans. by Lewis Thorpe (London: Penguin Classics, 1969), pp. 140–42. Copyright © by Lewis Thorpe, 1969.

them to compel them to move on. They went a little farther, and then they saw the Master of the King's Table, with his uniformed staff about him: and a third time they fell to the ground, imagining that this must be the Emperor. They were driven on once more until they came upon the Emperor's domestic servants, grouped in his private apartments, with the steward in their midst, and they had no doubt whatsoever that this man was the greatest of all mortals. The steward denied that he was anything of the sort; but he promised that he would use his influence with the nobles of the palace to ensure that the envoys should come into the presence of the august Emperor, if it should prove possible.

At long last there came servants direct from the Emperor's own presence, with instructions to introduce the envoys in an honourable way.

Charlemagne, of all kings the most glorious, was standing by a window through which the sun shone with dazzling brightness. He was clad in gold and precious stones and he glittered himself like the sun at its first rising. . . . Around the Emperor, like the host of heaven, stood his three sons, the young men who were later to share the Empire; his daughters and their mother, adorned with wisdom, beauty and ropes of pearls; his bishops, unsurpassed in their virtue and their dignified posture, and his abbots, distinguished by their sanctity and their noble demeanour; his leaders, like Joshua when he appeared in the camp of Gilgal; and his army like that which drove back the Syrians and the Assyrians out of Samaria. Had David been in their midst he would have had every reason to sing: "Kings of the earth, and all people; princes, and all judges of the earth; both young men and maidens; old men, and children: let him praise the name of the Lord." The envoys of the Greeks were dumbfounded. Their courage deserted them and they did not know which way to turn. Speechless and senseless they fell to the ground. In his great kindness the Emperor picked them up and tried to revive them with consoling words. . . . Charlemagne then swore to them by the King of Heaven that he would do them no harm. They took heart at this promise and began to behave with a little more confidence. In the end they went back home and never returned to our land again.

2. Monastery Church of St. Riquier at Centula, France, c. 800 (Gardner, pp. 332–33, ills. 8:20 and 8:21; Janson, p. 261, ill. 366–67)

The Song of Roland: "The Mighty Roland" and "Charlemagne and the Emir," early twelfth century

The monastery church of St. Riquier was built under the special protection of Angilbert, one of Charlemagne's most important advisers, and services in the church were attended by the emperor. Like the Palatine Chapel at Aachen, St.

Riquier had an elaborate western entrance, called the westwork. The westwork was a new feature of Carolingian architectural design. Consisting of two stair towers flanking the central portal and a raised gallery inside the church from which the emperor and his entourage could watch the service below, the westworks suggested the protective city gates and towers that guarded ancient cities. Symbolically, the westworks represented a Christian citadel protected by the king.

In the Middle Ages, Charlemagne was regarded as the model of a Christian king and emperor. His success as a ruler, however, depended in part upon his personal qualities of ambition and ruthlessness. In his determination to hold power, he proved himself ready to wage ceaseless wars against the external enemies of his realm, willing to eliminate internal rivals to his throne, including the sons of his brother, Carloman. At the same time, Charlemagne held the Christian church in high regard, considered himself accountable to God for the Christians entrusted to his governance, and believed it was the king's duty to spread the Christian faith among the heathen.

Charlemagne's reputation as the champion of the Christian faith is enshrined in the earliest surviving French epic, *The Song of Roland.* Intended to entertain a lay audience, the poem emerged from the oral tradition of northern Europe. Sometime between 1100 and 1130 the poem was recorded by an anonymous author. It is the best example of the literary genre called *chansons de geste* (songs of great deeds).

The Song of Roland is based upon an obscure historical event. In order to halt the Muslim raids from Spain into the Carolingian territories, Charlemagne had established a military district, called the Spanish March, in northern Spain. In 778, as the Carolingian army returned across the Pyrenees after a season's fighting in this region, Christian Basques attacked a Frankish rear guard. The Franks, led by Charlemagne's faithful vassal Roland, fought bravely but were annihilated. As time went on, the Basque ambush was transformed by the popular imagination into a heroic struggle between the Christian Franks and the Spanish infidels, and was embellished by an invented contest between Charlemagne and Baligant, the Muslim emir of Babylon. The tale was further enlivened by the inclusion of Bramimond, the Saracen queen who, according to legend, repudiated her religion and accepted Christianity. Two selections from *The Song of Roland,* "The Mighty Roland" and "Charlemagne and the Emir," are presented here.

The Song of Roland[11]

The Mighty Roland

Count Roland is a noble soldier,
Gautier de l'Hum a fine performer,
The old archbishop is another;

11. Reprinted, by permission of the publisher, from *The Song of Roland,* trans. by C. H. Sisson (Manchester, England: Carcanet Press, 1983), pp. 77–78, 123–26.

Each wants not to fail the others.
They are all in the thick of it.
A thousand Saracens on foot,
Forty thousand mounted, but
Not one of them dares to go near.
They throw their lances and their spears,
Arrows, darts and javelins.
Gautier is killed at once, Turpin
Of Reims has his shield holed,
His helmet smashed, his head mauled,
His hauberk pierced, the mail gone
And four spears right through his body;
His horse is killed under him;
With the archbishop down, things are grim.

Turpin sees he is on the ground
But four spears will not keep him down.
Rapidly he gets to his feet,
Looks at Roland, runs to meet
Him and says: "I am undefeated!
No surrender while I live!"
He draws Almace, his sword, and gives
More than a thousand thrusts and cuts.
Charles will see he didn't give up
When he sees around him four hundred,
Some wounded, some without heads,
Some of them stuck through the middle.
That is what one who was at the battle
Reports, it is all in the *Geste*
The noble Gilles, whom God so blessed,
Wrote it down in the abbey at Laon;
That's what the story is based upon.

Count Roland fights courageously
But his body is hot and sweaty,
He has a terrible pain in his head;
When he blew the horn, his temples bled.
But is Charles coming? He wants to know,
So once again, but feebly, he blows.
The emperor stops, listens and says:
"Things are not going well with us!
If the horn sounds so weakly it is
Because Roland has not long to live.

We must ride fast or he will be gone!
Sound the trumpets—every one!"
Sixty thousand of them blow,
The mountains ring, the valleys echo.
The pagans don't laugh at what they hear,
They know that Charles will soon be there.

Charlemagne and the Emir

Charles of Sweet France is valiant, the emir
Is not a coward or a doubter.
They brandish naked swords, each gives
Great blows upon the other's shield which
Cut the leather and double boards;
The nails fly out, the bosses[12] fall;
Unprotected except for their byrnies
They fight on; sparks as from a furnace
Rise from their helmets; and until
One admits he is wrong, they will.

The emir says: "Now, Charles, reflect
On the ill you have done to me, and repent!
You have killed my son, as well I know
And your claim to my country is hollow.
You should become my vassal, ready
To do me service faithfully
Both here and in the east." Charles says:
"It would bring shame to all of us.
Peace and love are not for pagans.
Receive God's law, the law of Christians
And I will begin to love you at once.
Serve and trust God's omnipotence."
Baligant says: "That is evil talk."
They took their swords again, and fought.
The emir with all his might and main
Strikes at the head of Charlemagne.
The burnished helmet breaks and splits;
The sword slices the scalp and it
Takes a handsbreadth of the flesh;
The bone shows, but Charles is not vanquished.
He totters, surely he must fall?

12. The thickened central part of the shield.

But no! for God wills his survival.
St. Gabriel comes back to him
And says: "Why hesitate, great king?"

The heat is great, the dust rises,
The pagans flee and fall under the eyes
Of the French, right into the town
Of Saragossa[13] where, high in her tower
Bramimond climbs with all her crowd
Of clergy, the men of the false law,

Untonsured, with no orders at all.
Seeing the Arabs in disarray
She cries: "Mohammed, give us aid!
Good king, our men are conquered now,
The emir shamefully brought us low!"
Marsilie hears and turns his face
Away, he weeps for his disgrace;
So dies of grief, in all his sins,
And yields his soul to living demons.

They are dead, the pagans, most of them
And Charles has won the battle. His men
Have battered down the massive gates:
Saragossa is left to its fate.
He knows it will not be defended,
He takes possession, the day has ended,
The victorious army settles down,
The king with the white beard is proud.
And Bramimond has given up
The towers to his guardianship,
The ten big ones, the fifty small.
Who trusts God may accomplish all.

The day has passed and it is night,
The moon is clear and there is starlight.
Saragossa has been taken.
A thousand Frenchmen search the place,
Its synagogues and mosques, and smash
With iron sledge-hammers and axes
The images and all the idols
Till nothing is left of all their lies.

13. Zaragoza, a city on the Ebro River in northeast Spain. The name is a corruption of the Roman name for the settlement, Caesarea Augusta.

The king believes in the God he serves.
The bishops speak their holy words
Over the water, and they lead
The pagans to the baptistry:
Any who opposes Charles's will
Is hung or burnt or otherwise killed.

A hundred thousand are baptised
True Christians, but the queen not at this time.
She is to go to France as a captive,
The king would have her converted by love.

3. Schematic Plan for a Monastery at St. Gall, c. 819 (Gardner, p. 331, ill. 8:19; Janson, p. 262, ills. 368–69)
The Rule of St. Benedict: "The Monastic Life," early sixth century

The plan of St. Gall was created for a Benedictine monastery, and exhibits the same qualities of order, clarity, and regularity that are exemplified by *The Rule of St. Benedict.* St. Gall demonstrates the growth of monasteries from small, isolated communities of the early Christian period into large feudal estates with vast complexes of buildings.

Monasticism sprang from the desire of the individual to encounter God by renouncing secular life and concentrating upon spiritual ideals. During the third and fourth centuries, Egypt was the center of the monastic movement, from which it moved slowly westward. But during the sixth and seventh centuries, there was an enormous growth of monasticism in Europe, and the number and size of monastic communities increased rapidly. As these communities assumed greater importance as social institutions, as well as religious centers, the need became apparent for a comprehensive code to regulate monastic life. This need was met by the Benedictine Rule.

Benedict of Nursia (c. 480–543) came from a wealthy family in central Italy, and was educated in Rome. Shocked by the licentiousness of city life, he became a hermit in a cave about forty miles east of Rome. He soon attracted many followers, who persuaded him to become abbot of a nearby monastery. Resenting Benedict's zeal, the monks there attempted to poison him, so Benedict, together with a few disciples, formed his own community at Monte Cassino, about halfway between Rome and Naples. Benedict wrote his *Rule* for this community.

Other monasteries quickly recognized the soundness of the Benedictine Rule. Charlemagne encouraged its adoption throughout Europe, and in 817, during the reign of Louis the Pious, the Diet of Aachen officially imposed the Benedictine Rule upon all monasteries in the Carolingian empire.

The Rule of St. Benedict offers both practical and spiritual advice on the formation and administration of a monastery and on the conduct of the spiritual life and daily activities of its members. According to the *Rule,* the principal focus of the life of a monk is the worship of God through common prayer and private devotions. Each monk is also required to perform some type of manual labor and to engage in religious study, and he is admonished to regulate his conduct according to his vows of chastity, poverty, and obedience. Finally, the *Rule* advises that the physical needs of the monks are to be met in a manner that is simple but sufficient. Benedict's provisions for food, clothing, and shelter are austere but avoid asceticism. A selection from *The Rule of St. Benedict,* "The Monastic Life," is presented here.

The Rule of St. Benedict[14]

The Monastic Life

Chapter 3: The Counsel of the Brothers

Whenever an important matter is to be undertaken in the monastery the abbot should call the entire community together and should set forth the agenda. After hearing the various opinions of the brothers, he should consider all and then do what he thinks best. . . . Everyone shall follow the *Rule* as his master. No one should rashly deviate from it.

Individual desires have no place in the monastery and neither inside nor outside the walls should anyone presume to argue with the abbot. If he dares do so, he should be punished according to the *Rule.* The abbot himself must do everything according to the *Rule* and fearing God, knowing that he will be held accountable for his reign to the highest judge, God.

Chapter 8: The Divine Office at Night (Matins)

During winter—from November first until Easter—the brothers shall rise at the eighth hour of the night as is reasonable; thus having rested a bit more than half the night, they will be refreshed. Any time left over ought to be used by the brothers to practice psalms or for reading.

From Easter until November first the hour for Matins should be arranged so that, after a very short break for going to the toilet, Lauds, which ought to be said at daybreak, may follow immediately.

Chapter 16: The Day Office

The prophet says: "Seven times daily I have sung Your praises" (Psalms 119:164). We will cleave to this sacred number if we perform our monastic

14. Excerpts from *The Rule of St. Benedict,* trans. by Anthony C. Meisel and M. L. del Mastro (Garden City, N.Y.: Doubleday & Company, Inc., 1975), pp. 51, 61, 66, 70, 80–81, 86. Copyright © 1975 by Anthony C. Meisel and M. L. del Mastro. Reprinted by permission of Doubleday & Company, Inc.

duties at Lauds, Prime, Tierce, Sext, None, Vespers and Compline. The same prophet says of the Night Office: "I arose at midnight to confess to You" (Psalms 119:62). In the Day Office, therefore, we ought praise our Creator for His just judgments, and at night we will rise to confess to Him.

Chapter 22: How the Monks Are to Sleep

All the monks shall sleep in separate beds. All shall receive bedding, allotted by the abbot, appropriate to their environment. If possible they should all sleep in one room. However, if there are too many for this, they will be grouped in tens or twenties, a senior in charge of each group. . . . When they arise for the Divine Office, they ought encourage each other, for the sleepy make many excuses.

Chapter 39: Food Apportionment

We believe that cooked dishes will satisfy the daily needs at each meal—at the sixth and ninth hours. If some brothers cannot eat one, then they may eat the other. Two dishes must be enough for all. A third dish may appear if fresh fruit or vegetables are available. Whether it be eaten at one meal or two (dinner and supper), a pound of bread will be allotted to each monk daily. . . .

Chapter 40: Drink Apportionment

"Everyone has his proper gift from God, one this, another thus" (I Corinthians 7:7). For this reason, we hesitate in apportioning others' food. If we are mindful of the sick, a *hemina*[15] of wine for each monk each day is adequate we believe. Those who have received the gift of abstinence will know they shall be especially rewarded by God.

Chapter 48: Daily Manual Labor

Idleness is an enemy of the soul. Therefore, the brothers should be occupied according to schedule in either manual labor or holy reading. These may be arranged as follows: from Easter to October, the brothers shall work at manual labor from Prime until the fourth hour. From then until the sixth hour they should read. After dinner they should rest (in bed) in silence. However, should anyone desire to read, he should do so without disturbing his brothers.

None should be chanted at about the middle of the eighth hour. Then

15. A quarter of a liter.

everyone shall work as they must until Vespers. If conditions dictate that they labor in the fields (harvesting), they should not be grieved for they are truly monks when they must live by manual labor, as did our fathers and the apostles. Everything should be in moderation, though, for the sake of the timorous.

OTTONIAN ART

1. *Otto III Enthroned Receiving the Homage of Four Parts of the Empire,* from the *Gospel Book of Otto III,* c. 997–1000 (Gardner, p. 338, ill. 8:28)
Christ Washing the Feet of St. Peter, from the *Gospel Book of Otto III,* c. 997–1000 (Jansen, p. 270, color plate 42, and p. 277, ill. 381)
Chronicon Novaliciense: "An Emperor Enthroned," c. 1060

Otto III (980–1002) was the fourth ruler in the Saxon dynasty that succeeded the Frankish dynasties of the Merovingian and Carolingian periods (476–887). Son of the Holy Roman Emperor Otto II and the Empress Theophano, a Byzantine princess, Otto III was elected to the throne in June 983, when he was only three years old, and was crowned in Aachen in December of the same year. In a bid for royal power, Henry the Wrangler, the duke of Bavaria, seized the young king, but an alliance of churchmen and princes forced the duke to surrender Otto to his mother. Theophano served as regent until her death in 991 and was succeeded as regent by Otto's grandmother, the dowager empress Adelaide.

In 994, shortly before his fifteenth birthday, the age of majority in Germany, Otto assumed control of the German territories and he quickly exerted his power over much of Italy as well. The death of Pope John XV in 996 presented Otto with the opportunity to name a successor to the Papacy. He arranged the election of his cousin, Bruno of Carinthia, as Gregory V. Gregory in turn crowned Otto as Holy Roman Emperor. In 998, Otto made Rome his official residence and the administrative center of his empire.

As a child, Otto had been strongly influenced by his Byzantine mother. He instituted elaborate Byzantine ceremonies in his court and sought to marry a Byzantine princess. Influences from Byzantine art can be seen in manuscript illuminations from the *Gospel Book of Otto III* such as *Christ Washing the Feet of St. Peter.* At the same time, Otto deeply admired Charlemagne and sought to model his reign on that of his great predecessor. Otto revived Charlemagne's dream of creating an international state in which the power and glory of the ancient Roman Empire would be realized in Christian forms. This state would be ruled by a theocratic emperor to whom the pope would be subordinate in religious as well as in secular affairs.

Otto's concept of kingship was revealed by the emperor's reverential visit to the tomb of Charlemagne in 1000. The visit was recorded by the chronicler of the monastery of Novalesa more than half a century later. It describes the appearance of the seated monarch, who in death was still holding the royal scepter and wearing the kingly crown.

The manuscript illumination *Otto III Enthroned Receiving the Homage of Four Parts of the Empire* depicts Otto in life in a similar manner, holding the symbols of church and state and flanked by his clerical and noble supporters. A selection from the *Chronicon Novaliciense,* "An Emperor Enthroned," is presented here.

Otto's reign ended in 1001. In January of that year, the Italian town of Tibur rebelled. Otto laid seige to the town and forced its surrender. However, his clemency in pardoning the inhabitants enraged the Romans, who in turn rebelled and besieged Otto's palace. After briefly placating the rebels, Otto withdrew to the monastery of St. Apollinaris near Ravenna, to do penance. He was unable to regain control of Rome and died of malaria as Henry of Bavaria, who was to succeed him as German king and emperor, marched to his aid.

Chronicon Novaliciense[1]

An Emperor Enthroned

We entered in unto Charles. He was not lying down, as is the manner with the bodies of other dead men, but sat on a certain chair as though he lived. He was crowned with a golden crown, and held a sceptre in his hands, the same being covered with gloves, through which the nails had grown and pierced. And above him was a tabernacle compact of brass and marble exceedingly. Now when we were come in unto the tomb, we brake and made straightway an opening in it. And when we entered into it, we perceived a vehement savour. So we did worship forthwith to him with bended thighs and knees; and straightway Otto the Emperor clad him with white raiment, and pared his nails, and made good all that was lacking about him. But none of his members had corrupted and fallen away, except a little piece of the end of his nose, which he caused at once to be restored with gold; and he took from his mouth one tooth, and built the tabernacle again and departed.

1. Reprinted, by permission of the publisher, from *The Cambridge Medieval History,* Vol. 3 (Cambridge: Cambridge University Press, 1924), pp. 213–14.

2. *Adam and Eve Reproached by the Lord,* from the bronze doors of Bishop Bernward for St. Michael's at Hildesheim, Germany, 1015 (Gardner, p. 335, ill. 8:25; Janson, p. 276, ill. 380)
Halitgar, *The Roman Penitential:* "Prescriptions of Penance," c. 830
Hrotswitha of Gandersheim, *Paphnutius:* "Renunciation of Sin," late tenth century

The scene depicted in relief on the bronze doors of St. Michael's, Hildesheim, represents Adam and Eve after the Fall. As the Fall of Humankind is described in Genesis, Adam and Eve were created by God and were sheltered in the Garden of Eden. All their needs were provided for, but they were forbidden to eat the fruit from the tree of the knowledge of good and evil. Tempted by the serpent, the woman ate the fruit and gave some to her husband as well. They were punished by God for their disobedience by being driven from the garden of paradise into the world of pain, toil, and death.

To the Christian church of the Middle Ages, Adam and Eve's expulsion from Paradise represented the penance that individuals performed to atone for their sins. During the first centuries of Christianity, the church recognized that sin was a universal and pervasive condition of humanity and urged all sinners to seek reconciliation with God by confessing and by performing penance. Through a series of public actions the sinner expressed personal sorrow for his or her deeds and achieved forgiveness and healing. By the third century, the church had developed penitential practices to test the repentance of its fallen members. Penitents made a public confession of their sins; wore sackcloth, a garment made of goat's hair to symbolize their separation from the sheep of Christ's flock; and covered themselves with ashes to commemorate Adam and Eve's expulsion from Paradise.

By the sixth century, this form of penance was no longer in use. To fill the vacuum, Irish monks developed and popularized a private system for confessing sins and doing penance. The penitent confessed privately to a priest, was given the priest's absolution, and then did penance, which usually consisted of fasting, reciting a number of prayers, or giving alms to the poor. Penances varied in length and severity, according to the status of the sinner and the nature of the sin. This system of penances was officially adopted by the Western church in the ninth and tenth centuries. Selections from two works, a penitential and a play, reflecting such practices in the medieval church, are presented here.

Penitentials were manuals intended to help confessors allot the penances appropriate for specific sins. The work of individuals, the penitentials relied for their acceptance upon their authors' reputations for sagacity and holiness. In 830, Ebbo, the archbishop of Reims, wrote to Halitgar (late eighth to early ninth centuries), the bishop of Cambrai, deploring the discrepancies among the penitentials then in use and urging Halitgar to write a new and authoritative one.

Halitgar died a year later. Among his literary works was a book entitled *The Roman Penitential.* The penitential is believed to have been compiled by Halitgar from older, Celtic sources. The title, with reference to Rome, may have been added to bolster the manual's authority. A selection from *The Roman Penitential,* "Prescriptions of Penance," is presented here. In it, Halitgar outlines a wide variety of sins committed by clerics and lay persons and recommends appropriate penances for each.

Paphnutius is a late-tenth-century play written by Hrotswitha of Gandersheim. Hrotswitha (935–c. 1000) was a nun at the convent of Gandersheim, a wealthy and important church community in Germany. In *Paphnutius*, Hrotswitha set out to describe the war between the flesh and the spirit and the long penance which must be observed by those who have yielded to desire. The play focuses on the relationship between its two central characters, Paphnutius and Thaïs. Paphnutius is a holy man troubled by the temptations caused to young men by the beautiful harlot Thaïs. Posing as a lover, Paphnutius confronts Thaïs and persuades her to renounce her ways. Thaïs agrees to enter a convent, where she observes a harsh penance. After three years of fasting and unrelenting mortification of the flesh, the dying Thaïs is visited by Paphnutius, who assures her she will soon be released from her earthly existence and will rejoice in God's mercy.

A selection from *Paphnutius*, "The Renunciation of Sin," is presented here. In this passage, Paphnutius convinces Thaïs of the sinfulness of her life as a courtesan, and Thaïs is led to repentance.

Halitgar, *The Roman Penitential*[16]

Prescriptions of Penance

If any bishop or other ordained person commits homicide. If any cleric commits homicide, he shall do penance for ten years, three of these on bread and water.

If [the offender is] a layman, he shall do penance for three years, one of these on bread and water; a subdeacon, six years; a deacon, seven a presbyter, ten; a bishop, twelve. . . .

If anyone slays a man in a public expedition without cause, he shall do penance for twenty-one weeks; but if he slays anyone accidentally in defense of himself or his parents or his household, he shall not be under accusation. If he wishes to fast, it is for him to decide, since he did the thing under compulsion.

If he commits homicide in time of peace and not in a tumult, by force, or because of enmity in order to take [the victim's] property, he shall do penance for twenty-eight weeks and restore to his wife or children the property of him whom he has slain. . . .

If anyone commits fornication as [did] the Sodomites, he shall do penance for ten years, three of these on bread and water.

16. Reprinted, by permission of the publisher, from *Medieval Handbooks of Penance*, trans. by John T. McNeill and Helena M. Gamer (New York: Columbia University Press, 1938), pp. 302–307, 310–14.

If any cleric commits adultery, that is, if he begets a child with the wife or the betrothed of another, he shall do penance for seven years; however, if he does not beget a child and the act does not come to the notice of men, if he is a cleric he shall do penance for three years, one of these on bread and water; if a deacon or a monk, he shall do penance for seven years, three of these on bread and water; a bishop, twelve years, five on bread and water. . . .

If anyone commits fornication with a nun or one who is vowed to God, let him be aware that he has committed adultery. . . .

If anyone violates a virgin or a widow, he shall do penance for three years. . . .

If anyone commits fornication with a beast he shall do penance for one year. If he has not a wife, he shall do penance for half a year. . . .

If a man has sinned with a goat or with a sheep or with any animal, no one shall eat its flesh or milk, but it shall be killed and given to the dogs. . . .

If any cleric is guilty of a capital theft, that is, if he steals an animal or breaks into a house, or robs a somewhat well-protected place, he shall do penance for seven years.

A layman shall do penance for five years; a subdeacon, for six; a deacon, for seven; a presbyter, for ten; a bishop, for twelve. . . .

If through necessity anyone steals articles of food or a garment or a beast on account of hunger or nakedness, pardon shall be given him. He shall fast for four weeks. If he makes restitution, thou shalt not compel him to fast.

If anyone steals a horse or an ox or an ass or a cow or supplies of food or sheep which feed his whole household, he shall fast as stated above. . . .

If anyone violates a tomb, he shall do penance for seven years, three years on bread and water. . . .

If anyone intentionally cuts off any of his own members, he shall do penance for three years, one year on bread and water.

If anyone intentionally brings about abortion, he shall do penance for three years, one year on bread and water.

If anyone exacts usury from anybody, he shall do penance for three years, one year on bread and water.

If any cleric commits perjury, he shall do penance for seven years, three of these on bread and water.

A layman, three years; a subdeacon, six; a deacon, seven; a presbyter, ten; a bishop, twelve. . . .

If one by his magic causes the death of anyone, he shall do penance for seven years, three years on bread and water. . . .

If anyone commits sacrilege—(that is, those who are called augurs, who pay respect to omens), if he has taken auguries or [does it] by any evil device, he shall do penance for three years on bread and water.

If anyone is a soothsayer (those whom they call diviners) and makes divinations of any kind, since this is a demonic thing he shall do penance for five years, three years on bread and water.

If anyone is a wizard, that is, if he takes away the mind of a man by the invocation of demons, he shall do penance for five years, one year on bread and water.

If anyone makes amulets, which is a detestable thing, he shall do penance for three years, one year on bread and water. . . .

If anyone eats blood or a dead body or what has been offered to idols and was not under necessity of doing this, he shall fast for twelve weeks.

If anyone wishes to give alms for his soul of wealth which was the product of booty, if he has already done penance, he has the right to give it. Here endeth.

Hrotswitha of Gandersheim, *Paphnutius*[17]

Renunciation of Sin

Thaïs. Why do you tremble? Why do you turn pale? Why do you weep?

Paphnutius. I shudder at your presumption. I weep for your damnation. How, knowing what you know, can you destroy men in this manner and ruin so many souls, all precious and immortal?

Thaïs. Your voice pierces my heart! Strange lover—you are cruel. Pity me!

Paphnutius. Let us pity rather those souls whom you have deprived of the sight of God—of the God Whom you confess! Oh, Thaïs, you have wilfully offended the divine Majesty. That condemns you.

Thaïs. What do you mean? Why do you threaten me like this?

Paphnutius. Because the punishment of hell-fire awaits you if you remain in sin.

Thaïs. Who are you, who rebuke me so sternly? Oh, you have shaken me to the depths of my terrified heart!

17. Reprinted, by permission of the publisher, from *The Plays of Roswitha,* trans. by Christopher St. John (London: Chatto & Windus, 1923), pp. 102–103, 108–10, 126–28.

Paphnutius. I would that you could be shaken with fear to your very bowels! I would like to see your delicate body impregnated with terror in every vein, and every fibre, if that would keep you from yielding to the dangerous delights of the flesh.

Thaïs. And what zest for pleasure do you think is left now in a heart suddenly awakened to a consciousness of guilt! Remorse has killed everything.

Paphnutius. I long to see the thorns of vice cut away, and the choked-up fountain of your tears flowing once more. Tears of repentance are precious in the sight of God.

Thaïs. Oh, voice that promises mercy! Do you believe, can you hope that one so vile as I, soiled by thousands and thousands of impurities, can make reparation, can ever by any manner of penance obtain pardon?

Paphnutius. Thaïs, no sin is so great, no crime so black, that it cannot be expiated by tears and penitence, provided they are followed up by deeds.

Thaïs. Show me, I beg you, my father, what I can do to be reconciled with Him I have offended.

Paphnutius. Despise the world. Leave your dissolute lovers.

Thaïs. And afterwards? What then?

Paphnutius. You must retire to some solitary place, where you may learn to know yourself and realize the enormity of your sins.

Thaïs. If you think this will save me, I will not delay a moment.

IX

Romanesque Art

1. St. Sernin, Toulouse, France, c. 1080–1120 (Gardner, pp. 346–47, ills. 9:4 to 9:6; Janson, pp. 280–81, ills. 383–86)
The Pilgrim's Guide to Santiago de Compostela: "Pilgrimage Roads," "Pilgrimage Experiences," and "Pilgrimage Attractions," twelfth century

The pilgrimage was an important focus of religious life during the Middle Ages. Christians began to make journeys to holy places as early as the second and third centuries. Sites associated with Christ's life, death, and resurrection in the Holy Land were especially venerable, but Europe also had places of devotion. The tombs of Saints Peter and Paul in Rome and the catacombs outside Rome drew steady streams of visitors. Another important pilgrimage center developed at the tomb of the Apostle Saint James the Greater in Galicia in northwestern Spain.

To the Christian population of Europe, James became the symbol of Christian resistance to the Muslims, and his name was the battle cry of warriors such as Roland and his men. According to a tradition which is now considered doubtful, James had visited Spain and had preached to the heathen; at his death, it was claimed, his body had been brought to Spain from Jerusalem by his disciples. In the ninth century relics attributed to James were discovered at Libredon (later Santiago de Compostela), and a church was constructed, later to be destroyed, rebuilt, and enlarged many times. Santiago de Compostela ranked with Jerusalem and Rome as one of the three holiest shrines in Christendom, drawing pilgrims from all over Europe.

Pilgrimages were undertaken for a variety of motives: to request special favors, such as a cure for a physical ailment, victory over an enemy, or success in a future endeavor; to give thanks for favors one had received; to do penance for a particularly grave fault; or to offer simple devotion. Whether they traveled alone or in groups, pilgrims were exposed to many hazards. Roads were rough and badly marked; robbers waited for travelers in deserted regions; and unscrupulous innkeepers found the pilgrims easy targets. To assist pilgrims on their journeys, travel manuals were written, offering information and advice.

The most famous of these travel books is *The Pilgrim's Guide to Santiago de Compostela,* written in France in the twelfth century. Most travelers reached Compostela by sea, but *The Pilgrim's Guide* was intended for those who chose the overland route. It offered practical advice on matters such as what to eat and drink, where to sleep, and how to avoid being cheated by the natives. *The Pilgrim's Guide* also provided information about the important churches and shrines to be visited en route.

The church of St. Sernin at Toulouse was closely connected with Santiago de Compostela. It was located along a pilgrimage route to Santiago de Compostela, and it was the model for the Romanesque cathedral begun in Santiago de Compostela at the end of the eleventh century.

Three selections from the *The Pilgrim's Guide to Santiago de Compostela* are presented here. The first, "Pilgrimage Roads," describes the major routes to Santiago de Compostela. The second selection, "Pilgrimage Experiences," describes the Basque (Navarrais) people who were encountered en route in northeastern Spain and who were despised by the French. The third selection, "Pilgrimage Attractions," describes the reasons to visit the church of St. Gilles at Arles, which, like St. Sernin at Toulouse, was located along one route to Compostela.

The Pilgrim's Guide to Santiago de Compostela[1]

Pilgrimage Roads

There are four routes leading to St. James[2] which merge into one at Puente la Reina in the region of Spain. One goes through St-Gilles, Montpellier, Toulouse, and Somport. Another proceeds by way of Notre-Dame du Puy, Ste-Foi at Conques, and St-Pierre at Moissac. Another passes through Ste-Marie-Madeleine at Vézelay, St-Léonard in Limousin, and the city of Périgueux. And another makes its way through St Martin's at Tours, St-Hilaire at Poitiers, St-Jean d'Angély, St-Eutrope at Saintes, and the city of Bordeaux. Those which go through Ste-Foi, St-Léonard, and St Martin's merge at Ostabat and, having crossed [the Pyrenees] through the pass at Cize, join at Puente la Reina the route which crossed at Somport and form one route from there all the way to St. James.

Pilgrimage Experiences

The people of Navarre dress disgracefully, and eat and drink disgracefully. Indeed, in the homes of the Navarrais the entire household—the servant as well as the lord, the maid as well as the lady—are all in the habit of eating together; and eating food mixed in the same pot, not with spoons but with their own hands, and drinking from one and the same cup. If you saw them eat, you would think they were dogs or swine feeding. And if you heard them speak, you would be reminded of the barking of dogs, for their language is utterly barbarous: they call God "Urcia," the mother of

1. From Aimery Picaud, *Le Guide du Pèlerin de Saint-Jacques de Compostelle* (Mâcon: Eds. Jeanne Vielliard, 1938), pp. 2–4, 26–30, 36–40, 46. Translated for this volume by Conrad Rudolph.

2. Santiago de Compostela; in medieval Spanish, Saint James was Sant' Iago.

God "Andrea Maria," bread "orgui," wine "ardum," meat "aragui," fish "araign," house "echea," the lord of the house "iaona," the lady "andrea," the church "elicera," the priest "belaterra"—because he expounds upon the Beautiful Land—wheat "gari," water "uric," the king "ereguia," St James "Jaona domne Jacue." This is a barbarous people, unlike all other people in their customs and very essence; full of malice to all, dark in color, hostile in appearance, vicious, perverse, treacherous, void of any trust and corrupt, licentious, given to drunkenness, well schooled in all forms of violence, fierce and wild, wicked and false, impious and harsh, cruel and contentious, uncultivated in any good thing, thoroughly knowledgeable in all vices and injustices, quite similar to the Getae[3] and Saracens, and hostile to us French in all things. For only one nummus[4] a Navarrais or Basque will kill a French person if he can. In certain regions of theirs, namely Biscaye and Alava, when the Navarrais warm themselves [in front of the fire] the men expose their private parts to the women and the women to the men. The Navarrais even practice unnatural sex with beasts: it is said that a Navarrais will arrange a device [similar to a chastity belt] at the rear of his she-mule or mare so that no one but himself may enjoy it. And so he offers his libidinous "kisses" to the vulva of both his woman and his mule. This is why the Navarrais are deserving of reproach by all people of experience.

Pilgrimage Attractions

The most worthy body of blessed Gilles,[5] most pious confessor and abbot, ought to be visited at Arles with the greatest diligence. For the most blessed Gilles, highly renowned through all regions of the world, is deserving to be venerated by all people, worthily honored by all, esteemed by all, invoked by all, and petitioned by all. After the Prophets and Apostles, no one is more worthy among the saints than him, no one more holy, no one more glorious, no one more quick with aid. . . .

Oh how beautiful and how valuable it is to visit his tomb! On the very day that one supplicates him with his whole heart, one will without doubt be abundantly helped. I myself am a witness of what I say here: once I saw a certain man of the town—on that day on which he invoked the saint—escape through the aid of blessed confessor from the home of one Peyrot, a shoemaker, when that extremely old house collapsed, completely destroyed. Who, therefore, will look further than his threshold? Who will

3. An ancient people of Thrace.

4. A small coin similar in value to a nickel.

5. The patron saint of blacksmiths, beggars, and cripples. Supposedly an Athenian, Gilles, who lived in the eighth century, became a hermit until Wamba, a Visigoth king, built him a monastery. His grave and remains were popular objects of veneration.

adore God in his most sacred basilica? Who will further honor his tomb? Who will kiss his venerable altar or tell the story of his most pious life? For a sick person puts on [the saint's] tunic and he is cured. By his unfailing virtue a certain person bitten by a snake is cured; another person possessed by a demon is freed; a storm on the sea stops; the daughter of Theocrite is restored to long sought for health; a sick man whose entire body was a stranger to good health is restored to sound condition after a long period of desire; a deer at first wild becomes domesticated and obeys his commands; the monastic order is augmented by that patronal abbot; one possessed by a demon is liberated; a sin of Charlemagne is revealed to him by an angel, and it is forgiven the king; a dead person is brought back to life; one who is disabled is restored to his former health. . . . I regret having to die without being able to tell of all his venerable actions—because they are so many and so great. After shining his rays upon the people of Provençe, this most brilliant star of Greece nobly lay himself down among them—not diminishing, but increasing; not losing his light, but giving it to all with double force; not descending to the nadir, but ascending to the heights of Olympus. [A description of the reliquary of Saint Gilles is given at length.] Those Hungarians who say they have his body ought to be ashamed; the people of St-Camelle who imagine that they have his entire body ought to be confounded; the inhabitants of Saints-Séquanais who exult that they have his head ought to languish away; the Normans of Coutances who brag that they have his entire body should also be afraid, since his most sacred bones are in no way able to be taken out of the region, as is attested by many. For certain people once tried to deceitfully take the venerable arm of the blessed confessor far away from the area of Gilles' home[6] but they were not at all able to go one step with it.

2. *Christ in Majesty,* St. Sernin, Toulouse, France, late eleventh century (Gardner, p. 356, ill. 9:24)
Apostle, St. Sernin, Toulouse, France, late eleventh century (Janson, p. 290, ill. 404)
Roger de Hoveden, *Annals:* "Heresy in Toulouse," late twelfth century

The church of St. Sernin in Toulouse was an important church along a pilgrimage route, and its surfaces were adorned with sculptures such as *Christ in Majesty* and the *Apostle* to aid the devout in worship. At the same time Toulouse was the center of one of the most widespread heresies of the Middle Ages.

Heresy is the belief in religious doctrines contrary to the articles of faith accepted by the church. The problem of heresy and the treatment of heretics by the church was almost as old as Christianity itself. The early Christian leaders

6. The region around St. Gilles du Gard.

favored peaceful persuasion as the means to return heretics to the orthodox faith. But during the early Middle Ages other methods, such as confinement in a monastery and "moderate persecution"—that is, the use of the whip and goad—were also introduced as ways to encourage heretics to renounce their unacceptable beliefs.

In the eleventh and twelfth centuries, the church increased its use of coercion. The earliest known instance of a heretic being burned at the stake occurred in 1022, and this practice became more frequent in the following centuries. In 1233, the Inquisition was instituted by Pope Gregory IX.

To the church, one of the most alarming heresies was that of the Albigenses, who derived many of their beliefs from Manichaeanism. Named for the town of Albi in Languedoc, France, where the movement was especially strong, the Albigensian heresy was based in part on the doctrines of the third-century Persian philosopher Mani. According to Manichaeanism, which was imported into the West in the 1040s, the universe was dualistic in nature. Instead of one God, there were two gods, a god of light, truth, and spirit and a god of darkness, error, and matter. The world, which consisted of spirit trapped in matter, was the evil creation of the god of darkness. The person who sought to achieve goodness had to purify his or her spirit from the material world. The Albigenses lived by an extreme puritanical code. They avoided the consumption of milk, eggs, and meat, and they condemned marriage and procreation. Because of their contempt for the material realm, they abhorred many practices of the pilgrimage churches, such as the use of pictorial imagery and the veneration of relics. In the view of the Albigenses, the Roman Catholic Church, with its lands, wealth, art, and possessions, was the shrine of Satan.

The Albigensian heresy flourished in southern France in the twelfth century. In 1176, Raymond V (1148–1194), count of Toulouse, appealed to Pope Alexander III, King Henry II of England, and King Louis VII of France for aid in suppressing the heretics in his lands. In 1178 a commission composed of representatives of the pope and the English and French kings arrived in Toulouse. The commission, which anticipated the Inquisition in its charge, was empowered to preach, to investigate, to condemn, and to use force as necessary against the heretics.

The actions of the commission are described in the *Annals* written by Roger de Hoveden, a clerk of Henry II. Because he was not present at Toulouse, Roger based his account on letters written by two members of the commission. A selection from the *Annals,* "Heresy in Toulouse," is presented here.

Despite the actions taken by the commission to suppress the heretics, the Albigensian heresy was not eradicated. Count Raymond VI, the son and successor of Raymond V, was a leading supporter of the Albigenses and a suspected heretic himself. When his agents murdered a papal legate, Pope Innocent III instituted a crusade against the Albigenses. A bloody war, lasting from 1209 to 1229, finally stamped out the Albigensian movement.

Roger de Hoveden, *Annals*[7]

Heresy in Toulouse

Accordingly, when the before-named cardinal[8] and the other Catholic persons had entered Toulouse, they found there a certain wealthy man, who possessed two castles, one within the city and the other without the walls of the city, who, before their coming, had confessed himself to be a sectary of the heretical corruption; but now, moved by terror, and desiring to screen this execrable sect, made pretence that he was a Christian. When the cardinal came to know this, he ordered the said wealthy person to be brought before him; on whose coming for the purpose of making confession of his faith, he was found to be in every article an antagonist of the Christian religion.

Accordingly, he was pronounced by the aforesaid cardinal and the bishops who were with him a manifest heretic, and condemned; and they gave orders that his property should be confiscated, and that the castles which he possessed, lofty and of great beauty, should be levelled with the ground. Upon seeing himself thus condemned, and his property confiscated, he came to the cardinal and the bishops, his associates, and prostrating himself at their feet, asked pardon, and, penance being enjoined him, was led naked and scourged through the streets and lanes of the city. After this, he swore that he would go to Jerusalem, and remain there three years in the service of God, and if after the said three years he should return home, his possessions were to be restored to him, on condition, however, that his castles should be levelled, in testimony of his heretical depravity; he was also to give to the count of Toulouse five hundred pounds of silver.

On these things taking place, many of the heretics, fearing lest they might be dealt with in a similar manner, came to the cardinal and his associates, and secretly confessing their errors and asking pardon, obtained mercy. In the meanwhile, it came to their ears, that certain false brethren, namely, Raymond, Bernard, the son of Raymond, and certain other heresiarchs, transforming themselves into angels of light, while they were those of Satan, and preaching what was contrary to the Christian faith, led astray the minds of many by their false preaching, and had dragged them with themselves to hell. These being summoned to come into the presence of the cardinal and his associates, for the purpose of making confession of their faith, made answer that they would come before them if they should have a safe conduct in going and returning. . . .

On being examined as to all the articles of the Christian faith, they

7. Reprinted from *The Annals of Roger de Hoveden,* trans. by Henry T. Riley (London: H. G. Bohn, 1853), Vol. I, pp. 471–76.

8. Peter, the papal legate.

made answer as to all the articles of faith as soundly and circumspectly as if they had been most sincere Christians.

Upon the count of Toulouse and others, who had formerly heard them preach what was contrary to the Christian faith, hearing this statement from them, being struck with the greatest astonishment and inflamed with zeal for the Christian faith, they arose and most clearly convicted them to their faces of having lied; saying that they had heard from some of them that there were two Gods, the one good, and the other bad, the good one having only made things invisible, and which cannot be changed or corrupted, the bad one the heavens, the earth, man and other things visible. Others again affirmed that they had heard at their preaching, that the body of Christ was not made by the ministration of a priest who was unworthy, or who had been convicted of any crime. Others also stated that they had heard them say, in their preaching, that a man and his wife could not be saved if the conjugal debt was satisfied. Others again said that they had heard from them that baptism was of no use to infants, and the utterance of numerous other blasphemies against God and the holy Church and the Catholic faith, which, by reason of their abominable enormity, it is better to be silent upon than to disclose. . . .

When, therefore, they had been convicted by many and competent witnesses, and many persons were still preparing to bear witness against them, because the Church is not wont to deny the bosom of mercy to those who return thereto, they [the legate and the bishops] carefully warned them, laying aside all heretical corruptions, to return to the unity of the faith. They also advised them, as they had been excommunicated by our lord the pope, and the before-named cardinal, and the archbishops of Bourges and Narbonne, and the bishop of Toulouse, on account of their perverse preaching and schism, to come to be reconciled to the Catholic faith, according to the forms prescribed by the Church. This, however, being warped into tortuous ways and hardened by abandoned habits, they refused to do, on which the said cardinal, and the above-mentioned bishops, together with the before-named bishop of Poitiers, and the other religious men who had assisted throughout, in the sight of the whole people, with lighted candles again denounced them as excommunicated, and condemned them, together with their prompter, the devil, and gave orders to all the faithful in Christ, thenceforth cautiously to avoid the before-named Raymond and Bernard, and their accomplices, as persons excommunicated, and handed over to Satan; and that if at any time in future they should preach to them any thing else than what they had confessed in their hearing, they should reject their preaching as false, and contrary to the Catholic and Apostolic faith, and drive them as heretics and forerunners of Antichrist to a distance from their territories.

3. Speyer Cathedral, Germany, begun 1030 (Gardner, pp. 348–49, ills. 9:7 and 9:10; Janson, p. 286, ill. 398)
Henry IV, Letter to Gregory VII: "The Deposition of the Pope," January 24, 1076
Gregory VII, Letter to Henry IV: "The Excommunication of the Emperor," February 22, 1076

Speyer Cathedral was the church of the German imperial family. Throughout the Middle Ages, the relationship between church and state was a changing and often volatile one. During the Carolingian and Ottonian periods, secular rulers had claimed the right to control the church within their own lands, but in the eleventh century the papacy, having increased its economic and political strength, sought to establish its independence from secular influence. The church envisioned the formation of a Christian realm in which the pope would be recognized as the rightful sovereign of all subjects and in which secular rulers would render him their humble obedience.

The conflict between church and state came to a head when Pope Gregory VII and Emperor Henry IV clashed over the issue of lay investiture—that is, the conferral of the symbols of spiritual authority on a prelate by a layman. In 1075, Henry defied the pope's decree forbidding lay investiture by nominating two favorites for vacant Italian sees. Gregory sent Henry a stern letter warning him against continued disobedience, but the emperor replied by summoning a synod at Worms and deposing the pope. Gregory countered by excommunicating Henry and absolving his subjects from their oaths of obedience.

The result was a general rebellion against the emperor in Germany, which forced Henry to seek a reconciliation with the pope. The emperor crossed the Alps and met the pope at the small Italian town of Canossa. For three days in January 1077, he stood humbly penitent and barefoot in the snow outside the castle where the pope was staying. Finally, Gregory lifted Henry's excommunication and readmitted the monarch to the church.

The scene at Canossa was a dramatic symbol of the submission of secular power to spiritual authority, but it did not resolve the conflict. Henry and Gregory clashed again, and in 1085 Gregory died in Salerno, after being forced into exile by Henry's armies. Twenty-one years later, Henry died in Liége, unthroned by a rebellious son. Still under the papal ban of excommunication, Henry was denied burial in consecrated ground. In 1111, Henry's body was finally transferred from an unconsecrated chapel in Speyer Cathedral to the family chapel in the imperial church which he himself had rebuilt.

Selections from two documents related to the controversy between Gregory VII and Henry IV are presented here. The first, "The Deposition of the Pope," is from Henry's correspondence with Gregory. In this proclamation, written on January 24, 1076, Henry addresses Gregory by his former name, Hildebrand, and denounces him as a "false monk." The second selection, "The Excommunication of the Emperor," is from Gregory's decree of February 22, 1076, in which the pope releases Christian subjects from their oaths of obedience to the emperor and places an anathema upon him.

Henry IV, Letter to Gregory VII[9]

The Deposition of the Pope

Henry, king not by usurpation, but by the holy ordination of God, to Hildebrand, not pope, but false monk.

This is the salutation which you deserve, for you have never held any office in the church without making it a source of confusion and a curse to Christian men instead of an honor and a blessing. . . . Our Lord Jesus Christ has called us to the government of the empire, but he never called you to the rule of the church. This is the way you have gained advancement in the church: through craft you have obtained wealth; through wealth you have obtained favor; through favor, the power of the sword; and through the power of the sword, the papal seat, which is the seat of peace; and then from the seat of peace you have expelled peace. For you have incited subjects to rebel against their prelates by teaching them to despise the bishops, their rightful rulers. . . . You have attacked me, who, unworthy as I am, have yet been anointed to rule among the anointed of God, and who, according to the teaching of the fathers, can be judged by no one save God alone, and can be deposed for no crime except infidelity. . . . Come down, then, from that apostolic seat which you have obtained by violence; for you have been declared accursed by St. Paul for your false doctrines and have been condemned by us and our bishops for your evil rule. Let another ascend the throne of St. Peter, one who will not use religion as a cloak of violence, but will teach the life-giving doctrine of that prince of the apostles. I, Henry, king by the grace of God, with all my bishops, say unto you: "come down, come down, and be accursed through all the ages."

Gregory VII, Letter to Henry IV[10]

The Excommunication of the Emperor

O blessed Peter prince of the Apostles, mercifully incline thine ear, we [sic] pray, and hear me, thy servant, whom thou hast cherished from infancy and hast delivered until now from the hand of the wicked who have hated and still hate me for my loyalty to thee. Thou art my witness, as are also my Lady, the Mother of God, and the blessed Paul, thy brother among all the saints, that thy Holy Roman Church forced me against my will to be

9. Reprinted from Oliver J. Thatcher and Edgar H. McNeal, *A Source Book for Medieval History* (New York: Charles Scribner's Sons, 1905), pp. 151–52.

10. Reprinted, by permission of the publisher, from *The Correspondence of Pope Gregory VII,* trans. by Ephraim Emerton (New York: Columbia University Press, 1932), pp. 90–91. Copyright © 1932 by Columbia University Press.

its ruler. I had no thought of ascending thy throne as a robber, nay, rather would I have chosen to end my life as a pilgrim than to seize upon thy place for earthly glory and by devices of this world. Therefore, by thy favor, not by any works of mine, I believe that it is and has been thy will, that the Christian people especially committed to thee should render obedience to me, thy especially constituted representative. To me is given by thy grace the power of binding and loosing in Heaven and upon earth.

Wherefore, relying upon this commission, and for the honor and defense of thy Church, in the name of Almighty God, Father, Son and Holy Spirit, through thy power and authority, I deprive King Henry, son of the emperor Henry, who has rebelled against thy Church with unheard-of audacity, of the government over the whole kingdom of Germany and Italy, and I release all Christian men from the allegiance which they have sworn or may swear to him, and I forbid anyone to serve him as king. For it is fitting that he who seeks to diminish the glory of thy Church should lose the glory which he seems to have.

And, since he has refused to obey as a Christian should or to return to the God whom he has abandoned by taking part with excommunicated persons, has spurned my warnings which I gave him for his soul's welfare, as thou knowest, and has separated himself from thy Church and tried to rend it asunder, I bind him in the bonds of anathema in thy stead and I bind him thus as commissioned by thee, that the nations may know and be convinced that thou art Peter and that upon thy rock the son of the living God has built his Church and the gates of hell shall not prevail against it.

4. Durham Cathedral, England, 1093–1130 (Gardner, p. 352, ills. 9:17 and 9:18; Janson, p. 284, ills. 391–93)
Roger de Hoveden, *Annals:* "The Insurrection at Durham," late twelfth century

At the same time that the church was expanding its temporal powers at the expense of the empire, European rulers were expanding their territorial holdings at the expense of neighboring peoples. In the eleventh century, German feudal princes moved aggressively against the pagan Slavic peoples in the East; Christian armies began to recover Spanish lands held by Muslim rulers; and the Normans sailed from Normandy to conquer Sicily, then ruled by the Muslims, and Saxon England.

The Norman conquest of England was led by William the Conqueror (c. 1028–1087), the illegitimate son of Duke Robert I of Normandy and his mistress Arlette, a tanner's daughter. As duke of Normandy, William claimed a connection to the English royal house through his father's marriage to King Canute's sister, Estrith, and considered himself the rightful successor to the English king, Edward the Confessor. On his deathbed, however, Edward nominated

William's rival, Harold, as king. In October 1066, William invaded England with an army of five thousand knights and defeated Harold at the battle of Hastings. William was crowned King of England in Westminster Abbey on Christmas Day.

Although the battle of Hastings was the decisive moment in the Norman conquest, the pacification of England took several years. In 1069 revolt broke out against William in the ancient kingdom of Northumbria in northern England.

The city of Durham, in northeastern England, became an important pilgrimage site when, in 995, the relics of Cuthbert,[11] one of the most popular English saints, were brought there from Lindisfarne. Growing unrest against the Normans caused William to dispatch an army, led by Robert of Comines, to the region. Robert ignored the warning from Egelwin, the English bishop of Durham, that an English army had assembled nearby. He decided to quarter his troops in houses in Durham, and he stayed in the bishop's house. On the night of January 27–28, 1069, the English army surrounded Durham, set fire to the houses, and massacred the Normans. William marched north to quash the rebellion, slaughtering the insurgents and burning the crops in the countryside as a lesson in the consequences of disobedience.

The Norman conquest ended the cultural insularity of England and irrevocably linked the island kingdom to the European continent. One of the most impressive monuments of the Anglo-Norman culture that emerged is Durham Cathedral. Built between 1093 and 1133 to replace an earlier church, which had been badly damaged during the revolt, Durham Cathedral displays Norman building and design methods at their best.

The events in Northumbria and the damage suffered by the earlier cathedral at Durham are described in the *Annals* written by Roger de Hoveden in the late twelfth century. A selection from the *Annals,* "The Insurrection at Durham," is presented here.

Roger de Hoveden, *Annals*[12]

The Insurrection at Durham

In the year 1069, being the third year of his reign, king William sent earl Robert of Comines against the Northumbrians of the country north of the Tyne; for they had all united in one determination, not to submit to the rule of a foreigner, and had resolved either to slay him, or else, all of them, to fall by the edge of the sword. On this approach, Egelwin, bishop of Durham, met him, and warned him to be on his guard against treachery; but he, thinking that no one dared this, despised the warning, and, entering Durham, with a large body of soldiers, allowed his men to act with hostility in all quarters, even to slaying some peasants belonging to the church; still,

11. Cuthbert (?–687) was an English monk who became Bishop of Lindisfarne and who had a reputation for great holiness. He was buried on Lindisfarne, but his remains were removed by the monks when they fled the Danes. After a century, he was reburied in the cathedral at Durham.

12. Reprinted from *The Annals of Roger de Hoveden,* trans. by Henry T. Riley (London: H. G. Bohn, 1853), Vol. 1, pp. 141–44.

he was received by the bishop with all kindness and honor. But the Northumbrians hastening onward all night, at daybreak broke through the gates with the greatest violence, and slew the followers of the earl in every direction, they being quite unprepared for the attack. The contest was waged most fiercely, the soldiers being struck down in the houses and streets, and the combatants attacked the house of the bishop in which the earl was entertained; but finding that they could not endure the darts of those who defended it, they burned the house together with those who were therein. So great was the multitude of the slain, that nearly every spot in the city was filled with blood, and out of seven hundred men only one escaped. This slaughter took place on the fifth day before the kalends of February, being the fourth day of the week. . . .

When king William was informed of this, being greatly enraged, he swore that he would pierce the whole of the Northumbrians with the single spear, and shortly afterwards, having assembled an army hastened with feelings of extreme irritation to Northumbria, and did not cease throughout the whole winter to ravage it, slay the inhabitants, and commit many other acts of devastation. . . .

While the Normans . . . were laying waste England, throughout Northumbria and some other provinces, but in the present and succeeding year, throughout almost the whole of England, but especially Northumbria and the provinces adjoining to it, a famine prevailed to such a degree, that, compelled by hunger, men ate human flesh, and that of horses, dogs, and cats, and whatever was repulsive to notions of civilization; some persons went so far as to sell themselves into perpetual slavery, provided only they could in some way or other support a miserable existence; some departing from their native country into exile, breathed forth their exhausted spirits in the midst of the journey.

It was dreadful to behold human corpses rotting in the houses, streets, and high roads, and as they reeked with putrefaction, swarming with worms, and sending forth a horrid stench; for all the people having been cut off, either with the sword or famine, or else having through hunger left their native country, there were not sufficient left to inter them. Thus, during a period of nine years, did the land, deprived of its cultivators, extend far and wide a mere dreary waste. Between York and Durham, there was not one inhabited town; the dens of wild beasts and robbers, to the great terror of the traveller, were alone to be seen. . . .

In the meantime, the king's army, dispersing in all directions, between the rivers Tees and Tyne, found nothing but deserted houses, and a dreary solitude on every side; the inhabitants having either sought safety in flight, or concealed themselves in the woods and among the precipices of the hills. . . .

The church of Durham was deprived of all its guardians and all ecclesiastical care, and had become like a desert, as the Scripture says, a refuge for the poor, the sick, and the feeble. Those who were unable to take to flight, turning aside thither, sank there under the influence of famine and disease. The resemblance of the cross, which was the only one of the church ornaments remaining there, (as on account of its large size it could not be easily removed by them in their haste) was robbed of its gold and silver, which were torn off by the Normans.

5. St. Étienne, Caen, begun c. 1067 (Gardner, pp. 350–51, ills. 9:14 to 9:16; Janson, pp. 283–84, ills. 390–94)
Orderic Vitalis, *Ecclesiastical History:* "The Death and Burial of William the Conqueror," c. 1109–1141

William the Conqueror died in 1087 in France. His last war began over a border dispute between Normandy and France. Enraged by French raids against Norman subjects, William stormed the French frontier town of Nantes and burned it. But his victory proved costly. As William was riding triumphantly through the flames, his horse stepped on a burning ember and stumbled. William was thrown violently against the iron pommel of his saddle and received an internal injury which was to prove fatal. He was placed in a litter and carried to his palace in Rouen, where he lingered in agony for six weeks.

At William's death, pandemonium broke out. William's nobles and churchmen fled the death chamber; his servants plundered the possessions of the dead king. The royal corpse was left, virtually naked, on the bare floor. At length, William's body was brought to Caen for burial at St. Étienne (St. Stephen), the church which William had founded. But disaster dogged the once-mighty Conqueror. The solemn funeral procession was interrupted by a fire breaking out along the route, and the service by the angry shouts of a man who claimed that William had confiscated the land on which St. Étienne was built without offering his family fair compensation. The final indignity suffered by William was the worst. At the conclusion of the service, the royal corpse was lifted down from its bier to be lowered to its stone sarcophagus, already placed in the vault. As the gravediggers tried to force William's corpulent body into the sarcophagus, the stomach exploded, and a nauseating stench filled the church. Even the most sincere mourners made haste to depart from St. Étienne and from William's presence.

William's death and burial are described in the *Ecclesiastical History* written by Orderic Vitalis between approximately 1109 and 1141. Orderic Vitalis (1075–c. 1142) was a monk who was born in England but who spent most of his life in Normandy. To the monk, the Conqueror's undignified end was a moral lesson illustrating the vanity of worldly wealth, pride, and position. A selection from the *Ecclesiastical History,* "The Death and Burial of William the Conqueror," is presented here.

Orderic Vitalis, *Ecclesiastical History*[13]

The Death and Burial of William the Conqueror

At last on Thursday, 9 September, the [dying] king awoke as the sun was beginning to shed its clear rays over the earth and heard the sound of the great bell in the cathedral church. When he asked what hour it was sounding, the attendants replied, "My lord, the hour of prime is being rung in the church of St. Mary." Then the king raised his eyes to heaven with deep devotion, and looking up with outstretched hands said, "I commend myself to my Lady, the blessed Mary, mother of God, that by her holy prayers she may reconcile me to her most dear Son, our Lord Jesus Christ." As soon as he had spoken these words he died. The physicians and others present, who had watched the king as he slept all night without a sigh or groan, and now realized that he had died without warning, were utterly dumbfounded and almost out of their minds. But the wealthier among them quickly mounted horse and rode off as fast as they could to protect their properties. The lesser attendants, seeing that their superiors had absconded, seized the arms, vessels, clothing, linen, and all the royal furnishings, and hurried away leaving the king's body almost naked on the floor of the house. Behold, I beg you all, of what earthly loyalty is made. Each one of them, like a bird of prey, seized what he could of the royal trappings and made off at once with the booty. So when the just ruler fell lawlessness broke loose, and first showed itself in the plunder of him who had been the avenger of plunder. . . .

At length the religious, both canons and monks, mustering their courage and coming to their senses, formed a procession and, clad in vestments with crosses and censers, moved to St. Gervase, where they commended the king's soul to God according to Christian rites. The Archbishop William decreed that the body should be taken to Caen and buried there in the church of St. Étienne the first martyr, which the king himself had founded. By then his brothers and kinsfolk had left him, and all his servants had shamefully abandoned him as if he had been a barbarian. So not one of the royal dependants could be found to prepare his body for burial. At last a certain country knight called Herluin was moved by natural goodness, and actively took charge of the funeral preparations for the love of God and honour of his race. He brought persons to lay out the corpse and bearers and a conveyance, paid for them out of his own resources, transported the king's body to the port on the Seine and, placing it on a boat, took it by water and land to Caen.

13. Reprinted, by permission of Oxford University Press, from Marjorie Chibnall, ed. and trans., *The Ecclesiastical History of Orderic Vitalis,* Vol. 4 (Oxford: Clarendon Press, 1973), pp. 101–107.

Then Dom Gilbert the abbot came out reverently in procession with all his monks to meet the bier, and with them came a great multitude of clergy and laity, weeping and praying. But soon a terrible disaster caused general panic. A raging fire suddenly broke out in one of the houses, sending up great balls of flame, and spread destruction through the greater part of the town of Caen. All, therefore, clergy and laity alike, rushed to put out the fire; the monks alone completed the half-finished office and, chanting psalms, escorted the king's body to the abbey church.

There at last all the bishops and abbots of Normandy were assembled for the funeral of the great leader and father of his country. . . .

When the Mass had been completed and the coffin had been lowered into the earth, but the body still lay on the bier, Gilbert, the famous bishop of Évreux, mounted into the pulpit and preached a long and eloquent sermon on the great eminence of the dead duke. . . .

Then Ascelin son of Arthur came forward from the crowd, and made this complaint in a loud voice, in the hearing of all, "This ground where you stand was the site of my father's house, which this man for whom you intercede, when he was still only duke of Normandy, violently took away from my father; refusing him all redress he founded this church in the fullness of his power. Therefore I lay claim to this land, and openly demand it, forbidding in God's name that the body of this robber be covered by earth that is mine or buried in my inheritance." . . .

Next, when the corpse was placed in the sarcophagus, and was forcibly doubled up because the masons had carelessly made the coffin too short and narrow, the swollen bowels burst, and an intolerable stench assailed the nostrils of the bystanders and the whole crowd. A thick smoke arose from the frankincense and other spices in the censers, but it was not strong enough to conceal the foul ignominy. So the priests made haste to conclude the funeral rites, and immediately returned, trembling, to their own houses.

6. Pisa Cathedral, 1053–1272 (Gardner, p. 353, ills. 9:19 and 9:20; Janson, p. 288, ills. 400–402)
Avicenna, *Metaphysica:* "The Necessary Existent," c. 1000
Al-Khwarizmi, *The Book of Algebra and Almucabola:* "Number and Units," "Six Rules of Algebra," and "A Word Problem," ninth century
Attributed to Geber, *Of the Sum of Perfection:* "The Six Metals," eighth–ninth centuries

Pisa Cathedral, built of black and white marble in a predominately Romanesque style, nevertheless displays a high pointed arch at the interior crossing, which was probably inspired by Islamic architecture.

For centuries, Western Europe regarded the Arabs as little more than illiterate marauders. But in the eleventh century, Europeans became aware of the high levels of learning achieved by the Arabs in such fields as philosophy, mathematics, and the natural sciences.

Arab accomplishments in many intellectual fields were based on Greek sources. The Arabs had translated into their own language the philosophical writings of Plato and Aristotle, the medical treatises of Hippocrates and his followers, and the mathematical teachings of Ptolemy.[14] Arab scholars had further extended this knowledge through their own intellectual efforts.

In the eleventh century, Europeans became eager to acquire a better understanding of Arab accomplishments. Sicily and especially Spain, with their mixture of Christian and Muslim inhabitants, became the two most important channels by which the achievements of Arab civilization were transmitted to the West. The pilgrimages and crusades undertaken by Christians provided other, though less important, channels of contact between the spheres of Islam and Christendom.

The Arab influence in the medieval West was profound. Although some Greek works were transmitted to the West by way of Byzantium, most entered medieval Europe through Latin translations of Arabic manuscripts. Arabic texts prompted a renewed interest in Greek philosophy; Arab mathematics resulted in the Western adoption of Arabic numerals and the decimal system; Arab experimentation with the properties of metals, called alchemy, gave rise to the modern science of chemistry. The writings of many Arab intellectuals were translated into Latin and widely disseminated throughout Europe. Three such scholars were Ibn-Sina, known in the West as Avicenna; Al-Khwarizmi; and Jabir ibn-Hayyan, called Geber in the West.

The great Persian intellectual Avicenna (980–1037) was both a diplomat and an intellectual. One of Avicenna's most important philosophical works is the *Metaphysica,* which formed a section of *The Book of Scientific Knowledge.* In this work, Avicenna interpreted Islam in Aristotelian terms. He defined God as the "necessary existent"—that is, the highest being in which essence and existence coincide. God, according to Avicenna, is the first cause, the highest intellect, and the highest love. Avicenna stressed that philosophical contemplation based on rational training and self-education is the best way to comprehend God. A passage from the *Metaphysica,* "The Necessary Existent," is presented here.

Al-Khwarizmi lived in the ninth century and was one of the most influential Arabic mathematicians. His name is the origin of the term "algorithm."[15] The title of his book, *Kitab al jabr wa'l mugubala (The Book of Algebra and Almucabola),* is the origin of the term "algebra."

Three passages from *The Book of Algebra and Almucabola* are presented here. In the first passage, "Number and Units," Al-Khwarizmi explains the principles of the decimal system; in the second selection, "Six Rules of Algebra," his rules

14. A second-century Greco-Egyptian astronomer, mathematician, and geographer (not to be confused with the Macedonian kings of Egypt, who were also called Ptolemy). The author of the standard textbook on astronomy, which declared the earth to be the center of the universe, Ptolemy was influential until the time of Copernicus.

15. By way of the form "algorism," which means specifically the Arabic system of numerals, and hence any system of numerical computation.

for algebra and elementary geometry are summarized; in the third passage, "A Word Problem," he suggests word problems that could be used to instill mathematical principles.

Geber was an eighth-century alchemist whose name became associated with a large corpus of later Arab alchemic writings. Alchemy is the ancient attempt to transform base metals such as lead and copper into precious metals such as silver and gold. It originated in Alexandria, Egypt, during the Hellenistic period and was compared to the spiritual processes by which the human soul experienced death and resurrection. Islamic practitioners advanced the alchemic knowledge and techniques inherited from the Mediterranean world. A selection from *Of the Sum of Perfection,* "The Six Metals"—attributed to Geber—is presented here.

Avicenna, *Metaphysica*[16]

The Necessary Existent

Wisdom in our opinion applies to two things: to complete knowledge and to perfect action. Complete knowledge in thought is displayed by recognizing a thing by its essence and by its definition. In a judgment, complete knowledge of a thing would be evident in assessing all of its causes correctly. Perfection, on the other hand, applies to an act which is determined. Perfection is that property which is present in the subject of perfection and in whatever is necessary to its existence. Whatever is necessary to continue the existence of the subject of perfection will exist as far as it is possible for it to subsist in It. Furthermore, that will also exist which is ornament and of benefit to It, although it may not be necessary. And the Necessary Existent knows all things as they are, even with respect to their complete causation, since Its knowledge of things comes not from second-hand information, from intermediaries, but from Itself, for all things and the causes of all things are due to It.

The Necessary Existence is thus the greatest perceiver in perceiving the greatest of the perceptibles—being Itself—which is most complete, having the highest glory, grandeur, and station. In Itself, therefore, It finds the state of the greatest pleasure since It has no need of anything external to It to endow It with beauty and grandeur. Unlike us, the absolute pure intelligences, those beings made complete in the first creation do not depend constantly on external things and on the perception of base things. They are occupied with their own perfection, which is intelligible to them, and with whatever they witness of the perfection and glory of the Necessary Existent which illuminates the mirror of their substance. Such is the

16. Reprinted, by permission, from *The Metaphysica of Avicenna (Ibn-Sina),* trans. by Parviz Morewedge (New York: Columbia University Press, 1973), pp. 70, 75–76.

ultimate pleasure. The joy they receive from perceiving the Necessary Existent is an addition to that which they obtain from contemplating their own perfection. They occupy themselves with pleasure and enrichment of the higher order since they never deviate from this higher order to the lower. Their dedication of their own selves to the beholding of the divine aura admits them to the highest glory and to the reception of pleasure of the highest degree. No vexation exists for them, for they lack the source of our vexation, be it an instrument which inflicts pain while it is active in another activity, or be it the evil inherent in the instrument. In brief, in order to experience vexation there must be a matter capable of undergoing change and whatever obeys a cause which relates to matter is changeable.

Fortunate is the man who seeks that state for his life which is attained when his "life-soul" leaves the body. He who seeks the opposite goal receives pain, rather than pleasure, though presently he has no idea of such a pain. He resembles that man who has not learned the pain of the burning fire but knows of it by hearsay. How well has Aristotle spoken on this topic, he who is the leader of the wise and the guide and teacher of philosophers, in asserting that the pleasure experienced by the Necessary Existent is due to Itself, for other things are due to It. He has affirmed:

"If the primary being has perpetually the same quantity of felicity in itself which we obtain from it, then whenever we conceive of it, when we meditate about its grandeur and present to ourselves a truth in relation to it, there will be a great felicity within us. There is no comparison between the amount of pleasure which we in our present possession of wisdom now receive, which our condition necessitates, and the amount of pleasure the Necessary Existent experiences due to Itself which is much more grand and marvellous. It is, indeed, the first being of pleasure which is complete in Its own nature. Perhaps one should not even name such a state 'pleasure,' but no commonly known word expresses this meaning in a more satisfactory manner."

Al-Khwarizmi, *The Book of Algebra and Almucabola*[17]

Number and Units

The Book of Algebra and Almucabola, concerning arithmetical and geometrical problems.

In the name of God, tender and compassionate, begins the book of Restoration and Opposition of number put forth by Mohammed Al-Khwarizmi, the son of Moses. Mohammed said, Praise God the creator

17. Reprinted from *Roger of Chester's Latin Translation of the Algebra of Al-Khowarizmi,* trans. by Louis Charles Karpinski (New York: Macmillan Co., 1915), pp. 67, 127, 125.

who has bestowed upon man the power to discover the significance of numbers. Indeed, reflecting that all things which men need require computation, I discovered that all things involve number and I discovered that number is nothing other than that which is composed of units. Unity therefore is implied in every number. Moreover I discovered all numbers to be so arranged that they proceed from unity up to ten. The number ten is treated in the same manner as the unit, and for this reason doubled and tripled just as in the case of unity. Out of its duplication arises 20, and from its triplication 30. And so multiplying the number ten you arrive at one-hundred. Again the number one-hundred is doubled and tripled like the number ten. So by doubling and tripling etc. the number one-hundred grows to one-thousand. In this way multiplying the number one-thousand according to the various denominations of numbers you come even to the investigation of number to infinity.

Six Rules of Algebra

First. When roots are equal to a number, divide the number by (the number of) the roots, and the quotient represents the desired quantity.[18]

Second. When squares are equal to a number, divide the number by (the number of) the squares, and the root of that which you obtain represents the desired quantity.[19]

Third. When roots are equal to squares, divide (the number of) the roots by (the number of) the squares, and the quotient represents the desired quantity.[20]

Fourth. When a number is equal to the sum of squares and roots, divide by (the number of) the squares. Take one-half of (the number of) the roots after the division and multiply it by itself. To this product add the number. The root of this sum less one-half of the number of roots, represents that which is sought.[21]

Fifth. When roots are equal to a number and squares, divide the roots and the number by (the number of) the squares. Take one-half of (the number of) the roots after the division, and multiply it by itself. From this product subtract the number; the root of the remainder subtracted from one-half of (the number of) the roots is the desired quantity. . . .[22]

Sixth. When squares are equal to a number and roots, on this side divide by (the number of) the squares. Take one-half of (the number of) the roots after the division, and multiply it by itself. To this product add

18. $ax = n$; $x = a/n$. (sic) [$x = n/a$ is correct.]
19. $ax^2 = n$; $x^2 = a/n$; $x = \sqrt{a/n}$ (sic) [$x^2 = n/a$ $x = \sqrt{n/a}$ is correct.]
20. $ax^2 = bx$; $x = b/a$.
21. $ax^2 + bx = n$; $x = \sqrt{(b/2a)^2 + n/a} - b/2a$.
22. $ax^2 + n = bx$; $x = b/2a \pm \sqrt{(b/2a)^2 - n/a}$.

the number; the root of this sum plus one-half of (the number of) the roots represents that which is sought.[23]

A Word Problem

A man is hired to work in a vineyard 30 days for 10 pence. He works six days. How much of the agreed price should he receive?

Explanation. It is evident that six days are one-fifth of the whole time; and it is also evident that the man should receive pay having the same relation to the agreed price that the time he works bears to the whole time, 30 days. What we have proposed, is explained as follows. The month, i.e. 30 days, represents the measure, and ten represents the price. Six days represents the quantity, and in asking what part of the agreed price is due to the worker you ask the cost. Therefore multiply the price 10 by the quantity 6, which is inversely proportional to it. Divide the product 60 by the measure 30, giving 2 pence. This will be the cost, and will represent the amount due to the worker.

Attributed to Geber, *Of the Sum of Perfection*[24]

The Six Metals

We now speak of Metallick Bodies, which are the Effect of these Principles of Nature. These are Six in number, viz. Gold, Silver, Lead, Tin, Copper, and Iron. Therefore we say, a Metal is a Mineral fusible Body, extensible with all Dimensions under the Hammer. But a Metal is (as we sayd) of a dense Substance, and of most strong and firm Composition. And Metals have great affinity each with other, yet the perfect perfects not the diminished, but its Commixtion. For if Gold be mixed in fusion with Lead, this Lead becomes not Gold, but vanisheth from the Mixtion, and is burnt; the Gold in the mean while stands the Tryal. So likewise, in instancing the other, it falls according to the Common Course. But, according to our Magistery, the Perfect helps the Imperfect; and the Imperfect, in our Magistery, by it self is Perfected, without the Administration of any Extraneous Thing. And through GOD, they alter each other, and are altered; and they perfect each other, and are perfected: and one only by it self is perfected without the help of another.

23. $ax^2 = bx + n$; $x = b/2a + \sqrt{(b/2a)^2 + n/a}$.

24. Reprinted from E. J. Holmyard, ed., *The Works of Geber,* trans. by Richard Russell (New York: E. P. Dutton and Co., 1928), pp. 62–63.

7. *The Last Judgment,* west tympanum, St. Lazare, Autun, c. 1130 (Gardner, p. 361, ills. 9:30 and 9:31; Janson, p. 291, ill. 407)
Peter the Venerable, *The Book of Miracles:* "The Besetting Demons," mid-twelfth century

The devil and his kingdom are represented frequently in medieval art. In *The Last Judgment* devils and demons vie for human souls and delight in inflicting torment on their pitiful human victims.

In the Middle Ages, the devil was believed to be the chief of the fallen angels, the foe of God and humans and the supreme spirit of evil. The Western concept of the devil came from widely varied sources, including Classical antiquity, Norse mythology, and the Old and New Testaments. The representation of the devil in art was also drawn from many sources, including popular Chinese art, Iranian carvings, Assyro-Babylonian reliefs, and the Classical depictions of gods, satyrs,[25] dryads, and fauns.[26]

According to medieval theology, the devil was at the head of a realm of demons, who were divided into hierarchies and who inhabited an underworld of darkness and gloom. The devil and his demons were permitted to trouble and torment humans and to exercise many other evil powers. They had the ability to influence the weather and destroy crops, to cause impotence in men and sterility in women, and to produce sickness and hasten death. The rite of exorcism was used by the clergy to free people from being possessed by an evil spirit.

The devil exerted a powerful hold on the popular imagination. Folktales, often recounted by monks, featured Satan in the form of a Moor, an ox, a black horse, a dog, and a toad, and even in the guise of a nun or a prior. The devil could appear anywhere, at any time of the day or night, offering temptations that caused the devout to abandon their devotions and the faithful to surrender their souls.

Many examples of stories about demonic spirits are found in *The Book of Miracles* by Peter the Venerable (1092–1156). Peter was the ninth abbot of Cluny, a powerful monastery and a major religious and intellectual center in Burgundy. Peter wrote *The Book of Miracles* in the mid-twelfth century in an effort to lift men and women from spiritual darkness by recording the wonders of Christian faith. A selection from *The Book of Miracles,* "The Besetting Demons," is presented here.

25. Satyrs are similar to fauns in their possession of both human and goatlike tails and ears. They lived in forests and were associated with the god Dionysus, rather than Pan, as were fauns. They had an appropriate liking for revelry, wine, and mischief.

26. For faunds and dryads, see Chapter Six, notes 21 and 22.

Peter the Venerable, *The Book of Miracles*[27]

The Besetting Demons

At another time another brother, who was a carpenter, lay by night in a place somewhat removed from the rest. The place was lighted with a lamp, as is customary in the dormitories of monks. While he lay on his bed, not yet asleep, he beheld a monstrous vulture, whose wings and feet were scarce able to bear the load of his vast body, labouring and panting towards him, until it stood over against his bed. While the brother beheld this in amazement, behold! two other demons in human form came and spake with that vulture—or rather, that fiend—saying, "What doest thou here? Canst thou do any work in this place?" "Nay," said he; "for they all thrust me hence by the protection of the cross and by sprinkling of holy water and by muttering of psalms. I have laboured hard all this night, consuming my strength in vain; wherefore I have come hither baffled and wearied. But do ye tell me where ye have been and how ye have prospered." To which the others made reply: "We are come from Châlons, where we made one of Geoffrey of Donzy's knights fall into adultery with his host's wife. Then again we passed by a certain monastery, where we made the master of the school to fornicate with one of his boys. But thou, sluggard, why dost not thou arise, and at least cut off the foot of this monk, which he hath stretched in disorderly fashion beyond his bedclothes?" Whereupon the other seized the monk's axe which lay under the bed, and heaved it up to smite with all his force. The monk, seeing the axe thus raised aloft, withdrew his foot in fear; so that the demon's stroke fell harmlessly upon the end of the bed; whereupon the evil spirits vanished forthwith. The brother who had seen this vision related it all forthwith, next morning, to the aforesaid father Hugh, who sent to Châlons and to Tournus to assure himself of the truth thereof. Here, searching narrowly into those things which the demons had asserted, he found that these ministers of lies had told the truth.

But some man will say: "Seeing that the evil spirits far surpass all human cunning in the subtlety of their malice (for their natural nimbleness is clogged by no bodily weight, whereby they are rendered free in all their motions and all the more sagacious by long experience), how is it that they betray their wicked designs or deeds to men's ears? Do they not understand how often men are saved from their most subtle snares by these revelations of their wiles, and the demons are thus frustrated of their purpose? Where-

27. Reprinted, by permission of the publisher, from G. G. Coulton, *Life in the Middle Ages* (Cambridge: Cambridge University Press, 1930), Vol. 4, pp. 110–11. Copyright (c) by Cambridge University Press, 1930.

fore, then, did they betray their evil deeds in the hearing of that brother, and confess themselves unable to work the wickedness that they desired?" To this we must answer that, great as are their powers for evil, and prompt as is their will to deceive us, yet by God's hidden disposition they are often-times so wondrously and incomprehensibly caught in their own false wiles, that they are sometimes compelled unwillingly to serve that human salvation which is always contrary to their desire.

8. *The Mission of the Apostles,* tympanum of the center portal of the narthex of La Madeleine, Vézelay, 1120–1132 (Gardner, p. 363, ills. 9:32 and 9:33; Janson, p. 292, ills. 408–409)
Urban II, speech delivered at the Council of Clermont: "Call to the Crusades," November 26, 1095
Usamah, *The Book of Reflections:* "A Muslim Account of the Crusaders," c. 1185

The eleventh century witnessed a religious renewal that had a far-reaching impact. The spiritual fervor of the period was evident not only in the increased popularity of pilgrimages and in the deepened dread of demonic spirits, but also in the enthusiastic response to the Crusades.

The term "Crusades" refers to the military expeditions organized by Western Christians between the eleventh and fourteenth centuries in order to win possession from the Muslims of the Holy City of Jerusalem. Jerusalem had been under Muslim rule since the eighth century, but Christian pilgrimages had been allowed to continue. However, in the eleventh century, Christians in the Holy Land began to be persecuted, and in 1009 the Holy Sepulcher was despoiled and profaned. In 1071 Jerusalem passed from the hands of the relatively tolerant Egyptians to Seljuk Turks. About 1090, the Byzantine emperor Alexius I appealed to Pope Urban II for aid against the Turks. Urban responded in his great speech at the Council of Clermont in 1095, in which he exhorted his hearers to go to war for the Sepulcher and promised a plenary indulgence—remission of all penance for sin—to those who heeded his call. The response of the crowd was instantaneous as cries of "*Deus vult*" ("God wills it") rang through the air, and men rushed forward to claim their places as crusaders.

The Crusades appealed to both the highest and lowest of motives—to the desire for wealth and adventure, and to the aspirations for Christian unity and personal salvation. Between 1095 and 1270 nine major Crusades and many smaller expeditions were undertaken. Of these successive expeditions, only the First Crusade realized its professed purpose. Leaving Europe in 1096, the main crusading force reached the Holy Land in 1097 and captured Jerusalem in 1099.

But the conquest was only temporary. In 1187 Saladin, the sultan of Egypt, recaptured Jerusalem. The Ninth Crusade, in 1270, was the last expedition that had the express purpose of retaking Palestine. Expeditions continued, however, until the end of the Middle Ages.

Vézelay is closely linked to the history of the Crusades. In 1095 Urban II had intended to preach there to the First Crusade, and in 1146 Bernard of Clairvaux did preach to the Second Crusade at Vézelay. In 1190 King Richard the Lion-heart of England and King Philip Augustus of France set out from Vézelay for the Third Crusade.

Two selections from documents related to the Crusades are presented here. The first, "Call to the Crusades," is part of the speech delivered by Urban to the Council of Clermont; the text presented here was recorded by Fulcher of Chartres. The second selection, "A Muslim Account of the Crusaders," is an excerpt from the writings of Usamah ibn-Munqidh. Usamah (1095–1188) was a well-educated Muslim aristocrat who had known many crusaders in Jerusalem. When he was almost 90 years old, he wrote his memoirs, *The Book of Reflections,* in which he recorded his impressions of the Franks from Western Europe.

Urban II, speech delivered at the Council of Clermont[28]

Call to the Crusades

Although, oh sons of God, you have promised the Lord more earnestly than heretofore to maintain peace in your midst and faithfully to sustain the rights of the church, yet it is necessary for you, newly fortified by the correction of the Lord, to show the strength of your righteousness in a precious work which is not less your concern than the Lord's. For it behooves you to hasten to carry to your brethren dwelling in the East, the aid so often promised and so urgently needed. For the Turks and the Arabs have attacked them, as many of you know, and have advanced into the territory of Romania[29] as far as that part of the Mediterranean which is called the Arm of St. George;[30] and penetrating farther and farther into the country of those Christians, already seven times conquered them in battle, have killed and captured many, have destroyed the churches and devastated the kingdom. If you permit them to remain for a time unmolested, they will extend their sway more widely over many faithful servants of the Lord.

Wherefore, I pray and exhort, nay not I, but the Lord prays and exhorts you, as heralds of Christ, at all times to urge men of all ranks, peasants and knights, the poor equally with the rich, to hasten to exterminate this vile race from the lands ruled by our brethren, and to bear timely

28. Reprinted from Oliver J. Thatcher, *The Library of Original Sources* (Chicago: University Research Extension, 1907), pp. 340–41.

29. The term refers to the whole Byzantine empire, including, but not restricted to, the area of modern Romania.

30. The reference appears to be to the south arm of the Danube delta, even though this is hardly part of the Mediterranean.

aid to the worshipers of Christ. I speak to those who are present, I shall proclaim it to be absent, but it is Christ who commands. Moreover, if those who set out thither lose their lives on the journey, by land or sea, or in fighting against the heathen, their sins shall be remitted in that hour; this I grant through the power of God vested in me.

Oh, what a disgrace if a race so despised, so degenerate, so entirely the slave of the demons, should thus conquer omnipotent God's elect people, rendered illustrious by the name of Christ! Oh, how many reproaches will be heaped upon us by the Lord Himself if you do not aid those who like ourselves glory in the name of Christ! Let those who have formerly been accustomed to contend wickedly in private warfare against the faithful, fight against the infidel and bring to a victorious end the war which ought long since to have been begun. Let those who have hitherto been robbers now become soldiers. Let those who have formerly contended against their brothers and relatives now fight as they ought against the barbarians. Let those who have formerly been mercenaries at low wages, now gain eternal rewards. Let those who have been exhausting themselves to the detriment both of body and soul, now strive for a two-fold reward. What shall I add? On this side will be the sorrowful and poor, on the other the rich; here the enemies of the Lord, there His friends. Let not the expedition be delayed. But let the warriors arrange their affairs and collect the money necessary for their expenses, and when winter ends and the spring comes, let them with alacrity start on their journey under the guidance of the Lord.

Usamah, *The Book of Reflections*[31]

A Muslim Account of the Crusaders

Mysterious are the works of the Creator, the author of all things! When one comes to recount cases regarding the Franks, he cannot but glorify Allah (exalted is he!) and sanctify him, for he sees them as animals possessing the virtues of courage and fighting, but nothing else; just as animals have only the virtues of strength and carrying loads. I shall now give some instances of their doings and their curious mentality. . . .

A case illustrating their curious medicine is the following:

The lord of al-Munaytirah wrote to my uncle asking him to dispatch a physician to treat certain sick persons among his people. My uncle sent

31. Reprinted, by permission of the publisher, from *Memoirs of an Arab-Syrian Gentleman,* trans. by Philip K. Hitti (New York: Columbia University Press, 1929), pp. 161–64. Copyright © 1929 by Columbia University Press.

him a Christian physician named Thabit. Thabit was absent but ten days when he returned. So we said to him, "How quickly hast thou healed thy patients!" He said:

"They brought before me a knight in whose leg an abscess had grown; and a woman afflicted with imbecility. To the knight I applied a small poultice until the abscess opened and became well; and the woman I put on diet and made her humor wet. Then a Frankish physician came to them and said, 'This man knows nothing about treating them.' He then said to the knight, 'Which wouldst thou prefer, living with one leg or dying with two?' The latter replied, 'Living with one leg.' The physician said, 'Bring me a strong knight and a sharp ax.' A knight came with the ax. And I was standing by. Then the physician laid the leg of the patient on a block of wood and bade the knight strike his leg with the ax and chop it off at one blow. Accordingly he struck it—while I was looking on—one blow, but the leg was not severed. He dealt another blow, upon which the marrow of the leg flowed out and the patient died on the spot. He then examined the woman and said, 'This is a woman in whose head there is a devil which has possessed her. Shave off her hair.' Accordingly they shaved it off and the woman began once more to eat their ordinary diet—garlic and mustard. Her imbecility took a turn for the worse. The physician then said, 'The devil has penetrated through her head.' He therefore took a razor, made a deep cruciform incision on it, peeled off the skin at the middle of the incision until the bone of the skull was exposed and rubbed it with salt. The woman also expired instantly. Thereupon I asked them whether my services were needed any longer, and when they replied in the negative I returned home, having learned of their medicine what I knew not before. . . ."

Everyone who is a fresh emigrant from the Frankish lands is ruder in character than those who have become acclimatized and have held long association with the Muslims. Here is an illustration of their rude character.

Whenever I visited Jerusalem I always entered the Aqsa Mosque, beside which stood a small mosque which the Franks had converted into a church. When I used to enter the Aqsa Mosque, which was occupied by the Templars who were my friends, the Templars would evacuate the little adjoining mosque so that I might pray in it. One day I entered this mosque, repeated the first formula, "Allah is great," and stood up in the act of praying, upon which one of the Franks rushed on me, got hold of me and turned my face eastward saying, "This is the way thou shouldst pray!" A group of Templars hastened to him, seized him and repelled him from me. I resumed my prayer. The same man, while the others were otherwise busy, rushed once more on me and turned my face eastward, saying, "This is the way thou shouldst pray!" The Templars again came in to him and expelled him. They apologized to me, saying, "This is a stranger who has only recently arrived from the land of the Franks and he has never before seen anyone praying except eastward." Thereupon I said to myself, "I have had enough prayer." So I went out and have ever been surprised at the conduct of this devil of a man, at the change in the color of his face, his trembling and his sentiment at the sight of one praying towards the *qiblah.*[32]

32. The direction in which all Muslims must pray is toward the *qiblah* (or *Kaaba*) shrine in Mecca.

X

Gothic Art

1. Abbey Church of St. Denis, Paris, 1140–1144 (Gardner, pp. 374–75, ills. 10:1 to 10:3; Janson, p. 302, ills. 422–23)
Suger, *On the Abbey Church of St. Denis and Its Art Treasures:* "The Beauty of the House of God," mid-twelfth century
Bernard of Clairvaux, *Song of Songs,* Sermon 83: "A Great Thing Is Love," 1135–1153.

St. Denis, located a short distance from the city of Paris, is one of the oldest abbeys in the French capital. Its history is inextricably linked with the history of the French kings, many of whom chose it as their burial place. Founded on the site where the martyred bishop Saint Denis[1] was buried in the third century, the abbey was endowed by King Dagobert I in the seventh century. Sections of the structure were rebuilt by Pepin the Short in the eighth century and by Charlemagne in the ninth. Louis VI (1081–1137) adopted the standard of Saint Denis as the banner of the French kings, and he chose Suger, the abbot of St. Denis, as his chief adviser.

Suger (c. 1081–1151) came from a humble family. He was pledged to the abbey of St. Denis at the age of ten. As an adolescent he attended the same school as the future King Louis VI, and the two formed a lifelong friendship. In 1122 Suger was elected abbot of St. Denis.

In practical matters of administration, Suger tried to reconcile the claims of church and state. In spiritual matters, Suger sought to deepen the individual's interior response to God. Suger was deeply influenced not only by the writings of the fifth-century Greek theologian Dionysius the Areopagite but also by the thought of the contemporary French reformer Bernard of Clairvaux. In 1127, in response to Bernard's call for spiritual renewal within the church, Suger reformed the abbey of St. Denis and restored the strict observance of Benedictine Rule.

Bernard of Clairvaux (1090–1153) came from an aristocratic family. At the age of twenty-two, he entered the Cistercian order, which was known for its strictness. His ability to sway people became evident when he persuaded about thirty relatives and friends, who had originally opposed his entering the order, to join him in taking religious vows. After only three years, he was chosen abbot for

1. Saint Denis, or Dionysius of Paris (died c. 258), was sent to convert Gaul to Christianity. He became bishop of Paris and was subsequently martyred, giving Montmartre its famous name. In the ninth century, he came to be identified mistakenly with Dionysius the Areopagite and therefore with the author of the Pseudo-Dionysian writings. He was the patron saint of France.

a new monastery at Clairvaux. His zeal was expressed in his polemics against the disciplinary decadence of other monastic orders in the Christian church.

Bernard was a prolific writer. His theology was imbued with the richness of his own genuine mystical experience. He believed that God was the source of all charity, and that God had, by love, created men and women and would, by love, redeem them. The believer, in Bernard's view, achieves a mystical state of union with God when he or she returns divine love. This union is attained when the soul accepts God, a state which Bernard alludes to as the bride accepting the bridegroom in mystical nuptials or spiritual marriage.

Bernard declared that his purpose in writing was "to penetrate hearts rather than to explain words." The same purpose can be ascribed to Suger in his reconstruction of St. Denis.

Two selections related to Suger and his architectural program at St. Denis are presented here. The first, "The Beauty of the House of God," is from Suger's text *On the Abbey Church of St. Denis and Its Art Treasures.* Here, Suger describes the reconstruction of the abbey church. He refers to the dazzling art works, such as the jeweled chalice and the cross that he commissioned to ornament the new structure, and he explains that the contemplation of their material beauty draws the worshiper toward the contemplation of the realm of immaterial beauty. The second selection, "A Great Thing Is Love," is from the collection of sermons entitled *Song of Songs,* composed by Bernard between 1135 and his death in 1153. In this passage from Sermon 83, Bernard describes the ardor of the worshiper for God.

Suger, *On the Abbey Church of St. Denis and Its Art Treasures*[2]

The Beauty of the House of God

Often we contemplate, out of sheer affection for the church our mother, these different ornaments both new and old; and when we behold how that wonderful cross of St. Eloy[3]—together with the smaller ones—and that incomparable ornament commonly called "the Crest" are placed upon the golden altar, then I say, sighing deeply in my heart: Every precious stone was thy covering, the sardius, the topaz, and the jasper, the chrysolite, and the onyx, and the beryl, the sapphire, and the carbuncle, and the emerald. To those who know the properties of precious stones it becomes evident, to their utter astonishment, that none is absent from the number of these

2. Reprinted, by permission of the publisher, from Erwin Panofsky, ed., trans., and annot., *Abbot Suger on the Abbey Church of St. Denis and Its Art Treasures,* second ed. by Gerda Panofsky-Soergel (Princeton, N.J.: Princeton University Press, 1979), pp. 63–65. Copyright © 1946; © 1973 renewed; second ed. © 1979 by Princeton University Press.

3. The French form of Saint Eligius (c. 590–660), patron of metalworkers. Eligius was a renowned mint worker to the Frankish kings; he later became a bishop.

(with the only exception of the carbuncle), but that they abound most copiously. Thus, when—out of my delight in the beauty of the house of God—the loveliness of the many-colored gems has called me away from external cares, and worthy meditation has induced me to reflect, transferring that which is material to that which is immaterial, on the diversity of the sacred virtues: then it seems to me that I see myself dwelling, as it were, in some strange region of the universe which neither exists entirely in the slime of the earth nor entirely in the purity of Heaven; and that, by the grace of God, I can be transported from this inferior to that higher world in an anagogical manner.

Bernard of Clairvaux, *Song of Songs,* Sermon 83[4]

A Great Thing Is Love

A great thing is love, but it has its degrees. The Bride stands at the highest. . . . The very being of the Bride, and her one hope, consists in love. In this she abounds and with this the Bridegroom is content. He seeks nought else of her, and she has nought else to give. It is for this that He is Bridegroom, and she is Bride. This belongs wholly to the wedded pair. . . .

Rightly then does she renounce all other affections, giving herself up wholly to love and to love alone, since it is to Love Itself that she must render love for love. For were she to pour forth all herself in love, what would that be compared to this ever-flowing and inexhaustible spring? Not with equal abundance flows that stream from the lover and from Love, from the soul and from the Word, from the bride and from the Bridegroom, from the creature and from the Creator; the thirsty wayfarer might then be compared with the spring. What then? Shall the vow of the betrothed, the desire of her heart, her loving ardour and her daring trust, shall all these perish and become of none effect because, forsooth, she cannot contend in swiftness with the Giant who runs his course, or dispute the palm of sweetness with honey, of gentleness with the lamb, of whiteness with the lily, of brilliance with the sun, or of charity with Him who is Charity Itself? No; for although, being a creature she loves less than He by whom she is loved, because indeed she is less, yet if she love with her whole self her love lacks nothing, since all she has is given. Wherefore, as I have said, to love thus is to enter into marriage. For she cannot love thus and yet be little loved, since in the mutual consent of two parties consists a full and perfect

4. Reprinted from Étienne Gilson, *The Mystical Theology of Saint Bernard,* trans. by A.H.C. Downes (New York: Sheed and Ward, 1940), pp. 138–40.

marriage. Unless perhaps someone should doubt whether the soul is not first loved, and with greater love than hers, by the Word? But we know well that in loving she is both anticipated and surpassed. Happy is the soul that merits to be prevented with the benediction of such sweetness. Happy the soul that experiences such sweet embrace, which is none other than a love holy and chaste, a love sweet and delightful, a love as sincere as it is pure, a love mutual, endearing, powerful, which makes of two, not one flesh indeed, but one spirit, as says St. Paul: He who is joined to the Lord is one spirit [I Corinthians 6:17].

2. Notre-Dame, Paris, 1163–1250 (Gardner, pp. 378–79, ills. 10:9 to 10:12; Janson, pp. 303–304, ills. 425–27)
Peter Abelard, *The History of My Calamities:* "Abelard's Love for Heloïse"; *Yes and No:* "The Dialectical Method," c. 1130–1140.
Thomas Aquinas, *Summa Theologiae:* "Human Reason and Divine Revelation," 1267–1272

Medieval universities emerged in the twelfth century as important intellectual centers. At the University of Paris, the first and most famous university located north of the Alps, classes were held at the schools connected with the cathedral of Notre-Dame and the churches of St. Victor and Ste. Geneviève. In the twelfth century by far the most popular teacher in Paris was Peter Abelard; in the thirteenth century by far the most influential scholar was Thomas Aquinas.

Because of their efforts to organize, analyze, and synthesize a vast body of learning, both men are known as scholastics. The medieval desire for unity is reflected in the systematic treatises of the scholastics and in the orderly plans of cathedrals such as Notre-Dame in Paris.

Peter Abelard (1079–1142) was famous in his own day for being a gifted teacher, a controversial philosopher, and the tragic lover of Heloïse. Born the son of a knight in Brittany in northwest France, Abelard was disinherited when he chose to study philosophy. He wandered from school to school, studying with the most renowned teachers of his day and quarreling with all of them. He settled in Paris, where he won renown as a brilliant public lecturer and a popular teacher. He also became tutor to the young Heloïse, niece of Canon Fulbert, one of the clergy of the cathedral of Notre-Dame, and fathered a son named Astralabe by his pupil. The lovers were secretly married, but, at Abelard's insistence, Heloïse entered a convent in Argenteuil outside Paris. This infuriated Fulbert. At his instigation, Abelard was attacked and castrated. Deeply mortified, Abelard retreated to the monastery of St. Denis.

At St. Denis, Abelard devoted himself wholeheartedly to theological studies. Although he unconditionally accepted the authority of revelation and of the church, Abelard was a medieval rationalist who believed reason to be more effective than intuition and experience in seeking truth. He deeply antagonized leaders of the church by appearing to give reason priority over authority. In his most famous work, *Yes and No,* Abelard collected passages from Scripture and from the writings of the Fathers that were unclear, inconsistent, or even contradictory. He argued that these apparent contradictions could be reconciled by logic and by an understanding of the nature of language. Bernard of Clairvaux led the traditionalist theologians in an attack on Abelard. Abelard was twice condemned for heresy, first in 1121 and later in 1140, by ecclesiastical councils in France.

In addition to being disputatious in his thought, Abelard was contentious in his personal life. His unpopularity with the abbey of St. Denis, caused by his disproof of the traditional identification of the abbey's patron with the earlier Dionysius the Areopagite, put his life in jeopardy. Abelard fled to Champagne in northeastern France for asylum. In 1125 he was elected abbot of a remote monastery in Brittany, where he claimed that the discontented monks within his community had tried to poison his communion wine. About 1135 Abelard returned to Paris and taught at St. Geneviève. He died in 1144, and when Heloïse died twenty years later, she was buried beside him.

Thomas Aquinas (1225–1274) was born in southern Italy, near Monte Cassino, of an aristocratic family. In 1244 he joined the newly founded Dominican Order. A brilliant pupil, he was sent to the universities of Paris and Cologne to study. After earning the degree of master of theology at Paris, he spent his adult life teaching in various places, including Rome, Bologna, Naples, and Paris.

Although he died before he was fifty years old, Thomas produced a prodigious amount of writing. Of his eighteen volumes, his most famous work is the *Summa Theologiae.* A vast ideological exposition, the *Summa Theologiae* seeks to harmonize various approaches to truth and to integrate all knowledge. The only other medieval treatise that has been as influential in Western intellectual history is Augustine's *City of God.*

Thomas wrote at a time when the introduction of Arabian-Aristotelian thought had stirred strong debate in Europe. Many European followers of Arab philosophers, such as Avicenna, believed that human reason could establish truth even though contradictory to faith. Traditional theologians, however, were skeptical of the value of reason in understanding spiritual truth and relied instead upon revelation as the avenue to wisdom.

Thomas sought to bridge the gulf between faith and reason harmoniously and to incorporate Aristotelian philosophy within Christian theology. He agreed with Aristotle that the universe is orderly and rational; he accepted the Aristotelian premise that reason could acquire knowledge from man's experience of the visible world; and he relied upon elements of Aristotelian physics in his discussion of man and nature. But Thomas also asserted that the natural world was only one part of the Christian world. To comprehend the supernatural world, reason must be guided by faith. Revelation established the principles on which faith is based, whereas reason demonstrated the truth of faith. When faith leads to a conclusion that defies logic, human reason has failed. But since both revelation and rational thought come from God, reason, properly exercised, will be in accord with faith.

Three selections from the writings of Peter Abelard and Thomas Aquinas are presented here. The first, "Abelard's Love for Heloïse," is from Abelard's autobiography, *The History of My Calamities,* written in the 1130s. In it, Abelard describes the stratagems by which he entered Fulbert's house and wooed Heloïse. The second selection, "The Dialectical Method," is from Abelard's prologue to

Yes and No, also written in the 1130s. Here, Abelard discusses his technique of juxtaposing apparently contradictory authorities in order to weigh their truthfulness. The third selection, "Human Reason and Divine Revelation," is from Thomas' treatise *Summa Theologiae,* written between 1267 and 1272. In it, Thomas poses a broad question about the relationship between theology based on revelation and philosophy based on reason and then marshals arguments on all sides. Thomas' method in the *Summa Theologiae* represents the ultimate development of the approach used by Abelard in *Yes and No.*

Peter Abelard, *The History of My Calamities*[5]

Abelard's Love for Heloïse

And so, all on fire with love for [Heloïse], I sought opportunity to enable me to make her familiar with me by private and daily association, the more easily to win her over. To effect this, through the intervention of some friends, I arranged with her uncle to receive me at his own price into his home which was near my school on the pretext that the care of my household greatly interfered with my studies and proved too heavy a financial burden. He was a very avaricious man and also most anxious that his niece advance in her literary studies. Because of these two traits, I easily gained his assent and got what I desired since he was all eager for the money and considered that his niece would profit from my teaching. On this latter point he strongly urged me beyond my fondest hopes, acceding to my wishes and furthering my love. He put his niece entirely under my control that whenever I was free upon returning from school I might devote myself night and day to teaching her, telling me to use pressure if I found her remiss. I was astonished at his simplicity in this matter and would have been no more astounded if he had been giving over a tender lamb to a ravenous wolf. . . .

What was the result? We were first together in one house and then one in mind. Under the pretext of work we made ourselves entirely free for love and the pursuit of her studies provided the secret privacy which love desired. We opened our books but more words of love than of the lesson asserted themselves. There was more kissing than teaching; my hands found themselves at her breasts more often than on the book. Love brought us to gaze into each other's eyes more than reading kept them on the text. And the better to prevent suspicion, I sometimes struck her not through anger or vexation but from love and affection which were beyond the sweetness of every ointment. No sign of love was omitted by us in our ardor and whatever unusual love could devise, that was added too. And the more

5. Reprinted, by permission of the publisher, from *The Story of Abelard's Adversities,* trans. by J. T. Muckle (Toronto: The Pontifical Institute of Medieval Studies, 1964), pp. 27–28.

such delights were new to use, the more ardently we indulged in them, and the less did we experience satiety.

Peter Abelard, *Yes and No*[6]

The Dialectical Method

Among the multitudinous words of the holy Fathers some sayings seem not only to differ from one another but even to contradict one another. Hence it is not presumptuous to judge concerning those by whom the world itself will be judged, as it is written, "They shall judge nations" (Wisdom 3:8) and, again, "You shall sit and judge" (Luke 22:30). We do not presume to rebuke as untruthful or to denounce as erroneous those to whom the Lord said, "He who hears you hears me; he who despises you despises me" (Luke 10:16). Bearing in mind our foolishness we believe that our understanding is defective rather than the writing of those to whom the Truth Himself said, "It is not you who speak but the spirit of your Father who speaks in you" (Matthew 10:20). Why should it seem surprising if we, lacking the guidance of the Holy Spirit through whom those things were written and spoken, the Spirit impressing them on the writers, fail to understand them? Our achievement of full understanding is impeded especially by unusual modes of expression and by the different significances that can be attached to one and the same word, as a word is used now in one sense, now in another. Just as there are many meanings so there are many words. . . .

We must also take special care that we are not deceived by corruptions of the text or by false attributions when sayings of the Fathers are quoted that seem to differ from the truth or to be contrary to it; for many apocryphal writings are set down under names of saints to enhance their authority, and even the texts of divine Scripture are corrupted by the errors of scribes. . . .

It is no less important in my opinion to ascertain whether texts quoted from the Fathers may be ones that they themselves have retracted and corrected after they came to a better understanding of the truth as the blessed Augustine did on many occasions; or whether they are giving the opinion of another rather than their own opinion . . . or whether, in inquiring into certain matters, they left them open to question rather than settled them with a definitive solution. . . .

In view of these considerations we have undertaken to collect various sayings of the Fathers that give rise to questioning because of their appar-

6. Reprinted, by permission of the publisher, from Brian Tierney, Donald Kagan, and L. Pearce Williams, eds., *Great Issues in Western Civilization,* second ed. (New York: Random House, 1972), Vol. I, pp. 412–14. Selection translated by Brian Tierney.

ent contradictions as they occur to our memory. This questioning excites young readers to the maximum of effort in inquiring into the truth, and such inquiry sharpens their minds. Assiduous and frequent questioning is indeed the first key to wisdom. Aristotle, that most perspicacious of all philosophers, exhorted the studious to practice it eagerly, saying, "Perhaps it is difficult to express oneself with confidence on such matters if they have not been much discussed. To entertain doubts on particular points will not be unprofitable." For by doubting we come to inquiry; through inquiring we perceive the truth, according to the Truth Himself. "Seek and you shall find," He says, "Knock and it shall be opened to you."

Thomas Aquinas, *Summa Theologiae*[7]

Human Reason and Divine Revelation

Article I. Is another teaching required apart from philosophical studies?

THE FIRST POINT. 1. Any other teaching beyond that of science and philosophy seems needless. For man ought not to venture into realms beyond his reason; according to *Ecclesiasticus,*[8] *Be not curious about things far above thee.* Now the things lying within range of reason yield well enough to scientific and philosophical treatment. Additional teaching, therefore, seems superfluous.

2. Besides, we can be educated only about what is real; for nothing can be known for certain save what is true, and what is true is identical with what really is. Yet the philosophical sciences deal with all parts of reality, even with God; hence Aristotle refers to one department of philosophy as theology or the divine science. That being the case, no need arises for another kind of education to be admitted or entertained.

ON THE OTHER HAND the second epistle to Timothy[9] says, All Scripture inspired of god is profitable to teach, to reprove, to correct, to instruct in righteousness. Divinely inspired Scripture, however, is no part of the branches of philosophy traced by reasoning. Accordingly it is expedient to have another body of sure knowledge inspired by God.

REPLY: It should be urged that human well-being called for schooling in what God has revealed, in addition to the philosophical researches pursued by human reasoning.

Above all because God destines us for an end beyond the grasp of reason; according to Isaiah,[10] Eye hath not seen, O God, without thee what

7. Reprinted, by permission of the publisher, from Thomas Aquinas, *Summa Theologiae,* trans. by Herbert McCabe (London: Eyre and Spottiswoode [Blackfriars], 1964), pp. 5–9.

8. One of the books of the Apocrypha, also known as *The Wisdom of Jesus, the Son of Sirach.* The quotation is from 3:23.

9. II Timothy 3:16.

10. Isaiah 64:4.

thou hast prepared for them that love thee. Now we have to recognize an end before we can stretch out and exert ourselves for it. Hence the necessity for our welfare that divine truths surpassing reason should be signified to us through divine revelation.

We also stood in need of being instructed by divine revelation even in religious matters the human reason is able to investigate. For the rational truth about God would have appeared only to few, and even so after a long time and mixed with many mistakes; whereas on knowing this depends our whole welfare, which is in God. In these circumstances, then, it was to prosper the salvation of human beings, and the more widely and less anxiously, that they were provided for by divine revelation about divine things.

These then are the grounds of holding a holy teaching which has come to us through revelation beyond the discoveries of the rational sciences.

Hence: 1. Admittedly the reason should not pry into things too high for human knowledge, nevertheless when they are revealed by God they should be welcomed by faith: indeed the passage in *Ecclesiasticus* goes on *Many things are shown thee above the understanding of man.* And on them Christian teaching rests.

2. The diversification of the sciences is brought about by the diversity of aspects under which things can be known. Both an astronomer and a physical scientist may demonstrate the same conclusion, for instance that the earth is spherical; the first, however, works in a mathematical medium prescinding from material qualities, while for the second his medium is the observation of material bodies through the senses. Accordingly there is nothing to stop the same things from being treated by the philosophical sciences when they can be looked at in the light of natural reason and by another science when they are looked at in the light of divine revelation. Consequently the theology of holy teaching differs in kind from that theology which is ranked as a part of philosophy.

3. Amiens Cathedral, c. 1220–1236 (Gardner, pp. 386–87, ills. 10:22 to 10:25; Janson, p. 307, ills. 430–32)
Guillaume Durandi, *Rationale Divinorum Officiorum:* "A Church and Its Parts," 1286–1291

To the medieval mind, the divine presence infused the material world. Nature was apprehended on two levels: on the literal level, it was the world of physical matter perceived through sense experiences; on the symbolic level, it was the revelation of the supernatural realm, understood through grace. Therefore, the material world consisted of an almost infinite variety of symbols suggesting the true meaning of the divine kingdom.

Amiens Cathedral represents the extraordinary engineering achievements of medieval church architecture. In it a system of skeletal construction was used that reduced the walls to mere screens of glass and suspended vaults at a height of 144 feet above the floor. At the same time, like other churches of its age, Amiens Cathedral discloses the intangible in the tangible. The complex symbolism of a Gothic church is described by Guillaume Durandi.

Guillaume Durandi (c. 1230–1296) was a respected canonist, liturgist, churchman, and administrator. Trained in canon law, Durandi was appointed one of the judges commissioned to hear cases of appeal brought to the Holy See. His most famous treatise, *Speculum Iudiciale,* written between 1271 and 1276, established him as an authority on canon law and court procedure. A later treatise by Durandi, *Rationale Divinorum Officiorum,* written between 1286 and 1291, made an original and lasting contribution to liturgy.

Rationale Divinorum Officiorum is a general discussion of the symbolism of churches, their ornaments, and their liturgical rites. Considered the most important medieval book on divine worship, Durandi's text exemplifies the dual comprehension of the visible world as spirit and matter, divine and mundane. A selection from *Rationale Divinorum Officiorum,* "A Church and Its Parts," is presented here.

Guillaume Durandi, *Rationale Divinorum Officiorum*[11]

A Church and Its Parts

First of all, let us consider a church and its parts. The word church hath two meanings: the one, a material building, wherein the divine offices are celebrated: the other, a spiritual fabric, which is the collection of the faithful. The Church, that is the people forming as assembled by its ministers, and collected together in one place by "Him who maketh men to be of one mind in an house." For as the material church is constructed from the joining together of various stones, so is the spiritual Church by that of various men. . . .

This is that House of the Lord, built with all strength, "upon the foundations of the apostles and prophets, Jesus Christ Himself being the chief cornerstone. Her foundations are in the holy mountains." The walls built upon these are the Jews and Gentiles; who come from the four parts of the world unto Christ, and who have believed, believe, or shall believe on Him. The faithful predestinated to eternal life, are the stones in the structure of this wall which shall continually be built up unto the world's end. . . .

The cement, without which there can be no stability of the walls, is made of lime, sand, and water. The lime is fervent charity, which joineth

11. Reprinted from William Durandus, *The Symbolism of Churches and Church Ornaments: Rationale Divinorum Officiorum, Book I,* trans. by John M. Neale and Benjamin Webb (London: Gibbings and Co., 1893), pp. 12–13, 17–18, 20, 22–25.

to itself the sand, that is, undertakings for the temporal welfare of our brethren. . . . Now the lime and the sand are bound together in the wall by an admixture of water. But water is an emblem of the Spirit. . . .

Furthermore, the church consisteth of four walls, that is, is built on the doctrine of the Four Evangelists; and hath length, breadth, and height: the height representeth courage, the length fortitude, which patiently endureth till it attaineth its heavenly home; the breadth is charity, which, with long suffering, loveth its friends in God, and its foes for God; and again, its height is the hope of the future retribution, which despiseth prosperity and adversity, hoping "to see the goodness of the Lord in the land of the living." . . .

The towers are the preachers and prelates of the Church, which are her bulwark and defence. . . .

The glass windows in a church are Holy Scriptures, which expel the wind and the rain, that is all things hurtful, but transmit the light of the true Sun, that is, God, into the hearts of the faithful. . . .

The door of the church is Christ: according to that saying in the Gospel, "I am the door." The apostles are also called doors.

The piers of the church are bishops and doctors: who specially sustain the Church of God by their doctrine. . . .

The beams in the church are preachers, who spiritually sustain it. The vaulting also, or ceiling, representeth preachers, who adorn and strengthen it. . . .

4. Chartres Cathedral, 1194–1220 (Gardner, pp. 382–83, ills. 10:15 to 10:17; Janson, pp. 305–306, ills. 428–29)
Our Lady's Tumbler: "The Tumbler's Service" and "The Virgin's Care," thirteenth century

The cult of the Virgin Mary had no rivals in popular piety of the Gothic period. Monastic orders, such as the Carthusian, Cistercian, and Carmelite orders, honored Mary. The cathedrals of many cities, including Amiens, Chartres, Laon, and Paris, were dedicated to her.

Chartres Cathedral was an especially important center for the veneration of the Virgin Mary. A garment, supposed to be her tunic, was kept there enclosed in a casket. During the twelfth and thirteenth centuries, vast throngs of pilgrims visited the cathedral to pay homage to Mary and to see the cathedral's most sacred relic.

Admiration for the Virgin found many different forms of expression. She was revered by the scholastics, such as Thomas Aquinas, who reverently addressed her as the Mother of God, the empress of the world, the queen of heaven, and the model of all virtues. Mary was eulogized by monks, such as Bernard of Clairveaux, who adored her for her charity, chastity, and heavenly glory. Poets strained the Latin language to phrase their admiration for Mary's beauty and benignity, and the common people implored her to act as a mediator between their souls and the Savior. In Mary, there was nothing harsh. She offered tender solace to all, softening the wrath of God toward sinners and winning merciful favors for her supplicants.

Medieval legends attest to the widespread devotion to Mary and to the popular faith placed in her intercession and her power to work miracles. One of the most famous legends is the anonymous French story *Our Lady's Tumbler,* written in the thirteenth century. Although it is set in the abbey of Clairvaux, the story was probably written in Picardy in France and may have been based upon a tale brought home from the Middle East by the crusaders.

According to the story, an acrobat, or tumbler, entered the monastery at Clairvaux. Because he was too uneducated to recite prayers or perform services, the tumbler felt that he was unable to serve God. Finally, he resolved to offer his skills as a tumbler secretly before the altar with its image of the Virgin Mary. When his activities were reported to the abbot by a surprised monk, the two clerics crept into the church to observe the tumbler's performance and the Virgin's response.

Two selections from *Our Lady's Tumbler* are presented here. In the first, "The Tumbler's Service," the tumbler is called to perform for Mary by the ringing of the church bell for Mass. In the second selection, "The Virgin's Care," the abbot is the astonished witness of Mary's benevolent concern for the tumbler.

Our Lady's Tumbler[12]

The Tumbler's Service

"By the Mother of God," [said the tumbler,] "this will I do, and never shall I be blamed for it. I will do that which I have learnt, and thus, after mine own manner, will I serve the Mother of God in her Church. The others do service with song, and I will do service with tumbling."

And he took off his habit, and then stripped himself, and laid his garments beside the altar, but so that his body should not be uncovered, he kept on a tunic, the which was very clinging and close fitting. Little better was it than a shift; nevertheless was his body wholly covered. And thus was he fitly clad and equipped, and he girded his tunic, and duly prepared him, and he turned him to the image, and gazed on it very humbly. "Lady," said he, "to your keeping I commend my body and soul. Gentle Queen and Lady, despise not that which I am acquainted with, for, without ado, I will essay me to serve you in good faith, if so be that God will aid me. How to sing, or how to read to you, that I know not, but truly I would make choice for you of all my best tricks in great number. Now may I be like a kid which frisks and gambols before its

12. Reprinted, by permission of the publisher, from *Of the Tumbler of Our Lady and Other Miracles,* trans. by Alice Kemp-Welsch (London: Chatto and Windus, 1908), pp. 8–12, 17–19.

mother. Lady, who art never stern to those who serve you aright,—such as I am, I am yours."

Then he began to turn somersaults, now high, now low, first forwards, then backwards, and then he fell on his knees before the image, and bowed his head. "Ah, very gentle Queen!" said he, "of your pity, and of your generosity, despise not my service." Then he tumbled, and leaped, and turned gaily the somersault of Metz. And he bowed to the image, and worshipped it, for he paid homage to it as much as he was able. And anon he turned the French somersault, and then the somersault of Champagne, and after that, those of Spain and of Brittany, and then that of Lorraine. And he laboured to the utmost of his power.

And after that, he did the Roman somersault, and then he put his hand before his face, and turned him with great grace, and looked very humbly at the image of the Mother of God. . . . "Lady," said he, "I do homage to you with my heart, and my body, and my feet, and my hands, for naught beside this do I understand. Now would I be your gleeman.[13] Yonder they are singing, but I am come here to divert you. Lady, you who can protect me, for God's sake do not despise me." Then he beat his breast, and sighed, and mourned very grievously that he knew not how to do service in other manner. And then he turned a somersault backwards. "Lady" said he, "so help me God, never before have I done this. Lady! How that one would have his utmost desire, who could dwell with you in your right glorious mansion! For God's sake, Lady, receive me there. I do this for your sake, and in nowise for mine own." Then he again turned the somersault of Metz, and tumbled and capered full many a time.

And when he heard the monks celebrating, he began to exert himself, and so long as the Mass dured, he ceased not to dance, and to jump, and to leap, until that he was on the point to faint, and he could not stand up, and thus he fell to the ground, and dropped from sheer fatigue. And like as the grease issues from the spitted meat, so the sweat issued from him all over, from head to foot. "Lady," said he, "no more can I do now, but of a surety I shall come back again.". . .

The Virgin's Care

And the abbot, watching there, observed all the service of the novice, and the divers somersaults the which he turned, and how that he capered, and danced, and bowed before the image, and jumped, and leaped, until that he was nigh fainting. And so greatly was he overcome of fatigue, that he fell heavily to the ground, and so exhausted was he, that he sweated all over from his efforts, so that the sweat ran all down the middle of the crypt.

13. A wandering minstrel.

But in a little, the Mother of God, whom he served all without guile, came to his succour, and well knew she how to aid him.

And anon the abbot looked, and he saw descend from the vaulting so glorious a lady, that never had he seen one so fair or so richly crowned, and never had another so beautiful been created. Her vesture was all wrought with gold and precious stones, and with her were the angels and the archangels from the heavens above, who came around the tumbler, and solaced and sustained him. And when that they were ranged around him, he was wholly comforted, and they made ready to tend him, for they desired to make recompense unto him for the services the which he had rendered unto their Lady, who is so precious a gem. And the sweet and noble Queen took a white cloth, and with it she very gently fanned her minstrel before the altar. And the noble and gracious Lady fanned his neck and body and face to cool him, and greatly did she concern herself to aid him, and gave herself up to the care of him; but of this the good man took no heed, for he neither perceived, nor did he know, that he was in such fair company.

5. *Ekkehard* and *Uta,* Naumberg Cathedral, c. 1250–1260 (Gardner, p. 406, ill. 10:54; Janson, p. 332, ill. 467)
Andreas Capellanus, *The Art of Courtly Love:* "To Talk of Love" and "To Act with Compulsion," c. 1170–1190
Gottfried von Strassburg, *Tristan:* "Love, Waylayer of All Hearts," c. 1210

While spiritual devotion for Mary was reaching its supreme expression in medieval religion, the courtly love for women was being elaborated in lay society. Courtly love first developed in the castles of southern France at the end of the eleventh century and flourished in aristocratic circles in the later Middle Ages. It expressed the ideals and values of an upper-class society in which women played increasingly important intellectual, economic, and political roles.

Courtly love idealized the well-born woman as an exquisite and refined being who possessed a nature more pure and more spiritual than any man. The lover of such a woman acknowledged the baseness of his nature but strove to win his mistress' affections by acting bravely and honorably in society, by following intricate rituals of courtesy toward women, and by undertaking whatever daring deeds were commanded by his beloved. Courtly love simultaneously ennobled and endangered the lover, for the noblewoman whom the lover both revered and desired was the wife of his feudal lord. Thus, courtly love involved an anxious and often precarious juxtaposition of sexual yearnings, spiritual aspirations, and personal jeopardy.

Three selections related to courtly love are presented here. Two selections are from *The Art of Courtly Love,* written by Andreas Capellanus between c. 1170 and 1190; the third selection is from *Tristan,* an epic poem by Gottfried von Strassburg.

Andreas (late twelfth century), a Frenchman who was sometimes described as chaplain to the king of France, codified the conventions of medieval courtly love. His book defines the nature and goals of love and offers a series of dialogues between men and women of different social classes. In the first selection from *The Art of Courtly Love,* "To Talk of Love," Andreas counsels a man of the upper nobility on how to speak to a woman of lesser nobility. In the second selection, "To Act with Compulsion," Andreas advises his reader on how to behave toward an unwilling woman of low social station.

Gottfried von Strassburg (early twelfth century) was one of the greatest medieval German poets. *Tristan,* which was written around 1210, is based upon a Celtic legend that reached Germany through French sources. The story revolves around Tristan's journey to Ireland to accompany Isolde back to England as a bride for his uncle, King Mark of Cornwall. On their return voyage, Tristan and Isolde mistakenly drink a magic love potion intended for the bride and her future husband, Tristan's uncle. Although each is bound by honor to serve King Mark, Tristan and Isolde are powerless to resist their passion and are doomed by their forbidden love. In the selection from *Tristan* presented here, "Love, Waylayer of All Hearts," Gottfried describes the effects of the magic potion on the unfortunate lovers.

Ekkehard and *Uta,* two statues from the choir of the German cathedral at Naumberg, represent important patrons of the church. Although the sculptures were carved long after the deaths of the feudal baron and his wife, the artist not only created a convincing portrayal of a powerful nobleman and his captivating wife, but also suggested the nature of their relationship.

Andreas Capellanus, *The Art of Courtly Love*[14]

To Talk of Love

When a man of the higher nobility addresses a woman of the simple nobility, let him use the same speeches that a nobleman and a man of the higher nobility use with a woman of the middle class, except that part dealing with the commendation of birth, and he must not boast very much of the fact that he is noble. In addition he might begin with this formula:

"I ought to give God greater thanks than any other living man in the whole world because it is now granted me to see with my eyes what my soul has desired above all else to see, and I believe that God has granted it to me because of my great longing and because He has seen fit to hear the prayers of my importunate supplication. For not an hour of the day or night could pass that I did not earnestly pray God to grant me the boon of seeing you near me in the flesh. It is no wonder that I was driven by so great an impulse to see you and was tormented by so great a desire, since the whole world extols your virtue and your wisdom, and in the farthest

14. Reprinted, by permission of the publisher, from Andreas Capellanus, *The Art of Courtly Love,* trans. by John Jay Parry (New York: Columbia University Press, 1941), pp. 91–92, 98, 100–101.

parts of the world courts are fed upon the tale of your goodness just as though it were a sort of tangible food. And now I know in very truth that a human tongue is not able to tell the tale of your beauty and your prudence or a human mind to imagine it. And so the mighty desire, which I already had, of seeing you and serving you has greatly increased and will increase still more.". . .

The woman says: "Even though I found you in every respect worthy of love, still we are separated by too wide and too rough an expanse of country to be able to offer each other love's solaces or to find proper opportunities for meeting. . . . Besides there is another fact, by no means trivial, which keeps me from loving you. I have a husband who is greatly distinguished by his nobility, his good breeding, and his good character, and it would be wicked for me to violate his bed or submit to the embraces of any other man, since I know that he loves me with his whole heart and I am bound to him with all the devotion of mine. The laws themselves bid me refrain from loving another man when I am blessed with such a reward for my love."

The man says: "I admit it is true that your husband is a very worthy man and that he is more blest than any man in the world because he has been worthy to have the joy of embracing Your Highness. But I am greatly surprised that you wish to misapply the term 'love' to that marital affection which husband and wife are expected to feel for each other after marriage, since everybody knows that love can have no place between husband and wife. They may be bound to each other by a great and immoderate affection, but their feeling cannot take the place of love, because it cannot fit under the true definition of love. For what is love but an inordinate desire to receive passionately a furtive and hidden embrace? But what embrace between husband and wife can be furtive, I ask you, since they may be said to belong to each other and may satisfy all of each other's desires without fear that anybody will object? . . .

"But there is another reason why husband and wife cannot love each other and that is that the very substance of love, without which true love cannot exist—I mean jealousy—is in such case very much frowned upon and they should avoid it like the pestilence; but lovers should always welcome it as the mother and the nurse of love. From this you may see clearly that love cannot possibly flourish between you and your husband. Therefore, since every woman of character ought to love, prudently, you can without doing yourself any harm accept the prayers of a suppliant and endow your suitor with your love."

To Act with Compulsion

But lest you should consider that what we have already said about the love of the [upper and] middle class applies also to farmers, we will add a little about their love. We say that it rarely happens that we find farmers serving in Love's court, but naturally, like a horse or a mule, they give themselves up to the work of Venus, as nature's urging teaches them to do. . . . And if you should, by some chance, fall in love with some of their women, be careful to puff them up with lots of praise and then, when you find a convenient place, do not hesitate to take what you seek and to embrace them by force. For you can hardly soften their outward inflexibility so far that they will grant you their embraces quietly or permit you to have the solaces you desire unless first you use a little compulsion as a convenient cure for their shyness. We do not say these things, however, because we want to persuade you to love such women, but only so that, if through lack of caution you should be driven to love them, you may know, in brief compass, what to do.

Gottfried von Strassburg, *Tristan*[15]

Love, Waylayer of All Hearts

Now when the maid and the man, Isolde and Tristan, had drunk the draught, in an instant that arch disturber of tranquillity was there, Love, waylayer of all hearts, and she had stolen in! Before they were aware of it she had planted her victorious standard there and bowed them beneath her yoke. They who were two and divided now became one and united. No longer were they at variance: Isolde's hatred was gone. Love, the reconciler, had purged their hearts of enmity, and so joined them in affection that each was to the other as limpid as a mirror. They shared a single heart. Her anguish was his pain: his pain her anguish. The two were one both in joy and in sorrow, yet they hid their feelings from each other. This was from doubt and shame. She was ashamed, as he was. She went in doubt of him, as he of her. However blindly the craving in their hearts was centered on one desire, their anxiety was how to begin. This masked their desire from each other.

When Tristan felt the stirrings of love he at once remembered loyalty and honor, and strove to turn away. "No, leave it, Tristan," he was continually thinking to himself, "pull yourself together, do not take any notice of it." But his heart was impelled towards her. He was striving against his own wishes, desiring against his desire. He was drawn now in one direction, now in another. Captive that he was, he tried all that he knew in the snare, over and over again, and long maintained his efforts.

The loyal man was afflicted by a double pain: when he looked at her

15. Reprinted, by permission of the publisher, from Gottfried von Strassburg, *Tristan,* trans. by A. T. Hatto (London: Penguin Classics, 1960), pp. 195–97.

face and sweet Love began to wound his heart and soul with her, he bethought himself of Honour, and it retrieved him. But this in turn was the sign for Love, his liege lady, whom his father had served before him, to assail him anew, and once more he had to submit. Honour and Loyalty harassed him powerfully, but Love harassed him more. Love tormented him to an extreme, she made him suffer more than did Honour and Loyalty combined. His heart smiled upon Isolde, but he turned his eyes away: yet his greatest grief was when he failed to see her. As is the way of captives, he fixed his mind on escape and how he might elude her, and returned many times to this thought: "Turn one way, or another! Change this desire! Love and like elsewhere!" But the noose was always there. He took his heart and soul and searched them for some change: but there was nothing there but Love—and Isolde.

And so it fared with her. Finding this life unbearable, she, too, made ceaseless efforts. When she recognized the lime that bewitching Love had spread and saw that she was deep in it, she endeavoured to reach dry ground, she strove to be out and away. But the lime kept clinging to her and drew her back and down. The lovely woman fought back with might and main, but stuck fast at every step. She was succumbing against her will. She made desperate attempts on many sides, she twisted and turned with hands and feet and immersed them ever deeper in the blind sweetness of Love, and of the man. Her limed senses failed to discover any path, bridge, or track that would advance them half a step, half a foot, without Love being there too. Whatever Isolde thought, whatever came uppermost in her mind, there was nothing there, of one sort or another, but Love, and Tristan.

This was all below the surface, for her heart and her eyes were at variance—Modesty chased her eyes away, Love drew her heart towards him. That warring company, a Maid and a Man, Love and Modesty, brought her onto great confusion; for the Maid wanted the Man, yet she turned her eyes away: Modesty wanted Love, but told no one of her wishes. But what was the good of that? A Maid and her Modesty are by common consent so fleeting a thing, so short-lived a blossoming, they do not long resist. Thus Isolde gave up her struggle and accepted her situation. Without further delay the vanquished girl resigned herself body and soul to Love and to the man.

Isolde glanced at him now and again and watched him covertly, her bright eyes and her heart were now in full accord. Secretly and lovingly her heart and eyes darted at the man rapaciously, while the man gave back her looks with tender passion. Since Love would not release him, he too began to give ground. Whenever there was a suitable occasion the man and the maid came together to feast each other's eyes. These lovers seemed to each other fairer than before—such is Love's law, such is the way with affection. It is so this year, it was so last year and it will remain so among all lovers as long as Love endures, that while their affection is growing and bringing forth blossom and increase of all lovable things, they please each other more than ever they did when it first began to burgeon. Love that bears increase makes lovers fairer than at first. This is the seed of Love, from which it never dies.

6. William of Sens and William the Englishman, Canterbury Cathedral, 1175–1184 (Gardner, p. 400, ills. 10:40 to 10:41)
Geoffrey Chaucer, *The Canterbury Tales:* The Clerk's Tale, "The Patience of Griselda" and "The Service of God," c. 1390–1400

Canterbury Cathedral commemorates a struggle between the Catholic church and the English state, which began in the twelfth century and continued until the sixteenth, when Henry VIII broke with Rome and formed the Church of England. The principal actors in the beginning of this struggle were Henry II, who tried to enlarge the prerogatives of the crown at the expense of the church, and Thomas Becket, who defended the supremacy of the church.

Henry II (1133–1189), king of England, was an able and energetic monarch, who established a reign of law and justice. His efforts to bring churchmen under the jurisdiction of the civil courts put him in direct conflict with Becket.

Thomas Becket (1118–1170), the son of a middle-class merchant, was an astute statesman and churchman. Appointed chancellor of England by the king in 1155, Becket loyally served Henry both in government matters and on the battlefield. In 1162, Henry appointed him archbishop of Canterbury, the highest church office in England. With the change in position, Becket underwent a radical transformation. He renounced the courtly life of luxury he had hitherto enjoyed and donned rough haircloth garments, ate coarse food, and subjected his body to severe forms of self-mortification. Moreover, the man who had once been the foremost champion of kingly power now became the ardent defender of papal authority.

On December 29, 1170, Becket was murdered at the high altar of Canterbury Cathedral by four knights in the king's service. Henry II was blamed for the deed. Four years later, Henry made a penitential pilgrimage to Becket's tomb, walking with bare and bleeding feet through the streets of Canterbury and submitting to a scourging by the bishop, abbot, and monks of the cathedral.

Becket was canonized by the church in 1173. Reports of miracles at his tomb had begun to circulate almost immediately after the archbishop's death, and drew pilgrims from all parts of England, Scotland, Wales, Ireland, and northern Europe. Fifty years after the martyrdom, Becket's relics were placed in a resplendent gold and jeweled shrine in the reconstructed Canterbury Cathedral.

The pilgrimages to the shrine of Becket were immortalized by Geoffrey Chaucer (c. 1340–1400) in *The Canterbury Tales.* Written in the 1390s, *The Canterbury Tales* consist of a collection of twenty-four stories told by a group of pilgrims to entertain each other during their journey to and from Becket's tomb in Canterbury Cathedral. The stories provide a description of English society in the late Middle Ages and reveal the thoughts and concerns of people on all social levels.

The Clerk's Tale is told by a pious student from Oxford University. The story, which the clerk claimed to have heard from the Italian poet Petrarch, concerns Walter, an Italian marquis, who married a humble country girl named Griselda. According to the clerk, Walter decides to test Griselda's devotion. After the birth of their children, he separates the mother from her daughter and son and secretly sends the infants away to be raised. When Griselda's love for him nevertheless proves constant, Walter devises still another test. He forges a bill of divorce and reintroduces their twelve-year-old daughter in his court as his future bride. Griselda humbly prepares the palace for the nuptials. Two selections are presented from The Clerk's Tale. In the first, "The Patience of Griselda," the clerk recounts how Griselda's humility finally causes the marquis to relent in his cruelty, to restore Griselda as his wife, and to return their children to their mother's affections. In the second selection, "The Service of God," the clerk concludes by advising his listeners that, even in adversity, they should serve God as faithfully as Griselda served her husband.

Geoffrey Chaucer, *The Canterbury Tales*[16]

The Clerk's Tale

The Patience of Griselda

And when this Walter thought of her patience,
Her glad face, with no malice there at all,
And how so oft he'd done to her offence,
And she aye firm and constant as a wall,
Remaining ever blameless through it all,
This cruel marquis did his heart address
To pity for her wifely steadfastness.

"This is enough, Griselda mine!" cried he,
"Be now no more ill pleased nor more afraid;
I have your faith and your benignity,
As straitly as ever woman's was, assayed
In high place and in poverty arrayed.
Now know I well, dear wife, your steadfastness."
And he began to kiss her and to press.

And she, for wonder, took of this no keep;
She heard not what the thing was he had cried;
She fared as if she'd started out of sleep,
Till from bewilderment she roused her pride.
"Griselda," said he, "by our God Who died,

16. Reprinted from Geoffrey Chaucer, *The Canterbury Tales,* trans. by J. U. Nicolson (New York: Crown Publishers, 1934), pp. 404–405, 406–407.

You are my wife, no other one I have,
Nor ever had, as God my soul may save!

"This is your daughter, whom you have supposed
Should be my wife; the other child truly
Shall be my heir, as I have aye purposed;
You bore him in your body faithfully.
I've kept them at Bologna secretly;
Take them again, for now you cannot say
That you have lost your children twain for aye.

"And folk that otherwise have said of me,
I warn them well that I have done this deed
Neither for malice nor for cruelty,
But to make trial in you of virtue hid,
And not to slay my children, God forbid!
But just to keep them privily and still
Till I your purpose knew and all your will."

When she heard this, she swooned and down did fall
For pitiful joy, and after her swooning
Both her young children to her did she call,
And in her arms, full piteously weeping,
Embraced them, and all tenderly kissing,
As any mother would, with many a tear
She bathed their faces and their sunny hair.

Oh, what a pitiful thing it was to see
Her swooning, and her humble voice to hear!
"Thanks, lord, that I may thank you now," said she,
"That you have saved to me my children dear!
Now I am ready for my death right here;
Since I stand in your love and in your grace,
Death matters not, nor what my soul may face!

"O young, O dear, O tender children mine,
Your woeful mother thought for long, truly,
That cruel hounds, or birds, or foul vermin
Had eaten you; but God, of His mercy,
And your good father, all so tenderly,
Have kept you safely." And in swoon profound
Suddenly there she fell upon the ground.

The Service of God

This story's told here, not that all wives should
Follow Griselda in humility,

For this would be unbearable, though they would,
But just that everyone, in his degree,
Should be as constant in adversity
As was Griselda; for that Petrarch wrote
This tale, and in a high style, as you'll note.

For since a woman once was so patient
Before a mortal man, well more we ought
Receive in good part that which God has sent;
For cause he has to prove what He has wrought.
But He tempts no man that His blood has bought.
As James says, if you his epistle read;
Yet does He prove folk at all times, indeed,

And suffers us, for our good exercise,
With the sharp scourges of adversity
To be well beaten oft, in sundry wise;
Not just to learn our will; for truly He,
Ere we were born, did all our frailty see;
But for our good is all that He doth give.
So then in virtuous patience let us live.

7. Gloucester Cathedral, England, 1332–1357 (Gardner, p. 402, ill. 10:46; Janson, p. 311, ill. 441)
Jean Froissart, *Chronicles:* "The Battle of Crécy," 1371–1404
Attributed to Henry VI of England, letter: "The Crimes of Joan of Arc," 1431

The present cathedral at Gloucester was constructed between 1332 and 1357. The great east window is a war memorial to the knights of Gloucester who were killed in France at the battle of Crécy in 1346 and in the siege of Calais in 1347.

William of Normandy's conquest of England in 1066 had united territories in France and England under a single ruler. His successors had later acquired other provinces of France through marriage and inheritance.

In the thirteenth century, the rising power of the French state brought England and France into direct conflict over the control of European lands, and many territories were wrested away from the Angevin kings of England. According to the peace treaty signed by Henry III of England and Louis IX of France in 1259, the province of Aquitaine was the sole French territory to remain in the possession of the English king.

In the fourteenth century, the positions of the two countries were reversed and English kings decided to recover the lost territories. The result was a long series of military campaigns known as the Hundred Years' War (1338–1453). In 1346 Edward III personally led his forces to Normandy and marched almost to the gates of Paris. He scored a decisive victory at Crécy in August 1346. In September of the same year, he laid siege to the port town of Calais and accepted its surrender in August 1347. In 1360 the French and English kings signed the Treaty of Calais, but the treaty was quickly repudiated by Charles V of France, and fighting resumed.

The war proved costly to both countries, but it was especially destructive to France. By 1420, the French had ceded most of France north of the Loire River to England. However, the English bid for domination was suddenly thwarted by a young peasant woman named Joan of Arc (c. 1412–1431). Inspired by visions, Joan believed that she had received a divine command to drive the foreigners from her native land. She rallied her French countrymen to her side. Dressed in men's clothing and armor, she joined the French troops in their defeat of the English at Orléans in 1429. The courage of her example and the sincerity of her belief in the French cause persuaded Charles, the disinherited son of the French king, to march to Reims. There, in 1429, in a simple ceremony attended only by three peers of France and by Joan, he was crowned Charles VII of France.

Joan was captured the following year, handed over to the English, and brought by the English before the Inquisition for trial on charges of witchcraft and heresy. Forbidden to hear Mass, Joan was chained to a wooden block in her cell. She was interrogated repeatedly, but she answered deliberately ambiguous and misleading questions with simplicity and common sense. She faltered briefly and appeared to recant, but her courage quickly returned, and she refused to compromise. On May 30, 1431, Joan was burned at the stake. Charles VII made no effort to rescue her. He went on to lead his armies to victory over the English and when the Hundred Years' War concluded in 1453, only Calais remained in English hands. Joan was canonized by the Catholic church in 1920.

Two selections related to the Hundred Years' War are presented here. The first is from the *Chronicles* written by Jean Froissart between 1371 and 1404. Froissart (c. 1337–1404) was a French historian, who based his account of the events in France from 1325 to 1399 largely on information furnished by eyewitnesses. The selection from the *Chronicles* presented here, "The Battle of Crécy," is typical of Froissart's attitude that the war was a long series of chivalrous adventures.

The second selection is from a letter attributed to King Henry VI of England and addressed to the German emperor and European rulers. In the selection presented here, "The Crimes of Joan of Arc," the monarch offers a justification of the execution of the Maid.

Jean Froissart, *Chronicles*[17]

The Battle of Crécy

The Englishmen, who were in three battles[18] lying on the ground to rest them, as soon as they saw the Frenchmen approach, they rose upon their feet fair and easily without any haste and arranged their battles. The first,

17. Reprinted from G. C. Macaulay, ed., *The Chronicles of Froissart,* trans. by Lord Berners (London: Macmillan and Co., 1904), pp. 104–106.

18. Divisions of the army.

which was the prince's battle, the archers there stood in manner of a herse[19] and the men of arms in the bottom of the battle. The earl of Northampton and the earl of Arundel with the second battle were on a wing in good order, ready to comfort the prince's battle, if need were.

The lords and knights of France came not to the assembly together in good order, for some came before and some came after in such haste and evil order, that one of them did trouble another. When the French king saw the Englishmen, his blood changed, and said to his marshals: "Make the Genoways[20] go on before and begin the battle in the name of God and Saint Denis." There were of the Genoways cross-bows about a fifteen thousand, but they were so weary of going afoot that day a [distance of] six leagues armed with their cross-bows, that they said to their constables: "We be not well ordered to fight this day, for we be not in the case to do any great deed of arms: we have more need of rest." . . .

When the Genoways were assembled together and began to approach, they made a great leap and cry to abash the Englishmen, but they stood still and stirred not for all that: then the Genoways again the second time made another leap and a fell cry, and stept forward a little, and the Englishmen removed not one foot: thirdly, again they leapt and cried, and went forth till they came within shot; then they shot fiercely with their cross-bows. Then the English archers stept forth one pace and let fly their arrows so wholly [together] and so thick, that it seemed snow. When the Genoways felt the arrows piercing through heads, arms and breasts, many of them cast down their cross-bows and did cut their strings and returned discomfited. When the French king saw them fly away, he said: "Slay these rascals, for they shall let and trouble us without reason." Then ye should have seen the men of arms dash in among them and killed a great number of them: and ever still the Englishmen shot whereas they saw thickest press; the sharp arrows ran into the men of arms and into their horses, and many fell, horse and men, among the Genoways, and when they were down, they could not relieve again, the press was so thick that one overthrew another. And also among the Englishmen there were certain rascals that went afoot with great knives, and they went in among the men of arms, and slew and murdered many as they lay on the ground, both earls, barons, knights and squires, whereof the king of England was after displeased, for he had rather they had been taken prisoners. . . .

This Saturday the Englishmen never departed from their battles for chasing of any man, but kept still their field, and ever defended themselves against all such as came to assail them. This battle ended about evensong time.

19. A harrow- or portcullis-like formation.
20. Genoese.

Attributed to Henry VI of England, Letter[21]

The Crimes of Joan of Arc

A certain woman whom the vulgar called *The Maid* had in fact arisen, who with an astonishing presumption, and contrary to natural decency, had adopted man's dress, assumed military arms, dared to take part in the massacre of men in bloody encounters and appeared in divers battles. Her presumption grew until she boasted that she was sent from God to lead their martial struggles, and that St. Michael, St. Gabriel, a host of other angels, with St. Catherine and St. Margaret, appeared visibly to her. So for almost a whole year she gradually seduced the people until the greater part turned away from the truth, put their trust in fables about the accomplishments of this superstitious woman which common report spread through almost the whole world. At last, taking compassion on His people whom He perceived to be stirred too easily by these dangerous and novel credulities, before receiving any proof that she was inspired by God, the divine mercy delivered this woman into our hands and power. Although she had inflicted many defeats upon our men and had brought great harm to our kingdoms, and it would therefore have been permissible for us to submit her forthwith to grave punishments, nevertheless not for one moment did we design to avenge our injury in that way or commit her to the secular authority for punishment. We were summoned by the bishop of the diocese in which she was captured to surrender her for judgment to the ecclesiastical jurisdiction, for she was commonly accused of grave and scandalous crimes hostile to the orthodox faith and the Christian religion. We therefore, as befits a Christian king reverencing the ecclesiastical authority with filial affection, immediately delivered the said woman to the judgment of Our Holy Mother Church and the jurisdiction of the said bishop. And certainly he, with all solemnity and most honourable gravity, after securing the collaboration of the vicar of the Inquisitor of Heretical Error, conducted this famous trial for the honour of God and the salutary edification of the people. After this woman had been for many days examined by the said judges, they submitted her confessions and statements to the decision of the doctors and masters of the University of Paris and many other learned authorities, and according to their advice they declared this woman to be manifestly superstitious, idolatrous, a prophetess, a caller up of demons, blasphemous towards God and His saints, schismatic and greatly erring from the faith of Jesus Christ. . . . Finally, as the ecclesiastical sanctions decree, to avoid the infection of the other members of Christ, she was

21. Reprinted, by permission of the publisher, from *The Trial of Jeanne d'Arc,* trans. by W. P. Barrett (London: Routledge and Kegan Paul, 1931), pp. 339–42.

given up to the judgment of the secular power which decided that her body was to be burned.

8. Florence Cathedral, Italy, 1296–1436 (Gardner, pp. 408–409, ills. 10:58 to 10:60; Janson, p. 315, ills. 449–51)
Dante, *The Divine Comedy:* Inferno, "Limbo," 1314–1321

By the end of the fourteenth century, the northern part of the Italian peninsula was dominated by three independent city-states—Venice, Milan, and Florence. During the preceding centuries Florence had grown steadily more powerful, enlarging its territories at the expense of neighboring towns and important families, and increasing its economic prosperity through expanded trade and banking relations with other states.

In the same period, Florence had also become an important center of artistic and architectural activity. Begun in 1296, Florence Cathedral is emphatically different from Gothic structures of northern Europe in its plan, proportions, and decorative elements. Its style blends elements of the Classical past with the native traditions of Romanesque architecture in Tuscany, the Italian province in which Florence is located.

The Classical past was also important to Dante Alighieri (1265–1321), a poet of Florence and one of the great forces in European intellectual life of the thirteenth century. Much of his poetry was composed in the vernacular Tuscan dialect rather than Latin, which, throughout the Middle Ages, was the language of churchmen, writers, and educated people. More than any other single author, Dante formulated the conventions of literary Italian and influenced its subsequent development.

Dante was the son of a Florentine money lender. Trained in the disciplines of grammar and rhetoric and drawn at an early age to poetry, Dante studied Classical authors, such as Virgil, Horace, and Ovid, and medieval scholastics, such as Thomas Aquinas. He was an acute observer of contemporary life. His involvement in Florentine politics led to his exile in 1301, and he never returned to the city he loved.

Dante's greatest work of poetry was *The Divine Comedy,* written between 1314 and 1321. The poem is a great sacred allegory about the progress of the soul toward God. It recounts an imaginary journey that Dante makes through the world beyond the grave. Led first by the Roman poet Virgil and then by the Florentine woman Beatrice, whom Dante revered, the poet visits Hell, Purgatory, and Heaven. He encounters the mythical and historical personages of past ages and the emperors, kings, queens, popes, and citizens of the contemporary world. Dante's bitter views toward his political enemies surface but do not distort the poem into a personal polemic. Instead, Dante finds in each of their souls, whether they be among the damned or the blessed, possibilities for the good and the evil that reside in everyone.

A selection from Canto 4 of *The Divine Comedy,* "Limbo," is presented here. Limbo is the first of nine descending circles of Hell, where Dante finds the virtuous pagans who cannot be admitted into Heaven because they were born before the advent of Christ. Accompanied by the poets of Greece and Rome, Dante enters the Citadel of Human Reason, the highest state man can reach without God. As impressive as it is to be in the company of Socrates, Plato, and Aristotle, Dante realizes that it cannot compare with being in the radiant presence of God.

Dante, *The Divine Comedy*[22]

Inferno

Limbo

"Let us descend into the sightless world,"
  began the poet[23] (his face was deathly pale):
  "I will go first, and you will follow me."
And I, aware of his changed color, said:
  "But how can I go on if you are frightened?
  You are my constant strength when I lose heart."

And he to me: "The anguish of the souls
  that are down here paints my face with pity—
  Which you have wrongly taken to be fear.

Let us go, the long road urges us."
  He entered then, leading the way for me
  down to the first circle of the abyss.

Down there, to judge only by what I heard,
  there were no wails but just the sounds of sighs
  rising and trembling through the timeless air,

the sounds of sighs of untormented grief
  burdening these groups, diverse and teeming,
  made up of men and women and of infants.

Then the good master said, "You do not ask
  what sort of souls are these you see around you.
  Now you should know before we go on farther,

they have not sinned. But their great worth alone
  was not enough, for they did not know Baptism,
  which is the gateway to the faith you follow,

and if they came before the birth of Christ,
  they did not worship God the way one should;
  I myself am a member of this group.

22. Reprinted, by permission of the publisher, from *Dante's Inferno,* trans. by Mark Musa (Bloomington, Ind.: Indiana University Press, 1971), pp. 98, 100–102.

23. Virgil.

For this defect, and for no other guilt,
we here are lost. In this alone we suffer:
cut off from hope, we live on in desire."

And as he spoke I heard a voice announce:
"Now let us honor our illustrious poet,
his shade that left is now returned to us."

And when the voice was silent and all was quiet
I saw four mighty shades approaching us,
their faces showing neither joy nor sorrow.

Then my good master started to explain:
"Observe the one who comes with sword in hand,
leading the three as if he were their master.

It is the shade of Homer, sovereign poet,
and coming second, Horace, the satirist;
Ovid is the third, and last comes Lucan.

Since they all share one name with me, the name
you heard resounding in that single voice,
they honor me and do well doing so."

So I saw gathered there the noble school
of the master singer of sublimest verse,[24]
who soars above all others like the eagle.
And after they had talked awhile together,
they turned and with a gesture welcomed me,
and at that sign I saw my master smile.

Greater honor still they deigned to grant me:
they welcomed me as one of their own group,
so that I numbered sixth among such minds.

We walked together toward the shining light,
discussing things that here are best kept silent,
as there they were most fitting for discussion.

We reached the boundaries of a splendid castle
that seven times was circled by high walls
defended by a sweetly flowing stream.

We walked right over it as on hard ground;
through seven gates I passed with those wise spirits,
and then we reached a meadow fresh in bloom.

24. The reference is probably to Homer.

There people were whose eyes were calm and grave,
whose bearing told of great authority;
seldom they spoke and always quietly.

Then moving to one side we reached a place
spread out and luminous, higher than before,
allowing us to view all who were there.

And right before us on the lustrous green
the mighty shades were pointed out to me
(my heart felt glory when I looked at them).

There was Electra standing with a group,
among whom I saw Hector and Aeneas,
and Caesar, falcon-eyed and fully armed.

I saw Camilla and Penthesilea;
across the way I saw the Latian King,
with Lavinia, his daughter, by his side.

I saw the Brutus who drove out the Tarquin;
Lucretia, Julia, Marcia, and Cornelia;
off, by himself, I noticed Saladin,

and when I raised my eyes a little higher
I saw the master sage of those who know,[25]
sitting with his philosophic family.
All gaze at him, all pay their homage to him;
and there I saw both Socrates and Plato,
each closer to his side than any other;

Democritus, who said the world was chance,
Diogenes, Thales, Anaxagoras,
Empedocles, Zeno, and Heraclitus;

I saw the one who classified our herbs:
Dioscorides I mean. And I saw Orpheus,
Tully,[26] Linus,[27] Seneca the moralist,

Euclid the geometer, and Ptolemy,
Hippocrates, Galen, Avicenna,
and Averroës, who made the Commentary.[28]

25. Aristotle.
26. Cicero.
27. Livy.
28. On Aristotle.

I cannot tell about them all in full;
  my theme is long and urges me ahead,
  often I must omit things I have seen.

The company of six becomes just two;
  my wise guide leads me by another way
  out of the quiet into tempestuous air.

I come into a place where no light is.

9. Giotto, *Lamentation,* c. 1305 (Gardner, p. 540, ill. 15:14; Jansen, p. 349, ill. 491)
Francis of Assisi, *The Canticle of Brother Sun,* c. 1226

Florentine artists excelled in painting and sculpture as well as in architecture. One of the most prominent artists in Florence in the late thirteenth and early fourteenth centuries was the painter Giotto. Two great sets of murals, one in the Arena Chapel at Padua and the other in the church of Santa Croce in Florence, are known to have been painted by him. A third cycle of murals, at the upper church of San Francesco in Assisi, has traditionally been attributed to Giotto, although modern scholarship has questioned this attribution.

The *Lamentation* is from the fresco cycle executed by Giotto in the Arena Chapel. The mural depicts the Virgin Mary, the disciples, and the holy women reverently displaying the wounds of Christ as they grieve over his lifeless body. Approximately eighty years earlier, Saint Francis of Assisi had been profoundly inspired by his own realization of Christ's suffering and had shared Christ's pain and his wounds.

Francis (1181/1182–1226) was the son of a wealthy textile merchant in Assisi. In his youth he had shown little inclination for a spiritual life, but in his twenties he experienced several visions that deeply stirred his religious nature. Renouncing all material possessions and family ties, Francis embraced a life of poverty. He began to preach to the common people. As disciples flocked to him, Francis founded the Franciscan Order. A second order, for nuns, was soon established and later, a society for lay members.

Throughout his life, Francis ardently strove to imitate the life of Christ and to carry out Christ's work in Christ's own way. His emulation of Christ was dramatically realized when, in 1224, he received the stigmata. One morning, as he prayed on the mountain of La Verna, Francis looked into the rising sun and saw Christ in the form of a seraph with outstretched wings nailed to a cross. The vision gone, Francis felt pain in his hands, feet, and side, and found marks on his body that corresponded to the five wounds on Christ's crucified body.

Never a great intellect or learned theologian, Francis inspired others by his humility in body and spirit, his deep compassion for fellow human beings, and his intense love for God and for all of God's creatures. In his most famous piece of writing, *The Canticle of Brother Sun,* Francis gave lyrical voice to his feelings. The canticle was written in the period after Francis had received the stigmata and expresses his belief that all nature is the mirror of God and that all creation shares in His divine grace and beauty. *The Canticle of Brother Sun* by Francis of Assisi is presented here.

Francis of Assisi, *The Canticle of Brother Sun*[29]

Most High, all-powerful, good Lord,
Yours are the praises, the glory, the honor, and all blessing.
To You alone, Most High, do they belong,
and no man is worthy to mention Your name.
Praised be You, my Lord, with all your creatures,
especially Sir Brother Sun,
Who is the day and through whom You give us light.
And he is beautiful and radiant with great splendor;
and bears a likeness of You, Most High One.
Praised be You, my Lord, through Sister Moon and the stars,
in heaven You formed them clear and precious and beautiful.

Praised be You, my Lord, through Brother Wind,
and through the air, cloudy and serene, and every kind of
weather
through which You give sustenance to Your creatures.
Praised be You, my Lord, through Sister Water,
which is very useful and humble and precious and chaste.
Praised be You, my Lord, through Brother Fire,
through whom You light the night
and he is beautiful and playful and robust and strong.
Praised be You, my Lord, through our Sister Mother Earth,
who sustains and governs us,
and who produces varied fruits with colored flowers and herbs.
Praised be You, my Lord, through those who give pardon for
Your love
and bear infirmity and tribulation.
Blessed are those who endure in peace
for by You, Most High, they shall be crowned.
Praised be You, my Lord, through our Sister Bodily Death,
from whom no living man can escape.
Woe to those who die in mortal sin.
Blessed are those whom death will find in Your most holy will,
for the second death shall do them no harm.

29. Reprinted, by permission of the publisher, from *Francis and Clare: The Complete Works*, trans. by Regis J. Armstrong and Ignatius C. Brady (New York: Paulist Press, 1982), pp. 38–39.

Praise and bless my Lord and give Him thanks
and serve Him with great humility.

10. Ambrogio Lorenzetti, *Peaceful City (Good Government in the City),* 1338–1340 (Gardner, p. 547, ill. 15:23; Janson, p. 328, color plate 55)
Bernardino of Siena, *Sermon 7: Why God Has Given Us a Tongue:* "The Tongue and the Nose," 1427

Siena is located in the Italian province of Tuscany. Through its success in agriculture, trade, and banking, Siena became a powerful economic rival to nearby Florence.

Commercial prosperity, however, fueled social and political unrest, and factions—representing the nobility, the merchants, and the middle class—clashed in almost constant struggles to control the government. In 1287, a merchant oligarchy closely allied with Florence established a Council of Nine to govern Siena. Ambrogio Lorenzetti extolled the virtues of the council in frescoes done for the Sienese city hall, the Palazzo Publico. *Peaceful City (Good Government in the City)* depicts the streets, stores, and houses of Siena teeming with activity, and it shows the merchants and farmers, noblemen and maidens enjoying the prosperity of the city and the surrounding countryside.

The citizens of Siena are also pictured in the pages of Saint Bernardino of Siena (1380–1444). Born in a small town in Sienese territory and raised in Siena, Bernardino founded a Franciscan monastery in the Tuscan city for himself and his followers.

Bernardino preached his first sermon in 1405 and was quickly recognized as the greatest preacher of his day. Invited by cities everywhere to come and preach, Bernardino spent most of his life traveling and preaching in northern and central Italy. He died on his way to evangelize the Kingdom of Naples in southern Italy. Wherever he appeared, vast throngs, sometimes numbering as many as thirty thousand, crowded the churches and assembled in the public squares to hear him.

Bernardino's sermons were popular because they were direct in style and down-to-earth in language. Throughout his preaching, Bernardino avoided theological issues and theoretical problems. He deals with the specific moral and religious concerns of his hearers, including crime, violence, vanity, avarice, lust, and deception. He fills his sermons with colorful anecdotes drawn from everyday life and with offhand comments directed to individuals in the audience.

Especially famous are the sermons that Bernardino preached in Siena during Lent in 1427. Delivered in the main plaza in front of the Palazzo Publico, the sermons were recorded by a tailor named Bartolomeo. In them, Bernardino alludes to every rank of Sienese society and to every profession and occupation—including princes and paupers, husbands, wives, and widows, shopkeepers, soldiers, and priests, farmers, innkeepers, and prostitutes—and he tirelessly exhorts them to aspire to their moral betterment. Sermon 7 is known as *Why God Has Given Us a Tongue.* A selection from Sermon 7, "The Tongue and the Nose," is presented here.

Bernardino of Siena, *Sermon VII: Why God Has Given Us a Tongue*[30]

The Tongue and the Nose

How many tongues hath man, and with how many tongues doth he speak? Never have I heard that any man had more tongues than one. . . . God hath given only one tongue to man; he hath not done so in respect of the other members, nor even of the other senses. God hath given man two eyes, he hath given him two hands, he hath given him two feet, he hath given him two nostrils to smell with. What doth it signify that he hath not given him more than one tongue? Why, I pray you? It must be for some right excellent reason. And knowest thou why? . . . because he wisheth that thou shalt do less with thy tongue than with the other senses.

O thou vain prattler, hearken! A sage giving counsel to mankind saith: If thou speakest, say little and speak seldom and speak low, do not shout; and verily this is a most useful saying! . . .

Woman, wouldst thou please thy husband? Yes. Then speak little, do not chatter as many women do—*chia, chia, chia, chia,*—who never cease in order to rest. O she is a bad neighbour, a chatterer. We have it that the Blessed Virgin spoke seven times in all the length of her life, and not more. I mean not to say that she never said more, but that of all those things which she said we know only seven.

Where is the root of the tongue? Tell me! Hast thou seen the tongue of swine, how it is fastened? So in like manner is ours fastened to the heart. What doth this teach thee? It teacheth thee this: that which thou hast in thy heart thou sayest with thy tongue, which is fastened to it and to it alone. . . .

The tongue is placed below the nostrils of the nose, so that when thou sayest aught about thy neighbour, first thou touchest thyself, to see whether thou hast the same fault. I know not whether thou hast given heed to this, that when one man wisheth to speak of another, first he toucheth his nose, and then commenceth to speak, proving first in regard to himself that he is full of the very fault of which he doth accuse his neighbour. And therefore do not point out that thou art good and thy neighbour bad; look first to thyself, and afterwards to thy neighbour. And of such as these speaks Saint Matthew, in the seventh chapter: Thou hypocrite, who wish-

30. Reprinted from Nazareno Orlandi, ed., *Saint Bernardino of Siena: Sermons,* trans. by Helen Josephine Robins (Siena: Tipografia Sociale, 1920), pp. 29–30, 33–34.

est to show that thou art esteemed a good man, cast out first the beam out of thy own eye, and then reprove others. Thou, on the other hand, who are reproved by some one for that which thou hast not done, but which he himself hath done, say to him: Wipe thy nose!

Hearken! I will tell you what befell once in Siena. At one time they used to sell flour by the barrel and a man wished to steal some here in the Campo at night, and he did steal it, and this was the manner of it. He hung a pouch down under him, and he took a little bell with him, and went on all fours; and when people heard the bell they supposed he was a pig, one of St. Antony's. He opened the vat, and took out flour from it two or three times in the night, and so he came and went, and carried it home. It happened that a thief had been taken and led to justice, and this man who stole the flour every night said: He deserves a thousand hangings. I say that he should work as hard as he may, and should do as I do. And he showed the hardened skin on his hand, which had been made there by his going on all fours. Now to that man might have been said when he spoke thus of the other: Wipe thy nose! In like manner one might speak so to the woman who hath led a most abandoned life, who heareth another spoken of, and accused of something infamous. Then she is very bold to reveal that infamous thing which is charged to the other, and she saith: They say . . . they say . . . what do they say? What do they say? Knowest thou what I say to thee? Go,—wipe thy nose!

11. Buonamico Buffalmacco or Francesco Traini, *The Triumph of Death,* c. 1350 (Gardner, p. 547, ill. 15:25; Janson, p. 353, ills. 497–98)
Boccaccio, *The Decameron:* "The Black Death in Florence," 1349–1351

The Black Death is vividly depicted in a fresco, *The Triumph of Death,* painted on the walls of the Camposanto, a cemetery building next to the Pisa Cathedral. The fresco, which illustrates various responses of Europeans to the dreadful epidemic, has been attributed to the Pisan painter Francesco Traini and, more recently, to Buonamico Buffalmacco.

The Black Death is the name given to the plague that swept over Europe between 1347 and 1351. The single greatest natural catastrophe in European history, the plague caused more deaths than any war or any other epidemic. The number of victims was staggering. It is estimated that one quarter of the population, or twenty-five million people, died from it and that, in some parts of Europe, as much as two thirds or three quarters of the population was wiped out.

The Black Death is caused by a type of bacillus which thrives in the stomach of fleas. These fleas, in turn, live in the fur of rodents, particularly rats. When the rodent host dies, the fleas readily transfer to human populations and plague epidemics erupt.

During the early fourteenth century, the plague spread throughout Asia, causing massive depopulation in China and Turkistan. Italian merchant ships carried the disease from trading settlements along the Black Sea to Mediterranean ports, where it spread inland. Sicily was struck in 1347; Italy, Spain, France, and England in 1348; Austria, Hungary, Switzerland, and Germany in 1349; Scotland and Scandinavia in 1350. Jews were popularly believed to have caused the epidemic by poisoning the wells, supposedly to provide victims for Passover services. Although the pope, Clement VI, vigorously denied these claims and instructed the clergy to protect their local Jewish communities, mass burnings of Jews occurred. Further outbreaks of the plague occurred in 1361–1363, 1369–1371, 1374–1375, 1390, and 1400.

The consequences of the Black Death were severe and longstanding. Many towns were abandoned, entire regions were depopulated. The shortage of laborers resulted in a decline of industry, in a depression of long-distance trade, in a decrease of the amount of land under cultivation, and in a heightening of social tensions, especially in cities. The plague also produced tremendous cultural and educational change. Europe's universities were depleted of their students and scholars; many important artists, such as Ambrogio Lorenzetti, died.

An account of the Black Death was written by Giovanni Boccaccio (1313–1375). Born in Paris and raised in Florence, Boccaccio witnessed the epidemic and its effects in Florence. He used the Black Death as a setting for *The Decameron,* a collection of a hundred tales written in the Italian vernacular. *The Decameron* opens with the flight of ten young people from plague-stricken Florence in 1348. The seven women and three men retire to a rich, well-watered countryside retreat, where they entertain each other with singing, dancing, conversation, and, most importantly, storytelling. In the preface to *The Decameron,* written between 1349 and 1351, Boccaccio provides a graphic description of the physical symptoms of the plague, the social havoc it wreaked, and the psychological responses of people to the threat of imminent death. A selection from *The Decameron,* "The Black Death in Florence," is presented here.

Boccaccio, *The Decameron*[31]

The Black Death in Florence

I say, then, that it was the year of the bountiful Incarnation of the Son of God, 1348. The mortal pestilence then arrived in the excellent city of Florence, which surpasses every other Italian city in nobility. Whether through the operations of the heavenly bodies, or sent upon us mortals through our wicked deeds by the just wrath of God for our correction, the plague had begun some years before in Eastern countries. It carried off

31. Reprinted, by permission of the publisher, from David Herlihy, ed., *Medieval Culture and History* (New York: Harper & Row, 1968), pp. 352–57. Copyright © 1968 by David Herlihy. Selection translated by David and Patricia Herlihy.

uncounted numbers of inhabitants, and kept moving without cease from place to place. It spread in piteous fashion towards the West. No wisdom or human foresight worked against it. The city had been cleaned of much filth by officials delegated to the task. Sick persons were forbidden entrance, and many laws were passed for the safeguarding of health. Devout persons made to God not just modest supplications and not just once, but many, both in ordered processions and in other ways. Almost at the beginning of the spring of that year, the plague horribly began to reveal, in astounding fashion, its painful effects.

It did not work as it had in the East, where anyone who bled from the nose had a manifest sign of inevitable death. But in its early stages both men, and women too, acquired certain swellings, either in the groin or under the armpits. Some of these swellings reached the size of a common apple, and others were as big as an egg, some more and some less. The common people called them plague-boils. From these two parts of the body, the deadly swellings began in a short time to appear and to reach indifferently every part of the body. Then, the appearance of the disease began to change into black or livid blotches, which showed up on many on the arms or thighs and in every other part of the body. On some they were large and few, on others small and numerous. And just as the swellings had been at first and still were an infallible indication of approaching death, so also were these blotches to whomever they touched. In the cure of these illnesses, neither the advice of a doctor nor the power of any medicine appeared to help and to do any good. Perhaps the nature of the malady did not allow it; perhaps the ignorance of the physicians (of whom, besides those trained, the number had grown very large both of women and of men who were completely without medical instruction) did not know whence it arose, and consequently did not take required action against it. Not only did very few recover, but almost everyone died within the third day from the appearance of these symptoms, some sooner and some later, and most without any fever or other complication. This plague was of greater virulence, because by contact with those sick from it, it infected the healthy, not otherwise than fire does, when it is brought very close to dry or oily material.

The evil was still greater than this. Not only conversation and contact with the sick carried the illness to the healthy and was cause of their common death. But even to handle the clothing or other things touched or used by the sick seemed to carry with it that same disease for those who came into contact with them. . . .

Such events and many others similar to them or even worse conjured up in those who remained healthy diverse fears and imaginings. Almost all were inclined to a very cruel purpose, that is, to shun and to flee the sick and their belongings. By so behaving, each believed that he would gain safety for himself. Some persons advised that a moderate manner of living, and the avoidance of all excesses, greatly strengthened resistance to this danger. Seeking out companions, such persons lived apart from other men. They closed and locked themselves in those houses where no sick person was found. To live better, they consumed in modest quantities the most delicate foods and the best wines, and avoided all sexual activity. They did not let themselves speak to anyone, nor did they wish to hear any news from the outside, concerning death or the sick. They lived amid music and those pleasures which they were able to obtain.

Others were of a contrary opinion. They affirmed that heavy drinking and enjoyment, making the rounds with singing and good cheer, the satisfaction of the appetite with everything one could, and the laughing and joking which derived from this, were the most effective medicine for this great evil. As they recommended, so they put into practice, according to their ability. Night and day, they went now to that tavern and now to another, drinking without moderation or measure. They did even more in the houses of others; they had only to discern there things which were to their liking or pleasure. This they could easily do, since everyone, as if he was destined to live no more, had abandoned all care of his possessions and of himself. Thus, most houses had become open to all, and strangers used them as they happened upon them, as their proper owner might have done. With this inhuman intent, they continuously avoided the sick with all their power. . . .

Many others held a middle course between the two mentioned above. Not restraining themselves in their diet as much as the first group, nor letting themselves go in drinking and other excesses as the second, they satisfied their appetites sufficiently. They did not go into seclusion but went about carrying flowers, fragrant herbs and various spices which they often held to their noses, believing it good to comfort the brain with such odors since the air was heavy with the stench of dead bodies, illness and pungent medicines. Others had harsher but perhaps safer ideas. They said that against plagues no medicine was better than or even equal to simple flight. Moved by this reasoning and giving heed to nothing but themselves, many men and women abandoned their own city, their houses and homes, their relatives and belongings in search of their own country places or those of others. Just as if the wrath of God, in order to punish the iniquity of men with the plague, could not pursue them, but would only oppress those within city walls! They were apparently convinced that no one should remain in the city, and that its last hour had struck.

Although these people of various opinions did not all die, neither did they all live. In fact many in each group and in every place became ill, but having given example to those who were still well, they in turn were abandoned and left to perish.

We have enough of these facts: that one townsman shuns another; that almost no one cares for his neighbor; that relatives rarely or never exchange visits, and never do they get too close. The calamity had instilled such terror in the hearts of men and women that brother abandoned brother, uncle nephew, brother sister, and often wives left their husbands. Even more extraordinary, unbelievable even, fathers and mothers shunned their children, neither visiting them nor helping them, as though they were not their very own. . . .

With these and others dying all about, the city was full of corpses. Now a general procedure was followed more out of fear of contagion than because of charity felt for the dead. Alone or with the help of whatever porters they could find, they dragged the corpses from their houses and piled them in front so, particularly in the morning, anyone abroad could see countless bodies. Biers were sent for and when they were lacking, ordinary planks carried the bodies. It was not an isolated bier which carried two or three together. This happened not just once, but many biers could be counted which held in fact a wife and husband, two or three brothers, or father and son. . . .

Every hour of every day there was such a rush to carry the huge number of corpses that there was not enough blessed burial ground, especially with the usual custom of giving each body its own place. So when the ground was filled, they made huge trenches in every churchyard, in which they stacked hundreds of bodies in layers like goods stowed in the hold of a ship, covering them with a bit of earth until the bodies reached the very top.

12. Doge's Palace, Venice, c. 1345–1438 (Gardner, p. 411, ill. 10:64)
Ca' d'Oro, Venice, 1422–c. 1440 (Janson, p. 317, ill. 455)
The Travels of Marco Polo: "Khan-balik," 1298

Venetian architecture incorporates strong influences from the Orient into Gothic structures such as the Doge's Palace and the Ca' d'Oro. At the height of its power, Venice was more a world power than an Italian city-state, and this power was based, in large part, on its thriving long-distance commerce.

In contrast to the incessant party strife that disrupted most Italian city life, Venice enjoyed a stable government. The city was rigidly controlled by the merchant class, which elected the doge and the Council of Ten to govern the state. The main object of government policy was to promote Venetian commerce. Protected by swift naval vessels, Venetian fleets sailed through the eastern Mediterranean and the Black Sea and regularly visited northern Europe.

One of the most extraordinary of Venetian merchants was Marco Polo (1254–1324). Born into a family of adventurous merchants, Marco was a small boy when his father, Niccolo, and his uncle, Matteo, set out for the East in 1260. Their prolonged journey took them to China, where they were welcomed at the court of Kublai Khan (1215–1294), the first Mongol emperor of China, in Khan-balik, modern Beijing (Peking).

Led by Genghis Khan (1162–1227), the Mongols had conquered a vast territory in Asia stretching from the Pacific Ocean to the borders of Western Europe. The Polo brothers were among the first Europeans to visit China, since the earlier Islamic conquests had made the Far East inaccessible to Westerners. Kublai had welcomed them and questioned them about their religious beliefs. At their departure, he entrusted them with letters to the pope, in which he requested that missionaries come to his lands and instruct his subjects in the Christian faith.

The Polo brothers returned to Venice in 1269. Two years later, they set out again for the East, taking with them fifteen-year-old Marco and two Dominican missionaries. The priests soon abandoned so arduous a missionary effort but after a long overland journey, the Polos arrived in China, and in 1275 they presented themselves to Kublai Khan at his summer palace at Shang-tu.

Marco Polo remained in China until 1292. He studied the Mongol language and became an official in the Khan's government. Kublai apparently trusted Marco and sent him on various missions to different parts of his kingdom. An astute observer, Marco made careful notes about the regions which he visited and the people he encountered. Marco's notes became the basis of a book, *The Travels of Marco Polo,* written in 1298.

After a twenty-five-year absence, Marco Polo, his father, and his uncle returned to Venice in 1295. In 1298, Marco served as a naval officer in the Venetian fleet during the conflict between the republic and the rival trading city of Genoa, and was captured by the Genoese. During his imprisonment, which lasted less than a year, he met a fellow prisoner, Rustichello of Pisa, a writer of romances. Marco dictated the story of his adventures and Rustichello transcribed them in his own style. Although Marco's European contemporaries were skeptical about Marco's accounts of the Orient, modern scholarship has generally confirmed their accuracy. A selection from *The Travels of Marco Polo,* "Khan-balik," is presented here.

In the fourteenth and fifteenth centuries, commercial ties between China and Europe were disrupted by the gradual disintegration of the Mongol empire and by the destruction of the trading cities by Tamerlane. However, the obstacles that blocked the use of overland trade routes led to the search for sea routes to the exotic Orient. The quest to establish these routes was the stimulus for the voyages of Vasco da Gama to India and Columbus to the Americas.

The Travels of Marco Polo[32]

Khan-balik

The multitude of inhabitants and the number of houses in the city of Khan-balik, as also in the twelve suburbs outside the city (corresponding to the twelve gates), is greater than the mind can comprehend. The suburbs are even more populous than the city, and it is there that the merchants, and others whose business brings them to the capital, stay. Wherever, indeed, his Majesty holds court, there these people flock from all quarters in pursuit of their several objects.

In the suburbs there are also as handsome houses and stately building as in the city, with the exception only of the palace of the Great Khan. No corpse is suffered to be buried within the city; and those of the Idolaters whose custom it is to burn their dead are carried to the usual spot beyond the suburbs. There likewise all public executions take place. Women who live by prostituting themselves for money dare not, unless secretly, exercise their profession in the city, but must confine themselves to the suburbs, where, as has already been stated, there reside above 25,000; nor is this number greater than is necessary for the vast throngs of merchants and other strangers who are continually arriving and departing.

To this city everything that is most rare and valuable in the world finds its way; and more especially does this apply to India, which furnishes precious stones, pearls, and various drugs and spices. From the provinces of Cathay itself, as well as from other provinces of the empire, whatever is of value is brought here to supply the demands of those multitudes who establish their residence in the vicinity of the court. The quantity of merchandise sold exceeds also that of any other place; for no fewer than a thousand carriages and pack horses loaded with raw silk come here daily; and an immense quantity of gold tissues and silks of various kinds is manufactured here.

In the vicinity of the capital are many walled and other towns, whose inhabitants live chiefly by the court, selling the articles they produce in return for whatever they need.

32. Reprinted from Milton Rugoff, ed., *The Travels of Marco Polo* (New York: New American Library, 1961), pp. 152–53. Copyright © 1961 by Milton Rugoff. Reprinted by arrangement with the New American Library, New York, N.Y., and Milton Rugoff.

Bibliography

The reader is referred to the bibliographies in Gardner and Janson for further studies of the various periods of Western art. The bibliography that follows contains suggestions for further reading on the aspects of social history that are discussed in this volume.

I: The Art of the Ancient Near East

Botteró, Jean, et al. *The Near East: The Early Civilizations,* 3 vols. (London: Weidenfeld and Nicolson, 1967).

Bright, John. *A History of Israel* (Philadelphia: Westminster Press, 1959).

The Cambridge Ancient History, Vols. 1–2, 3rd ed. (Cambridge: Cambridge University Press, 1970–71).

Frye, Richard N. *The Heritage of Persia* (London: Weidenfeld and Nicolson, 1963).

Gurney, Oliver. *The Hittites* (London: Penguin Books, 1952).

Hallo, William W., and William K. Simpson. *The Ancient Near East: A History* (New York: Harcourt, Brace, Jovanovich, 1971).

Kenyon, Kathleen M. *Archaeology in the Holy Land,* 4th ed. (London: Methuen, 1985).

Kramer, Samuel N. *The Sumerians, Their History, Culture and Character* (Chicago: University of Chicago Press, 1964).

Mellaart, James. *The Neolithic of the Ancient Near East* (New York: Scribner, 1975).

Oates, Joan. *Babylon* (London: Thames and Hudson, 1979).

Olmstead, Albert T. *History of Assyria* (Chicago: University of Chicago Press, 1975).

Oppenheim, A. Leo. *Ancient Mesopotamia* (Chicago: University of Chicago Press, 1964).

II: The Art of Egypt

Aldred, Cyril. *Akhenaten, Pharaoh of Egypt: A New Study* (London: Thames and Hudson, 1968).

———. *The Egyptians* (London: Thames and Hudson, 1961).

Breasted, James Henry. *A History of Egypt* (New York: Scribner, 1905).

The Cambridge Ancient History, Vols. 1–2, 3rd ed. (Cambridge: Cambridge University Press, 1970–71).

Emery, Walter Bryan. *Archaic Egypt* (London: Penguin Books, 1961).

Frankfort, Henri. *The Birth of Civilization in the Near East* (London: Benn, 1951).

Gardiner, Sir Alan H. *Egypt of the Pharaohs* (Oxford: Oxford University Press, 1961).

Giles, Frederick J. *Ikhnaton: Legend and History* (London: Hutchinson, 1970).

Hallo, William W., and William K. Simpson. *The Ancient Near East: A History* (New York: Harcourt, Brace, Jovanovich, 1971).

Hayes, William C. *Most Ancient Egypt* (Chicago: University of Chicago Press, 1965).

———. *The Scepter of Egypt* (Cambridge, Mass.: Harvard University Press, 1953–59).

Redford, Donald B. *Akhenaten: The Heretic King* (Princeton: Princeton University Press, 1984).

Steindorff, George, and Keith C. Steele. *When Egypt Ruled the East,* 2nd ed. (Chicago: University of Chicago Press, 1957).

Van Seters, John. *The Hyksos: A New Investigation* (New Haven: Yale University Press, 1966).

Wilson, John A. *The Culture of Ancient Egypt* (Chicago: University of Chicago Press, 1951).

III: The Art of the Aegean

The Cambridge Ancient History, Vols. 1–2, 3rd ed. (Cambridge: Cambridge University Press, 1970–71).

Hood, Sinclair. *The Home of the Heroes: The Aegean Before the Greeks* (London: Thames and Hudson, 1967).

———. *The Minoans: Crete in the Bronze Age* (London: Thames and Hudson, 1971).

Hutchinson, Richard Wyatt. *Prehistoric Crete* (London: Penguin Books, 1962).

McDonald, William A. *Progress into the Past: The Rediscovery of Mycenaean Civilization* (Bloomington, Ind.: Indiana University Press, 1969).

Mylonas, George E. *Mycenae and the Mycenaean Age* (Princeton: Princeton University Press, 1966).

Pendlebury, John D. S. *The Archaeology of Crete* (London: Methuen, 1979).

Vermeule, Emily T. *Greece in the Bronze Age* (Chicago: University of Chicago Press, 1964).

IV: The Art of Greece

Andrewes, Antony. *The Greeks* (London: Hutchinson, 1967).

Burn, Andrew R. *Persia and the Greeks* (New York: St. Martin's Press, 1962).

Bowra, Cecil M. *The Greek Experience* (London: Weidenfeld and Nicolson, 1957).

Bury, John B. *A History of Greece to the Death of Alexander the Great,* 4th ed. (London: Macmillan, 1975).

The Cambridge Ancient History, Vol. 3, 2nd ed. (Cambridge: Cambridge University Press, 1982). Vols. 4–6, 1923–39.

Cary, Max. *A History of the Greek World from 323 to 146 B.C.,* 2nd ed., rev. (London: Methuen, 1951).

Claggett, Marshall. *Greek Science in Antiquity* (New York: Collier, 1963).

Copleston, Frederick. *A History of Philosophy,* rev. ed. Vol. 1, *Greece and Rome* (Westminster, Md.: The Newman Press, 1955).
Cornford, Francis M. *Greek Religious Thought from Homer to the Age of Alexander* (London: Dent, 1923).
Forrest, William G. *The Emergence of Greek Democracy, 800–400 B.C.* (London: Weidenfeld and Nicolson, 1966).
Guthrie, William K. C. *A History of Greek Philosophy,* 3 vols. (Cambridge: Cambridge University Press, 1962–81).
Hammond, Norman G. L. *A History of Greece to 332 B.C,* 2nd ed. (Oxford: The Clarendon Press, 1967).
Jones, Arnold H. M. *Athenian Democracy* (New York: Holt, Rinehart and Winston, 1966).
———. *The Greek City from Alexander to Justinian* (Oxford: The Clarendon Press, 1940).
Kagan, Donald. *The Outbreak of the Peloponnesian War* (Ithaca: Cornell University Press, 1969).
Lloyd, Geoffrey E. R. *Early Greek Science: Thales to Aristotle* (London: Chatto and Windus, 1970).
Snodgrass, Anthony M. *Archaic Greece: The Age of Experiment* (Berkeley: University of California Press, 1981).
———. *The Dark Age of Greece* (Edinburgh: The University Press, 1971).
Starr, Chester G. *The Origins of Greek Civilization, 1100–650 B.C.* (New York: Knopf, 1961).
———. *A History of the Ancient World* (Oxford: Oxford University Press, 1965).
Tarn, William W., and E. T. Griffith. *Hellenistic Civilization,* 3rd rev. ed. (London: E. Arnold, 1959).

V: Etruscan Art

Pallottino, Massimo. *The Etruscans* (London: Penguin Books, 1956).
Randall-MacIver, David. *Italy Before the Romans* (Oxford: The Clarendon Press, 1928).
Richter, Gisela M. A. *Ancient Italy* (Ann Arbor: University of Michigan Press, 1955).
Strong, Donald. *The Early Etruscans* (New York: Putnam, 1968).
Whatmough, Joshua. *The Foundations of Roman Italy* (London: Methuen, 1937).

VI: Roman Art

The Cambridge Ancient History, Vols. 8–12 (Cambridge: Cambridge University Press, 1923–39). Vol. 7, 2nd ed., 1982.
Earl, Donald C. *The Age of Augustus* (London: Paul Elek, 1968).
Hammond, Mason. *The Antonine Monarchy* (New York: American Academy, 1959).
Jones, Arnold H. M. *The Later Roman Empire, 284–602,* 3 vols. (Oxford: Blackwell, 1964).
Rostovtzeff, Michael I. *The Social and Economic History of the Roman Empire,* ed. by P. M. Fraser (Oxford: The Clarendon Press, 1957).
Scullard, Howard. *A History of the Roman World from 753–146 B.C.,* 4th ed. (London: Methuen, 1980).

VII: Early Christian, Byzantine, and Islamic Art

Alfoldi, Andras. *The Conversion of Constantine and Pagan Rome* (Oxford: The Clarendon Press, 1948).

Barker, John. *Justinian and the Later Roman Empire* (Madison: University of Wisconsin Press, 1966).

Baynes, Norman H., and A. St. L. B. Moss, eds. *Byzantium: An Introduction to East Roman Civilization,* 3rd rev. ed. (Oxford: Oxford University Press, 1962).

Boak, Arthur E. R., and William G. Sinnigen. *A History of Rome to A.D. 565,* 6th ed. (New York: Macmillan, 1977).

Brockelman, Carl. *History of the Islamic Peoples* (New York: Putnam, 1947).

Brown, Peter. *Augustine of Hippo* (Berkeley: University of California Press, 1967).

———. *The World of Late Antiquity, A.D. 150–750* (New York: Harcourt, Brace, Jovanovich, 1971).

The Cambridge History of Islam, Vols. 1 and 2 (Cambridge: Cambridge University Press, 1970).

The Cambridge Medieval History, Vols. 1 and 2 (Cambridge: Cambridge University Press, 1936). Vol. 4, 2nd ed., 1964–75.

Chadwick, Henry. *The Early Church* (London: Penguin Books, 1967).

Chejne, Anwar G. *Muslim Spain, Its History and Culture* (Minneapolis: University of Minnesota Press, 1974).

Duchesne, Louis M. O. *Early History of the Christian Church,* 3 vols. (London: J. Murray, 1909–24).

Gibb, Hamilton A. R. *Studies on the Civilization of Islam* (Boston: Beacon Press, 1962).

Gilson, Etienne. *The Christian Philosophy of St. Augustine* (New York: Random House, 1960).

Grant, Michael. *History of Rome* (New York: Scribner, 1978).

Hussey, Joan M. *The Byzantine World,* 4th rev. ed. (London: Hutchinson University Library, 1970).

Jenkins, Romilly J. H. *Byzantium and Byzantinism* (Cincinnati: University of Cincinnati Press, 1963).

Jones, Arnold H. M. *Constantine and the Conversion of Europe* (London: Penguin Books, 1949).

———. *The Decline of the Ancient World* (New York: Holt, Rinehart and Winston, 1966).

Lietzmann, Hans. *A History of the Early Church* (London: Lutterworth Press, 1950–52).

Nicholson, Reynold A. *A Literary History of the Arabs* (Cambridge: Cambridge University Press, 1966).

O'Callaghan, Joseph F. *A History of Medieval Spain* (Ithaca: Cornell University Press, 1975).

Schaff, Philip. *History of the Christian Church,* 7 vols. (New York: Scribner, 1907–12).

Southern, Richard W. *Western Society and the Church in the Middle Ages* (London: Penguin Books, 1970).

Vogt, Joseph. *The Decline of Rome: The Metamorphosis of Ancient Civilization* (London: Weidenfeld and Nicolson, 1982).

Von Grunebaum, Gustave E. *Medieval Islam,* 2nd ed. (Chicago: University of Chicago Press, 1953).

Watt, William Montgomery. *A History of Islamic Spain* (Edinburgh: The University Press, 1965).

———. *Muhammed: Prophet and Statesman* (Oxford: Oxford University Press, 1961).

Whitting, Philip D. *Byzantium: An Introduction* (New York: New York University Press, 1963).

VIII: Early Medieval Art

Bark, William C. *Origins of the Medieval World* (Garden City, N.Y.: Doubleday, 1958).

Barraclough, Geoffrey. *The Crucible of Europe* (Berkeley: University of California Press, 1976).

Bauml, Franz H. *Medieval Civilization in Germany, 800–1273* (London: Thames and Hudson, 1969).

Bloch, Marc. *Feudal Society,* 2 vols. (Chicago: University of Chicago Press, 1961).

Boussard, Jacques. *The Civilization of Charlemagne* (New York: McGraw-Hill, 1968).

Brondsted, Johannes. *The Vikings* (London: Penguin Books, 1960).

Bullough, D. A. *The Age of Charlemagne* (London: Paul Elek, 1965).

The Cambridge Medieval History, Vol. 3 (Cambridge: Cambridge University Press, 1964).

Dawson, Christopher. *The Making of Europe* (New York: Meridian Books, 1956).

Duckett, Eleanor S. *The Gateway to the Middle Ages,* 3 vols. (Ann Arbor: University of Michigan Press, 1961).

Fichtenau, Heinrich. *The Carolingian Empire: The Age of Charlemagne* (New York: Harper & Row, 1957).

Gallagher, John J. *Church and State in Germany under Otto the Great* (Washington, D.C.: The Catholic University of America, 1938).

Hodgkin, Thomas. *Italy and Her Invaders, 376–814,* 8 vols. (New York: Russell and Russell, 1967).

Laistner, M.L.W. *Thought and Letters in Western Europe A.D. 500–900* (Ithaca: Cornell University Press, 1957).

Lewis, Archibald R. *Emerging Medieval Europe, A.D. 400–1000* (New York: Knopf, 1967).

Lopez, Robert S. *The Birth of Europe* (New York: Evans, World, 1967).

Musset, Lucien. *The Germanic Invasions* (University Park, Pa.: Pennsylvania State University Press, 1975).

Richards, Jeffrey. *Consul of God: The Life and Times of Gregory the Great* (London: Routledge and Kegan Paul, 1980).

———. *The Popes and the Papacy in the Early Middle Ages* (London: Routledge and Kegan Paul, 1979).

Ryan, John. *Irish Monasticism* (Ithaca: Cornell University Press, 1972).

Sawyer, P. H. *The Age of the Vikings* (New York: St. Martin's Press, 1963).

Southern, Richard W. *The Making of the Middle Ages* (New Haven: Yale University Press, 1953).

Stubbs, William. *Germany in the Early Middle Ages, 476–1250* (New York: H. Fertig, 1969).

Thompson, James Westfall. *Feudal Germany,* 2 vols. (Chicago: University of Chicago Press, 1928).

Tierney, Brian, and Sidney Painter. *Western Europe in the Middle Ages, 300–1475,* 3rd ed. (New York: Knopf, 1978).

Wallace-Hadrill, J. M. *The Barbarian West,* rev. ed. (New York: Harper & Row, 1962).

———. *The Long-Haired Kings* (New York: Barnes and Noble, 1962).

IX: Romanesque Art

Artz, Frederick B. *The Mind of the Middle Ages,* 3rd ed. (Chicago: University of Chicago Press, 1980).

Baldwin, John W. *The Scholastic Culture of the Middle Ages, 1000–1300* (Lexington, Mass.: D. C. Heath, 1971).

The Cambridge Medieval History, Vols. 5 and 6 (Cambridge: Cambridge University Press, 1911–36).

Clanchy, M. T. *From Memory to Written Record: England, 1066–1307* (Cambridge, Mass.: Harvard University Press, 1979).

Erdmann, Carl. *The Origin of the Idea of Crusade* (Princeton: Princeton University Press, 1977).

Erickson, Carolly. *The Medieval Vision* (Oxford: Oxford University Press, 1976).

Hollister, C. Warren. *Medieval Europe: A Short History,* 5th ed. (New York: Wiley, 1982).

Hoyt, Robert, and Stanley Chodorow. *Europe in the Middle Ages,* 3rd ed. (New York: Harcourt, Brace, Jovanovich, 1976).

Jeffrey, Burton Russell. *Medieval Civilization* (New York: Wiley, 1968).

Left, Gordon. *Medieval Thought: St. Augustine to Ockham* (London: Penguin Books, 1958).

Oakley, Frances. *The Medieval Experience* (New York: Scribner, 1974).

Peters, Edward. *Europe, the World of the Middle Ages* (Englewood Cliffs, N.J.: Prentice-Hall, 1977).

Runciman, Steven. *A History of the Crusades,* 3 vols. (New York: Harper & Row, 1951–1954).

Southern, Richard W. *Western Views of Islam in the Middle Ages* (Cambridge, Mass.: Harvard University Press, 1962).

Stephenson, Carl, and Bryce Lyon. *Medieval History,* 4th ed. (New York: Harper & Row, 1962).

Sumption, Jonathan. *Pilgrimage: An Image of Medieval Religion* (London: Faber and Faber, 1975).

Tellenbach, Gerd. *Church, State and Society at the Time of the Investiture Contest* (New York: Harper & Row, 1970).

Tierney, Brian. *The Crisis of Church and State, 1050–1300* (Englewood Cliffs, N.J.: Prentice-Hall, 1964).

Wakefield, Walter L. *Heresy, Crusade, and Inquisition in Southern France, 1100–1250* (Berkeley: University of California Press, 1974).

X: Gothic Art

Brooke, Christopher. *The Twelfth-Century Renaissance* (New York: Harcourt, Brace, Jovanovich, 1969).

Brucker, Gene. *Florentine Politics and Society, 1343–1378* (Princeton: Princeton University Press, 1962).

The Cambridge Medieval History, Vols. 7 and 8 (Cambridge: Cambridge University Press, 1911–36).

Chenu, M. D., O.P. *Nature, Man and Society in the Twelfth Century* (Chicago: University of Chicago Press, 1968).

Cobban, A. B. *The Medieval Universities* (London: Methuen, 1975).

Copleston, F. C. *A History of Philosophy.* Vol. 2, *Medieval Philosophy, Part II: Albert the Great to Duns Scotus* (Garden City, N.Y.: Doubleday, 1962).

Fortini, Arnaldo. *Francis of Assisi* (New York: Crossroad, 1981).

Gilson, Étienne. *Heloïse and Abelard* (Ann Arbor: University of Michigan Press, 1960).

Haskins, Charles H. *The Renaissance of the Twelfth Century* (Cambridge, Mass.: Harvard University Press, 1927).

———. *The Rise of Universities* (Ithaca: Cornell University Press, 1957).

Huizinga, Johan. *The Waning of the Middle Ages* (Garden City, N.Y.: Doubleday, 1954).

Painter, Sidney. *French Chivalry* (Ithaca: Cornell University Press, 1957).

Index

SMALL CAPITALS indicate authors of readings in the text